TERENCE CONRAN'S
NEW
HOUSE BOOK

TERENCE CONRAN'S
NEW
HOUSE BOOK

Conran Octopus

Contributors

A Taste for Simplicity	Terence Conran, interviewed by Stephen Bayley
Assessment	Colin Robinson
Planning	John Thackara
Structural Alterations	Martin Lazenby and Elizabeth Wilhide
Architectural Character	Gillian Darley
Exteriors	Joyce Lowrie
Heating	Mary Trewby
Storage	Jeremy Myerson
A Sure Sense of Style	Susan Collier
Floors	Jane Lott
Surfaces and Finishes	Neal Morris
Fireplaces	Mary Trewby
Windows and Doors	Caroline Clifton-Mogg
Lighting	Nonie Niesewand
Entrances, Halls and Staircases	Lance Knobel
Living Rooms	Hilary Green
Kitchens	Nigel Walters
Eating Rooms	Jan Burney and Lewis Blackwell
Bedrooms	Caroline Clifton-Mogg
Bathrooms	Rebecca Eliahoo
Children's Rooms	Diana Harris
Work and Activity	Steve Braidwood
One-room Living	Suzanne Slesin
Outdoor Rooms	Mary Keen and Michael Miller
Safety	Sally King
Design for Disabled People	Sally King
Electricity	Barrie Evans
Security	Jeanne Griffiths
Maintenance	Neal Morris

All available information about photographs
is given in the Acknowledgments on page 365.
Conran Octopus cannot provide further details.

First published in 1985 by
Conran Octopus Limited
37 Shelton Street
London WC2H 9HN

This paperback edition published in 1996 by Conran Octopus Limited

Reprinted 1992, 1993, 1994, 1995, 1996

Copyright © Conran Octopus Limited 1985

ISBN 1 85029 375 9

Typeset by Tradespools Limited

Printed in China

Project editor
Hilary Arnold
Project consultant
Stafford Cliff

Editorial
Senior editor	Mary Trewby
Contributing editors	Frances Kennett
	Julian Worthington
	Susan Conder
Editorial assistant	Katherine Dunn
Editors	Vicky Hayward
	Elizabeth Wilhide
	Jane Walker
	Sarah Litvinoff
	Yvonne Rees
	Anne Dobell
	Catherine Carpenter
Index	Richard Bird and Hilary Bird

Picture research
Picture editor	Philippa Lewis
Picture researchers	Shona Wood
	Marian Price

Design
Art director	Douglas Wilson
Art editor	Stephen Bull
Designers	Paul Burcher
	Karen Bowen
Art assistant	Neil Haines
Illustrator	Mulkern Rutherford
Production	Michel Blake

Consultants
	Ray Porfilio (United States)
	Lance Knobel
Technical	David Holloway
	Martin Lazenby
	Tessa Hunkin
	Tony Wilkins
Ergonomics	Jane Dillon
Heating	C.M.J. Sutherland Associates
Botanical	Jasmine Taylor
Lighting	John Phillips
	Royal Society for the Prevention of Accidents
	Metropolitan Police (New Scotland Yard)

CONTENTS

HOW TO USE THIS BOOK

The contents list gives a detailed breakdown of the topics covered on each page and should be used in conjunction with this general outline.

PART 1
DESIGN FOR LIVING

This first section of the main text looks at the fundamentals of home design. It explains how to work out your precise requirements so that you can decide not only what changes to make to your present home but also how to select a new one. Guidance is given on planning changes, with advice on time, money and all other practical considerations. There are also chapters on aspects of home design which affect all others: altering the structure and layout of a building in order to use it to its best potential; architectural style and exterior appearance; heating and storage.

PART 2
DECORATING THE HOME

This section should be used as reference for all decorating decisions. It opens with a chapter giving an overview of style, colour and pattern. Then each separate element involved in decoration – floors, walls, doors, lighting and so on – is looked at in turn. The range of options available is described so that decorating decisions can be based on budget, function and visual effect.

PART 3
CREATING ROOMS

With a chapter devoted to each room in the house, the third part of the book explains how to design rooms so that they work for the specific activities which will take place in them. Guidance is given on layout, fixtures and furniture, as well as on style and atmosphere.

PART 4
ESSENTIALS

This section deals with the essential services and other topics related to the safe and effective running of a home; diagrams and charts expand the information given.

The salon of a musician's Provençal house. Yellow walls and ochre tiles provide the quintessential Mediterranean ambience. Sparse furnishing and decoration include local antique pieces painted grey, a portrait by Palmero and pride of place for the grand piano.

A TASTE FOR SIMPLICITY

TERENCE CONRAN

*The demure simplicity of a rustic
bedroom in Greece and the grand
simplicity of fine bed-linen in a stark
modern room.*

I have a taste for austerity and utility, but that's certainly not to say I have no appetite for pleasure. Quite the contrary. I firmly believe that plain, simple things are superior to flashy, complicated ones, precisely because ultimately they are more pleasurable. Something that is simple *and* satisfying is a greater achievement than something fussy that attracts attention only because it's over-complicated.

I find a plain glass milk bottle more pleasing than an intricate silver gilt ewer. There are lots of perfect objects in this world that could not be improved no matter how hard you tried. So much of what is wrong with the things we buy is that they have been 'designed up', given unnecessary frills instead of actually being conceived with honesty, integrity, simplicity and guts. It's not decoration itself that is wrong, it's phoney, artless, witless decoration.

It is exactly the same with interiors. My taste in interior design is in part a reaction to the clutter that most of my generation grew up with. I was lucky because when I was a child my mother decided what the house should look like and her taste was for Ambrose Heal's furniture. We had some of that, together with quite good, hand-me-down, antique furniture. She achieved great simplicity. I remember big, chunky sofas in a real 1930s interior, which enjoyed an exceptional quality of light. The few objects that were in it seemed to be in sharp focus: you saw them with an intensity you can't appreciate in a cluttered room. I've been trying to recreate that atmosphere of luxurious simplicity every since.

One of my earliest memories concerns colour. I remember the shock and excitement I felt when I spilt a

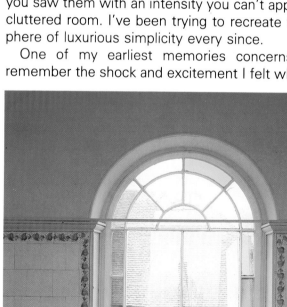

The subtle shades of the spurge hawk and privet hawk moths.

A window in the dairy at Uppark, an English mansion.

12

can of bright green paint over the terracotta floor in my mother's kitchen: the combination was horrible. My taste in colour and pattern was formed in part from another childhood experience – a deep interest in wild flowers, butterflies and moths which I developed at the age of about twelve. My particular interest was the hawk moth family, about which I was *passionate*. This childhood hobby helped me develop an ability to discriminate between shapes, colours and textures.

The dairy at Lanhydrock in Cornwall – slate runnels beside the tiled walls and round the marble-topped table carried spring water to keep fresh foods cool.

It was at Bryanston School, where they took great interest in the arts, that I became aware of interior design. We were taken to West Country stately homes such as Montacute and Stourhead. While we were being called upon to admire this or that fine painting or exquisite architectural detail, I was perversely drawn to the dairies and the servants' quarters. On the whole, I remember finding the grand rooms rather fake and wondering how anybody actually lived in them; it seemed to me that, in terms of environment, the servants were actually better off.

The grand salons and dining rooms of the historic country mansions are a magnificent artistic endeavour,

A section of the scullery at Lanhydrock, showing the open storage of sturdy kitchen utensils – both practical and simple.

but it seemed to me that they were intended for more stilted theatrical performances than for living in. There was so much visual impact, so much ornate detail, I wondered how anybody could have concentrated on a conversation or even managed to taste the food in such decorative environments. The work rooms, however, the dairies and kitchens with their stone floors and simple, unpretentious furniture, seemed to me a far more attractive setting for real life.

The below-stairs world of the great country houses was furnished not by the great cabinet-makers of the day, but by artisans who used materials and skills perfected over generations. What they made had to be basic and functional; they stripped their furniture to its bare essentials. The unfussy shapes and the honest materials used in laundries, dairies and kitchens harmonized perfectly with the plain colours of these rooms.

Altogether, they seemed the most attractive areas in these great houses. Nobody tried too hard to impose any

The laundry at Beningborough Hall in North Yorkshire where every element is strong, functional and very beautiful.

synthetic aesthetic quality on these objects. They were intended only to perform their function as honestly, efficiently and economically as possible. Upstairs, exotic timbers were tortured with intricate carving and then treated with finishes that made the furniture delicate, vulnerable and precious.

It is ironic that in the twentieth century, when life has become more relaxed and egalitarian, that bourgeois taste has often tried to imitate the life above stairs, so that a pretentious gentility has become the norm.

It's amusing to reflect how very *uncomfortable* the contrived posturing of the grand salons must have been. The dedicated followers of fashion of the seventeenth and eighteenth centuries were dressed so ornately that sitting down at all was a problem; it was compounded by frail chairs that were desperately impractical, into which they had to be stuffed like mannequins. The servants, however, after a hard day's work, enjoyed eating and conversation in an easier, more stimulating and altogether more natural way. These qualities of relaxation, comfort, naturalness, seem to have far more to do with life as we live it today than the affectations of upstairs.

Of course, the people responsible for creating those functional rooms were not aware, in any self-conscious way, of what they were doing, but their work was, I believe, a greater contribution to civilization than the tapestries, ormolu and paintings that added 'prestige' to life above stairs.

Gobelins, tapestries, Savonnerie carpets: life upstairs at Newby Hall is a display of status.

The essence of good interior design is the ability to ask simple questions: good design is ninety-eight per cent common sense, two per cent aesthetics. For instance, ask yourself: how do I want my family to live, and how do I want my friends to feel when they visit me? You have to define the problem; the solution then comes very easily if you follow some basic rules.

I think the most comfortable rooms are almost always the simplest ones. If you go into a *ryokan*, a traditional Japanese inn, you sit at floor level on *tatami* mats in serene surroundings with only the decoration of tiny, jewel-like chrysanthemums. Rooms like these, with light suffused through paper screens, can have a terrifically calming effect. In a traditional Japanese room, the austere and dignified design allows what little colour and texture there is to focus your attention. Put a beautiful pot of marguerites in the salon at Montacute and you would probably never notice them. Put the same spray in a *ryokan* and it becomes an object of intense beauty. Anyone can put simple furniture and objects to work for them. My visits to Japan confirm many of my assumptions about how interiors should be, but the greatest influence on my taste was nearer home – France.

Designer and architect Charles Eames built this house in Santa Monica with his wife Ray in 1949. It became a shrine to his principles of simplicity and restraint in design.

Modern, minimal American room with strong Japanese influence.

Japanese stone garden.

The calm simplicity of a traditional Japanese interior.

My guide to France was photographer and *bon vivant* Michael Wickham. We travelled there in 1952 in his open Lagonda. It was my first trip abroad and Michael's inquisitive eye taught me a lot.

My parents had left the country maybe three or four times in my life, and when I was growing up it was still unusual for people to go on family holidays abroad. We

Provence – the perfect setting for the perfect outdoor room.

The cornucopia of a French food market.

usually went to Swanage, or Bembridge, or some other lovely seaside resort. I remember the boatyard at Bembridge: as a child, I found it the most seductive place, because of the wonderful shapes of the yachts, the subtle colours, stacks of rope, and the pervasive smell of wood and varnish. And perhaps, most of all, the environment created when skilled artisans were at work.

But generally my upbringing in wartime Britain was bleak. You rarely saw bright colours. Suddenly seeing a French foodmarket with stacks of fresh produce in abundance was a great shock. The French present their food in a style that is at once natural, seductive and mouthwatering: colours and shapes are arranged to give visual pleasure, just like the best interiors. In France, a poor, thin Englishman, brought up on a public-school diet lacking in colour and texture, found himself in heaven. The market-places, the shops, the architecture of provincial France! In cafés, everything was so simple and beautiful: a white table-cloth; heavy, plain porcelain dishes with a slice of charcuterie; a few vegetables; a sturdy carafe of wine – everyday things had the quality of what, in England, we could only appreciate as art.

An English boatyard.

I suppose if there's one thing I'm proud of it's that through design and through the shops I've been able to bring something of those experiences I had in post-war France back to Britain. But those lessons I learned over thirty years ago could have been learned by anybody.

The enormous impact of France had stemmed from the fact that it was abroad and I was on holiday. When you are on holiday, just take a minute to sit and reflect about exactly *why* you're enjoying yourself. Of course, you haven't the usual work pressures and the weather's probably fine and there's interesting food and drink in abundance. But just as important, I think, is the environment. We select beautiful landscapes to relax in, be it Mexico or the South Pacific, Scotland or New England. It goes beyond the landscape, though. I am particularly drawn by the Mediterranean; Mediterranean cultures understand environment and nature at a very fundamental level and that's why I enjoy myself so much when I go to France, Italy, Greece or Spain.

What are the qualities that make a place wonderful? When you're sitting under a vast blue sky on a lovely floor of terracotta tiles against stark white, roughly plastered walls, consider whether the objects you covet so much at home would improve your holiday scene. Maybe you would feel even better with your own possessions around you, but somehow I doubt it. I think if you're honest with yourself you would realize, when you got home, that it's ridiculous to return to a carpet with a pattern that looks as though it was actually *designed* so

A Greek house shows a sensitive interpretation of traditional Mediterranean style.

Mediterranean builders use materials that mellow with age.

The perfect mixture of old stone, flowing water and tubs of brightly coloured flowers.

that people could be sick all over it and it wouldn't show. (I've never understood why some people say that complex patterns are sensible because they hide dirt. Personally, I prefer to see dirt so I know when to get rid of it.) Instead of bringing back souvenirs, which would only add to the clutter of your home, what you should take home from your holiday is a memory of the environments you have enjoyed.

Holiday experiences can be a genuinely salutory lesson in interior design. Too often modern architects have forgotten something that Mediterranean artisan/builders have always known: the importance of using materials that age well, so that buildings gain style and quality as they get older. Experience tells us that we like the patina of age, both for direct reasons and for reasons of association. Probably the great country houses looked horrible when they were new – imagine a glistening mansion with fresh paint and newly planted gardens. Part of our enjoyment of old houses comes not only from the pleasure of rich and varied textures due to weathering and ageing, but also from the comforting feeling of stability that their very age suggests. The problem with having an absolutely brand new house is that the only sensation you're likely to have is: 'It's getting old and dirty and losing its pristine quality.' But you need courage. Remember that buildings are alive and even the most unlikely modern materials improve with age. We

Ice-cream colours, rich textures, simple forms – quintessential Mediterranean qualities.

A modern interpretation of traditional Mediterranean architecture, softened with linen curtains and given great style by the strong grid of the concrete and wood floor.

now appreciate early plastic objects, old cars; even rust can be beautiful.

I certainly don't want to decry modern architecture, because the great architects of the 1920s and 1930s were pioneers of much of what is excellent in modern design. Their rules about truth to materials and the relation of form to function are valid and useful guides to pleasing design.

Since the Second World War, architects have come in for a lot of criticism, often unfairly. Many modern buildings are bad, particularly public-housing projects and local government offices. Most of Europe suffered a downward spiral of mediocrity, because the developers and public authorities who commissioned the work cared nothing for good design or lasting quality. They were often only interested in maximizing profit in the shortest possible time. These buildings were made with mean materials, cheap details and a lack of generosity in proportion and space. In contrast, the United States has some of the finest modern architecture in the world, alongside its fair share of bad buildings. Some of the best are those buildings commissioned for city centres by

The Deere & Company Building in Moline, Illinois, designed by Eero Saarinen; built in 1964. The rusting iron has the qualities of strength and beauty found in living materials.

The ever-changing reflective facing in bronze, marble and glass of Mies van der Rohe's Seagram Building, built in New York 1956–9.

wealthy corporations. The priority has been to erect fine buildings and in creating them the architects inspired one another to greater heights.

Sadly, few people get the opportunity to fully experience the very best in modern architecture and interior design. A restaurant is possibly the closest contact most of us have with a room which has been created by an interior designer. The restaurants we enjoy have not happened by accident – they are planned by professionals. Restaurants help to form people's tastes not just about food. They must look good and work well. The functional considerations are complex; staff have to be able to move around with ease, while the customers must be able to reach their tables, be comfortable when seated and enjoy the food without distraction but with visual stimulation. Careful planning, flexibility, lighting and atmosphere are of equal importance. Certainly, for me, some of the greatest of all pieces of interior design are to be found in cafés and restaurants. You can learn a great deal from them. The 'Grand Véfour' in Paris is simply one of the most beautiful rooms that I know, unchanged since the early nineteenth century.

The 'Grand Véfour' restaurant in Paris – an ageless interior that excites admiration and appetite.

Michael Chow's chic contemporary restaurant in Los Angeles exemplifies the best in professional design; the style of decoration and Richard Smith's hangings perfectly suit the oriental metropolitan cuisine.

Certain types of food go with certain types of interior. You are going out for the evening: do you want a country meal, a Greek one or, perhaps, high-tech fast food? Terracotta tiles and whitewashed walls, with a *Chiavari* chair, can suggest only bouillabaisse and Italian food. Similarly, it's absurd to think of *nouvelle cuisine* being served in a gilt and swagged restaurant: you want rococo food, you go to a rococo restaurant. Thinking about this is one way of appreciating the difference between design and style. Design is the skeletal structure of a room. How do you get in and out? How is it lit? How do the parts fit? Without it being well considered, no matter what style you add, the end result will be unsatisfactory. If you like, style is the flavours of the food, the spice of life, while design is the quality of the ingredients. Style is what gives you the thrill, upsets some people, pleases others, and, of course, the difficult thing is to achieve the right balance between design and style.

Cooking and decoration are much the same thing. Imagine going into a kitchen and finding all the ingredients laid out on a working surface, ready to be combined together to make a well-balanced meal. The problem is exactly the same if you are designing an interior. In an ideal menu you can enjoy something luxuriously rich and complicated as long as it is followed by something fresh to clean the palette. This contrast is as fundamental to design as it is to cooking. The aim should be to achieve and preserve a balance. You should have a base of simplicity with the contrast of rich tastes.

An enticing combination of ingredients and sunlight through an open window – a balance of good elements is equally important in interior design.

Master chef Michel Guérard was inspired by the traditional grand kitchens of France when he created this one for his home.

Making the most of a wonderful location on America's West Coast, the architect has designed the house around the windows.

The generous proportions of a Windsor chair.

Design really *does* matter, because if people are satisfied with their home life they feel comfortable, pleasant and relaxed. If their friends come into their houses, coo with admiration and say, 'You've done a wonderful job here, how clever you are,' it adds to the pleasure of life. I can't think of many easier ways to improve your life. Alas, a lot of people think it's terribly *nouveau* and anti-intellectual actually to bother about the environment you live in. To me, that's real snobbery. I think that people who would disdain a trashy book or un-serious music, but ignore their clothing or environment, even their food (but often not their wine!) – people who don't accept that the eyes and the tongue are at least as important as the mind – take a very narrow view of culture. The contents of the mind can be expressed through all the senses; at its best, a house can be very much more than just a home. When it comes to the practical business of designing a house interior, I think it helps to consider objects you find pleasing and those you do not, and to work out why. I admire traditional Windsor chairs, made to proportions that were *generous.* A work of total conviction. If you look at their present-day counterparts you'll see that economic factors have rid the chairs of all these elementary, but important, charac-teristics. The original energy has disappeared and the result is emasculated and dull. But that is all you might expect when most modern furniture is designed by people of no great aesthetic judgment, people who haven't learnt to 'do it simply'. One test of quality when looking at furniture is to ask yourself: 'Is this the best of its kind; can I detect any sense of compromise?' Too often modern furniture is loaded with compromise. I

Shaker furniture built in America in about 1815.

enjoy interiors which display conviction and dislike those that are the result of compromise.

The best advice I've heard on cooking was Elizabeth David's instruction *'faites simple'*. In cooking and interior design we distrust simplicity and plain common sense seems to leave people when they begin to plan their homes. Simplicity doesn't mean environments which are stark and inhuman. On the contrary, if you have chosen the basic shapes and forms of a room with simplicity in mind, then any decorative, elaborate objects you have will work better in conjunction with them. Take, for example, a piece of sculpture. It looks superb on a plain plinth in an empty room, suffused with even light. Whatever is on top, if the plinth beneath is simple and there is sufficient empty space around it, you'll be able to look at it with enjoyment. If you took a Corinthian column and put a Brancusi on top you would have two confusing, contrary arguments.

Sheer magic: a swirl of Fortuny-inspired fabric.

The second bit of practical advice is to *be honest* with yourself. Don't try to achieve any effect – even one of simplicity – only because you feel you should. Don't do anything because you fear your mother-in-law or your neighbours or your boss would be critical of your house. The basic part of any design is *thinking*: think about who you are and how you want to express this in your home environment. Unless you do this your house will be synthetic, dull and boring.

Conservatism and tradition are very different things. Most people are innately conservative in their approach to home design; they tend to reproduce what their relatives had, rather than think through what they want themselves. People are prepared to live in ugly and uncomfortable surroundings merely because they won't upset anyone; straying from convention requires a great deal of strength of character.

Confident colour makes for great style – a famous fashion designer's house in Marrakesh.

Flowers are one option for adding style once the basics are absolutely right; like all details, they can change as you change.

A beautiful antique Austrian cupboard.

Personal style is confidence; knowing what you like and not being afraid to put it on display. People seem to find it very hard to express their personalities in their own homes, usually because they are afraid they will stand out. Men, in a reactionary sort of way, find it particularly difficult even to take an interest and seem to think home design is a woman's subject, as if playing rugby and choosing curtains don't mix. People who can express their personal style confidently, dressing with enormous flair, often live in predictable and unattractive homes.

Fashion is easier to handle than home design, because clothes are more ephemeral than furnishings and on the whole cost less. Also, you are given far more choice with clothes: the fashion industry is highly developed and the shops offer such a wide range of inspiring choices, a range magnified by the profusion of magazines and newspapers which treat fashion as an everyday concern. There is no reason why you should not care about fashion in the home too. Few of us want to live for the rest of our lives in the same tweed suit we had at eighteen and why should our homes be any different? I once heard the great Italian designer Ettore Sottsass ask, 'Why *should* homes be static temples?' I agree. Too often people think they have to furnish a home not just for their own lifetime, but for the one succeeding it as well. This leads to dull, middle-of-the-road decisions, often euphemistically described as 'practical'. Style in clothes is that knack of putting things together in a certain way and wearing the right accessories; it's the same with rooms. First get the basics absolutely right and pay very close attention to the essential details: from a good floor to the right door handle. Hide the wires! Budget wisely; spend most on the things that receive the most wear and you really want to last, the ones you will use constantly. Choose sober and classic furnishings and basic decoration to provide the stage set, then add personality, excitement and fashion through the things that are easily changed: fabrics, wall colours, rugs, lampshades. In this way you can constantly keep a room fresh and provide a new focal point, a new style. Just as you'd add a piece of fine old jewellery to lift a beautifully cut plain black dress and make it fantastically stylish, so you can change the visual impact of a room dramatically by using a lovely rug, bright cushions or a great bowl of flowers. Contrasts and surprises are *very* important.

Creating a home should be a labour of love; certainly, it's one of life's great pleasures. Sharing a home should involve compromise and discussion, not conflict and argument. My wife and I both have strong tastes which do not always coincide. We compromise on rooms we share, but she has a room of her own creation and I like going in there because it reflects her personality. There are plenty of things which I can admire even when I don't necessarily want them for myself; I admire any sort of honest interior. The most important thing is that what is done should be done with conviction. You should be able to enjoy going into other people's rooms and enjoy other people coming into yours.

Rustic minimalism in a French country house, using a modern fireplace that works well in traditional surroundings.

*A room should always reflect a personality and this alcove is full of favourite
objects that give strong hints to the character of the owner.*

Sir John Soane's use of 'hazard and surprise' appeals to me. To enter a small room from a large doorway, or to enclose a large space with a lowered ceiling – such choices bring vitality to an interior.

It can be very depressing to go into somebody's house and find it's got no personality, but only a sort of dull respectability. But it's exciting to go into somebody's house and to find yourself thinking suddenly, 'I know this person rather better now', because the interior design tells you something more about the personality of the owner.

When you think of the influence the space you live in has over your life, it's surely worth the expense of experimenting a little to try to find the design that pleases you most. After all, you only have one life; you may as well try to make it something special. I always think that Sir John Soane's ideas about hazard and surprise – coming from a big space through a small door into a small space, popping out into a huge space, getting vistas, reflections and terminals where you don't expect them – are some of the best aims of interior design. Hardly anyone can afford to build a house like Soane's, but you can achieve much the same stimulating effects with light, moving from bright areas into semi-darkness and back into light again. Textures of floors can do the same thing. So can the actual furnishings; imagine moving from a very cosy room with lots of objects into a very spare, monastic cell. This sort of contrast can make a house more interesting to live in.

In a domestic interior, unless you are warm and sitting comfortably you cannot relax. Many times I've been into rooms and had to sit on such excruciatingly uncomfortable sofas that, no matter how great the pictures on the wall were, I've had no sense of well-being. It's the same in restaurants: no matter how good the food might be, if the chairs are diabolically uncomfortable, or the room is too noisy, or you're seated in a draught with waiters banging into you and the lights are too bright, then you cannot enjoy yourself. Colour and pattern can add to this distress. I've been into many a room where the wallpaper dazzles you and makes it impossible to look at anything else. People often become so obsessed with practicality, that things must be invulnerable to fingermarks. In the process, they make their rooms look like airport lounges that could be hosed down after a nasty incident. I enjoy small imperfections, signs of wear, the patina of age. Little noises help; the hiss of a traditional gas fire, or the spit and crackle of logs.

But, above all, I think light is most important. We don't think about lighting anything like enough, particularly when you consider that most of us spend more time at home in artificially lit surroundings than in natural light. A room painted a sour, heavy beige can feel sad; the same room, painted pale lemon yellow, catching the early

The fine architecture of this San Francisco house built in 1940 creates a beautiful setting for a superb object – a Sung Dynasty granary jar.

A Kentish garden at dawn. Observing the play of natural light on a landscape is the best possible inspiration for designing illumination indoors.

morning sun, can be transformed. Even cluttered rooms can look marvellous in the right light; the most elegantly minimal ones can look barren and gloomy with the wrong quality of light. If you can get the lighting right, many other things become less important, and you can actually afford to have fewer things of better quality. Look outdoors; stop to appreciate the light in the country and it will help you learn a great deal about artificial lighting. Natural daylight shows you the importance of shadow, the importance of modulations from hard to soft, and how light reacts when filtered or directed. With the huge range of lighting equipment available on today's market, it is possible to recapture almost any natural effect with artificial light.

Curiously, because I should be professional about it, my own approach to colour stems from a certain lack of confidence. When I move into a new house I usually take the obvious approach of painting everything white, so that I can add colour and pattern later. This gives you a plain skeleton on which to build. It is tremendously important to remember that if you do enjoy something rich and luxuriously patterned, you can admire it that much more in simple surroundings.

The most important material part of an interior design is the floor. It is the base which supports all the other elements in the room. The floor covers a large area and it will probably have to outlive other design decisions; it is far easier and cheaper to change the colour of the walls or the curtains or to rearrange the lighting than it is to dig up, re-lay or otherwise completely re-do the floor.

Whether it is going to be carpet, tiles or stripped wood, see to it that the floor is beautiful. Certainly see that all the surfaces are flush, the wires chased-in, or hidden behind the skirting (baseboards). Details that are visible,

This window offers gentle light by day and a calming view by night.

The effect of natural light through an open doorway is ever changing, as night follows day – when choosing finishes, such as flooring, consider how they will be enhanced by natural and artificial light sources.

The enviable quality of this room comes not only from the sybaritic luxury of a
sunken bath but also from the less exotic elements of sunlight, fine surfaces
and textures and carefully chosen accessories.

The building and this room within it are magnificent; even more character is added through the owners' delight in displaying personal treasures such as these dolls' houses and the billiard table.

architraves and plasterwork, should be as well done as you can possibly afford. The same with the walls. Have them lined, papered or painted to the very best of your ability. It is false economy to skimp on these things because with shoddy floors, cheap plaster and a spaghetti of wires you cannot possibly have a successful interior, no matter how many superb objects you have.

When you begin to plan an interior, it will be easier to cope with the enormous range of choices on offer if you use some of the many magazines that deal with interiors – tear out of them images that inspire you. The variety available means there's every opportunity for people to discover what they want. You can add holiday snapshots to create a visual diary. I think *Avenue* (Dutch), *La Maison de Marie Claire* (French), *The World of Interiors* (British), *Schöner Wohnen* (German) and *Metropolitan Home* (American) are among the best sources for tear sheets.

With the tear sheets, snapshots and samples of fabrics you are considering, sit around in the empty room for quite some time. Try to understand it. Try to appreciate its essential nature. You absolutely don't *have* to respect any qualities you find in a room, but it's unlikely you'll make a success of decorating unless you realize they're there, and have made a positive and considered decision about them.

Trying to completely finish a room immediately is rather like meeting someone on the train and deciding between stations you want to marry them. There may be an immediate attraction, but you have to know a lot more about them before you make any serious commitment. When you have understood the skeleton of a room, you should go out window shopping, scrapbook in hand; spend a lot of time looking, and come back to the room with the image of your purchase in mind *before* you make an expensive decision.

Never consider one element of a room in isolation; it is

hard to imagine its effect out of context. Take home the largest carpet samples and fabric swatches and live with them in the room you are designing. Never buy something, or decide on a colour, or choose a style of furniture, until you know you really like it and want to live with it.

Buying a sofa is a big decision. I'm constantly amazed that people often do it without considering any of the things that will go with it. Never be afraid of rolling up the rug that will lie in front of the sofa and taking it along to the shop; it is so important how things work together. You wouldn't buy a pair of shoes without thinking what clothes they would go with.

Interestingly, I have noticed a marked increase in the sales of sofas since we offered them in plain calico – people can put on their own loose covers after considering the sofa in their own rooms. It is so much easier this way than either understanding the shape of the sofa when it is covered with someone else's choice of fabric or imagining, while you're in the shop, what it would be like with the fabric of your choice.

A modern kitchen reflects the style and simplicity of those great below-stairs rooms of grand country houses.

Sadly, we are not educated in these essential practicalities, even though making choices for our homes has an economic as well as an aesthetic significance. I do not believe you will design a better home after watching *The Nutcracker* ballet, or visiting an art gallery. Certainly, you will widen your vision, taste and style, but what is more likely to improve your house is considering things in terms of function, economy, ease of movement, comfort, practicality and visual impact.

The rules for designing the entire house are fundamentally the same as the rules for designing an individual room. That's to say, think about it before you make any irreversible decisions. For instance, do you *really* need a dining room? Kitchens seem to me to be the heart of any house; unless you lead the sort of life where you have to do a lot of formal entertaining, I'd suggest you spend your time and money making the kitchen a more pleasant place than anywhere else. Why not knock down a wall and make your dining room into a part of the kitchen? Most of the things you use in a kitchen can be

The draping and folding of fabric on a sofa makes a strong sculptural form in a room.

I like to paint interiors all white while I decide exactly what colours to introduce – if any. A subtle but dynamic use of colour in Finnish designer Ristomatti Ratia's Helsinki apartment.

At first sight you are overwhelmed by the exotic jungle location and spacious luxury of this outdoor room, but look again – its beauty and impact also derive from its utter simplicity.

pleasant objects in themselves; they don't *have* to be hidden away in cupboards. People buy too many bits and pieces that get stuck away and never used because they have commodious kitchen cabinets. I always prefer a kitchen where most things are on display, with utensils that are in everyday use easily to hand.

Privacy and relaxation are important in bedrooms so it surprises me that so many people make them the most fussy, decorative and stylized rooms in their house. They go mad with floral patterns, flounces of fabric, matching details and often put more thought and planning into the bedroom than the living room. Think about the amount of time you are going to spend in a room and what the activities will be there. Spend most and take most trouble over the areas you will use most.

Planning and thinking are essential to all design in the home. Consider how to plan a family room so that someone can read while a child watches television, or so that, on another occasion, the whole family can be together to talk, or so that the room may cater for a crowded party with friends. Plan a room so that it will contain a variety of activities and work well for all of them. *Think* about the sort of life you want to live and make your home fit into it. Formal interiors do it the other way around; their strict structure limits the range of the inhabitants' activities.

Any sort of design, but particularly design in the home, is more about common sense than about style. You should think what it is you *want*; homes are for people; your home is for you and your style.

Your 'home sweet home' is what you make it.

PART 1

DESIGN
FOR LIVING

Hugh Newell Jacobsen designed this house to suit the clients' needs and to blend into a location amidst old Pennsylvania town houses. An eighteenth-century-style façade, echoing local Amish buildings, appears to be a terrace of seven small houses, with this magnificent glazed gable end. The couple who commissioned the house thought the design was too big, too modern and impossible to construct, but bravely went ahead; now they feel it's an ideal home. The vast expanse of mirrored glass is a heat trap in winter, but is shaded by dogwood trees in summer.

ASSESSMENT

We shape our homes in an infinite variety of ways, ranging from simple placing of furniture to designing and building from scratch; in return, and with equal variety, the homes we live in structure our day-to-day lives.

Considering how much potential there is for creative change, many of us approach making alterations to our homes in a surprisingly piecemeal fashion. Simply overwhelmed by the complexity of it all, we go by what 'feels right'.

The feel of a new plan or home, though certainly significant, is not enough. Choices about home changes are complicated; they are also of paramount importance. Major alterations may disrupt the life of your household for months or years. Simple redecoration will result in changes that you will have to live with until you have the energy or resources to pick up a paintbrush again. Buying a house involves the largest financial transaction you will probably ever make.

Assessment is the means to deciding what you want and need from a home and the route to establishing what options are available. A methodical step-by-step analysis is the best way of ensuring satisfactory results.

Levels of change

Selecting the level of change that is right for you entails identifying how you want to live, as well as your practical requirements, and then assessing how these can be met in the simplest, cheapest and least disruptive way.

Broadly speaking, there are three possible levels of change. In ascending order of magnitude, these are:
- redecorating and/or refurnishing;
- making structural alterations;
- moving.

In many cases the calculations will be straightforward. If the only problem in your home is that the living room is dingy, then redecorating is probably a better bet than moving. If your job has moved to another city, the reverse will almost certainly hold.

But imagine, for instance, that you need another bedroom because of the arrival of more children. You may then have to decide between extending or moving your home. Consider the range of factors this choice would involve:

Layout and structure Would the best solution be to change the function of an existing room to provide the extra bedroom? If not, is there scope for extension in the existing layout? If you have a solid, single-storey garage attached to your house or an airy attic then, planning permission or zoning regulations notwithstanding, this may not present a problem. If you are on a middle floor of a high-rise it almost certainly will.

Cost How much money can you raise? If you're making structural alterations and re-decorating, can you afford to buy good quality materials? Will the work mean expensive changes to the electrical system? Would it be more economical to go for a new mortgage on a different home than attempt to finance costly structural alterations?

Investment value Which option best protects the capital you have already invested in your home? As a general rule it is not a good idea to sink large sums into redesigning properties in poor or declining areas; it may be difficult to recoup your outlays when you come to resell.

Disruption Whichever option you adopt, disruption is inevitable. But it will vary in kind and degree. The noise, dirt and lack of privacy involved in altering your home may be difficult to live with. But will the travails of selling your home, finding another, packing up, moving and resettling be any easier?

Long-term plans What about the longer term? Might your requirements change again in a few years' time when your children get older or elderly relatives appear on the scene? Is it better to move now or extend for an interim period?

Your practical requirements

A detailed profile of your practical requirements is an essential foundation for major home decisions. By working through the checklist opposite you can chart this profile.

The art of the possible: the humble ruins of a fortified tower, built on the southern Italian coast by the Spanish in 1586, transformed into an impressive modern house. Fragments of the old tower have been incorporated into great vertical elevations of the new walls, which faithfully reconstruct the outline of the original fortress.

The building has an imposing grandeur inherited from its ancient predecessor, and its design is perfectly suited to the remote coastal location. A high central window bisecting the seaward wall of the house ensures ample natural light inside without the use of conventional windows, which would have destroyed the fortress-like exterior. Reflected light is increased by the dominant use of white, especially a floor of white ceramic tiles. The open-plan interior incorporates the full height of the tower and three floor levels have been created, spanned by an industrial-style grid staircase.

TABLE OF PRACTICAL REQUIREMENTS

LOCATION

- Do you want your home to be near:
  - employment?
  - public transport?
  - schools or nurseries?
  - friends or relatives?
  - hospitals or doctors?
  - shops?
  - night life?
  - parks and playgrounds?
  - youth clubs?
  - sports facilities?
  - libraries?
  - countryside or sea for recreation?

SPACE

How many rooms?

- How many bedrooms do you need?
- Do you want a:
  - separate kitchen and dining room?
  - combined kitchen and dining room?
- Do you want more than one living room?
- Do you want more than one bathroom?
- Do you want a:
  - nursery?
  - garage?
  - workshop?
  - study/library?
  - laundry?
  - guest room?
  - store room?
  - breakfast room?
  - porch?
  - garden shed?
  - conservatory (sunroom)?
  - greenhouse?
  - dressing room?
  - games room?
  - swimming pool?
  - sauna?
  - jacuzzi?
  - solarium?

What size rooms?

- Which rooms do you want to be spacious?
- Do you want high ceilings?
- How much and what size furniture do you want in each room?
- How much storage space do you need in each room?

What position?

- Which rooms do you want to be close to each other (eg, kitchen and dining room)?
- Which rooms do you want to be kept apart?
- What time of day would you prefer sunlight in each room?
- Which rooms do you want to have access to the garden?
- If you have a view, from which rooms would you like to see it?
- Are there rooms which need to be on the ground floor (eg, for elderly or disabled people)?

SERVICES AND FITTINGS

Heating

- What type of fuel do you want:
  - gas?
  - electricity?
  - oil?
  - solid fuel?
  - solar?
- Do you want:
  - open fires?
  - radiators?
  - storage heaters?
  - gas or electric fires?
  - air conditioning?
  - warm-air ducts?
  - a solid-fuel kitchen range with boiler?
- What level of insulation do you want:
  - cavity wall?
  - loft lining?
  - draught stopping?
  - double glazing?
- Do you want your heating control to be:
  - room by room?
  - centralized?
  - both?
- How many electric socket outlets do you need in each room?
- How many wall or ceiling light leads do you want in each room?
- Do you need high-voltage circuits for cooking, immersion heaters etc?
- Do you want a separate meter for off-peak electricity?
- Do you want an exterior electricity meter?
- Do you need a separate meter for rented accommodation?

Gas and oil

- How many gas points do you want in each room and in what positions?
- Do you want an exterior gas meter?
- Do you need a tank for oil or liquid gas storage:
  - above ground?
  - below ground?

Plumbing

- How many water outlets, hot and cold, do you need and in which rooms?
- Do you want:
  - water points for a washing machine or dishwasher?
  - an external tap?
  - a water softening unit?
  - a waste disposal unit on sinks?
  - a direct mains water supply?

Built-in cabinets

- Do you want built-in units in the kitchen?
- Do you want storage units in bedrooms or elsewhere?

LIGHT AND NOISE

- Do you want areas with lots of natural light?
- Do you want areas that are quiet?
- Do you want to insulate rooms against noise?

ACCESS

- How many access points do you need?
- Do you want separate access points to different areas?
- Do you want direct access to the garden or patio and from which rooms?
- Do you want covered access to the garage?
- Do you need access to attic, roof or cellar?
- Do you need access to fire escapes?
- Should any access areas not have steps?
- Do you need doors and halls that are wide enough for a wheelchair?
- Do you need an elevator?
- Do you need access for bulky furniture?
- Do you need access for fuel delivery or rubbish collection?

SECURITY

- Do you want:
  - to be close to a police station?
  - an alarm system? If so, what type?
  - dead locks on all exterior doors?
  - locks on internal doors?
  - locks or bars on windows?
  - unbreakable glass in doors and windows?
  - to be overlooked by neighbours?
  - a lockable garage?
  - a wall safe?
  - secure boundaries around your property?

SAFETY

- Do you need:
  - child-proof windows and doors?
  - child-proof electric socket outlets?
  - heating outlets that are safe for children?
  - storage areas out of reach of children?
  - unbreakable glass in doors?
  - garden gates and fences to protect children?
  - lighting on stairs and steps?
  - handrails for elderly or disabled persons?
  - an alarm system for summoning help?

MISCELLANEOUS

- Do you need space or access for pets?
- How many telephones do you need? Where?
- Do you need:
  - an external TV aerial?
  - a satellite receiver?
  - facilities for a home computer?
  - provision for cable TV?
  - a telex machine?

Home options

Most of us adopt a highly conservative approach to the homes we live in, for good reason: borrowing, renovating and reselling are more straightforward with a standard house or apartment.

And certainly conventional housing works – designs have been fine tuned as they have been handed down through the centuries. If you live in a house or an apartment, you can make the home specifically your own by changing it in simple ways without having to resort to major structural changes.

But playing safe also has its price. It may be hard to avoid the boring or find a bargain. For those prepared to go for something different, a galaxy of interesting alternatives is available.

Around most cities a lot of industrial and commercial property is now available at low prices. Provided that planning departments and money lenders will co-operate, the option for creating a home in old factory buildings, warehouses, offices or shops has never looked more attractive.

Empty churches are dotted around the towns and cities. Find out what is available for conversion from communion to communal living through the offices of your local church diocese.

Many people are now happily ensconced in railway stations, signal boxes and even carriages. Would-be trackside tenants can find out what remains by contacting the property boards of the railway networks.

Farmers are feeling the squeeze and for those looking for unusual rural accommodation inquiries about vacant or under-utilized farm outbuildings may prove profitable.

Outbuildings in the urban environment also offer considerable potential. Old garages, workshops, even gazebos and greenhouses can be converted to create unusual and attractive living space.

From windmills to lighthouses, from castles to barges, anything with weatherproof walls and roof can provide a home for the daring and creative. The risks may be high. But the returns can be spectacular.

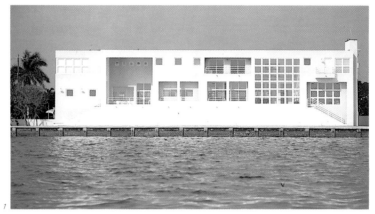

1

1 A romantic house on Biscayne Bay in Miami creates the illusion of an ocean liner.
2 A Victorian warehouse in London's dockland has been converted to modern apartments.

2

3 The ultimate isolated coastal house, built on the end of a pier above the Indian Ocean on Australia's western seaboard.
4 Raised on stilts above the waters of Lake Lacaneau in south-west France, these wooden holiday cabins are reminiscent of Asian waterside buildings.

3

4

5 Once grand, but then allowed to fall into sad decay, this house is being converted to self-contained units.
6 The generous proportions of a late nineteenth-century mansion put no limitations on space.
7 This English nineteenth-century shopfront now provides a living room with a wide view across a city square to an ancient cathedral.
8 Casa pronto: stylish prefabricated living, quickly assembled from a neat box the size of the middle section.
9 The traditional simplicity of a country cottage with trellised porch.
10 The restored façade of a Venetian church hides a contemporary home.
11 Intricate iron railings on a New Orleans terrace, 150 years old.
12 The classic geometry of the Colonial architectural style in Williamsburg, Virginia.

Assessing a new home

A home can be restructured or redecorated but, unless you are in the market for a caravan (house trailer) or a houseboat, the location is something you will be stuck with until it is time for you to move again.

The location

In general terms, location means the district or area where the property is situated. Its facilities – shops, transport, schools, hospitals and parks – together with its 'character' – well-heeled or run-down, improving or declining, mainstream or backwater – will largely determine the price of a home and its potential as investment.

You might decide you can live in a derelict area with no trees, no shops and no transport. But there is little point transforming a simple dwelling in a slum area into an elegant town house in the hope of increasing its value: property prices are not calculated in isolation. On the other hand, the desirability of an area is not static and you might be able to exploit this by finding a home at a low price in an area which is just starting to improve.

On a more specific level, the immediate vicinity is also important. Are nearby houses in sound or poor condition? Are builders or decorators at work on them? Are the roads and open spaces well maintained and are local shops flourishing? Is there pollution from nearby industrial units, noise from factories, night-clubs and pubs, or roads with heavy traffic?

How is the property itself situated? Will you be able to park your car nearby? Will it be safe for your children to cross the roads?

Look at the direction the property faces. Many people prefer bedrooms and kitchens that get sun in the morning, with living rooms on the opposite side of the house for warmth and light later in the day. If the property is in an exposed position, try to check how it squares up to the prevailing winter wind.

The structure

Before purchasing a home you must make yourself fully aware of the state of its structure. That means that at some point before buying you will have to obtain a survey from a qualified surveyor or house inspector. But it is a good idea to do your own preliminary survey (see the checklist opposite).

Any potential mortgagee will commission a survey of the property before lending money on it, but remember such a survey is only designed to establish if the place is worth more than the amount of the proposed mortgage – which may be considerably less than you are paying for the property.

The value

Real estate agents normally fix a price on the basis of comparison with similar properties on the market. It will then be adjusted for specific features:

The size Smaller properties which match family patterns – young couples, families with one or two children, pensioners – are in most demand and, therefore, more expensive room by room.

But size is not merely a question of floor area; numbers of rooms can also be a critical factor. A 'three-bedroomed' house may fetch a higher price than one with two bedrooms, even though they are identical in area.

The condition While a well-designed interior will bump up the price, the most important aspect is the structural condition of the property: if there is something wrong structurally you should drastically reconsider your assessment of the property's value.

Other points that add to the asking price include the size and condition of the garden, a modernized kitchen, newish bathroom suites and a garage.

Viewing a home

Viewing potential homes requires a mixture of method and imagination. You may have only a few hours to decide on something you will have to live with for many years. Don't be pressured into making a quick decision.

Any serious home-hunter needs to be armed with a limited but useful range of equipment: a pair of binoculars for inspecting the roof; a notebook for sketching plans; a tape measure; a camera (with flash); a penknife for poking into suspected damp or rot; a compass for checking the siting of the rooms; a flashlight for checking dark corners; and, most important of all, a copy of the checklist opposite.

It is usually preferable to be shown around a home by its occupants than by a real estate agent; the owners will know the place better and are less likely to be skilled at disguising faults and amplifying virtues.

Don't be afraid to ask questions. Ask why the owners are selling, how long they have inhabited the property, how much its running costs are, what they like and dislike about it, and what maintenance they have carried out.

Take your time when viewing a home. Make sure you see hidden corners under stairs, sinks or the roof. These are often the best places to find tell-tale signs of rot and damp. If you are serious about purchase, return several times – preferably not at the same time of day: a building will look quite different on a dull day or at night.

EXTERNAL FEATURES

Foundations

- Do the foundations appear level?
- Are there cracks in foundation walls?
- Is there earth banked against the walls?
- Is the building near large trees whose roots could undermine the foundations?
- Is water from downpipes (downspouts) and overflows channelled away from the property?
- Is there an adequate damp-proof course?

Drains

- Is the drain cover (clean-out) accessible?
- Is the concrete cracked around the cover?
- Does water rush or dawdle below the cover?
- Are rainwater drains free of debris?

Walls

- Do walls stand straight?
  Look at corners and for bulges.
- Are there cracks in the stone- or brickwork?
- Do brick courses run straight?
- Is mortar between bricks loose?
- Is render (stucco) firmly attached?
  Tap it to see if it sounds hollow.
- Are weatherboards (clapboards) rotting?
- Are there stains on walls below guttering, windows or roof?

Exterior doors

- Are doors warped?
- Are there any traces of rot?
- Is caulking around doors sound?
- Is the door furniture of good quality, and securely fastened?
- Are doors properly finished?
- Are the doors architecturally appropriate?

Windows

- Are windows warped?
- Are window frames in good condition?
- Is putty around frames in good condition?
- Is glass cracked in a way that suggests movement?
- Are the windows architecturally appropriate?
- Are screens, storm windows fitted properly?
- Have the windows been double glazed?

VIEWING A HOME CHECKLIST

Roof

- Has the roof been replaced or renovated recently?
- Does the ridge of the roof sag?
- Are there loose slates or tiles?
- Is the sheet-metal roofing rusted or loose?
- Are weatherboards in sound condition?
- Are joints around chimneys or dormers cracked?
- Are chimney stacks straight and in good condition?
- Is guttering sound and free of debris?

Porches, conservatories (sunrooms) and outbuildings

- Is the porch or conservatory (sunroom) firmly attached to the building?
- Are wood and external walls in good condition?
- Is the conservatory properly ventilated?
- Are outbuildings conveniently located?

Garden and paths

- Is the garden well designed and maintained?
- Does water drain properly from patios, terraces and paths?
- Are the fences and gates in good condition?
- Have paths been maintained?
- Are steps and railings secure?

INTERIOR FEATURES

Walls and ceilings

- Are the walls and ceilings straight?
- Are there cracks in the plaster?
  Look especially in corners.
- Are the wall surfaces in good condition?
- Are there gaps between skirting (baseboards) and walls?
- Do the skirting boards and architraves match?
- Are there any stains or bulging?

Stairs

- Are stairs and banisters solid?
- Are stairs too steep or too narrow?
- Is there adequate headroom above stairs?
- Are there light switches at the top and bottom of stairs?

Floors

- Do the floors slope?
  Placing a marble on the floor will sometimes reveal an otherwise undetectable slope.
- Are joists below floorboards in good condition?
  Look for loose boards that can be lifted for inspection and check in basement.
- Do floors feel spongy or sound hollow when tapped?

Basement

- Does the basement smell musty (a sign of dry rot)?
- Are there signs of damp on walls or floor?
- Is untreated wood in contact with earth?
- Is wiring and plumbing tidy and in good condition?
- Is basement properly ventilated?

Attic

- Are rafters and beams sound?
- Can you see light through the roof?
- Can you see damp, especially around chimneys, skylights or along walls or under valleys?
- Are there signs of infestation by birds, bats or insects?
- Is the attic ventilated and insulated?

Kitchens

- Are there signs of damp around the sink?
  Look inside cabinets.
- Are cabinets and surfaces in good condition?
- Are there sufficient electric socket outlets and are they sited conveniently?
- Are the cooker (stove) and sink well positioned?
- Is there adequate ventilation?

Bathrooms

- Are there traces of damp around fittings?
- Are the fittings in good condition?
- Does the toilet flush properly?
- Are there cracks in ceramic tiles?
- Is grouting on tiles sound?
- Is there adequate ventilation?
- Is the electricity safe?

Fireplaces

- Are there signs of damp around fireplaces?
- Do the chimneys draw properly?
  Test by holding a piece of lighted paper in them.
- Are tiles around fireplaces in good condition?
- If the fireplaces have dampers, do they close properly?
- If the fireplaces have been boarded up, are they safe to open up again?

Plumbing

- Are there signs of leaks in pipes (identifiable by rusting or crusting)?
- Are there clanking noises when a tap is turned on?
- Is the water flow adequate?
- Are copper water pipes linked to a galvanized-iron water cylinder (creating the danger of electrolysis)?
- Do sinks, basins and baths drain quickly and without bubbling?
- Do taps drip after they have been turned off?
- Does the hot-water system operate quietly?
- Is there an adequate-sized boiler?
- Are there overflow pipes from tanks and are their outlets clear of walls?
- Is the stop cock for the water supply working and accessible?

Heating

- Is the property heated with:
  - gas?
  - electricity?
  - oil?
  - solid fuels?
  - solar?
- Is the ventilation from the central-heating boiler adequate?
- Has the boiler been serviced regularly?
- Is there room-by-room control of heating?
- Is the thermostat positioned out of draughts?
- Is the home effectively insulated?

Electricity

- Is the wiring old?
  Tell-tale signs are rubber insulation and messy leads around the distribution box.
- Do lights flicker when turned on or off?
- Is the meter conveniently located?

Redesigning your home

Sketching a floor plan of your home will help you to familiarize yourself with what you have already got. But a plan will only show the layout of a building, not how it works. To assess this you need to walk around your home asking yourself questions about the spaces within it.

First consider how space is used by you and your family. What sort of activity takes place in each room, who uses it, for what and when? Try to assess which activities happily coexist and which conflict. Look also at whether rooms are used to their full potential.

Map out the routes around your home. How much space is used for circulation? Is the amount of space taken up by stairs, halls and landings excessive and, if so, could it be used for other purposes as well, for storage or work areas perhaps?

Look at how the various spaces interact with each other. Which rooms are isolated and which need to be located close to each other for related activities such as cooking and eating? Are there adjacent rooms with incompatible uses? Does circulation interfere with room space or vice versa?

Next review what you like about each room. Are the rooms a pleasing size and shape? Do they have sufficient light; are noise levels satisfactory? Perhaps there is nice detailing in the ceiling plasterwork or around the fireplace. Now consider if these positive features are complemented or highlighted by the decoration and furnishing. Does the furniture fit in?

List the least attractive elements of each room. Is there a lack of light, an ugly window, or a cramped and cluttered feel?

The decor should suit the purpose of the room. Are the surfaces in children's rooms and kitchens washable? Does the purple and orange flocked wallpaper on your bedroom ceiling appear frequently in your nightmares?

The external decoration should be in keeping with the architectural style of the building. Does the interior complement it?

Think once more about the overall character of your home; about whether everything goes together and produces a satisfying feeling of wholeness.

Options for change

This process of assessment will give you a fairly clear idea about what – if anything – is wrong with the way your house works and looks. The next stage is to decide how to solve your particular design problem. Acquaint yourself with the widest possible range of ideas: consult books and magazines, talk to retailers, professional designers, archi-

tects and builders. Ask friends with first-hand experience how they've carried out their own home improvements.

This shouldn't be as daunting as it might sound. The purpose is not to test how much you know about design, but to look hard at the drawbacks of your own home in the light of the options available. The object of redesigning your home is to make the space within it work better for you – both functionally and aesthetically. You should aim to make the optimum use of space in the simplest possible way, and any changes should involve the least cost and disruption.

In general terms, there are four basic options in home redesign:

Changing the function of rooms Whether it is making a nursery from a store-room or a spare bedroom in the garden shed, this can be an easy home design solution. It may require only the moving of furniture.

Changing the appearance of rooms Space is a vital element in the appearance of rooms. Try imagining the rooms in your home devoid of all furniture and then mentally letting through the door only those pieces you like and use. Different lighting patterns or changing the colour and texture of finishes on your walls, ceilings and floors may also do much to improve a space. Redecoration can transform your home – often at levels of expenditure and effort considerably lower than those required for any structural change.

Changing the shape of rooms Awkward-shaped or cramped rooms can often be greatly improved by cutting through a dividing wall; additional rooms can be created by erecting partitions. And ceilings and floors can be raised or lowered to improve the building's spatial quality.

Adding on If your need is simply for more space, you may have no choice but to extend, either within the building – in unused cellars, for example – or outside, linking up outbuildings, perhaps, or going up from the roof.

Completing the assessment

Other chapters discuss in detail *how* to change your home. For now – using your list of practical requirements and your analysis of the way the home functions and looks – you can decide exactly *what* you want to change.

All that remains to be done is to make some rough plans, arrange loans, call in architects, builders, plumbers and carpenters, deal with legal and planning matters, shop for materials, tolerate impossible levels of noise and dirt, and then clear everything up before settling down to normal life again. Congratulations. The difficult part is over.

The owner of a Dublin town house is restoring it to the state it was in when completed in 1743 – with a concentrated passion for accuracy, based on solid research. He and his family occupy it while work progresses, surrounded by inherited portraits and treasures as well as inexpensive recent acquisitions.

Structural repairs are being carried out first and all materials removed are stored for future use. Taking time enables more informed choices. The owner will make his own hand-blocked wallpaper for each room when the time comes. Meanwhile, the house is a dramatic setting for daily life, hinting at past glory. Built for the Earl of Ely, it was then a bishop's town house and a barracks, and later a run-down tenement before being rescued.

Restoration: four approaches

The four homes illustrated here are basically identical nineteenth-century terraced houses (1) on a north London street. The photographs reveal four very different approaches to home design: pictures 2, 5, 9, 13 were taken from the same position in each house.

The classically elegant terraces were built between about 1840 and 1860 as spacious family homes for respectable professionals. In the 1930s a cigarette factory opened nearby, homes were converted to 'rooming houses' in which workers rented rooms and shared cooking and washing facilities; the buildings went into serious decay. From the mid-1960s onwards the district again attracted young professionals who were faced with major renovation and redecoration.

2 This house was intact: the lovely double doors and the original decorative plaster mouldings were easily renovated. The owner followed a popular pattern, using the back as the kitchen and the front parlour as a dining room. The traditional furniture and decoration complement the building style.

3 Upstairs, in the 'drawing room', dividing doors were discovered beneath hardboard and the room's original proportions and atmosphere were restored.

Thorough renovation was needed for this building, which had been rented out as rooms. In the dining room (5) the original double doors have been stripped down to the natural pine. Beyond them is the spacious modern kitchen where structural alterations include the removal of the wall between kitchen and hall and a glass extension housing a utility and store room. In the hall (4) and dining room the original plaster ceiling mouldings were carefully restored and highlighted, while upstairs (6, 7), layer upon layer of paint was removed from the decorative plasterwork. The window frames, architraves and shutters were stripped and polished to match the double doors. A smaller door, originally leading to the landing, was found to be blocked and left that way. Close attention to detail has created rooms of cool harmony.

Removing walls on the ground floor of this house has radically altered its atmosphere and function. The owners admit that the open-plan kitchen/dining room (9) has its drawbacks: their privacy is sometimes invaded because the front door opens directly on to the hub of the house. The staircase (8), now part of the room, provides an attractive focal point and the area below it has been well used for storage space and to house the washing machine.

For six years the couple who own this house (12) have been working with painstaking care towards turning a decayed and neglected building into a beautifully decorated and fitted home. The husband has done much of the work himself. They have also used skilled carpenters and joiners to carry out their own design ideas. The kitchen units, which can be glimpsed beyond the dining room (13), are one example of this. The kitchen window is a faithful but enlarged version of the original and offers a full-length view over the garden.

The addition of a two-storey extension (10) provided the family with an extra sitting room (11). It has fine details, including hanging slate tiles on the exterior, and unusual, full-length arched windows.

14 Upstairs, work is in progress and at this stage the final tasks requiring access under floorboards are being completed. This room has become the workshop and storage area for tools, equipment and materials.

15 On the top floor, fitted wardrobes are based on period drawings, but the vanity unit is a modern departure.

PLANNING

Once you have decided what you want to change in your home, there is an overwhelming temptation to leap straight in and start work immediately.

But it is wise not to be too hasty. House improvements and alterations can be satisfying to carry out, and a good investment of time and money; they can also turn out to be a costly nightmare, disruptive of work, family life and even health.

Building work needs careful planning and supervision: after all, houses are not just inert stacks of bricks or wood but a composite of heating, plumbing and electrical networks contained within the structure of the building. All these systems – and the people who interact with them – can be affected by even quite minor alterations.

Another reason for planning is that it is often more difficult, and therefore more costly, to change buildings than might at first appear. It may seem sensible to move a bathroom from one place to another – but it might also prove, upon investigation, to be illegal or impractical, or it might be ruinously expensive to do so.

The Chinese have a most advanced attitude to planning problems. Before a single brick is touched they will consult a *feng shui* expert, a sort of philosopher-designer, who advises not only on such details as room plans and orientation, but also on how, when and where everything should be carried out. *Feng shui* is about thinking through the fundamentals first – a characteristic of all good and effective planning.

The planning process

Hiring a philosopher may seem too extreme for most of us, but thinking *is* what planning is all about: thinking about your needs, about the condition and potential of your property, and about possible design solutions.

Planning is both an exact process and a flexible one; it does not necessarily involve drawing up a blueprint for every single item of work. That would be impossible, and inappropriate: a plan fixed rigidly from the start will be an inhuman one. Your plan should start loose and amorphous, and become more refined, more detailed, more complete, as you go along.

The previous chapter outlined how you should establish what you want to change about your home. If you have followed this procedure you will know what features you need and will have pinpointed the house's functional and aesthetical deficiencies; as well, you should list any repairs necessary to the building's structure.

These are the minimum requirements of your plan of work. They are the starting points for any alterations.

Working out the options

By now you will have a rough floor plan of your home. Make several copies of the plan on which you can mark all the different possibilities you are considering.

On one copy, mark all the necessary repairs, plus structural and technical features such as retaining walls, plumbing, and so on, so that you can price this work separately.

You should try to keep an open mind about the options. It is always a good idea to have several alternatives ready in case your first choice is just not workable.

Feasibility study

Now you need to measure the available options against what is practically possible. At its simplest, this means asking of each plan the following questions:

Can I afford to pay for it? You must decide not only whether you could raise enough money to carry out the work, but also whether it would be a good idea to do so: the improvements might not add much to the property's resale value, or it might be a better investment to commit less money to your home and keep some back for holidays or entertainment.

Can I afford the time and trouble? You should be extremely conservative in estimating how much you intend to do personally. This may well mean that some items in your 'wants' list may prove too expensive; better to face this now than find your social life in ruins in eighteen months' time as you struggle to install a bathroom or hang complicated kitchen units off a partition wall.

Hiring professional help, such as a builder or architect, may seem an unnecessary luxury, but remember, in letting them do the work you also shift a good deal (but not all) of the day-to-day management and administrative responsibilities too.

Is it practical? Is it technically possible? All kinds of apparently sensible house modifications can turn out to be physically impossible upon close examination. If in any doubt, get expert advice before starting.

Also find out now whether the proposed work is legal: big jobs such as additions and attics usually need to meet a variety of structural, planning and zoning requirements – but unlikely small changes can be affected too. Repainting the front door of your listed or landmark house a different colour can be illegal, for instance.

Having compared what you would like, ideally, to do, with what is feasible, you will probably encounter a number of contradictions. Sorting these out should not be too complicated: for example, if your major priority is three bedrooms, then the fact that this conflicts with your wish for a study simply means you don't get a study, unless you adapt an under-used dining room, for instance, to play a more useful dual role.

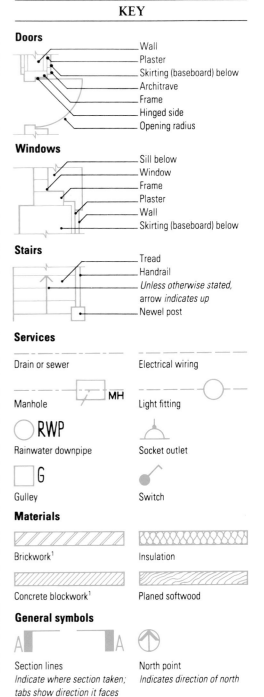

KEY

Doors
- Wall
- Plaster
- Skirting (baseboard) below
- Architrave
- Frame
- Hinged side
- Opening radius

Windows
- Sill below
- Window
- Frame
- Plaster
- Wall
- Skirting (baseboard) below

Stairs
- Tread
- Handrail
- *Unless otherwise stated,* arrow *indicates up*
- Newel post

Services

Drain or sewer   Electrical wiring

Manhole   MH   Light fitting

RWP

Rainwater downpipe   Socket outlet

G

Gulley   Switch

Materials

Brickwork[1]   Insulation

Concrete blockwork[1]   Planed softwood

General symbols

A   A

Section lines   North point
Indicate where section taken; tabs show direction it faces   *Indicates direction of north*

[1]United Kingdom only

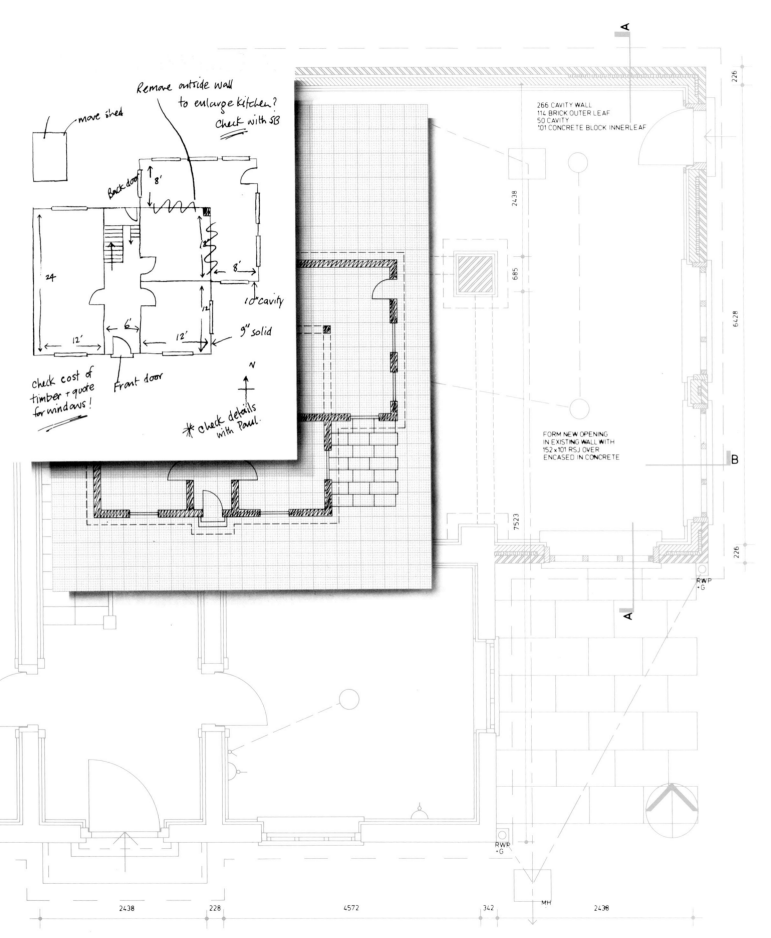

266 CAVITY WALL
114 BRICK OUTER LEAF
50 CAVITY
101 CONCRETE BLOCK INNERLEAF

FORM NEW OPENING
IN EXISTING WALL WITH
152 x 101 RSJ OVER
ENCASED IN CONCRETE

move shed

Remove outside wall
to enlarge kitchen?
Check with SB

Back door ↑ 8'

24

10" cavity

9" solid

12'   6'   12'

Front door

N

check cost of
timber + quote
for windows!

✳ check details
with Paul.

Money

There is virtually no limit to the amount of money you could spend on your home. That's why it is so important to impose budgetary control over the whole process: estimating the likely costs accurately, working out where the money for the work will come from, and monitoring the actual progress of the project against your budget and schedule.

Establishing your budget

It is easier to estimate the cost of building a complete house or a new wing than it is for rebuilding or a conversion. Complications often arise after work has started: you might, for instance, discover rot or other deterioration that needs to be remedied once walls are removed. And it is the nature of refurbishing work that the detailed specification changes as work progresses. An example: once the plumbers move in you might decide to put in one or two extra basins. The psychological urge to 'get it all done while they're here' is a strong one – it can also prove financially dangerous!

Indirect costs

These include architectural and legal fees and the costs of other professional services you purchase.

Although professionals might seem expensive, they can often save you more than they cost you – what you are buying, after all, is their specialized knowledge and their years of experience.

Direct costs: alterations

You should get detailed estimates of the costs of labour and of materials for every step of your proposed project. Also budget for fixtures and finishes: remember to allow for the 'small' items needed to finish off your new bedroom when the builders leave – the beds, light fittings and so on.

In addition, it's essential to add a 'fudge factor' of say ten or twenty per cent. This contingency allowance is considerable; but contingencies are not optional – it is rash in the extreme to base your financial planning on the fixed estimates.

Direct costs: necessary repairs

Necessary repairs – repairs to the structure of the house, plumbing and electrical maintenance, and work to bring the property in line with planning or zoning requirements – should be budgeted for separately. In the end, you might find that they are all you can afford to do. Be sure to cross reference your list of repairs to the list of improvements and alterations – inevitably there will be some overlap between the two.

Getting the figures It may be worth paying an architect to go over your various outline plans and give you a broad idea of the costs involved. This will help eliminate the totally impossible; you can then obtain detailed figures for feasible projects.

Ask a builder or contractor for a rough estimate of what it will all cost: you will need to provide a sketch of the proposed work and as detailed a list of fixtures and fittings as you can manage. It should be made clear that the builder will be asked to put in a formal tender with two or three other firms.

FINANCIAL PLANNING
GENERAL

- Can you afford:
  - experts' fees?
  - labour?
  - materials?
  - redecoration?
  - new furnishings?
  - a holiday (after the turmoil)?
- Have you costed the basic work?
- How much will resulting extra work cost?
- Have you added money at each stage for possible unseen developments, such as discovering dry rot?
- Are you intending to use capital or to borrow?
- What percentage of your income can you afford to invest in this work, through repayment of loans, and over what period?
- Will loan(s) be long or short term and how much will repayments be?
- Is there a possibility of tax relief?
- Are your employment and long-term plans stable?
- Can you do any of the work yourself?
- Would it be better to work overtime in order to pay someone else to do the work?
- Have you left yourself enough money for finishing decoration, furnishings, fixtures?
- Will the altered home cost more to run?
- Do you expect the market value of the building to increase?

CREATING A BUDGET
TWO EXAMPLES

A new lighting scheme

- Can you afford the expertise of a lighting designer?
- If not, first read *LIGHTING* in this book and work out your fittings (fixtures) options:
  - pendant(s)
  - downlights
  - dimmer switches
  - spotlights
  - table lamps
  - floor lamps
- How will you achieve the correct effects:
  - general?
  - task?
  - atmospheric lighting?
- How will this lighting affect existing furnishings and decoration?
- Are you going to create extra costs?
- Will the room need:
  - rewiring?
  - replastering?
  - repainting?
  - wallpapering?
  - other repairs?
- Can you re-use existing fittings?
- Have you obtained estimates from three electricians and fittings suppliers?

Building an extension

- Why do you need an extension?
- Would it be financially advantageous to move house rather than extend your present one?
- Will the extension have special requirements such as soundproofing?
- Will it entirely fulfill extra space requirements?
- Will it increase the market value of the property?
- Do you require:
  - structural survey?
  - building licence?
  - neighbours' consent?
  - planning permission?
  - development permit?
  - a more realistic plan?
- Do you need to comply with:
  - preservation area regulations?
  - listed or landmark building restrictions?
  - local health, safety and water regulations?
- Will you need an architect or can your builder provide architectural drawings?
- Have you obtained three estimates via architects or from:
  - builders?
  - electricians?
  - plumbers?
  - decorators?
- Do you understand your contract(s)?
- Will the extension be covered by your present insurance policy?

Operational costs

There are two additional costs which you should consider before commissioning or starting work: the cost of borrowing money to do the work and the maintenance costs once work is complete. For instance, build as much insulation as possible into the new work, as a hedge against rising heating costs.

The chances are that you will be faced with a gap between what you can spend and what you would like to do. But you can reduce costs by planning ahead, and through choosing alternative design solutions. This book is filled with a variety of cost-saving hints which you should consider at the planning stages; also consider the following general points:

● Avoid major restructuring of the site (and garden): shifting earth and rubble is always expensive, so where possible work within the existing landscape and topography.

● Keep the plan simple: avoid meandering corridors, complicated roof forms and the like; but if you are intent on unusual design features, price them particularly carefully, and only use them if they match the style and character of the building.

● Consider prefabricated components: they are often cheaper than ones which are custom-made. Investigate using second-hand materials – they might cost more to install, but could increase the property's value if they match the original materials and features.

● The choice of materials can affect the budget considerably: their costs should be considered at this planning stage. But remember that good quality materials are often better value in the long term.

● Building techniques also influence final costs: specify unusual or non-standard work only when absolutely necessary.

Financing: raising money

The amount of money available to you, now and in the future, represents the limits to the amount of work you can plan on carrying out.

'Money' does not just include cash in hand; also calculate into the amount available:

● short-term credit – that is, money available through overdrafts, credit cards and personal loans; these will be limited to small sums;

● the monthly amount you are prepared to spend repaying a home improvement loan;

● the potential value of your home, less the mortgage you owe on it (this is the equity – the part you own).

Even if you do have large sums of cash available – enough, say, to convert an attic or build a small addition – you may be better advised to borrow money in any case. Discuss this with your bank or accountant.

Budget planning

Your next step is to decide what you can afford to do immediately, and what will have to be deferred. When setting priorities, remember that you may, conceivably, be faced with a change of circumstances and wish to sell the house unexpectedly. So, unless you are particularly sure about the future, avoid planning to leave work unfinished pending finance; it is better to design the work in stages to be completed one at a time.

DIVIDING YOUR MONEY
ALLOCATING FUNDS

Whatever your plans may be, it will help to work out first your total budget and then the amount of money you can allocate to each specific area of work or expenditure.

Always add a contingency sum to each area of expenditure to cover unplanned developments and possible difficulties which will cause further expense.

The following examples provide general guidance only. Unless stated, the cost of the building is not included.

Converting a derelict farm building
Be prepared for living off-site (that is, affording two homes at once), or in messy discomfort, for some time. An option for the rich, perfectionists, idealists, or obsessives only.

Restoring a period family house
Giving new life to an old house you have enjoyed living in for years. Large-scale disruption to family life and routine. Major financial commitment for long-term investment.

A small, modern apartment
For first-time buyers who plan to move on soon. Accept the fabric and as much of basic decoration as possible and spend any spare funds on movable furnishings.

A house for retirement
Expensive initial investment, preferably little redecoration or alteration required. Maintenance/running costs important.

Converting a derelict farm building

Restoring a period family house

A small, modern apartment

A house for retirement

KEY

Major structural alterations/repairs, such as new roof, large extension, complete restoration, supplying services (water etc)

Altering internal layout, such as removing walls, moving staircases and landings, adding windows and doors

Improving use of space, such as building small extension, moving/adding a bathroom, converting attic, enlarging kitchen

Modernizing and improving, such as rewiring, landscaping garden, installing central heating, replastering

Renovation, decoration and maintenance, such as repainting, repairing decorative plasterwork, installing new flooring

Adding assets, such as the latest kitchen fittings, a swimming pool, a conservatory (sunroom), a tennis court

Who does what?

Most people will employ an architect and a builder or contractor to carry out major structural work associated with alterations and improvements. Some of us would rather have professionals do all the work. But if you are reasonably well organized and practically minded, you should be able to remove the odd partition wall or replace skirting (baseboards) – but only attempt to replace a roof or build an addition if you are very experienced.

You might not be able to afford to employ others, but in the long run it is certainly far better to modify your overall plans than to embark on major works yourself which may prove impossible to handle, and, in some cases, even dangerous.

Your options are much wider when it comes to finishing jobs on the interior of the house, the range of work which includes simple carpentry, tiling walls, filling cracks, painting and decorating.

New technology has made this work far easier to do. Take painting, for example: paints have been developed (in fact 'engineered') to an extraordinary extent. Until a few years ago, achieving a smooth result on a door painted with gloss finish was a matter of skill and considerable patience. Today, non-drip paints put a reasonable finish within the range of most amateurs so long as they follow the basic instructions.

If you do tackle any electrical or plumbing work, however, it is essential that you have it checked over by a professional – heating and plumbing installation needs to comply with local building regulations; a mistake in the wiring can easily put a home, and lives, at risk through fire.

But beware. The important thing is not to take on more than you know you can manage. For it is a cast-iron rule of home improvements that all work turns out more time-consuming and extensive than you have anticipated.

Before you decide to tackle a job, you should ask yourself: Is this work necessary? Can I carry it out? Do I really want to do it? Do I have the time to do so? Would it be cheaper – in terms of both time and money – to employ a professional?

Get in perspective exactly what you are competent to do. The secret of success is not to aim too high by taking on work which is too long-term, too difficult, or too complicated to handle comfortably. And it's important to remember that you could be spending your time more profitably earning money at something in which you are skilled in order to pay professionals to work on your home.

BUILDING

Straightforward

- sealing cracks around windows and doors
- installing draught proofing
- installing loft insulation

Semi-professional

- laying foundations
- repointing brickwork
- replacing damaged bricks
- doing basic brick- and blockwork
- removing non-loadbearing walls
- building new partitions and extensions
- cutting small openings in walls (ie, for extractor fan)
- attaching insulation to walls
- facing walls with stone
- removing or installing fireplaces
- erecting prefabricated chimneys
- refurbishing roof space

Professional

- putting in or repairing damp-proof courses and airbricks
- repairing settlement cracks
- removing structural or loadbearing walls
- laying concrete floors
- doing decorative stonework
- installing cavity-wall insulation
- cutting large openings in walls (ie, for doors and windows)
- replacing and installing lintels
- repairing chimney stacks and flues
- demolishing or building chimney stacks and flues
- installing roof tiles, slates, iron etc
- structurally altering roof or attic space

The experts

- builder
- bricklayer
- roofing contractor
- specialist loft company

PLUMBING, CENTRAL HEATING AND AIR CONDITIONING

Straightforward

- replacing tap washers
- clearing blocked sinks, drains and gullies
- installing plastic guttering and downpipes (downspouts)
- insulating water tanks and pipes
  All gas work must be done by a gas company or utility

Semi-professional

- making simple extensions to plumbing systems (ie, pipework)
- repairing burst or split pipes
- renewing ball valves
- fitting new taps and shower extensions
- plumbing in washing machine, dishwasher etc
- installing waste systems for sinks, bath, washing machines etc
- installing stop-taps or cocks
- installing metal guttering and downpipes (downspouts)
- installing packaged central-heating systems
- servicing central-heating system (excluding boilers)
- installing thermostat and time controls for central-heating system
- cleaning and replacing air filters

Professional

- laying drains
- installing water mains and mains drainage (done by water board or utility only)
- installing baths, sinks, toilets etc
- fitting complete shower systems
- installing storage tanks or cylinders
- fitting immersion heaters
- installing waste systems for toilets
- installing custom-built central-heating systems
- installing and servicing boilers for hot water and central heating
- installing expansion tank for central-heating system
- installing and servicing air-conditioning system

The experts

- plumber
- water board or utility
- central-heating engineer
- central-heating supply company

ELECTRICS/ELECTRONICS

Straightforward

- replacing fuses and light bulbs
- changing plugs
- installing battery-operated bells and buzzers

Semi-professional

- replacing appliance cords
- fitting or replacing switches and socket outlets
- making simple extensions to lighting
- putting up light fittings
- fitting electrically operated bells, buzzers and burglar alarms
- installing battery-operated fire alarms
- installing outdoor lighting
- installing radio and television aerials
- installing extractor fans and hoods
- installing ceiling fans

Professional

- laying mains cables
- installing electricity meters (done by electricity board or utility only)
- installing consumer units and distribution (fuse) boxes
- installing cables from mains supply
- wiring and rewiring work
- installing lighting and power circuits
- running supply to sheds and outbuildings
- installing telephone cables and extensions (done by telephone company only)
- installing a cooker (stove) and hob
- installing under-floor, storage and other electrical heating systems
- installing electronic burglar alarms

The experts

- electrician
- electricity board or utility
- telephone company
- security company

WOODWORK

Straightforward

- putting up shelving
- erecting packaged furniture
- treating light infestation of woodworm etc

Semi-professional

- fitting shutters and louvre doors
- repairing window and door frames
- making cupboards and small items of furniture
- putting up cupboards
- hanging doors
- repairing stairs and staircases
- fixing mouldings, architraves and skirting boards (baseboards)
- treating structural timbers affected by woodworm etc
- installing kit built-in furniture
- repairing wooden furniture

Professional

- laying floorboards
- fitting or replacing windows and doors
- replacing staircases
- repairing structural timbers
- inserting floor joists
- treating dry rot
- building in furniture
- repairing antique and valuable furniture

The experts

- carpenter (structure)
- joiner (fittings and fixtures)
- specialist timber treaters
- furniture restorer

GLAZING

Straightforward

- installing simple-kit double glazing
- hanging mirrors
- putting up mirror and glass shelves

Semi-professional

- cutting, drilling and fitting window and door glass
- replacing louvre-window glass
- repairing stained-glass windows
- installing secondary-frame double glazing
- fitting sealed double-glazed units
- fixing mirror tiles
- cutting and drilling mirrors
- smoothing plate-glass window and mirror edges
- fitting glass blocks
- fitting glass or mirror tops to work surfaces

Professional

- installing custom-built double glazing
- repairing leaded windows
- cutting plate-glass windows
- reglazing mirrors
- fixing large areas of mirror

The experts

- glazier

FITTINGS AND FINISHES

Straightforward

- painting interiors
- applying wall coverings
- laying ceramic tiles on walls
- laying carpet, cork, vinyl floor tiles
- sealing timber floors
- filling cracks in walls and ceilings
- fitting curtain and blind tracks
- fitting window and door furniture

Semi-professional

- applying exterior decorative wall finishes – eg, masonry paints
- applying timber panelling or boarding to walls
- patching damaged areas of plasterwork
- putting up coving between walls and ceiling
- laying foam-backed carpets
- laying stair carpets
- levelling concrete floors with screeding compound
- laying quarry tiles on floors
- sanding and preparing timber floors for final finishes

Professional

- plastering and replastering walls and ceiling
- replacing ceilings
- stretching and laying fitted carpets
- laying terrazzo and slate floors
- replacing floorboards
- painting iron and corrugated asbestos roofs

The experts

- painter and decorator
- plasterer
- builder
- carpet fitter
- tiler

Employing others

You must make a detailed evaluation of what professional help your budget can support; it is better to stagger the schedule (and therefore payment) of work rather than take things on that you are ill-equipped to handle.

Employing others will not solve all the problems associated with home alterations – if you are unlucky, the opposite can be the case. But if you plan and manage professional help in a sensible way, you can achieve excellent results and off-load a large amount of day-to-day responsibilities.

Remember when using outside help, you are employing experts to carry out your wishes; it's not for them to decide what your needs are or to impose their own ideas on your home. By all means take professional advice in deciding what you want, but if you don't agree in advance with solutions, almost certainly trouble will follow.

Planning and preparation

As outlined earlier, you need to negotiate several stages before building work can commence; these are just as important as the actual construction. They include: preliminary planning and outline design; a feasibility study of options; drawing up draft proposals and budgets, detailed working drawings and a schedule of work; obtaining estimates and necessary permissions; compiling a detailed financial budget.

You can carry out all these preparatory stages yourself; there are numerous books and guides that tell you how. However, do not underestimate the tasks – detailed working drawings or specifications are far beyond the capabilities of most people.

Getting the work done

Once you have reached the state when building work is ready to begin, you should consider how best to manage the project.

If you are employing an architect, your main role at this stage is to make doubly and trebly sure that you both understand each other. You will have agreed plans, drawings, budgets and schedules: from here on, you need not be too involved on a day-to-day basis – although this does not mean that either the architect or builder should intimidate you out of keeping an eye on progress! It is your money, after all. But don't interfere unnecessarily, particularly when it comes to technical questions.

However, if you have done your own planning and design, or have used an architect to draw up plans but not to manage the work, you now have to find and work with a builder and other contractors.

Planning/preparation

Architects

The best way to choose an architect is through personal recommendation. Failing that, architects' professional bodies, such as the Royal Institute of British Architects or the American Institute of Architects, maintain registers of members – get in touch with the local section of the organization. If you see work you like, ask who the architect was.
Architects fees Most architects are happy to give you preliminary advice at the planning stage for a standard fee per hour.

Before you employ an architect, check with the architects' professional association for the recommended scale of fees for the various types of work.

Full architectural service will usually work out between six and thirteen per cent of the total price of the job, but fees do vary widely depending on such factors as the size and complexity of the work, and the extent of the responsibility involved. Fees are usually higher for conversion or renovation than for new building.

Surveyors/house inspectors

You employ a surveyor or house inspector to check over the building's structure, its services, finishes, and so on, and to suggest what, if anything, needs to be done in the way of repairs. A surveyor could also give you a rough estimate of how much it would cost to carry out any alterations you want to make, and then supervize the work. But essentially, surveyors and house inspectors know about structure and building work – if you need advice on design, go to an architect. The survey the mortgagee commissions on a building you

want to buy may reveal basic faults, but is intended to establish the property's value, not its condition. You can also get a full structural survey done which could be useful when bargaining over the property's price. There is no standard scale of charges; it's worth shopping around.

Legal matters

If you decide to employ an architect to manage the whole project, then he/she will look after all the paperwork. Or the builder may do it. The ideal person to handle this is a solicitor or lawyer.

Consents, prior to work commencing, may involve:
● your landlord;
● lessees/tenants;
● insurancer/morgagee;
● adjoining property owners/easements;
● local authorities, eg, re zoning, statutory building and drainage regulations, building license;
● planning/highway authorities;
● fire department;
● gas board/supplier;
● electricity board/supplier;
● telephone company;
● water board/supplier;
● transport authorities/river/harbour boards;
● community groups.

It is essential to establish whether any of the above need to give their consent to work – obtain this before you start. Many regulating bodies react adversely to property owners who start work too soon; in some cases – for example, with foundations or plumbing – work may be impossible for their inspectors to pass, if other work has progressed in the interim.

Allow time for obtaining consents; treat them as a priority.

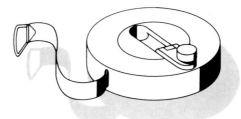

Getting the work done

Builders/contractors

The safest way to find a reliable builder is by personal recommendation; if a builder has done a good job for someone you know, the chances are you will get good results too. Failing this, if there is a national building trade organization, the local branch should have lists of members.

Always ask a builder for details of at least two previous clients – find out from them how the builder performed. If a builder refuses to divulge these details, keep on looking for one that will.

Builders' estimates Always obtain estimates from two or three builders or contractors. As well as the total cost of the job, you should establish when they would start work, and the time the job will take.

Carefully consider any qualifications on the estimates – as well as price – before finally deciding on a builder.

Most builders will start a job with great enthusiasm, but as the job approaches completion they are already working on new contracts and things might slow down: to avoid this, consider tying the estimates to agreed completion dates.

The plan of work To safeguard all parties, no builder or contractor should be asked for an estimate for a job without being given a written specification of what you want done and to what standard. This, and any drawings you submit, will form an important part of the contract between you and the builder.

The moment you give any builder leeway to choose a size, or height, or detail, is the moment trouble starts. So, if you are planning to write your own specifications, leave nothing to the builder's discretion. You do not need to spell out how the work is to be done – but you must spell out, in great detail, what you want at the end: if you simply asked for the removal of a partition wall, for example, you could find that the extensive 'making good' required was not included in the price.

Any subsequent changes must be confirmed in writing – verbal instructions may be misinterpreted by the builder.

For some projects, the builder may also need drawings. An architect will supply these, or a draughtsperson will prepare the necessary drawings for a small fee, given a careful brief.

Paying the builder On small contracts, lasting less than four or five weeks, most builders will not expect payment until after work is completed.

On bigger jobs, it is usual to make interim payments as work progresses: you pay agreed percentages of the total estimated cost at specified stages of the building work.

Some estimates will include provisional sums . These are normally used for work the builder has to sub-contract and has not obtained firm estimates for. Always ensure you are consulted before a provisional sum is converted into a firm price.

You are entitled to retain up to ten per cent of the total cost of the job for a period of between three and six months after work has been completed – provided you tell the builder your intention at the estimate stage – to cover the cost of any defects that may arise due to faulty work.

Make/stay friends with your builder Before the work starts, completely clear the rooms likely to be affected.

Agree on a convenient place where ladders, scaffold boards and other equipment and materials can be stored during the work; and set some rules about tidying up when work is completed every day – not tramping through the place in dirty boots, washing dirty dishes, and the like. Provide facilities for meals, making cups of tea or coffee, and somewhere to shelter in bad weather if the builders are working outside.

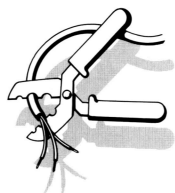

Electricians' work

Local electricity boards or utilities will usually take on any domestic electrical work, but they tend to be a little more expensive than private contractors.

If the board does do the work, it will not question it afterwards; however, you can make an independent contractor responsible for ensuring that all the work complies with local codes. To safeguard yourself, get this agreement in writing.

As always, make sure you know exactly what you are getting for your money before you agree the price: the quickest and cheapest way might not be the best – cables fixed up along skirting boards, for example, may not have been what you had in mind at the start.

Always use a professional.

Plumbers

It is illegal to make any alterations or additions to the plumbing or drainage of a building without reference to the local building department.

Bureaucratic interest in your plumbing arrangements is mainly

confined to traps and vents and falls; their main purpose is to prevent you and your neighbours coming down with unpleasant diseases because the drains aren't working properly.

In order to estimate for a plumbing installation, plumbers need to be supplied with a detailed specification indicating which fixtures are to go where. As always, get at least two or three estimates and try to use firms which have been recommended.

Interior and landscape designers

If you are going to pay an interior decorator or landscape designer, you should satisfy yourself first that she or he has got talent and ability. Insist on seeing work already completed and talk to some former clients if possible.

Agree – on paper – at the start exactly how much the bill is going to be, find out on what basis fees are calculated, and what you will get for your money.

Order of work

Preliminaries

Clear the decks

- Area to be altered cleared of furniture, carpets etc.
- Unaffected areas protected from dust, debris etc.

Demolition

- Floors, partitions and walls propped where loadbearing sections are to be altered or removed
- Unwanted structure demolished, redundant plumbing, electrics, fittings and finishes stripped out and rubbish removed

Special treatments

- Plaster hacked off walls around areas where damp-proof course is to be put in
- Damp-proof course put in
- Floorboards lifted for timber treatment (approximately every fifth board)
- Timber treatment carried out (to prevent woodworm and beetle attack all timber structures should be sprayed, including roof, floors and stairs)
- All timber structure affected by dry rot cut out and surrounding brickwork sprayed
- Chimneys and flues swept out and relined if required for new appliances

New construction and services

Basic construction

- Trenches evacuated for drains, foundations and incoming services
- Manholes built and new underground drains laid

Adding services

- Water, gas and electricity mains and telephone cables laid

Building up

- Walls built up to groundlevel (incorporating new damp-proof course)
- External walls pointed (brickwork)
- Ground-floor slab laid (incorporating damp-proof membrane and insulation)
- Trenches around building filled in
- Walls built up with lintels, door and window frames and insulation incorporated (provision made for external meters, extractors, waste pipes etc.)
- New floor joists built in

Water/plumbing

- Cold-water storage tank installed and connected to mains supply
- Cold-supply pipes from cold-water storage tank installed for baths, bidets, toilets, showers, dishwashers, washing machines (if cold-fill)
- Water softener installed
- Feed pipes from mains supply for kitchen sinks installed (for drinking water)
- Hot-water cylinder, immersion heaters etc. installed with feed from cold-water storage tank
- Feed pipes from hot-water cylinder installed for kitchen, bathroom, laundry (if washing machine is hot-fill) installations
- Soil pipes installed
- Waste pipes from baths, bidets, basins (sinks) and toilets connected to soil pipes and gullies

Central heating

Wet system
- Expansion tank installed and connected to mains supply
- Boiler (can also supply hot water for household use) installed with feed from expansion tank
- Feed pipes from boiler and expansion tank installed for radiators

Warm-air system
- Air-heater (furnace) installed and connected to energy source
- Air ducts from air heater installed
- Return air duct installed

Gas

- Meters installed
- Supply pipework from meters installed for gas appliances (including boiler, if applicable)

Electricity/telephone

- Meters and distribution (fuse) boxes installed
- Cables from meters installed for lighting and power circuits, freezers, refrigerators, washing machines etc., via distribution box
- Telephone lines from underground cables installed

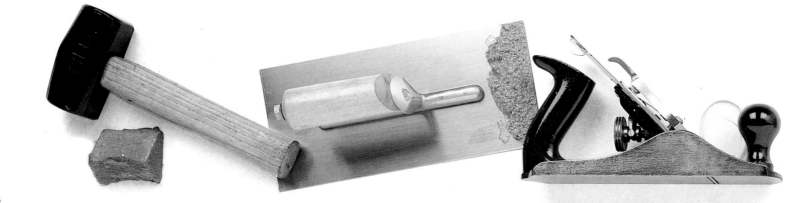

Finishing

Floors and roofing

- Sub-floors and floorboards laid; grilles for warm-air central-heating system installed
- Roof structure (with access) built
- Insulation installed, if used here
- Roof finish laid
- Soil pipes, drainpipes, downpipes (downspouts) and guttering installed

First finishes

- External walls finished – plastered, painted etc. – if applicable
- Windows glazed
- Walls and ceilings plastered, tiled, boarded or panelled
- Doors hung and windowsills, skirting (baseboards), architraves, mouldings etc. fitted
- Built-in floor finishes – quarry tiles, wood strip etc. – installed; floorboards sanded etc.
  Floor finishes may be done before or after fitting out and decoration, depending on the type of flooring

Fitting out

- Kitchen and bathroom units, wardrobes, cupboards etc. built in
- Baths, bidets, toilets, showers etc. installed and connected to hot- and cold-water supply and to waste pipes
- Radiators installed and connected to feed pipes
- Cookers (stoves), refrigerators, washing machines etc. installed and connected to supply

Decoration

- Backgrounds to final finishes – lining papers, paint undercoats, battens for stretched fabrics etc. – applied
- Final finishes – paint on ceilings, walls and woodwork; paper or fabric on walls and ceilings; mirror cladding etc. – applied
- Last fittings – switch (socket) cover plates, door handles and locks, window catches etc – installed
- Curtain tracks fitted

Furnishing

- Floor finishes – underlays, carpets etc. – laid
- Curtains and blinds hung
- Light fittings hung
- Furniture put in position
- Pictures and mirrors hung

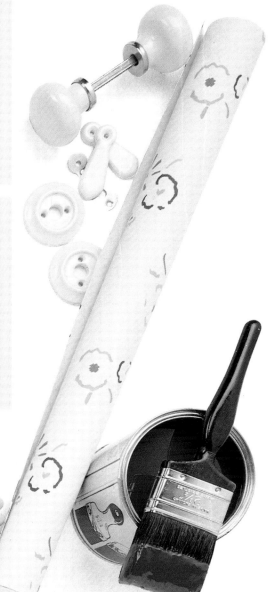
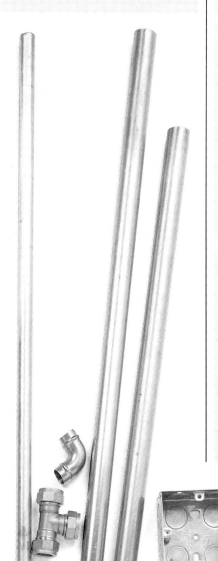

STRUCTURAL ALTERATIONS

Interiors hacked apart and stripped of all character, and unsympathetic additions tacked on with no thought for the original building, have earned conversions something of a bad name. Then, too, there are those depressing tales of bad workmanship, months of disruption and hefty bills.

But altering the structure of your home may be the *only* way to improve its spatial quality or to increase its area. It can be remedial, a logical reorganization of what you already have. It can be a good investment, better and cheaper than moving. It can even dramatically change the way you live.

Spatial quality

From the simple removal of an internal wall to a full-scale roof conversion, all structural alterations are 'architectural treatments' – real changes in volume – often primarily concerned with improving spatial quality. You can achieve this by:

● enhancing existing space, through removing or erecting walls and partitions, altering door and window positions, changing floor and ceiling levels;
● converting unused space, such as attics, basements, hallways, and so on;
● adding new space, ranging from extending porches to building new floors and wings.

What is a structural alteration?

If you remove an internal wall, you may not necessarily be making an alteration that will affect the structural stability of the building; if you knock through an outside wall to create a window, you definitely will be. The difference concerns the way buildings hold together, and can have an important bearing on the cost and scale of difficulty of the work.

Wherever you live, your home almost certainly has outside walls, internal partitions, floors and a roof. No matter of what material it is constructed, the basic principles do not vary. The roof rests on the external walls, which also, in conjunction with some inside ones, support the weight of the floors; all of this load, in turn, is carried on the foundations. Because they span between the walls, the upper floors and the roof are also integral to the overall structure of the building and act to tie it together. As a general guide, any internal wall carrying the joists of the floor above will be structural – in timber floors, the joists run at right angles to the floorboards. But even if a partition is not carrying the joists, it may well be carrying the weight of walls immediately above it.

Structural change is any alteration that affects the way in which any of these loads

is carried. Any building work to outside walls, loadbearing internal partitions, upper floors or the roof will therefore constitute structural alterations. Because such work involves putting back some strengthening element, such as a beam, to compensate for the loss, say, of an area of loadbearing wall, inevitably it will be more complicated and, therefore, more expensive than any nonstructural building work.

Permissions

Although structural principles are universal, the legal restrictions on what you are allowed to do vary from place to place. The basic aim of all such official restrictions is to prevent you from endangering the stability of a building, from creating a health or fire hazard or from adversely affecting the environment.

Structure Additional loads put on a building or altering the methods of support will probably be subject to approval.

Planning Alterations to the exterior of your home may need to be approved by planning or zoning authorities to ensure that these are not detrimental to the character of the district or unacceptable to neighbours, or that provision of additional rooms does not exceed density limits. You must also check whether there are any deed restrictions.

Health Where the internal layout is altered, laws regarding the size and height of rooms, the treatment of staircases, the amount of ventilation or light, and so on, may apply.

Fire Regulations will stipulate how the structure of a building should be protected. Internal layouts may have to be arranged to allow escape via smoke-free passages or stairs.

Historical interest Buildings of recognized historical or architectural interest or ones located in designated historic districts may be listed and subject to stringent conditions.

Cautions

Before any alterations begin, you need to identify the structural elements of the building. This is work for an expert – an architect, engineer or qualified surveyor or house inspector; don't rely on a builder.

Professional help is certainly invaluable at all stages, not least as a preventive measure. The effects of bad design, planning or building can be devastating; putting it all right again may be difficult and expensive.

Another important point: a major structural change may have considerable effect on the resale value of your property. A highly individual built-in feature is more likely to offend prospective buyers than an unusual selection of outrageous wallpaper.

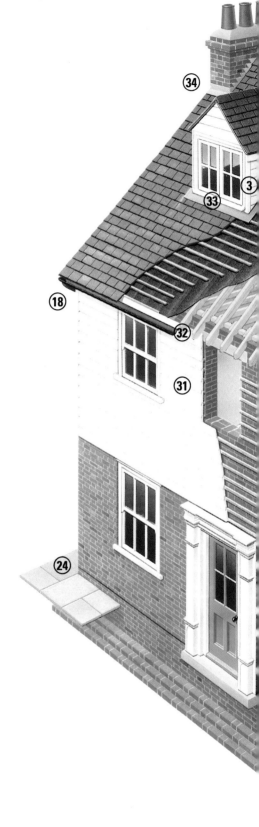

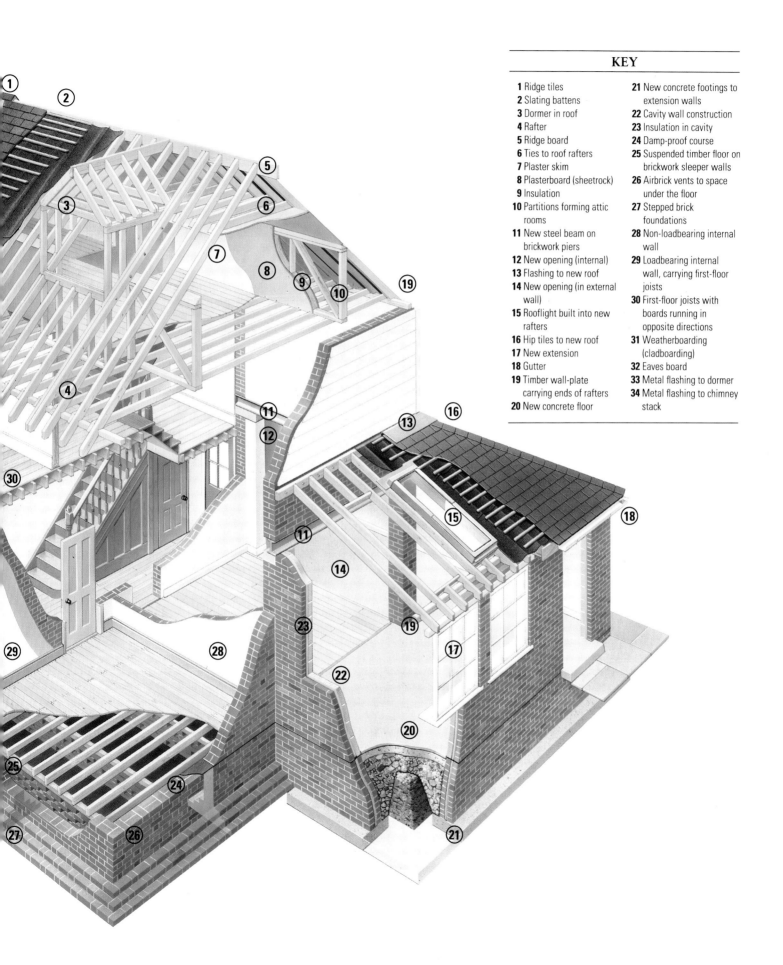

KEY

1 Ridge tiles
2 Slating battens
3 Dormer in roof
4 Rafter
5 Ridge board
6 Ties to roof rafters
7 Plaster skim
8 Plasterboard (sheetrock)
9 Insulation
10 Partitions forming attic rooms
11 New steel beam on brickwork piers
12 New opening (internal)
13 Flashing to new roof
14 New opening (in external wall)
15 Rooflight built into new rafters
16 Hip tiles to new roof
17 New extension
18 Gutter
19 Timber wall-plate carrying ends of rafters
20 New concrete floor

21 New concrete footings to extension walls
22 Cavity wall construction
23 Insulation in cavity
24 Damp-proof course
25 Suspended timber floor on brickwork sleeper walls
26 Airbrick vents to space under the floor
27 Stepped brick foundations
28 Non-loadbearing internal wall
29 Loadbearing internal wall, carrying first-floor joists
30 First-floor joists with boards running in opposite directions
31 Weatherboarding (cladboarding)
32 Eaves board
33 Metal flashing to dormer
34 Metal flashing to chimney stack

Internal layout

Making a few simple alterations to the internal layout of your house or apartment can be radical in effect. Basic rearrangement of doors or walls could make better use of the space available and lighten up dark areas. You can use new partition walls to create private areas; new openings will introduce internal vistas or set up intriguing contrasts of scale between one room and the next.

A certain degree of caution is required before you go ahead and remove all the walls. The open-plan living of the 1960s and 1970s, itself a rather extreme reaction against the repetitive planning of many homes, both old and new, is now being modified to include specifically defined rooms. Whatever your preference, it is important to have a balance between community and privacy: parents and children each need their own spaces; rooms with special functions, such as home offices, work rooms, playrooms or guest rooms, are probably best separated from general living areas.

Practical implications

The complexity of the work will depend on whether you need to alter a structural wall. If you do, a steel joist or a reinforced concrete or timber beam must be inserted to carry the load from the floor or roof above, in place of what has been removed. At lower levels, because the walls must carry more weight, the beams will have to be stronger than those at upper storeys.

Aside from this, the major part of the work will involve repairing ('making good') finishes and decoration – always check this is included in the estimate – and adjusting heating, lighting and drainage services to suit the new layout.

Reorganization

Reorganizing the space is probably the easiest type of change you can make to your home; it may involve no more than taking down a non-structural wall or blocking up a door. Even making new door openings is comparatively simple, but it does need additional caution if the wall is structural.

There may be a lot of scope for this type of improvement. In older homes particularly, hallways can be wasteful of space and simple changes can provide room for storage or even a small office or dining room.

Provided it already has kitchen and bathroom facilities, self-containing an area of a house to form a separate apartment can be achieved fairly easily by building a new partition wall and making an extra entrance (but, depending on local regulations, a fire door may have to be installed between the units).

Alterations to electrical or plumbing services can be disruptive and expensive; changes to ground-level drainage are often extremely complicated. If you want a larger bathroom or kitchen, it may be more sensible to take space from an adjoining room, rather than totally relocate it. Sometimes, however, the only way to improve other areas is to move a bathroom back from the exterior wall to the interior of the building; in such a case, you will have to install some sort of ventilation. If you are relocating a bathroom on an upper level, check that the floor structure is strong enough to carry the additional load of a bathful of water.

Dividing up

At the cost of a reduction in floor area, dividing a room with a new partition wall will provide two new areas that can be used for different purposes, extra wall surface (useful for shelving) and privacy. Make sure that what you will end up with will be habitable and well proportioned – there's no advantage in creating two dim and poky cells. Plan carefully where the partition will go; don't slice a window or a delicate plaster ceiling in half. Also be sensitive to the fine details – the mouldings should match, and so should the skirting or baseboards, for instance.

The partition can be built up off the existing floor, although this may need to be strengthened. If the floor is timber, strengthening might consist of 'doubling up' the joists – placing a second joist alongside the existing one, underneath the new wall, and bolting the two together to provide the extra support.

In lofts or purpose-built apartments the floors will probably be strong enough to carry partitions in almost any position. Given this freedom, walls need not follow the usual rectilinear layout but can be arranged to create a free flow between areas. In fact, the only fixed point you need to have is a centralized 'service core' in which the kitchen and bathroom are grouped.

Even in more conventional layouts, new partitions don't have to follow straight lines; curves are not really much more difficult to build – although they will be more expensive – and can provide a counterpoint to the main walls. Partitions can also be built to half-height, giving a degree of privacy without splitting up a room completely; this might be appropriate for a bedroom shared by two children. Similarly, partitions could be staggered down a long room to create alcoves defining different areas.

Dividing up an area can lead to more complex alterations; for example, a new room may need a new window (if it hasn't one already this will be a legal requirement, unless the room is a bathroom). Do take care to blend the new partition in with the existing building.

Opening out

This is a way of introducing dramatic spatial changes relatively easily – by taking down walls or changing or creating new openings – but bear in mind that you may sacrifice peace as well as privacy. There are many possibilities: two rooms can be united or hall-space absorbed, walls beside stairs can be removed and door openings enlarged. At its most complicated the work should only involve inserting a new beam.

If you do not want to lose entire walls, you might consider making internal 'windows' to provide a visual connection between different rooms. Openings need not be square or rectangular, although a lintel – a horizontal beam – will almost always be required.

A degree of restraint is advisable. Take care not to ruin the proportion of the original rooms or eradicate their character. An enlarged opening between two rooms will generally be more successful if you retain some of the existing wall on each side to act as definition and support the new beam; hanging large double doors in the new opening gives you the option of closing off the rooms as before.

1 *Depth and simplicity are given to this opening by the use of black and by the symmetrical waist-high cabinets fitted at either side.*
2 *Angled alcoves create some privacy without destroying the light, airy quality of the original loft space.*
3 *In a Chicago apartment, built about 1910, the spirit and atmosphere of the original building have been retained, despite extensive renovations. The curved opening in the wall between the kitchen and dining room is more sympathetic to the room than a stark hole and its shape echoes that of the kitchen ceiling.*

4 *Tall and elegantly narrow, this dramatically accented passage between rooms was made by opening out a chimney breast.*
5 *Floor levels in the cellar of a converted farmhouse on a hill near Florence follow the slope of the land; they also naturally define the different functions of the room – the dining, social and work areas. The beams of the vaulted ceiling are highlighted.*

6 *Interior walls on one side of an Australian villa have been demolished to make an open kitchen/living area. The steel beam and joist inserted as structural support have been left exposed and picked out with colour.*

Levels

Changing levels – adding or removing floors and ceilings – is a largely unexplored area for home improvement. Nothing else can give such a sensation of height or volume or provide such dramatic lighting effects. Building up the floor or lowering sections of the ceiling can create intimate, private alcoves within a large, open room; removing part of a floor can make an internal light-well, a gallery or a soaring double-height space.

The main reason why such alterations are relatively uncommon is that most homes cannot afford a loss of floor area.

Practical implications

Simply changing the level of a ceiling – which is only a finish applied to the underside of a floor – is not a major alteration.

Floors, on the other hand, are a primary structural element in any building, and if a section of one is removed a suitable alternative method of support must be provided for the remaining areas. Because floors also give stability to the building as a whole, additional strengthening or bracing may be needed for the external walls. If you alter floor levels, you may need to change windows, external doors, internal doors and finishes.

Ceilings and floors

Since the ceiling is purely cosmetic, it can easily be lowered to define an area or remodelled into a more interesting shape – such as a slope or vault – just by applying a plaster or timber finish to a light frame suspended from the floor above. If a large, high room has been divided into smaller units, lowering the ceiling can adjust the proportions of the new rooms to a more appropriate scale.

Mezzanines

An intermediate level – or mezzanine – is a good way of providing a semi-private space within a large open area without sacrificing all the qualities of the original room. The space underneath the new level could be used either for storage or for an intimate alcove. The joists of the new floor must be adequately sized and the walls may have to be strengthened to carry the extra loading.

Cutting away

Cutting away part of an upper floor to give a double-height room with a gallery is a device much loved by architects, and there is no doubt that, especially when combined with a rooflight, such a treatment introduces a very special kind of spatial dynamic. Buildings with extremely low ceilings can benefit particularly from this type of alteration. The advantages are aesthetic ones, however, and should be offset against the loss of usable floor area.

How complicated the building work is will depend on the extent of the area removed; a small section may only require a timber beam to hold up ('trim') the ends of the remaining joists, whereas a large opening will probably need a new steel beam to be built into the structural walls. To fully exploit the 'light-well' effect possible with this kind of alteration, it is worth enlarging existing windows or introducing new high-level openings or rooflights.

Stairs

Most of these changes will require either new sections of staircase or modifications to the original stairs. Building a new staircase is relatively easy as it spans between, and is carried by, the floor structure at the top and bottom. Stairs in older houses are notorious for taking up too much space; rebuilding to a new layout will certainly gain you some room – a new section of floor may have to be built over the old stairwell and a corresponding area opened up somewhere else.

Ladders can provide access to galleries or platforms but are often inconvenient and should be seen as temporary; they are certainly not as safe as conventional staircases, and in some cases may be illegal. For maximizing space, spiral stairs are a good option; because the full weight of the stair is carried on a single point, some extra support – a structural wall, column or beam – may have to be built in underneath.

Basements

An existing basement may only need a few simple improvements to turn it into a useful living space. Increasing the size of the openings in the external walls will improve daylighting; cutting away the ground outside will give access to the garden.

Another option, though not the most straightforward, is to create a new basement. Many older homes have fairly deep space under the ground floor; this could be extended and waterproofed.

The critical factor will be the headroom; to make the space habitable, the ground may have to be excavated. Such a procedure is likely to involve a lengthy, complicated and expensive process known as 'underpinning', in which the existing foundations are propped up by new sections of concrete to prevent them from being undermined when the excavation takes place. The complication of this process, together with almost certain disruption of the drainage, makes the creation of a new basement a last resort.

1 *A high-flying space cut down to size with an imaginative platform providing badly needed extension of floor space; below, the jagged screen hides the kitchen area.*

2 *A conversion about variety of levels. The open stairway and the lack of internal doors emphasize the quality of space.*

3 *Sculptural spiral stairs provide dramatic access to the upper level without sacrificing too much floor space.*

4 *A floor that literally opens up. When no children are about it can be safely lifted to wonderful effect.*

5 *A small Edwardian terrace has been impressively altered by removing internal walls and floors to create a basement room.*

Roof extensions and conversions

The most useful extra space in many homes is right under the roof. Adding a new storey or converting an existing attic can be the most appropriate way of extending a home in the city, where space is often restricted at ground level. Roof extensions and conversions can provide unique living spaces, creating spectacular views as well as roof gardens and terraces.

Practical implications

There are a large number of practical and, possibly, official constraints on this type of alteration. How the work will affect the overall structure and appearance of the building is the prime consideration; such changes may also be subject to neighbours' agreement and will certainly require planning approval. And, as with any major building work, there may be considerable disruption to the normal routine of the household.

Obviously, if it isn't strong enough already, the building must be made capable of supporting the new construction. You will also have to provide a suitable staircase, and perhaps increase headroom, daylighting and ventilation, and comply with fire regulations. Building up another storey may mean you have to alter existing chimney stacks and exterior walls as well as relocating water tanks and rainwater pipes.

Because of the involved nature of the building work, you should employ a professional consultant to negotiate the practical hurdles and to produce an architectural solution in tune with the construction and character of your house.

Converting an attic

There is enough attic space under many pitched roofs to make conversion a fairly easy exercise. Access is the main problem; if the existing staircase cannot be extended you will have to build a new stair, which may involve altering the layout of some rooms.

The ceiling joists are unlikely to be strong enough for the increase in loading so larger joists will have to be installed alongside them to strengthen the floor.

Adapting the roof structure

A pitched roof relies for support on the strength of its triangular framework, which is comprised of rafters, ceiling joists, posts and struts. Even in the simplest attic conversion, some parts of this structure will need to be removed to create clear space, and the rafters given an alternative method of support. Since loads in a roof are relatively light, this should not present too many difficulties; at worst, new steel beams may have to be built in between the loadbearing external walls.

Cutting out small sections of roof for rooflights provides daylight but does not increase the headroom; you may need to build in dormer windows to make a habitable bedroom or living area.

If you cut away sections of the rafters to make a roof terrace, you will have to take into account where the drainage will run and of course enclose the opening. Another possibility is to cut away the ceiling joists to add the volume of the roof to the top-floor rooms. This kind of alteration, together with new rooflights, is as dramatic as a gallery but involves no loss of usable floor area.

Adding a new floor

Taking off the roof and replacing it with another of a different profile, or adding on a completely new floor, could radically affect the appearance of the building and its relationship with adjacent properties, and you would certainly need planning permission. Typical requirements are that existing parapets or eaves lines must be maintained or that the new roof is set back to comply with light angles. If your property is terraced or semi-detached, the neighbours' formal consent may be required.

Existing external walls and party walls will have to be raised to give the extra height; in turn, this may affect chimney stacks, boiler flues, rainwater pipes and drainage pipework. The extra load of the new floor on the rest of the building – exterior walls, internal structural walls and foundations – will also have to be taken into account. 'Trial holes' dug to expose the foundations will help to assess their bearing capacity if this is in doubt; if there is evidence of instability, underpinning may be required to strengthen them.

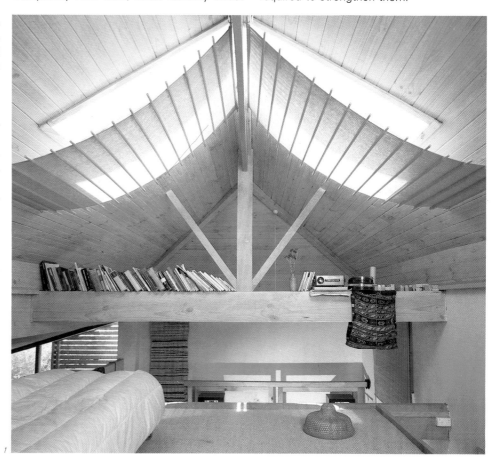

1 *The ceiling has been completely removed here. On one side of the airy space, a platform has been built and the central supporting beam now provides a useful shelf for books and other objects. Tongue-and-groove timber panelling covers the roof and the room has been decorated and fitted to match this. The large skylights are covered with sweeping wood and canvas blinds.*

2 *A roof section has been opened up and the new roof-top room incorporates a walk-out dormer window and (3) dramatically defined roof trusses.*

4 *A new storey was built up from this flat London roof-top. There are windows on two sides, so that natural light floods the new room (5) from more than one direction.*
7 *A glass-topped roof extension is hardly noticeable against a busy skyline; inside (6), a new bedroom/ bathroom has been created.*

External walls

Changing internal walls or floors often involves altering exterior walls as well: repositioning partitions, for instance, may mean creating a new window or blocking up an existing opening. The installation of a new window can radically improve lighting, make use of a good view or a sunny aspect; a new door often simplifies access, especially to a garden or terrace. The size or shape of an opening can be altered to provide a point of interest; going further, making a new external opening is a major part of the work involved in adding on a balcony or a simple extension such as a basic conservatory, or sunroom.

The important point to consider is the effect such changes will have on the external appearance of your home. While the safest course of action – and many would argue, the only proper approach – is to harmonize the new opening with existing ones by taking care over scale, decorative treatment and position, striking contrasts between old and new have also been successful. The aim should be to avoid glaring incompatibility but this does not necessarily mean shunning a bold treatment.

Practical implications

Such alterations are relatively simple to carry out; however, because walls hold up the floors and roof, caution is obviously necessary. If you make a new opening or change the width of an existing one, you will need to build in a beam or lintel to compensate for the loss of loadbearing wall.

Official permissions may be required, both in respect to the structural stability of the building and to approve the changes to the outside appearance or 'elevation'. If the building is of recognized historical interest, or in a designated historical district, you may not be allowed to make any external changes at all.

Making and altering openings

Blocking up a door or window is fairly easy. In the case of brickwork walls, for example, the new brick addition is simply bonded into the old structure at either side, although the floor and wall will have to be propped while the old lintel is removed. It is worth taking the trouble to blend in the new work with the old, since contrasts here hardly ever prove interesting. Bricks can even be stained to ensure an exact match; so can mortar.

The simplest way to change a door to a window or vice versa is to retain the same height level and width, and either remove the area beneath the sill or build up from the floor. This area of wall is not loadbearing and

alterations will not affect the structure of the building. If you're changing a ground-level door into a window, it may be advisable to build up the new section of wall off a new section of foundation.

If you want to enlarge a window or doorway – for access to a balcony, for instance – and the existing opening is not wide or tall enough, a new lintel will have to be built in. This will entail propping up the floor and wall above while the old lintel is being replaced with a new one. The wider the opening, the stronger – and therefore larger – the lintel necessary: very wide openings will need a steel or reinforced concrete beam and, because of the consequently heavier load on the walls at either side, the foundations may have to be strengthened by underpinning.

As with blocking up, the style and treatment of such alterations should be taken just as seriously as the structural consequences. In the brick- or stonework walls of older properties, for example, there is often an arch over the windows or doors, sometimes plastered, sometimes in contrasting material. To reproduce this detail, build in the new lintel on the inside face of the wall only and add the arch on the outside.

The opposite approach is to consciously contrast the treatment of your alterations with the style of your property, but you'll need a good eye – or a good architect – to get this right. So long as the surrounding structure is adequately strengthened there is nothing to prevent you from extending window areas through two or more floors or installing automatic up-and-over doors to open the house into the garden; such large-scale openings can be the ideal complement to the spatial changes suggested in *Levels*, completely transforming the internal volumes and lighting. A less extreme option is to avoid the traditional rectangular format and go for round, semicircular or triangular windows. Narrow, arrow-slit openings could light a dark interior if the view is less than spectacular.

Extending

Once you have opened up an exterior wall, you can extend your home in a number of simple ways – with a conservatory, or sunroom, for example. This type of addition need not be restricted to ground level; a balcony or upper-level conservatory can be created by extending the existing floor structure and bolting on either new timber joists or new steelwork on to it for support. This could be ideal for an upper-floor apartment which lacks a garden and where extra space would be extremely desirable.

1 *A simple, spacious sunroom, built in metal and glass, is reached through an extended and curtained opening from the house.*
2 *This glass door, strongly constructed with a wide canopy and designed to roll open, replaces a whole section of an external wall and provides an open-ended room with direct access to the garden.*

3 *An intensely colourful and airy extension to an Australian home. It is linked to the main house by an unusual, sculptured opening which, from inside the house, creates an interesting frame for the landscape beyond.*

4 The feeling that the garden extends from this room has been created by a glass door that opens conventionally or swings up across the roof, and by using the same stone tiles on both the patio and the lower inside floor.

Simple extensions:
5 *a lean-to conservatory;*
6 *an Edwardian-style glasshouse;*
7 *a new dining area on a lower floor level, created by roofing over an outdoor passage.*

Additions

Adding on to your home can improve the rooms you already have or create entirely new accommodation. A new kitchen or bathroom will not only provide extra facilities but may relieve congested space in the rest of your home; an addition can give the room for anything from a studio to self-contained living quarters for grandparents or grown-up children. And this type of alteration is one of the best ways of adding value to your home – if it is well carried out.

The essential prerequisite is sufficient ground area. But however much land you have, you will have to balance the loss of outside area with the gain in living space. If your garden is precious, consider a roof extension instead. Another option would be to convert an adjoining garage or build an extra storey on it.

Since additions demand careful siting, planning and design, it is always a good idea to consult an architect.

1 A wood and brick extension to a stone country cottage gives this old building an extra bedroom, workshop and wood store, as well as a new entrance.
3 An important feature of the brick extension that provides a study (2), is the expansive window incorporating an open corner, which is supported by metal poles.

Practical implications

Alterations to external walls are likely to form a major part of the work. In some cases, new loading may be put on to walls, especially if the addition is more than one storey high. When building on top of an existing structure, you can avoid having to strengthen the foundations by using a light timber or metal framework. New drainage and services or alterations to existing arrangements may also be required.

You must check whether there are any legal restrictions about what you can build.

5 *A typical Toronto house has been transformed by this large extension built of glass bricks. The broad balcony is defined by a window frame added for visual effect. The oak tree provides shade in summer, but during the long winter months the room receives maximum light and sunshine. Inside, the original back door has been fitted with a sliding screen, visible at the back of the room (4), which emphasizes the Japanese atmosphere created by the flat surfaces of varying textures and the filtered light.*

4

Local legislation may affect not only the style and type of addition but also its location, size, the materials of which it can be constructed and its relation to other buildings.

Building on

The options for building directly on to your home range from extending an existing room with a custom-built addition in materials chosen to match the original building to putting up a prefabricated off-the-shelf unit.

No matter how the work is carried out the new area will require drainage, heating and electricity. Careful planning is essential to minimize disruption to existing drainage and rainwater pipes and to avoid blocking out light from other rooms in the home. If some loss is unavoidable, introducing rooflights or high-level windows is a good way of bringing light back into the centre of the building.

Linking up

The way of ensuring that light is not blocked off is to plan the extension around a court-yard, with openings into both the new build-ing and the old. Alternatively, an outbuilding or garage could be converted and linked to the main house, with the space between turned into a courtyard – and perhaps even glazed over. Since this type of alteration will have little or no effect on the structure of your home, a greater freedom in the treatment of both the outbuilding and the link between the two is possible, together with the opportunity to create interesting indoor/outdoor spaces, contrasts of style and materials.

The type of addition

What type of addition is appropriate will depend on the size, style, location and im-mediate surroundings of your house; as well, it will depend on what local planning legisla-tion will allow.

Take as much care inside the building over the continuity of old and new. If, for example, the new addition is to share access and circulation with the main house, it will have to be planned to make use of present access points and stairs – and to make the best use of space and resources.

As far as the style of the addition is concerned, the two extremes of treatments might be expressed as follows: on the one hand, a new wing for a period house, which so exactly matches it in every detail that it appears to have always been there; on the other, an aluminium and glass addition so skilfully and sympathetically designed that it perfectly complements a building quite differ-ent in character.

5

ARCHITECTURAL CHARACTER

Understanding how your home was meant to look is essential if you want to restore, modify, or decorate it in a way which is sympathetic to the original style.

Today buildings of architectural and historical note are often protected against demolition; alterations that change original architecture and details are also forbidden. What is designated as listed or landmark varies from country to country: it can be groups of buildings, such as a row of brownstones in New York City or a medieval village in rural England, or an individual building, a Modernist apartment block or a Colonial house.

It is not just listed or old buildings which are worth restoring; if your house was built in the 1950s, say, do not assume that it is devoid of architectural merit.

Your home may be documented in some general way – in maps which show the development of the area, perhaps – but more specific information may also be available. Your local library may hold records or, if not, should be able to point you in the direction of historical associations and the local government archives; the library is also a useful source for reference books on architectural periods and styles. As well, look at the houses around you: often there will be similar buildings to yours in the district – these may give you clues about the date of your home, and, if you find one that has not been altered, how it would have looked originally, both inside and out.

The exterior of a building will carry some of the basic clues for assessing its age. Various details – the shape of the doors and windows, for example – belong to particular architectural periods. Always look behind the façade: sometimes only the front elevation was altered to give it a 'modern' feel, and the back of the house will still reveal the true date of construction.

The older the building, the more likely that it has been altered – in some cases, many times. Obviously, some of these renovations will have improved the original and there will be no question of changing them back; others you might just have to live with.

If you have chosen an older home then it is probably sensible to emphasize its features rather than disguise them. Try to use traditional materials and keep the intrinsic qualities of the building. It is best to find a builder and an architect who specialize in restoring old houses. Above all, do nothing that is irreversible without consulting an expert and avoid new 'wonder' products when renovating – they haven't stood the test of time, unlike your home.

When he designed this
Italian apartment,
architect Paolo Farina
was inspired by Leon
Battista Alberti's
statement that a
dwelling should be in
the image of a city. This
room is based on the
outside of a stone
building, a restrained
example of the vogue
for using architectural
details inside. There are
some ironic touches,
such as the bases of
the wooden columns
against the bookcases
finished to resemble
stone rustification, the
keystones on the
arches housing
loudspeakers for the
stereo system. A
minimum of furniture
holds the illusion of a
building rather than a
room – classic modern
chairs, a fine old rug
and a simple but
ornamental desk.

The exterior

Textures and surfaces of the walls, the way windows and doors are placed and proportioned, the shape of the roofline and chimneys, the detailing and condition of the ornamentation, all affect the way we see a building, the pleasure we get from it.

Many otherwise beautiful houses have been ruined because their wooden sash-window frames have been changed to aluminium ones, or the early twentieth-century leaded panes have been replaced with a modern 'picture' window. Even if the original glass and glazing bars have gone – as is likely – the proportions, dimensions and positions of the windows are still characteristic of whatever period house you have. The Colonial sash, the Regency bay or the Arts and Craft oriel window, the cast-iron patterning of Gothic Revival windows, and the more recent stained-glass windows within leading are all precious survivals. Always consider repair before replacement; it is not necessarily more expensive. If you must replace them, look for windows which correspond to actual historical examples, rather than spurious 'Georgian', 'Colonial' or 'Tudor' models.

If a building is to be given the right feel, then getting the approach and entrance details correct is a priority. The type of entrance is quite specific to each architectural style. An English terraced town house of the late eighteenth century, for example, built on a very narrow site, would have had railings on either side of the steps, and a path to the front door that was related to the internal plan of the house. In an Australian wooden bungalow built a century later, the doorway was defined by broad low steps and a deep verandah which was used as an outdoor room in the hot weather. And certain details were usually included – the doorways, for instance, would have incorporated panels of stained glass to light the front halls.

Important too are the texture and pattern of exterior walls. Brick, stone and wood are the most commonly used materials. They were either left in their original state or painted, plastered, clad with timber boarding or hanging tiles or slates – as an 'improvement' or as part of the original building design.

Do beware of 'protective' surfaces, which can very often ruin not only the look but, more importantly, the structure of the building by interfering with the natural qualities – such as the porosity – of the materials.

Finally, don't forget the important contribution careful choice of colour can make. Choosing the best colours for the exterior can be as difficult as deciding on a scheme for indoors; see *EXTERIORS* for ideas.

1 *The plain stone exterior of a Regency terrace in Cheltenham is offset by delicate cream-painted ironwork.*
2 *Important early-Georgian elements carefully preserved: fenestration, brickwork, iron railings and doorcases.*
3 *Clever paintwork on nineteenth-century San Francisco houses.*
4 *1930s details proudly retained.*

5 The charm of a nineteenth-century French country house comes from the balanced use of brick and stucco.
6 An Irish cottage with traditional whitewashed walls. The gravel path is in character and adds texture.

7 The unpretentious picturesque ideal of the rural cottage stands unaltered: lattice windows and thatched roof.
8 An early twentieth-century house in a Suffolk seaside village.

Exterior details

If you want to restore the exterior of your house to its former glory, it's important to get the small details correct. The building won't look right if the ornamentation is missing, if the originals have been replaced at any stage, or if styles have been mixed. Once you start researching these details, the chances are you will soon become fascinated with the building methods and styles of the past. Often, too, the way a building was decorated – both inside and out – will tell you a lot about the people who lived there originally.

Details which people dispense with, often without much thought, are the characteristic ornamental stucco work of the late eighteenth century onwards, such as brackets, parapets and cornices, and, then in later nineteenth-century houses, terracotta decoration, which sometimes took the form of panels of sunflowers or rosettes set into a porch or over lintels.

If there is any of the original ornamentation on the building it should be kept. Without such flourishes – the interlaced wrought-iron work on a house in New Orleans, for instance, or the terracotta ridge tiles and finials on an Edwardian terrace – many houses are far less appealing; it is worth looking out for replacements if the original details are missing when you move in. You may have to search demolition yards to get the right pieces, although, in some cases – with terracotta, for example – reproductions may be available. Another alternative is to find someone who specializes in such work who will make them up for you, possibly working from a section of the original; or a contemporary pattern book of the period will be a good source of reference.

Other classical details such as pilasters and keystones are also worth looking out for. Heavy stucco brackets, both at parapet level and sometimes under windowsills, can be replaced. In a terrace or in an area that was developed as one unit, you can pick up clues from your neighbours if your house has been stripped of details.

Often, the roof is completely ignored. When you are adding lofts or attic rooms, try to keep to the original roofline by setting the alterations well back. When reroofing, use the traditional materials (which can include plain tiles, stone slates, wooden shingles, corrugated iron, and even thatch) or, if that is impossible, choose replacements which will not seem out of place. Reroofing is expensive, however you do it, but a good job done with traditional materials will be a great bonus to the appearance, the value and the structure of your house.

1 *Early nineteenth-century stucco details, in the Egyptian style, have been well preserved and give character to this house and the street it stands on.*
2 *Finding the right replacement details or conserving original elements ensures that the architect's original intention is preserved – this garden gate is integral to the Art Deco design.*
3 *The pleasing patina of use and age on this French farmhouse offers a powerful case against over-restoration.*
4 *A nineteenth-century porch of individuality and character, which has been carefully looked after.*
5 *This porch has a lead-sheeting roof; the choice of red for the door cleverly reflects its oriental character.*

6 *A building of rare architectural merit, this Colonial clapboard house in Massachusetts has been preserved intact.*
7 *Never undervalue the importance of traditional tile and brick.*
8 *The lace curtains add to the traditional charm of a French window and balcony.*

9 *The strong lines of this 1930s apartment building are best left to their own design.*
10 *A New York brownstone is improved and complemented by ivy foliage.*
11 *Australian colonial architecture: a sweeping verandah with corrugated iron roof and carved wood pillars.*
12 *Well-restored ironwork on a clapboard house.*

The interior

If previous owners of your home have removed all traces of the past – creating large spaces from small rooms, perhaps, or discarding the distinctive ornamentation – then there is little point in elaborately recreating a period impression. You might as well remain in the present. But careful use of any existing detail, together with, perhaps, some authentic colour and furnishings, will create the feel of the period.

In any case, it is unlikely that you would want to emulate the exact way in which rooms in an older house were used originally. Nowadays, for instance, most people eat in the kitchen or in a room adjacent to it: servants and dumb waiters are part of the past. And generally we seem rather fonder of sun-baked rooms than our predecessors were; many of them even fought shy of natural light. So some alterations might be necessary to make darker rooms lighter (see *STRUCTURAL ALTERATIONS*).

It is possible, in an old building, to pay great attention to authenticity and somehow miss the point. A stark, bare-boarded room with stiff-backed chairs around the walls, or an over-stuffed sitting room might have every last detail historically correct. But a home is not a museum; it has been built to be lived in, and it's only natural that, over the years, it will be modified as occupants, needs and feelings change.

The important thing is to keep the building's rhythm, rather than imposing on its essential character. Don't force a small two-bedroomed suburban house to look like a New York loft; if that's what your heart is set on, then it would be better to move. On the other hand, this doesn't mean faithfully reproducing a period piece: a soaring lightwell cut through two levels of a Victorian terrace house need not be inappropriate, and there is certainly no reason why a Bauhaus chair, a glass and chrome table or an espresso machine should be a stranger in a rambling Colonial house. The key to being successful is keeping everything in proportion and using sympathetic materials and textures.

It is advisable to live in your home – whatever its state – while you consider how to go about repairing, decorating and furnishing it. By living there you will begin to understand it and the period in which it was built and how your needs relate to it: once you know exactly how the building functions, how it feels, it will be more obvious what to do, what looks right and what looks wrong. Time and its companion, patience, are invaluable ingredients when you are putting a house to rights.

1 *Ornament can inspire decorative treatments. In this nineteenth-century French hallway, a beautiful mosaic floor and colourful glazed double door prompted rich marbling for the walls and ceiling.*
2 *The simplest architectural feature has been strongly emphasized. Allowing the window frame to stand out unadorned strengthens the 1930s character which is also enhanced by the elegant wall treatment, a custom-made rug, and fine modern furniture.*

3 *An elegant late-Georgian room painstakingly restored, decorated and furnished in the style of the period. The original wooden shutters are retained to complement the fine window.*

4 *In the same house, the plaster ceiling and cornice detail are based on an Egyptian theme, a popular influence at the time the building was constructed. Modern lights and hand-built bookcases suit the style of the room.*

5 *The ability to mix styles in a period room can reveal the character of objects more successfully than when they are surrounded by products or a setting of their own time. Here, the combination works well and the design qualities of different periods contrast effectively.*

Interior details

Attention to detail makes all the difference in sustaining the sense of period when you are renovating or redecorating. If you are looking for guidance, don't rush in; look at some books on interiors, and, perhaps, visit museums where rooms of a similar period have been faithfully recreated. These will give you examples of absolute accuracy which you can then adapt to your own tastes. One point to keep in mind: it is important not to be anachronistic – there is no harm in having an early-Victorian grate in a Georgian or Colonial house – after all, houses take on the additions of each successive generation – but a Georgian fireplace in a Victorian house is not such a good idea.

Staircases are the first thing you see in many houses. Their shape and details – the balusters, newel posts, as well as the shape of the treads themselves – are very characteristic of the period of your house. Whether you expose or paint the handrail, carpet the treads or just use a runner will have a great bearing on the overall feel of the house.

Too often the floors are treated rather like poor relations. Any old rug may be thrown down, or else wall-to-wall carpet is fitted indiscriminately throughout the entire house. Wall-to-wall carpets did not come into use until the mid-nineteenth century; before then rugs were used over boards, while stone or slate, used in great slabs, often floored halls and the areas most used around the house. Later on, encaustic (decorated glazed earthenware) tiles were popular for hallways, and bricks or tiles for kitchens.

Think carefully before you coat a stone or slate floor with any kind of protective surface; it might be impossible to remove, except by a destructive process of chipping it off, and in addition it could discolour the original surface. Even the vast ranges of sealants and colourants for wood should be approached with care: wood simply stained and polished with wax or scrubbed with salt and water looks best.

Flat, smooth walls will look wrong in a country cottage, which once had bulging plaster walls with no sharp corners. Matt or silky paints are always closer to the old wash and oil finishes than modern gloss paint. It is possible to stay quite close to the spirit of the original, given the range of paint colours and finishes available, and the widespread interest in decorative finishes such as stippling and sponging. And you can get traditionally patterned wallpapers and fabrics.

Papers have often been used to divide the wall into sections, with frieze and dado papers marking top and bottom. The dado – paper or panelling which runs around a room from the floor to about windowsill height – and the area above the picture rail can, therefore, be treated differently from the rest of the wall. Wooden panelling was always used in early eighteenth-century houses; you will also find it in many of the houses built this century in the Georgian or Colonial Revival styles. It acts as insulation, and is an attractive surface in its own right.

Cornices, the carved or moulded plaster band hiding and strengthening the junction between walls and ceiling, and the ceiling roses (originally meant for gaslight fittings) vary from the simple to the florid. If they are damaged, you should be able to match the pattern and shape with reproduction work.

You might find every detail of your house in period – except the doors, architraves and skirting, or baseboards, which may have been 'modernized'. It is well worth having replacements made which match the originals, although they will be more expensive than standard, off-the-shelf models.

When replacing a fireplace, which often acts as a focal point, take into account the proportions of the room, its period, and make sure of getting a grate of appropriate style.

It is worth investigating these finer points; inevitably, if there is only one detail in a room that is wrong, everyone will notice it.

1 *An idiosyncratic carved wooden handrail looks best against paintwork rather than stripped balusters.*
2 *The form and material of a curved stainless-steel bannister highlights the elegance of an English Art Deco hallway, which has been beautifully restored.*

5 *The strong beauty of eighteenth-century wood panelling is matched with good furniture from the same period.*
6 *Small details evoke great character as shown by the original glass and window catches in an old English country house.*

3 *The Edwardian detail of the ceiling plasterwork is complemented by the moulded Lincrusta dado panel of the staircase.*
4 *An eighteenth-century stair bannister painted traditionally.*

7 *Brussels 1912: the original leading and coloured glass of the window precisely conveys the style of the period, which is echoed in the chair.*
8 *Glazed doors with decorative ironwork grilles and pretty tie-back sheer curtains that filter daylight.*

EXTERIORS

It is worth remembering that you can increase the value of your house by the way you decorate its exterior. The wrong treatment can very easily highlight ugly features or obscure positive architectural character. Many masterpieces of the 1930s Modern Movement, for example, have lost their impact because the colours chosen by their architects to underline the planes and voids of the buildings have been ignored subsequently.

Even if your home is not particularly old, in order to give it the right feel and balance it's important to know how it was treated originally (see *ARCHITECTURAL CHARACTER*). By following the original scheme, you might surprise yourself by turning what seemed an unremarkable, even clumsy, house into one of considerable charm and character.

However, it is not only the cosmetic effect of colours and textures you need to consider when decorating; also important is the protective qualities of paints and preservative-based stains, and the insulating value of materials such as weatherboards and plaster.

Almost every neighbourhood has its own mood and it's sensible to follow this when decorating your house – unless the area is run down and needs a bit of drama to liven it up.

Houses of a similar style, and those which are semi-detached or terraced, obviously lend themselves to unifying treatments. For semi-detached houses – especially ones that are mirror images of each other – get together with the neighbours and decorate both at the same time; or do your side so enchantingly that they will copy you next time round. Use the same colours, materials and textures throughout, but keep your own identity by painting each front door a different colour. Individual treatments can work too, particularly if the houses are different, but there often needs to be some common points.

The charm of terraces (row houses) is the rhythm they create; it's all too easy to disrupt this with an idiosyncratic decorative scheme. Brick and stone terraces work well when the wood- and metalwork are all painted the same with only the front doors and other small details in different shades. If the walls are painted, one colour can be used for the entire terrace; another option is to paint the walls of every house differently, using colours with a similar depth of tone.

Of course, if you live screened in by trees or a wall, or if the neighbourhood has no architectural unity, you can simply decorate your house on its own merits, emphasizing its good features, and playing down whatever is wrong about it. Understatement is usually preferable to a fussy treatment.

Architect George Woo took full advantage of a stunning view over the Gulf of Acumal in Mexico and created a dramatic structure against the rugged splendour of the landscape, enhanced by the theatrical effect of natural light. Irregular-sized windows and varying height in the main housing blocks give alternate areas of light and solid shapes that are unified by the gleaming white stucco of the walls.

Walls

The usual reasons for decorating the outside walls of a house are to improve its appearance and/or to provide better protection against the weather. But before you start, the first step is to make sure that the walls are in good condition (see *MAINTENANCE*).

Paints nowadays are much easier to apply and last longer than those used in the past. Nevertheless, about every seven years they will need renewing, so it's worthwhile considering alternatives when doing up the exterior of your house. Instead of trying to brighten up dowdy looking walls of natural materials with paint, you could concentrate on the windows, the doors and other architectural features and try to divert attention away from the wall surfaces. Or faced with, say, an aggressive or patchy brick that will never mellow with age, disguise it by planting creepers. For planting to be effective all the year round, use evergreen climbers – flowering shrubs such as *Lonicera halliana*, *Clematis armandii*, 'Rosa mermaid' and *Hydrangea integerrima* are good choices. You can let the plants climb freely or, for a more ordered effect or to alter the balance of the elevation, train them to grow over trellising. Trellising by itself can be an excellent disguise; the French use it in a very adventurous way.

Brick- and stonework

If brick- or stonework needs repointing, be sure the mortar mix is right both in colour and consistency. Unless you are maintaining a specific vernacular practice – such as using bricks of two colours in diaper work – the walls should present a texture rather than a pattern. A mortar close in tone to the brick or stone usually works best: test a sample in an inconspicuous part of the wall and let it dry out. All mortar will grey down in time.

Sometimes walls are in such bad condition that even repointing won't rescue them. If whole areas of the wall have spalled off, the only answer may be to render (plaster) the surface – although not necessarily of the whole house. A traditional treatment is to limit the rendering to the lower walls at ground-floor and basement level; this will not only brighten up a dull-looking house and make a tall skinny one seem wider but, depending on the colour it's painted, could reflect light back off the walls. Another advantage is that the rendering will be reasonably accessible to maintain.

You can either render and then paint wall surfaces, or else use tinted render. Paints and render come in a wide variety of textures. Smooth finishes will discourage dust and soot dirtying the surface. Rougher textures help disguise uneven surfaces, but the effect should be regular, not busy waves or spirals.

If you do decide to paint brickwork, make sure you choose a permeable finish; this allows any moisture trapped in the walls to escape, and, at the same time, protects the face of the building. Damp trapped behind impermeable paint can cause bubbles, splits and, finally, the paint skin to peel off.

Cladding

Other methods of decorating and protecting the exterior of your home – weatherboarding and slate- and tilehanging – are more expensive initially, but are more permanent. They also have the advantage of providing a certain amount of insulation. Cladding introduces a horizontal emphasis to the façade, spreading the lines of the house and making it appear to lie longer and lower. It can also disguise the patchiness of an altered façade.

Depending on the type of timber, weatherboarding need not be painted or even treated with a preservative; some woods, such as elm and cedar, develop an attractive colour as they age. Stains will not mask the grain of the wood, and permeable, preservative-based types are available. If you are painting weatherboarding, a more easily maintained alternative to conventional oil-based paint is one with a permeable finish. Preservative-based and opaque in appearance, it looks very much like a semi-gloss oil paint, but because it penetrates right into the fibre of the wood, the painted surface never cracks or peels – it simply powders away with age.

Once installed, tile- and slatehanging demand no regular attention. But badly done, they can ruin a pretty house as easily as they can give interest to a dull one. Tiles should match those on the roof in colour and texture, if not precisely in form. Slatehanging on walls occurs in slate areas only, so, unless you live in one of those areas, hang tiles on the walls.

Occasionally, mock half-timbering, render, pebble-dash, even tilehanging and weatherboarding, appear on the same house – for a less fussy effect, the tilehanging and the main wall material can be left in their natural state and the rest painted in one colour.

Colours

When choosing paint colours, take into account the age and character of your house and any regional traditions there may be. Tracings of the house's outline, taken from an enlarged front-on photograph, can be used to try out various colours. The most startling viridian greens, brilliant blues, rich browns and yellows have often been used for house walls, as have glowing intense pinks and ochres and soft cream and pink washes. The right colour will be related to the house's surroundings. If you live in a dark or remote setting, or simply want the house to stand out, light reflective colours are best. Bright colours usually work well in places with lots of strong sunshine. And colours that look best by the sea might not suit a grey-brick town or a lush farming area.

1 *Although unity in the decoration of façades is often considered advisable, there are times when bold conjunctions of different tastes can make an impact. These late nineteenth-century houses in California seem to have distinctive personalities, witty and forceful.*
2 *A beautiful clapboard house on Prince Edward Island, Canada, benefits from the local custom of brightening a harsh wintry climate with colourful exterior walls.*
3 *Low-cost housing on the edge of Lille, France, has been individualized with colour by planners; an inexpensive way to inject cheer and character into a new neighbourhood.*

Windows

One of the fastest ways to devalue a house is to replace its original windows with modern metal, timber or plastic ones – beware of the overtures of double glazers with their 'patio doors' and promises of lower heating bills. If the existing windows are beyond repair, make sure the replacements are as close to the originals as possible. With buildings of considerable architectural value, it really is unforgiveable to upset the balance of the façade by introducing windows which are of the wrong size, shape and materials; with houses of little distinction, consistency is just as important, because it helps to pull the building into some sort of order.

Frames

Instead of installing double-glazed replacement windows, have secondary frames, or storm windows, fitted inside – it's important to make sure that their framing members carefully coincide with those of the existing windows (see *HEATING*).

The innate beauty of many a window has been all but lost behind the wrong coloured paint. Small-paned sash and patterned cast-iron windows show their glazing patterns to best advantage when painted white or a light colour. On the other hand, the frames of single-pane sash windows and of large metal studio-type windows suit dark greens and browns or black.

Tinted preservative stains are a practical solution for new door and window frames. For a more solid effect, you can use products with the same permeable qualities but which have an appearance similar to the original, traditional oil paint.

Sills and lintels

If the sills and lintels are brick or stone, they are better left unpainted; if wood, the sills should be painted in with the window frames. Plastered lintels and sills should be painted to match any other decorative plasterwork that may be on the building.

The metalwork of traditional window boxes, railings and balconies should rarely be painted anything but black or white. Black emphasizes the delicate tracery of wrought iron, but it can make cast iron look heavy. Very dark blue or dark green suits modern metalwork.

Problems

Mis-matched windows

From the outside, glass appears as black or dark grey, so, if your house has windows of varying shapes, sizes and pane proportions, the window frames and glazing bars can be painted white and white blinds or curtains hung behind them. Or you can paint the outer frames white and the inner frames black or dark grey, so the glazing pattern virtually disappears. If the walls of the house themselves are white, the entire frame could be painted dark grey or black – but make sure you don't hang white blinds or curtains in the windows.

Windows that are too small

Make small windows appear bigger by using white paint on the frame and reveal (the brick- or stonework that surrounds the window), preferably rendering (plastering) the reveal first.

Louvred or panelled shutters make narrow windows seem wider; they will look best if the shutters are exactly half the width of the window itself; the shutters can then be painted the same colour as the window frames and the reveals.

Pale-coloured stone or plastered mouldings framing windows will add emphasis – it's a treatment that appears frequently both on formal and vernacular buildings. A moulded heading used alone will lengthen a squat window. A window box painted to match the frame will also have this effect; however, if it is painted in a contrasting colour, it will have the effect of widening the window.

1 *Wooden templates gave the standard replacement windows for this cottage harmony with the adjoining chapel when the two were converted into one house.*
2 *A classic Georgian sash window brought to life with geraniums.*

Large windows

In the great houses of the Modern Movement, the architects took great trouble to carefully balance the solidity of the walls with the voids created by the large windows they favoured, as well as to introduce rhythms in the framing itself that give considerable aesthetic pleasure. But soon, because this aesthetic geometry was badly misinterpreted, it became the fashion for almost every new house to incorporate large picture windows and patio doors, usually without any sense of composition.

The situation is not always beyond repair, however. A pergola, its horizontal framing set just over the window head and forward over a paved terrace, will help absorb large rear windows; at the front of the house, you can run trellising across the walls, up to the height of the door head, to disguise picture windows and then the whole effect can be softened by growing climbing shrubs over them (see *Walls*).

If a window is introducing too much light, louvred shutters can be inserted over one or more sections and painted to match the window frames.

Adding and altering windows

If you need to provide more light inside the building, one option is to widen existing windows. Or consider adding extra windows at the side or back, rather than the front of the house. In either case, the important thing is to try not to disturb the balance of the main façade: the new windows should look as though they have been there as long as the house itself.

Take care to match the pane sizes and proportions as closely as possible. Err on the slightly larger size for panes if you can't match them exactly – over-small panes do tend to introduce a fussy note. If the new windows are the same sizes as the existing ones, take care to line up their heads and sills; otherwise, you should match up the head heights.

Dormers

Dormers should match the framing pattern and glazing scale of the other windows. If you want to diminish the impact of dormers, paint their frames and side panels to blend in with the roof colour, irrespective of the colour used for the windows below; a single colour above the gutter is not so distractive. However, the frames and woodwork of small traditional dormers always seem to look best if they are painted to match the other window frames in the house.

3 *A stark modern extension is intelligently combined with the old house. Original windows can be seen behind the large new ones.*
4 *Windows in a restored Nash terrace reflect their counterparts opposite.*
5 *Concertina metal shutters on a pair of French windows provide adjustable cover, ventilation, a source of decorative colour and security – without looking hostile.*
6 *Elegant fenestration that requires no further embellishment.*

Doors

Although it is the windows of a house that create the pattern of the façade, it is the front door that provides its focus. The grander the house, the more emphasis is placed on the entrance, with elaborate detailing, pediments, porches and columns. It should always be immediately obvious where the entrance is, even if it's at the side of the house; then, the path leading to it should make its position evident.

If all the external doors are painted the same colour, the impact of the front door will be lost, especially when a bright or strong colour is used. Garage doors are a particular problem since they are large and so tend to dominate a façade; as with other service doors, these are better painted to blend in with the wall colour, while glazed garden doors and French windows should match the window frames.

But before you get as far as painting, make sure the existing doors are the right ones for the house (see *ARCHITECTURAL CHARACTER*). It is just as important to fit the appropriate door furniture – hinges, locks, handles and so on – carefully placing it on the axis of the framing members to create a comfortable symmetry.

Unless the door is made from wood that can stand weathering – oak, elm or teak, for example – or is protected by a fairly deep porch, it is better painted or stained rather than varnished. The door and its frame should be painted the same colour only when white is used and the window frames are white too. Paint the door frames to match window frames, with the door a contrasting colour, otherwise the effect is of a dead void with none of the modelling and detail of the opening expressed. And relate the colours to those of the surrounding walls: cool against warm is a good general principle – but, as always, some 'outrageous' exceptions can look wonderful.

Porches

With a porch, there are two basic choices: painting it to match either the front door or the window frames. The former treatment works well with a modest door and comparatively small porch because it makes the whole entrance seem more important. A larger scale door and porch will look more delicate if the porch matches the window frames.

Paving

The paving used for paths, driveways, patios and terraces should have an affinity with the house – cool grey or cream slabs, for example, would look good with warm-coloured brickwork. Creamy grey slabs look less chilly on wet winter days than plain grey. If the house is built of stone or has stone dressings, match the slabs to this. If you want brick paths use paviors (pavers), which can take frost and weathering, and aim for darkish tones and some overburnts in the mixture. Generally, the size of the paving slabs should relate to the extent of the terrace; in other words, you should use small slabs for small patios, and larger slabs for wide terraces.

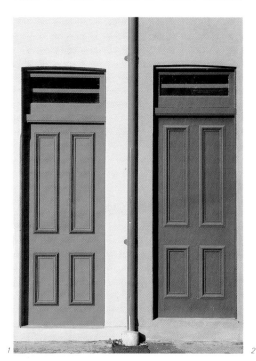

4 *A Chelsea town house given an urbane treatment: glossy black pillars and co-ordinated railings. A touch of red in the paintwork and for the flowers tubs enlivens the effect.*
5 *Seafront architecture can sustain bright colours because of the clarity of light – as here in Cornwall.*

1 *Together neighbours can inspire schemes for colourful façades.*
2 *Porches and fencing integral to a house and on a small scale look good painted in one colour, or else there's a danger that the exterior could become broken and fussy.*
3 *From opposite sides of the colour spectrum, red and green vividly balance each other, and are further brightened by the sunlight of southern France.*

6 *This open-air walkway, separating a bedroom from the living area of a warehouse conversion in Sydney, was inspired by Balinese temple architecture.*

Roofs

Roofs that are thatched or covered with shingles are steeply pitched so the rain runs off quickly. With clay and slate roofs, pitches are shallower, while with sheet materials, such as corrugated iron, the angle is even flatter. Flat roofs were traditionally made of lead or zinc, and, lately, of asphalt or bitumen roofing felt.

When existing finishes fail, replacing them is not necessarily the best or the only solution. If you have a handsome old slate or tiled roof with an attractive patina, it is possible to bond it together underneath, using a flexible plastic material that holds the tiles or slates safely together in a waterproof homogeneous whole. However, never use the type of bonding that is applied to the *top* of the roof – it will mask the patterning of the tiles or slates, completely destroying their aesthetic qualities, and cannot be removed.

If it is impossible to rescue the roof, try to match up the existing finish with salvaged materials. You may be able to reuse some of the old slates or tiles; if so, group them together on the most visible elevation and use the replacements on the inner slopes of the valleys and other less prominent positions. Brush the new slates or tiles with a slurry of manure, sour milk or liquid plant food; within six months the active organisms will take over and soften the contrast between the old and new materials. Soot rubbed on will help to darken them down.

Lead is expensive and could be replaced by zinc, copper or aluminium, although none of them will look quite right; if you have to use any of these materials, try to confine them to the parts of the roof which can't be seen. Replacement shingles – usually Canadian cedar or the thicker Western red cedar type – are readily available.

Repairing corrugated metal roofs is a straightforward matter of replacing worn-out sheets with new ones. If you are reroofing the entire building, consider using metal that has been enamelled, but avoid the textured type, which will spoil the look of your house.

Gutters and downpipes

Traditionally, gutters and downpipes (downspouts) were painted black, and it's a treatment that works well. But when there is a maze of pipes, attention can be diverted away by painting them a softer version of the wall colouring if the building is unpainted; if it has been, match the paint colour exactly. When replacing gutters and downpipes, try to rationalize the pipework itself: aim for fewer pipes and arrange them to run down at the corners of the building or, on detached and semi-detached houses, they should be grouped on a side wall.

Decorative details

Decorated ridges are often an attractive feature of old buildings, and the ornamented tiles with their piercings and fretted profiles are still available from salvage companies; so, too, are elaborately ornamented finial tiles used at the ends of ridges and at junctions of the roof and handsome old chimney pots that look like giant chess pieces.

On a house with white walls, curved bargeboards decorating the gables can match the front door – as long as that is a quiet or dark tone. Against brick, stone or coloured walls, barge-boarding looks better painted to match the windows and other woodwork.

1 *Australian tin roofs highlighted by striped painting and wooden trims. A fine example of sympathetic public housing design.*
2 *Weathering adds character to the complex of roof shapes and shingled gable end in a New York city house.*

3 *Remarkably fine barge-boarding, 1892, in Somerset merits meticulous conservation. Replacement roof tiles or slates can be 'aged' by treating with manure slurry or sour milk.*
4 *On this villa in the south of France, replacement pantiles have added texture and interest.*

5 *Atmospheric Gothic splendour in this American clapboard house is accentuated by a monochrome colour scheme, which tones with the roofing.*
6 *Slate roofs are rare in Holland, except for a small area to the south. The owners of this château, which has sixteenth-, seventeenth- and eighteenth-century sections, opted to maintain the exterior as perfectly as possible, while furnishing the interior in a more eclectic, modern style.*

HEATING

If you are to maintain your house in good condition and yourself in health and comfort – ideally, warm in winter and cool on hot summer days – you need to strike a balance between insulating and heating or cooling, and, at the same time, provide adequate ventilation for comfort.

For heating, you will probably consider a centralized system as a possibility; but although it is the ideal system in many situations, it is not always the right one. It depends on a number of factors: what kind of house you live in; where it is situated; what level of insulation it has; and what fuels are available, at what price. It may be more economical, for example, just to use individual heaters, or to have a central-heating system in part of the house combined with separate heaters in rooms you don't use all the time. In hot climates, it will make sense to incorporate air conditioning into the system; alternatively, you might decide against central heating and for air conditioning, using open fires or individual heaters when necessary.

Comfort and economy should not be at the price of appearance. Fireplaces and stoves will be the focal point of a room, and should be chosen with that in mind. For central heating, whether you want to emphasize the sculptural qualities of your radiators or hide all evidence of the heating and cooling system, you should incorporate all the pipework into the house's structure or in fixtures – under floors, in walls, cupboards, and skirting (baseboards) and behind grilles, for example.

Arbitrarily placed and clumsily designed radiators or a badly proportioned fireplace will irritate you long after the heating engineers and the builders have left, so it's worth planning the system carefully. Before installing an expensive system, thoroughly research all the possibilities; an architect will give you advice on the options available, which is the best system for your house and lifestyle, and such details as the siting of radiators or grilles and the size of boilers.

Insulation plays the dual role of keeping heat in during the cold weather and keeping the house cool when it's hot outside. The most sensible approach is to incorporate as much into the structure of the house as you can. After all, it is false economy to invest in an expensive heating system and then not insulate your house; the better insulated, the more efficient the system will be – and the more comfortable it will be for you.

1 *A stove positioned prominently in a living room becomes a sculptural object and an integral part of the architecture. Stoves are more efficient heat sources than open fireplaces and many combine the functions of warming rooms and providing a glowing focal point with heating the water.*

2 *In an open-plan, high-ceilinged apartment, these slim finned radiators are positioned vertically, spanning the height of the room and merging with twin bookcases. They give a good expanse of heat without disrupting the strong design of the room. Other, flat-panelled radiators are set along the lower walls.*

Central heating

Wet systems

Water is heated in a boiler; the hot water is circulated through pipes to radiators or other heat emitters and then back to the boiler for reheating. Usually, the system is also used to heat the domestic hot water (see below).

Most wet systems work on the small-bore principle: a small circulator pump is used to force the hot water through the pipework and radiators; it enables pipes of a fairly small diameter – usually of about 15mm ($\frac{5}{8}$in) – to be used for the final pipe runs. Water flowing through pipes can be easily controlled: each radiator can have a separate thermostat, rather than be controlled centrally.

Domestic hot water

Hot water for domestic use is heated in a cylinder by hot pipes running from the central-heating boiler. The water for the heating system and for domestic use is carried in completely separate circuits of pipes; however, the bathroom heating should be connected to the same pipe circuit as the domestic hot-water cylinder, so that heat is availale for towel airing in summer when the main heating system is out of use. Some form of thermostatic control must be applied to the domestic hot-water storage cylinder, usually in the form of a strap-on cylinder thermostat acting on a motorized valve set into the pipework.

Warm-air systems

In these systems, air ducts circulate warm air through the house. A fan is used to draw the air through a heater and then to circulate it through ductwork to the rooms, where it is emitted through grilles. The grilles can be fitted to the floor, wall or ceiling; purpose-made grilles are required for each location – they are all shaped differently so that they will direct air into the area to be heated efficiently.

A return air path is provided through further grilles to enable at least some of the air to be returned to the heater, and warmed again before being sent back to the rooms. Electrostatic air cleaners can be used to deodorize the air; even so, return air grilles should not be installed in the kitchen, bathroom or toilet. The supply and return air grilles must be positioned so that the warm air is able to circulate freely around the room before being withdrawn.

There are several disadvantages with a warm-air system, however. Firstly, sounds tend to carry along ductwork, and particularly through the return air path. Secondly, it is more difficult to control the flow of air through the ducts than it is to stop and start water flowing through pipes, as in a wet heating system. Generally, it is only possible to control the air heater, usually in conjunction with a central thermostat.

Air conditioning

A great advantage of warm-air systems is that air conditioning can usually be incorporated. A cooling coil put in the ductwork cools the air as it is circulating around; alternatively, when the air heater is turned off, most of these systems can distribute cool air. In addition, the level of humidity in the air can be adjusted as it passes through the system.

Electric systems

These are not, strictly speaking, centralized systems, because each heater can be operated independently of the others; but they are called 'central' if used throughout the house. There are several types:

Storage heaters Electricity is expensive, although most suppliers offer cheaper off-peak current, usually during the small hours of the night. Although electricity is unstorable, it produces heat, which can be stored. However, you need to predict accurately what the temperature is going to be the next day in order to decide what charge the heater should receive at night. Obviously, it is easy to get it wrong, so a back-up system with on-peak electric heaters is needed; the best idea is to have storage heaters in some rooms, while rooms that are only used occasionally have on-peak heaters only.

Storage heaters are now much slimmer; they are available with individual thermostats, or can be linked to a central thermostat.

Oil-filled radiators These are generally uneconomical, but do sometimes have an application where operating costs are unimportant and the installation of alternative forms of heating would be difficult.

Under-surface heating Heating cables are set into either a floor or ceiling and can be run off on- or off-peak electricity. If the underfloor heating is set in a concrete floor slab, the system will respond slowly to controls and is best used to supply background heat.

Fuel

In both wet and warm-air heating systems, there is a centralized source of heat; in a warm-air system it is an air heater (furnace), in a wet system it is a boiler, or a back boiler. (A back boiler is incorporated into the back of an open fire or a stove to provide domestic hot water and/or central heating; the boiler and the fire should be able to operate independently, as well as together.)

Gas

Used for both wet and warm-air systems

In most areas, gas has low operating costs; it has a great degree of flexibility, combined with automatic operation.

Gas boilers are now highly efficient and take up very little space – some are not much bigger than a hat box. As with all gas installations, they must be installed and serviced by a fully trained fitter.

Flues Nearly all gas appliances must have flues; they can be connected to either a conventional flue run through the chimney or to a balanced flue run directly to the outside from the rear of the appliance. Balanced flues can be fan assisted, which enables gas boilers or air heaters to be positioned 3m (10ft) or more away from the external wall.

Solid fuel

Used for wet-system boilers and back boilers

Semi-automatic heating can be provided if a gravity-fed boiler is used, and operating costs are competitive; a smoke-consuming appliance burning cheap bituminous coal is even cheaper to operate. Solid-fuel appliances must have really good flues, and cleaning is very important.

Wood

Used for wet-system boilers and back boilers.

These can be either individual units or back boilers, sometimes combined with cookers (stoves) or room heaters. The availability of wood for fuel varies very considerably from area to area and costs and long-term supplies need to be carefully considered. However, most wood-burning appliances can be easily converted to burn solid fuel.

Electricity

Used for wet-system boilers; limited use in warm-air systems

Electric boilers for wet systems can be based on off-peak storage; these require considerably more space than other types of boilers and very careful output sizing (that is, working out whether the storage core is big enough to heat the house). They do have an advantage over gas boilers in not requiring flues; this is true, too, of boilers based on the use of on-peak electricity, which are very small, but very expensive to run.

Storage furnaces can propel warm air through ductwork, but can become exhausted and are really only suitable for heating a smallish area.

Electrically powered heat pumps can be used to extract low-grade energy from a source such as a stream and convert it into usable heat for the home. They can provide cooling as well as heating. Careful sizing is required, because the heat produced is at a slightly lower temperature than that produced by a boiler or warm-air furnace. Capital costs are quite high; running costs are dependent on local electricity prices.

Alternative energy

Solar energy can be used successfully where there is adequate sunlight. But capital costs are high in relation to the amount of heat produced, and home heating can be difficult by this means. Solar energy is an excellent way of providing low-temperature heat on a seasonal basis – swimming-pool heating, for example.

Oil

Used for both wet and warm-air systems
Oil-fired boilers are usually fired by pressure-jet burners, and are reliable but may be a little noisy. Air heaters using oil are very similar to the ones that are gas fired. Oil-fired boilers are usually more expensive to buy than gas-fired ones.

Liquefied petroleum gas

Many ordinary gas-fired boilers can also be used with LPG.

Controls

Most appliances have built-in controls to regulate the amount of heat produced; these are usually automatic, but, in the case of solid-fuel back boilers, are often manually operated. In addition, there are several other types of controls that can be used with central-heating systems:

Room thermostat A simple control used in most forms of central heating. The thermostat is wired to the circulating pump and boiler, or to a warm-air furnace, and is programmed to switch them on, at pre-set times, to meet the pre-set temperature, and off when this has been achieved. Although inexpensive and reliable, it will only sense the temperature of the area it is installed in.

Radiator thermostat Installing thermostatic radiator valves on all radiators is more expensive than installing a room thermostat, but operating costs will be lower because the temperature of each room is individually controlled. The best system is to have radiator thermostats and a central thermostat.

Frost stat A second thermostat can be fitted in the coldest part of the house or outside, and set so that it will switch on the heating, overriding all other controls, if the tempera-

ture drops below a certain level – usually near freezing point.

Motorized valve This is used in conjunction with a room and hot-water thermostat and time switches, to control circulation on a temperature and time basis. It can be used to control a separate heating zone (for example, downstairs or upstairs), or to bring an additional zone into the circuit. The different zones can be controlled by separate room or radiator thermostats.

Outside sensor A thermostat that is sited outside, usually on a north-facing wall (or south-facing, in the Southern Hemisphere). It produces an even level of heat and reduces costs, by comparing outside and inside temperatures and adjusting heat to the internal temperature required.

INSULATION

There is little sense in spending a great amount of money on a heating system if all the warmth escapes through the walls, through cracks in the windows and so on. Insulation can be expensive, but what is important is the increased comfort it will provide. And it's worth remembering that it will also keep the house cool when the weather is scorchingly hot.

Heat rises, so the best approach is to keep the bottom of the house warm, insulate the walls and windows, and then try to stop the heat going through the roof.

But do beware of 'superinsulating': you must have a supply of fresh air for both health and safety. Most houses have enough cracks for adequate infiltration of fresh air. But remember that fuel-burning appliances need air for combustion, usually a purpose-designed air supply path unless they have balanced flues. If in the slightest doubt, get expert advice.

Lofts

The first step is to make sure that the loft space is well insulated. Lay 100 to 150-mm (4 to 6-in) thick mineral fibre matting between the joists. Any exposed pipes should be well insulated – 35-mm (1⅜-in) thick lagging is required. Insulate the water storage cisterns – including the cold-water cistern to prevent freezing – but leave their bases uncovered and take the insulation down to join the loft-floor insulation.

It is important to keep the loft space well ventilated, by leaving room for air to enter under the eaves – otherwise condensation will collect and cause rot in the roof structure.

Walls

Thirty-five per cent of heat loss is through the walls, so wall insulation is a good investment. It is important to make sure that the walls are completely dry before insulating – damp walls are cold, and moisture will diminish the effectiveness of the insulation.

Cavity-wall insulation is very worthwhile, but it must be done well to be effective, so you should get specialist advice on this. In older buildings with solid or timber walls, the internal walls could be lined with boards or panelling, if appropriate to the style of the house.

Windows and doors

Weather stripping the doors and windows is one of the most cost-effective ways of saving heat. Shutters and curtains will also contribute to the level of insulation.

Double glazing is expensive and is rarely worth installing in money-saving terms. It would be better to install a secondary window. The wider the gap left between the two, the less effective the insulation is against the weather but the better against noise – a gap of 200mm (8in) between windows that are 6mm (¼in) thick will reduce the noise level by 44 decibels. But if you are installing double glazing, make sure that the framing of the double-glazing panels is matched to that of the existing window, and remember, if the panels are permanently fixed, you won't be able to open the window – which could be dangerous if there is a fire.

Floors

It may be possible to insulate the ground-level floor from the underside. Otherwise, layers of insulation – carpets, for example – can be laid on top of the floors.

Hot-water pipes and cylinders

Hot pipes below ground-floor level and in unheated areas should be insulated; pre-formed sectional lagging can be used and sealed around the pipes, bends and valves. Pipes that carry hot water from the boiler to the cylinder and are used for summer and winter water heating should be insulated along their entire length.

The insulation of the hot-water storage cylinder is also important. Thick jackets, available at low cost, save a great deal of heat.

Heaters

Heat emitters

Whichever type of central-heating system you have, you can mix the types of heat emitters, although, because they react differently, they will need individual thermostats. Grilles for warm-air systems are not considered here.

Heaters can produce radiant or convected heat, or a combination of both. The output from radiant heaters comes directly from the hot surface of the appliance, while convectors produce a warm air current.

There is a certain amount of debate about where radiators should be sited. One school of thought recommends placing them underneath windows – generally, the coldest part of a room – to counter heat lost through the external walls and draughts off the cold window panes. The opposite view is to place the radiators along an inside wall, where there will be considerably less heat lost; also, installation costs are lower because there is quite a saving in pipe runs.

The radiator should not be blocked by furniture or heavy curtains, otherwise the radiant heat it produces will be shielded from the area to be heated – therefore, a long radiator occupying one wall will limit where you place the furniture; likewise, if a radiator is placed under a window you will need a window covering that does not hang over it.

Heat emitters that produce convected heat should be positioned to suit their warm-air output.

It is always advisable to get several opinions about the placing and sizing of heat emitters.

Radiators Normally these are steel-panel, but more expensive cast-iron and aluminium ones are also used. Finned steel-panel radiators are more efficient than ordinary steel ones, because the metal surface that can be heated is increased. The number of radiators required varies according to the size of the room, the type of radiators used and where they are placed. It is something you should get several opinions on.

Skirting (baseboard) heaters These give out very even heat and mean there are no problems positioning furniture.

Fan convectors Although they produce hot air, these convectors are normally only connected to wet systems. Warm air is blown by fan through a heat exchanger in the unit, through which water flows. They enable a large amount of heat to be distributed into a large area from a very small wall space. They are ideal in kitchens, where there is a shortage of wall room; a kick-space fan-convector heater can be installed under kitchen units.

Radiators come in all sizes and shapes so make sure you see the full range before deciding what to buy. You should be able to find ones that integrate with any style of interior.

1 In this kitchen, the radiator is set neatly under a shelf below the window.

2 A room that takes its style from the past has an old-fashioned radiator, painted pink, prominently placed as a divider between bedroom and bathroom.

3 Upright radiators with their expanse of heated metal warm a room without intruding too much on wall space at a level where furniture might stand. The vertical lines give a sense of height which is lost with lower, horizontal radiators.

4 An equally unobtrusive and stylish alternative is slimline skirting (baseboard) radiators. Here, they are emphasized in black – a good match to the chrome of the table and matt black of the loudspeaker unit.

5 An alcove radiator cleverly covered with wooden slats, which let the heat out and provide a frame for a cosy built-in seat.

6 An aluminium floor with electrical socket outlets; warm-air vents provide a design detail as well as a heat source.

7 *1930s style – an old chrome electric room heater beautifully offset by a metal cover for an old fireplace.*

8 *A modern version of an old-fashioned wood-burning stove merges well in a stylish up-to-the-minute apartment.*

9 *A simple towel rack in a bathroom – heated to warm towels and keep the room temperature up.*

10 *A charming room of quirky oddments is the ideal home for a old-style wood stove.*

11 *A traditional stove within a tiled cylinder provides sculptural emphasis for this room.*

12 *A room planned to include this wood-burning stove with windows on either side of the central flue.*

Room heaters

Many people don't want to heat the whole house from one source, but instead prefer to install individual heaters in the rooms that are not used all the time. So these are often found in houses or apartments that are heated by a centralized system – especially in the case of open fires.

Solid fuel

Open fire You should make sure that the size of the fireplace is suitable for the chimney above it; in addition, there must be an adequate supply of air to the fire, preferably direct from the outside, otherwise the chimney will draw off a large proportion of the warm air that the open fire has produced.

Stoves There are many types of stoves available to suit almost all types of rooms. Far less hot air is lost through the flue than in the case of an open fire; another advantage is that the heat output is generally higher.

Gas

Gas fires Generally, these are less attractive than open fires and solid-fuel stoves, but they are automatic and do not require attention. They can produce either radiant or convected heat, or a combination of both. Decorative 'fake-log' open fires, which can be very difficult to distinguish from the real thing, are relatively expensive to run – this is because they are open and heat is lost up the chimney, as with open fires.

Gas fires no longer have to be fitted to a chimney; they can be connected to an ordinary balanced flue, or flued through a 50-mm (2-in) diameter pipe run at skirting (baseboard) level to outside.

Gas-fired convection wall heaters are balanced-flue appliances, and they can heat large rooms or hallways. With a time-switch control and if fitted in all rooms, they operate in much the same way as a normal centralized heating system.

Electricity

There is a wide variety of electric-powered radiant, convection, and combined radiant/convection heaters available to choose from. They are all extremely efficient, but are usually expensive to run.

Liquefied petroleum gas

Propane and butane-powered portable 'cabinet' heaters are very popular, but are quite bulky and tend to cause condensation. Generally they are not flued, so care must be taken to make sure that there is adequate ventilation in the rooms they are used in.

STORAGE

The dream homes lavishly photographed in glossy magazines are invariably distinguished not only by their style but also by simplicity, lack of clutter and sometimes an apparent total absence of possessions. Real life simply isn't like that. All households have possessions. The things we own, and how, when and where we use them, are factors which shape our living arrangements. The key to a neat, smooth-running home environment is to ensure that what is displayed is there to be seen and used, and the rest is kept out of sight.

With a well-designed storage system for the home, your possessions will be under your control and not creating unwanted mess. This does not mean that absolutely everything has to be hidden away; rather that it all has its particular place and is where you want it to be.

The advantages of good storage are many. The most obvious one is less stress – from not having to stare clutter in the face and from being able to find things without fighting

STORAGE
CHECKLIST

- Do you want built-in or free-standing storage?
- Do you want storage units you can take with you when you move house?
- Is there a single room or area which could be made into a storage-only room?
- What extra space can you utilize for storage?
- What objects need to be stored away?
- Do certain items need to be stored in particular rooms?
- Is there storage space for sports and hobby equipment?
- Are there some items you need but can never find?
- Do you need somewhere to put things you want to keep but not necessarily look at constantly, such as souvenirs from holidays, letters, and treasured collections?
- Are there some items you use more often in summer or in winter, so that you can organize storage on a seasonal basis?
- Do some of your possessions suffer from the way they are stored, such as:
  - tools that get rusty?
  - clothes that get crumpled?
  - fragile things that get broken?
  - papers that get muddled?
- How much can you spend on storage?
- Will the storage facilities you plan increase the value of your house or apartment?

your way through a tangle of excruciating muddle. Most of us have drawers or other receptacles full of all manner of items without a proper home. This leads to near fury when the car keys are needed and must be extracted from stashes of loose change, cotton reels entwined with that useful piece of string, a varied collection of pens and pencils, discarded badges, postcards from last summer, the contents of a broken matchbox and some rusty screws. Take this clutter one step further and you find more obtrusive items are without a home: hallways have become obstacle courses of bicycles, boots and junk mail; living rooms are piled high with records, homework, and so it goes on.

Keeping things in order and easily accessible means they are kept in good condition, so they last longer. And another premium from good storage is the space you create. Relieved of unwanted clutter, rooms reveal assets you may not have realized they had – clean lines, fine architectural details and a feeling of spaciousness.

1 *What was originally a solicitor's filing cupboard now provides an unusual but ideal display space for a collection of antique glass. With the wide shelf and small, deep drawers, there is ample space for more mundane objects.*
2 *The 'Miscellanea' chest in this harness room adjoining an English country house was specially created by local craftsmen to fit the curved walls and complement the traditional rural style of its setting.*

Storage systems

After thoroughly examining your requirements, look at the storage systems available. These can be grouped into three basic categories.

Free-standing furniture: bookcases, cupboards, chests, wardrobes. They are often inherited, can be bought secondhand, can go with you when you move house, but do waste space.

Built-in units: they are there for good, can be expensive, save space and can be chosen to suit the style of your rooms. Ideal for awkward and unused spaces, such as underneath stairs and in attics.

Modular systems: shelving and cupboards can be added to as needs demand and budget allows; they often come in kit form to be assembled at home.

There are another three options when it comes to creating the storage system of your choice:
● buy manufactured products off the shelf;
● design and build a system yourself;
● commission a professional to build a custom system to your specification.

You can, of course, mix all the options to good effect. Hand-built items have obvious advantages in that the choice of materials is far wider than when choosing from manufactured units; you can be sure they fit and serve your needs; they can be made to match the period and details of your home. Using professional cabinet makers can be expensive; doing it yourself can save money if not time.

Adjustable shelving
Shelving is the staple of the storage system. It comes in all shapes, sizes and styles, with varying degrees of adjustability. Assess what you want in terms of materials – wood, aluminium, steel – and consider how they are attached to a wall: it may be better to choose a system that has its own backing rather than one hung directly on to a wall.

Industrial storage ideas
An excellent source of durable, practical storage ideas for the home is the office, shop or factory. Several items, such as trolleys, steel lockers, filing cabinets, revolving racks and pegboards, have made their way into domestic use. They can conflict with your style if not carefully selected, but it is worthwhile looking at the wares of commercial and industrial suppliers. A simple solution to clothes storage may be a shop dress rack if you want open display, and heavy tools and appliances in the work-room may be best served by tough, braced industrial shelving. Even the most seemingly inappropriate pieces of equipment could have storage uses in your home – bicycle stands, plastic racks, steel bins which revolve or run on castors, and wire merchandise baskets. Tubular steel structures can also be used effectively, and, coupled with roller blinds, can provide space-saving, large-scale facilities.

Storage interiors
What happens inside a storage unit is largely dependent on its type and external framework. Manufactured units usually come with internal fittings and partitions: these include many alternatives to drawers and shelves – the options range from wire trays to wicker baskets, from steel hooks to string cord.

Plan the inside of a storage unit in relation to your possessions, not in isolation from them. That way you can ensure not only a place, but a purpose-designed place for each item. For example, wire shoe racks can be bought to fit inside cupboards, and hooks and small rails can be used to take anything from ties to sewing equipment.

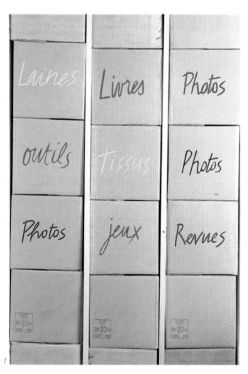

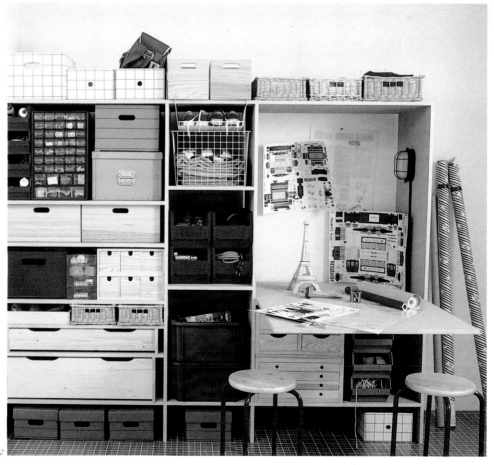

1 *Stacked cardboard boxes have been brightened with multi-coloured writing.*
2 *All storage ideas in a simple unit, with built-in worktop, using wood, board, metal, basket and plastic containers for visual liveliness and easy identification.*

3 *Merging attractively into the style of the apartment, this free-standing cupboard was purpose-designed inside and out. It is profiled to fit under the sloping eaves of the roof in a converted attic. The shelves were designed to store music cassettes at the top, video tapes in the centre and long-playing record albums below – each displayed for easy selection.*
4 *The narrow space below these stairs has been well utilized for storing shoes and boots of every description. High boots hang in deeper compartments and two sections have been allocated for cleaning brushes and shoe polish. Fitted storage must be carefully planned so that it looks good from the outside and suits the particular objects that are kept in it; merely building a below-stairs closet and then finding a use for it would not have resulted in such systematic and practical storage.*

5 *In the mezzanine bedroom of this imaginatively converted top-floor apartment, a small wardrobe with a plastic roll-down front provides hanging space for clothes.*
6 *Industrial lockers are spacious storage solutions in a room created over a closed stairwell; the original balustrades have been retained to ironic effect.*

Storage masterplan

It is crucial to avoid making piecemeal decisions about storage. Tidying one room and then sorting out what is left could be a waste of time. A masterplan should be formulated which takes into account the entire house. Start by making a list of all the items – from books to barbecues – which could be stored away. Scrutinize this list; often possessions which you automatically put away should be left out because of frequent use. Conversely, some things left on view create clutter and would be best put away. Then there are other objects which should be thrown away – be brutal with yourself and separate what you really want to keep from what you have simply got used to having around. If you cannot remember what is in a cupboard or attic, it is probably because you never use or need the items there.

Finally, make sure you have not ignored the obvious: you might forget the large and bulky items, such as luggage, that should be a priority when planning storage.

Think about where you could add storage facilities in your home. Space is a luxury – particularly for those who live in small apartments – but the smaller your living environment, the more organized you need to be. Adding storage units may mean losing a valued corner or section of a room, but the advantages will almost certainly outweigh that loss.

Divide your list of items to be stored into levels of priority for ease of access, depending on frequency of use. You may give top priority to cereal packets, shoes and telephone books, and less to Christmas decorations, camping equipment and much-appreciated but rarely used gifts. And note specific requirements, such as dry storage for tools that could rust and safe storage away from children for dangerous objects.

Now you can begin to devise a system of storage for particular objects and particular rooms or areas. But before you start looking for storage fittings, think about possible problems so you keep them in mind at all times.

If space is tight, consider the sort of storage which will not involve hinged doors – sliding doors, retractable doors, small double doors, even blinds can be used. Cupboards can be fitted into unused areas such as chimney breasts and alcoves, under stairs or beneath beds. Also, there is no point in using high-level storage if things cannot be reached. And remember that deep shelves can be less efficient than narrow ones that store a single row of accessible items rather than several rows, half of which you can't see or reach with ease.

When you are deciding where to locate storage units, remember not to block off electric sockets (outlets) or important taps and switches. Also check the strength of a wall if you are going to place shelving or other storage units on it, and consider weight when choosing those units.

Lighting is important for walk-in or other large-scale units – groping in the dark for your tennis shoes is no fun. Small but highly effective light fittings can now be found to fit into even the smallest cupboard.

In this London apartment, built late last century and chosen for its spacious period style, an ingenious storage system was devised by the architect. Classical and imposing, the system was designed as an integral part of the building and takes careful account of the needs of the owners. The result has been maximum storage space in a quiet, uncluttered atmosphere.
1 A beautifully proportioned and finely detailed wall of book shelves in the library. Behind the glass doors, the upper shelves are adjustable, and slim drawers have been included in the system.

2 *The folding doors of the fitted, panelled wardrobes save space and echo the style of wooden shutters. Blankets and other bulky items are stored in the top cupboards in this small bedroom (**3**).*
4 *An old sideboard and collector's box provide large and small free-standing storage in the living room.*
5 *In the library, the fitted cupboards extend to the bay window and radiators are concealed in the panelling. The desk chair is set on a plinth for working in comfort at an old ledger desk.*

6 *A hall of cupboards fronted with modular panels based on the design of classical exterior stonework. A curved alcove provides visual relief (**7**). The curve is repeated in the bathroom door (**8**), where the use of perspex (acrylic) panels complements the overall style.*

Storage style

Storage demands as much ingenuity and flair as other, more overtly creative aspects of home design. The ability to innovate and experiment will produce far better storage results than holding fast to domestic conventions, so attack storage problems with imagination as well as common sense. Practical improvisation will save space and money.

The history of interiors is a series of broken conventions. Old pine dressers slowly came up from below stairs, where they were used to store crockery and utensils, and found pride of place in the living room. Now furniture stores stock new versions of the old kitchen dresser, designed to match your other living-room furniture, so the transition is complete. Similarly, 'high-tech' styling has allowed materials and finishes associated with industry to reach the kitchen and other rooms. If you find you are lacking storage for particular items, look away from conventional solutions and you may well find the answer.

Visual impact

When choosing storage it is essential to create a visual impact without completely overpowering the interior of a room. A well-chosen storage unit can merge effectively with the room. Alternatively, it can be hidden altogether using paint finishes or other decorative methods.

Storage units can be used themselves to hide an uneven sloping wall or to fill an ungainly alcove. They can be used to divide spaces, to change the proportions of a room, box in and hide unsightly pipes or block off an unused door. And there are now many ingeni-ous and attractive space-saving items of furniture which store themselves – fold-down beds and tables, and workbenches that reduce to a neat contraption which you can hang from a wall.

Whatever you choose, remember to consider the room as a whole. You may find the perfect cupboard in terms of capacity and colour, but with handles that do not match your other ideas in the room – the simple solution is to change the handles.

Many different finishes can be applied to doors and sides of storage units using plastic laminates, wood veneers and paint finishes. And large storage furniture which is bulky can be made less obtrusive by carefully matching a finish that blends with the rest of the room. Always avoid contrasting materials, unnecessarily ornate finishes and mouldings and a proliferation of knobs and handles.

If you build in storage fittings, try to match the character of the room. Drawings can be copied by good cabinet makers so, if you are adding cupboards in an old house, find an illustrated example of a cupboard from the period and use this as the basis for your design. Continue any decorative mouldings or other details across the front of units which break the continuity of a room. Poorly positioned storage will damage a room's visual balance, but if situated correctly it could add visual interest.

Some items of storage will be chosen for this very reason – in order to display items to visual effect. Make sure they are suitable for those things on display and not only show them to best effect but enhance them.

1 *Venus of the wood pile: classical inspiration to fan the flames in an Amsterdam town house. The far wall of a small backyard has been stacked with wooden boxes and crates for efficient use of space. The juxtaposition of the sculpture's smooth texture with the roughness of the timbers gives a vitality and dramatic focus to what could very easily have been an unattractive and cumbersome problem.*

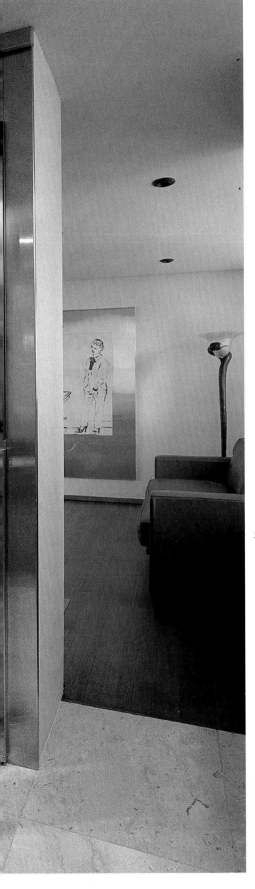

2 *A gleaming stainless-steel storage unit fits into a small corner in the most sophisticated of apartments. It also conceals plumbing for the toilet and water fountain.*

3

4

3 *In the home of a family of professional musicians, deep shelves have been designed to carry music scores and reference books. Walls have been removed, leaving structural pillars that neatly incorporate storage for tapes.*
4 *Flexible home-assembled units allow for inexpensive but stylish customized storage. Basic cubes can be used to create various shapes and fill awkward corners. Clutter can be hidden while more attractive objects are displayed, using a mix of doors, drawers, shelves and spaces.*

Storage rooms

Perhaps the best possible solution to most people's storage problems would be to have a room in the home especially reserved for this purpose. The best candidates would be small rooms, not suitable for other uses because of lack of natural light, perhaps, or odd dimensions. If you are carrying out major alterations, converting an attic or basement or extending a house, consider creating a storage room as part of your overall planning.

When fitting out a room of this type, remember you won't be entertaining guests there or using it as a place to relax, so make your priorities not the finish of the walls but the room's capacity to hold objects, offer you easy access to possessions and keep things in good condition. Make sure it is adequately ventilated, waterproof and has effective lighting. Nothing is more disheartening than clambering into a freezing attic clutching a torch, stepping carefully from joist to joist to avoid breaking through a ceiling below, searching for ages for that long-lost instruction manual to the food mixer so you can complete the dinner, only to find a sodden mass of rotting paper, ruined during a blizzard when snow was blown into the roof space.

An attic or basement is not suitable unless converted. Fit the storage room to suit the items it will hold. Use adjustable shelving and place objects in wire baskets or other containers that are not too heavy to carry when full. Mark all containers clearly so things can be found and always store objects that are used more regularly so that they are easily and immediately accessible.

Furniture should be covered to prevent damage in storage and all breakable items should be packed in the same way as you would if moving home.

If you have the space and the storage room is accessible, it could also be the ideal location for large items, such as a freezer, or for storing tools, paints and other decorating equipment. If the temperature is consistent, this could also be the place for storing wine: milk crates turned on their sides provide a cheap solution to wine racks. In addition, you can store bulk purchases of items such as toilet rolls or washing powder.

The room may become filled to the ceiling and provide an excuse for never throwing anything away. Keeping clutter under control includes keeping storage space under control. It will not be of great use if too full, since nothing will be accessible. Keep a note, perhaps on the inside of the door, showing precisely what is stored in the room and approximately where.

STORAGE
SAFETY AND COMFORT

Basic common sense is often ignored in storage planning. In a kitchen, for example, high shelves are frequently made too deep for a normal height person to see what is stored at the back, even when stretching.

Keep high shelves narrow, one-object deep, to avoid difficult rummaging and knocking things down. If this is not possible, store small objects in front of taller containers.

A lower shelf which allows you to look over the contents without strain can afford to be deeper, with objects ranged in rows. The ideal height for such shelves depends on the individuals using them.

 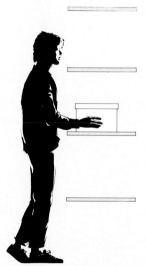

For storing less-used objects, a top shelf should be accessible at full stretch, before tip-toe. Only light objects, such as folded blankets or empty suitcases, are sensibly kept at this height to avoid accidents.

Objects stored at ground level should be easily retrieved, particularly if they are bulky or heavyweight. Attach wheels, or wheeled bases, and a big strap or rope to pull boxes out. Avoid crawling and straining.

Heavier objects are best stored on suitably sturdy shelving at waist height, not on the floor which causes back strain. Lifting at waist height enables you to use all muscles, distributing the weight evenly.

1 *When converting this building (2), the owners removed the staircase, replacing it with spiral stairs. The space saved allowed them storage room for their vast collection of books. The library extends through three storeys, with simple wooden slats used for flooring. Each section is kept light and airy with a large opening on to the adjoining stairwell. The ground floor contains a small study in what was once a hallway.*

3 *When commercial buildings are cleared, useful fittings can be found for storage rooms, such as these wooden lockers, originally used in an Australian tobacco factory.*
4 *Sturdy old furniture and shop fittings turn a box-room into a dressing-room.*
5 *Home-produced fruits and vegetables are kept in the rafters of this kitchen store-room, alongside wine, bulbs and other bulky objects, making good use of a cool, airy space.*

Hidden benefits

1 *A ready-made storage unit designed to adapt to various uses. Electric wiring for lights and gadgets is built into the system. High narrow shelves can be fitted with small plastic containers and a wide central shelf doubles as a worktop with more wide shelves below. The ironing board folds away and the concertina doors save space, too.*

2 *Large mobile storage units, custom-designed and built for an open-plan apartment; they can be placed in a group or lined up separately against a wall. This idea would work well in a work space where several people have quite different requirements.*

3 *A new linen chest in a French Alpine house is made to a traditional design; a fine example of purpose-built furniture. Table linen sits on pull-out glass shelves.*

4 *Classical concealed storage in an early Victorian house, where the limed oak panelling continues over the doors and up to the ceiling so that the line of the wall is unbroken, in keeping with the proportions of the room. Liming lightens the wood, and therefore prevents too heavy an effect.*

5 *The finely finished, fitted cupboards create a deep reveal to the door, well utilized for bookshelves. The skirting, or baseboard, unifies the cupboards and walls.*

113

PART 2

DECORATING THE HOME

Stencilled wild flowers, Cornish thrift, decorate an old farmhouse in Cornwall. When the walls were stripped, strong pinks and blues were discovered to have been the original colours; they were merely softened with a wash of white emulsion. Woodwork was dabbed with various colours and the floor stencilled with a chequered design.

A SURE SENSE OF STYLE

Designing a pattern may seem far removed from decorating a home but they both involve making choices about difficult abstract considerations, such as colour, balance, harmony and style. I spend my time, with other members of our team, choosing and painting patterns and have done so for over twenty years. Painting the designs and working out colour combinations take an enormous amount of time and concentration. As we experiment over a long period, ideas develop and come to life! When decisions are finally made, they seem simple and instinctive and we feel sure they are right. Without allowing the time for sifting the imagination, close focusing, 'sleeping on it', nothing confident or personal could be achieved.

The same is true of most other creative processes – none more so than the decoration of your home. Your home has to be designed for the way you want to live, so it is essential, before you begin decorating, to make a list of what you expect to *do* in your home.

You will most likely have moments of doubt when you have to make decisions about how to decorate a room. You could even feel paralyzed by the thought: 'I can't make a decision'. You may have started with confidence, with clear ideas about how you want the room to look, but often external influences cloud that initial vision. You may feel assessed and judged from outside and

pressurized by doubt from within. An immediate response to this indecision is to look elsewhere for reassurance, to consider what others have done, what you can see on the pages of magazines and books, what friends have done. This tends to sap your initial impetus and with it your confidence in your own ideas.

Discovering what you like involves developing a keen sense of your surroundings and with it the ability to judge your reactions. Test yourself in the room where you are reading this book – look up, make a list of the first five positive features you like about the room – a window, a box, a colour? Immediately, without bringing in judgment, make a list of features you don't like – a patch of damp, the door handle, the way the books are out of order, a colour, a texture? By becoming conscious of how you react to what you see, you are building a bridge between your abstract ideas about interiors and the practical execution of those ideas.

Develop the habit, every time you enter a room, of considering: 'Do I like it – yes or no?' Make a list of all those aspects you find likeable and those you find chilling. Do any of these rooms come near to your ideas of how you want your home to be?

Try to define the essential quality of a room and the ingredients that give it that particular feel, mood or atmosphere. Merely saying somewhere is 'stylish' or 'pleasant' is not

helpful unless you know what you understand by those words. If you respond to a room with a positive feeling and it expresses a way of living that appeals to you – it may be 'welcoming' or 'chic' or 'ethnic' or 'relaxed' or 'Mediterranean' – identify from your list the elements that inspired your definition and can inspire ideas for your own rooms.

Other sources of inspiration will be found in books and magazines, and in shop displays, television programmes and so on. All these usually express elements of current fashion. New fashions are exciting, they come and go, and they awaken us to change – new architectural and decorative materials, new ways of living, new furniture ideas and new priorities for interior design. Today we are bombarded by a myriad of choices. The advantage is that we can do virtually anything we like in interior design, but the paradox is that *choosing* is far more difficult than ever before. It is essential to make personal choices and not be dominated by what is presented as fashionable by sophisticated mass-marketing techniques. Be aware of what it is you are being persuaded to do and make up your own mind – take from fashion those elements you like, embellish and use them. Personal taste is something you alone can develop. Decorate your home with a sure knowledge of exactly how you respond to details, objects, textures, patterns, colours and space.

1 *Daylight filters through glass bricks into a restrained room, which is 'cool' rather than 'cold' because of the woven wall hanging and whimsical pink trolley.*

2 *A room filled with personal treasures. The handmade quilts, embroidered cushions, worn rug and comfortable proportions suggest 'warmth'.*

3 *A semi-basement room in a period Queen Anne house in London, inspired by journeys to warm countries. The coolness of the large ceramic floor tiles and the simplicity of the whitewashed plaster walls in a naturally rustic room imply. 'Mediterranean'.*

4 *With finely moulded decorative plasterwork picked out in gold, this imposing symmetrical room is made 'elegant' rather than grand by the witty use of classic Matisse shell chairs, canvas floor covering, a small table with a snake leg and a streamlined glass table.*

5·*'Minimal' rooms such as this leave nothing to chance. Each colour, shape and proportion is carefully considered and all objects stored out of sight. The lifestyle of the owners must be suitably restrained.*

Understanding colour

1 *This blue bedroom is warm, gentle and welcoming in the morning light, despite being decorated with a colour usually described as 'cold'. The tone of blue chosen, the dappled daylight, the touches of pink and green and the soft textures of the lace, fine-cotton quilt and hand-painted wooden chest allow it to be warm.*
2 *Monet's use of yellow, in his house at Giverny, also contradicts the usual preconceptions about the colour. Yellow is so strong it tends to engulf a room and dominate all other colours, but here it has been controlled by an imaginative and disciplined room design. Where the blue room was given softness, this dining room is given strong lines: the table is covered in unabsorbent oil cloth, the pictures have black frames, the fireplace and floor carry austere checks and the chairs bring a repeated curve to the room. They all combine to counterbalance the yellow.*

Colour is so powerful that we tend to approach it looking for rules. 'Blue and green should never be seen' was an old childhood chant in our neighbourhood. Yet there are *no* hard and fast rules. Feeling at home with colour takes time and effort, trial and error. Choosing a colour is finding the right version of that colour and understanding how it will look when you use it.

A colour is affected by everything else around it—especially light and shadow, and other colours. Light affects the tone, warmth and clarity of colour. A deep colour in a dark corner tends to look black, while in a brightly lit area the same colour can evaporate.

The effect of one colour on another is formidable. Some colours completely absorb others, some dominate and hold all those around them in suspense. Some versions of colours, such as those tinged with grey, are invariably co-operative and will work with most others.

If you haven't watched colour changes before, try this experiment. Use several coloured papers, say red, blue, yellow and grey: take a 225-mm (9-in) square of one and a 75-mm (3-in) square of another. Place the smaller square centrally on the larger, and watch the change. Then try two at a time – perhaps the large red and the small grey. (Incidentally, if your smaller shape is a pattern, say heart-shaped, the colour change is more difficult to see.) When you come to decorate, experiment. Paint a patch of a wall and consider it at various times of day, in different qualities of light. Imagine that colour around the whole room. Consider that patch, or, similarly, a fabric or a carpet sample, against other objects that will be in the room. Do the colours work together or against one another?

An off-white room will look one way with cream ceramic floor tiles; quite different with cream carpet and different again with a coloured linoleum floor. As well as the difference in colour tones of these various elements, there is a difference in texture which also affects their impact. The soft colour of the carpet is having one impact, the more reflective surface of the tiles another.

Off-white is a good example because it seems so simple yet, in practice, it can vary so much. How do you choose the right off-white for your purpose? The first step is to find the version of off-white you think you want – not on a paint colour chart but on an object or within a fabric, on a sheet of paper, a book jacket or a piece of pottery. It will not be simply 'off-white', it will be reddish, yellowish, greenish, blueish or greyish, warm or cool, strong or muted, bright or flat. Consider

2

off-white and think of it in each of these ways. Make a habit of considering the precise nature of any 'plain' colour that you like.

Make a list of objects you own whose colours you value – these objects will be far more use when selecting colour schemes for rooms than paint colour charts.

You may discover that a favourite colour is not the one you want to use in large quantities to cover whole walls, but it can have an important place in the room when included in another way, to bring a room either restful or dramatic emphasis. The colour may be contained in an earthenware pot or a pale green wicker basket, a bright woven shawl or a glossy red lamp, which will live in the room. You can use it in proportion and enjoy it. Do not feel that a favourite tone is devalued if it is not generously applied to vast areas of a room – the pale green of the wicker basket

will have just as positive an impact on the room as the colour you decide on for walls.

Colour can transform the quality of a room in terms of harmony and mood so, once you have chosen a version of a colour and have decided the proportion in which it will be happiest in the room, also consider the times of day you use the room and what you will want to do in that room.

The right version of a colour is the one with which you are comfortable. Certain colours can make you depressed, others lift the spirits, so, before you start choosing paint colours or selecting fabrics, make sure you know the shade of the colour you want, that you have lived with it and like it. The most innocent of off-whites could make you uncomfortable, pinks can be cold, blues can be warm and can lift you to contentment, while beige can damage your health. Even if you

would be happy relaxing or romping at night in a black bedroom, waking up there on a sunny morning would be a travesty. Strong pure colours, red and black, may work best for you for formal occasions, such as in a formal dining room, whereas less dominating colours are generally easier to live with in rooms used for family gatherings. If you want a room in flamingo pink, it can be *made* to work – one way is to find the exact version of pink you like contained in a multi-coloured fabric. The colour combination you enjoy in the fabric can inspire you to find other colours for the room to work with pink, perhaps using that fabric for curtains with turquoise flooring and grey-painted furniture. A quite different effect would result from lavender paintwork and a yellow floor. But there are no rules; your own response to particular colours must be the basis of your choices.

Using colour

1 *White, like any colour, has many versions and is as difficult to choose in precisely the right shade. The textures of a room affect the colours and reflective surfaces give quite different effects from those which absorb light. In a considered white room with natural muslin mosquito nets over camp beds, the rugs on the floor and the nets combine textures to produce a feeling of simplicity, and the wooden floors and earthenware pots introduce a feeling of warmth.*
2 *A pre-Raphaelite painting is well-placed in a Gothic corner – highly stylized windows, carved furniture and floor pattern are unified by a flat white to give an architectural quality.*
3 *The enchanting quality of this attractive window bay with a stunning view has been achieved by various textures of white: oak panelling and carved wooden furniture that have been limed, white linen upholstery and a thick white lace cloth.*

4 *An off-white room has walls containing yellow and upholstery tinged with grey, allowing an important turquoise ceramic collection to be an integral part of the whole room.*

4

5 *Clean and shiny and bright, bright white. In this harbourside house, white has been used as a spartan background against which every object and detail is defined. Clear, white artificial light against reflective walls, stainless-steel skirting (baseboards) and a pale polished floor give a gleaming quality.*

5

Understanding pattern

Pattern seems essential to our state of well-being, whether we wear it, use it or live with it. People have decorated themselves from their earliest days, imitating the markings of beetles, snakes and butterflies. It is worth noting that a lack of decoration, a lack of pattern, is traditional in mourning, in depression, in recession. Pattern can communicate origins or status – tartan cannot fail to imply Scottish; floral chintz is associated with English grandeur. Some pattern is traditionally made for ritual occasions – layers of ornate white lace speak of purity, modesty, weddings; wonderful Hungarian folk dances are performed in heavily embroidered dresses, and intricate, lacy henna patterns are painted on the hands of Indian brides.

Once, making things at home was part of everyone's familiar tradition. Pattern was something you made. Now that production is no longer domestic but industrial, the choice of patterns has become enormous and distanced from our individual experience.

The revival of stencilling, wall painting, marbling or stippling offers the chance to fulfil our need to make pattern. But usually we choose it ready-made, and our power to choose is influenced by what we are offered and how it is 'sold' to us.

There have been mass-produced patterns for furnishing fabrics since the end of the eighteenth century, when copper rollers and block printing made it possible to reproduce sketches and drawings in a repeating pattern. The early, unknown artists who drew those patterns imitated and embellished designs from the East – richly embroidered Kashmiri shawls, Indian and Turkish embroidery – and also made copies of copperplate illustrations and paintings of the period.

Now, as then, a large percentage of printed patterns are adaptations of earlier prints – traditional chintz is an obvious example. Major manufacturers frequently rely on prints inspired by and based upon archive designs for a large part of their output.

Pattern painted in our time and for our time for decorative furnishings was pioneered by innovative manufacturers who led a post-war revolution in using the work of contemporary painters and the creations of a new breed of textile designer. Printed fabric carried designs to be appreciated in their own right, to be seen flat and not merely in the folds of a fabric as a repeating detail.

The range of fabrics available today is wide, but remember that it is limited to the manufacturers' choices. For example, by choosing which archive designs they wish to adapt, manufacturers are choosing for us. They tend to select those designs which speak of affluence, calm, rhythm and order – stylized motifs of nature where no lizard sneaks, no insects buzz, no petal drops. It is assumed we do not want butterflies or insects perching on our bed-linen, but we can be allowed to see them in an unnatural form on curtains. Early floral designs quite happily included more realistic observations of natural life.

Co-ordination has become too easy for us with the marketing of whole ranges of household products carrying the same design – bed-linen, towels, wallpapers, shower curtains, tea services, plates, table-cloths, place mats, picture frames, soap dishes, writing papers and even saucepans. This acknowledges the human need for pattern, but implies that co-ordinating one pattern over many surfaces is the right solution for decorating and that co-ordination in itself is essential. The effect may be lifeless and you may not enjoy living with it.

Do not underestimate the power of pattern in decoration. Pattern drawn with warmth and coloured harmoniously can bring you warmth and harmony, and can give a room rhythm, drama, vigour, comfort, serenity and a sense of life. Pattern drawn harshly and coloured insensitively will undermine you just as certain colours can.

1

2

1 *The stepped walls of the water hole at Tonk, near Jaipur in India.*
2 *The same pattern occurs on a silk dhurry made close by.*

3

Architect Charles Jencks uses symbolic motifs as an integral part of his interior design; his inspirational themes appear throughout his buildings as decorative devices. This house in California is a converted ranch, using the main house with adjoining 'pavilions', and has become a small private village. The theme of the buildings and the decoration is the four elements: earth, water, fire, air.

3 *This bedroom is in a guest house named 'Hermitage' and has a spiritual atmosphere evoked by the Gothic shapes of the carved wood. For the design of his California home, Jencks has created the LA Order; the LA column motif can be seen on the bedstead.*

4 *The detail shows a stencilled design used in the Aer Pavilion, which contains the poolside master bedroom – the motif carries symbols of the four elements and part of the design is based on the California palm.*

4

Fabric design

1 *The traditional ogee shape on a mid sixteenth-century Spanish silk velvet altar fontal.*
2 *Isphahan woven fabric by William Morris, 1888, hand-loom jacquard.*
3 *A panel imported from India, c. 1820 – block print made with vegetable dyes.*
4 *A jacquard pattern woven at Paisley in Scotland, c. 1880. It is a fanciful interpretation of the traditional Indian imported textile.*
5 *Painted paisley design – Collier Campbell, 1983.*

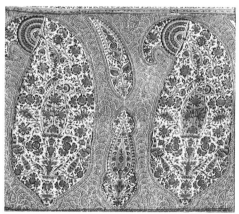

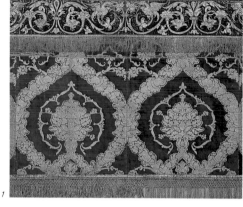

6 *Crewel embroidery – a detail from a sixteenth-century decorative furnishing cloth.*
7 *English block print, c. 1780.*
8 *A modern chintz design by Colefax and Fowler.*
9 *A sprig design printed on a copper roller in Manchester, c. 1820.*
10 *A modern sprig pattern by Laura Ashley.*

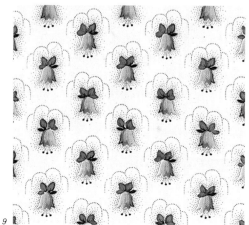

11 *Repeating pattern from illustrations by May Gibb for a series of stories – 'The Gum Nut Babies' – printed on English cotton in 1929 by Turnbull and Stockdale.*
12 *Post-war textile by painter John Piper.*

13 *Eighteenth-century 'warp' printed woven icat from Afghanistan.*
14 *'Bedouin Stripe' – Collier Campbell, 1983.*

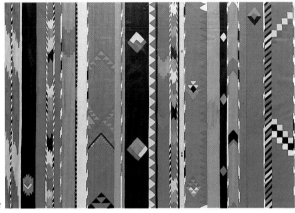

15 *Abstract design named 'Foxtrot' – Collier Campbell, 1984.*
16 *Motif of folding ribbons – 'Havannah', Collier Campbell, 1982.*

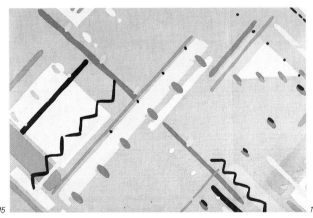

17 *'Côte d'Azure', painted design – Collier Campbell, 1982.*
18 *'Barge Roses' – painted design based on decorative stencilled motifs used for river barges, Collier Campbell, 1979.*

Using pattern

Pattern is present in a room not only in the obvious ways of printed fabrics and wallpapers, woven rugs and decorative plasterwork; it is also there in textures and surfaces. Sisal has a pattern as does embossed wallpaper, and the same is true of inlaid tables, lace table-cloths, carpet and plain woven coverings for chairs.

Consider the ways we use texture, decoration and applied pattern. Many decorative items are designed for a useful function – to keep out draughts or disguise faults and dirt. We use pattern to enliven dull surfaces. Historically, it was often used to disguise poor-quality base fabrics.

List the decorative features in the room where you are now sitting and ask yourself if the decoration on the feature affects the function, either by making it more simple, more pleasurable or more impractical. As far as you know, is the design directly from a culture other than your own? Is it derived from another discipline – for example, fabrics printed in a woven pattern? Is it machine made or hand-crafted? Are decorative surfaces or objects fulfilling their original design function or have you adapted their use to your needs and preferences – for example, are you using an antique shawl as a wall hanging or a chamber pot as a flower planter?

Pattern is used in different ways for different styles of room. Fabric printed with a bold design can be used in a minimal dining area as a single focal point. In a dramatically patterned room it will be used as part of the general decorative rhythm. In a room of similar, muted shades, pattern adds texture and interest. The affect of the pattern in a room depends not on particular designs but on how the colours blend or contrast with other objects and textures, and the amount and type of pattern used.

The effects of pattern are important and choosing a pattern in isolation is difficult because it is so powerful. We may select a pattern because of its attractive design, the colour combinations and its style, but it must also be chosen for its impact on a room. Patterns in a room should be balanced. If you look at the classic pattern mix of Dutch Old Master flower paintings, you will see the floral 'pattern' balanced by the geometric form of a basket, or the single coloured shape of a ceramic vessel, unified on a sympathetic coloured 'ground'. Quite often other less important decorative elements are implied in these paintings, such as architectural ruins and patterned insects. Balanced and unified, pattern, texture and colour will provide harmony in a room, as they do in a painting.

1

1 *An austere, simple room with decorative textured surfaces: Portuguese floral embroidered rugs, cushions covered in woven kelims, heavy white embroidery on white cloth on a large armchair, and intricately carved table legs. The variety of surface design is held firmly together by the strong black lines of some of the chairs, by the ceramic objects displayed and by the severe glass table-top.*

2 *The decorative zig-zag pattern of the stairway, without embellishment, makes a witty counterpoint to the dramatic, painterly quality of the bed-linen design.*

3 *Almost every surface in this study is 'patterned'. The bamboo blinds break up the light, the patina of time has mottled the surface of the 'plain' table and leather books, the cupboard and desk are carved, the picture frame moulded – even the flowers seem dappled.*

4 *An exuberant and sympathetic use of multiple pattern and texture in the tradition of English interiors. The heavily woven upholstery, richly patterned carpet, lighter lace refinements, carved wood, handmade quilts and decorative ceramic pots are all held in harmony by the simple device of painting the lower wall strong red.*

Gathering ideas

No one can look at a room and instantly decide on its final appearance. It helps to collect together some positive aids to making decisions about decorating. These things are best described not as influences but as suggestions, to think about over a period of time while ideas gather themselves. The obvious sources are not necessarily the best; magazines, books, shop displays are important and can be useful, but they are created by other people. Start by trying to formulate your own ideas rather than looking immediately outside your frame of reference.

Look around your home and carefully isolate the objects that give you visual pleasure – nothing is too small or too lowly. They may include something you have owned since childhood that brings with it a strong association of security and familiarity, something you wear because it always looks good, something you have had standing on a shelf and enjoy looking at. Become aware of details, of how each object was made. Wash the object, clean it or polish it, get to know its qualities better. Did you choose it for yourself or is it part of your home by chance? Some of what is natural to your taste has come by choice but much of it has come by accident. Look at what your accidents have provided you with – a length of fabric intended for a curtain which still beautifully covers the table

it was first laid on, or a cushion, received as a gift, which has given new life to a sofa and a pleasing focal point to an area of the room.

Start to think about those things in relation to the room to be decorated – the colours and textures – and see if they suggest a theme.

It can be helpful to gather 'inspirational' colours and textures together in a small container. Take a wicker basket, a wooden tray or something similar, and fill it. Pieces of fabric, a string of beads, a swatch of wool, embroidery thread, fruit, nuts, decorated glass, wrapping papers, corks, shells, pottery.

Do this slowly over a period because you will want to take things away and add other elements. You may find you want to arrange some of the objects into a still-life in order to see how the textures, colours and patterns work together.

Pictures from magazines, postcards, paintings can all have inspirational value, studied together or seen alone. A picture, though, is an illusion, so consider it in terms of patches of colour and texture, harmony and contrast, rather than hoping to reconstruct a room which exists only on paper. For example, you may find a still-life inspirational, a murky olive plate with lemons and oranges against a green wall; it is the artist's use of certain colours and shapes that you are appreciating and can adapt for your own use.

Name a collection of objects and pictures by their dominant quality. It may be 'glossy' because of the texture, 'dramatic' because of the powerful or contrasting colours you are selecting, 'natural' because you have placed natural substances in a group, or 'soft' because that is the general ambience of your collection. By providing a name or finding a theme, you can focus your ideas and expand and clarify them with further objects, colours, fabrics and furniture. Begin building up inspiration from your collection, inspiration which will lead to real decisions about how you want your room to look.

We are not always conscious of inspiration – you can absorb influences without being aware of it. But try and make yourself alert to potential influences when you are excited by something visually. Theatre sets can be fine inspiration, as can restaurants, where you have time to linger and think about the way the room has been planned, decorated and lit. Travel opens our eyes to the colours and patterns, the qualities of light and drama of other cultures. Driving from an airport in India past yellow and red muslin saris, turquoise bangles, white turbans, dusty trees, grey cattle is as exciting visually as all other ways. Ideas come from the new, the existing, the hidden or the familiar – keep your mind open to all these potential sources.

1, 2 *The worn Afghan wall hangings, the texture of the rafia dish, the presence of old books and the pink and yellow ceramic in the still-life provoked this rich and diversely decorated room. It invites and permits any amount of activity and family untidiness and could include yet further decorative collections. Much of the ornament is hand-crafted, so the rhythm of the room is human and therefore relaxed.*

3, 4 *The hallway is in an eighteenth-century house with rustic Queen Anne panelling and cottage-like proportions. The wood on the cupboard door had layers of paint and these were stripped to prepare the door for new paint. However, once taken back to the state where part of the original paint was adhering stubbornly to the surface, stripping stopped. It was left for some time; that effect of old, knobbly, worn wood became a positive feature of the hall and it was decided to leave it.*

The walls were painted white to lighten the area and to provide a neutral background while further decoration was considered. The still-life began when, in a room adjoining the hall, an old brown and cream slipware bowl was placed on a white cotton cloth with shells and seed pods. A friend's necklace was added and then a photograph was seen in a magazine which showed an interior painted with brown dots – a traditional American house interior. It exactly created the effect of brown objects on a white background. After dots were painted on the hall wall, the final touch was the wavy cream lines up the stairway – done without truly realizing that they matched exactly the pattern of the old slipware bowl that had provided the initial inspiration.

3

4

Ideas into practice

Collect together those things you really like and want to keep for the rest of your life – such as rugs, pictures, ceramics – and with your colour/texture inspirations distribute them as central themes in their appropriate rooms.

If you can't afford to replace existing furnishings that you dislike, consider what adaptations can be made to improve their look and diminish their negative impact: for example, dyeing a hideous but expensive carpet, or compensating for well-fixed but offensive bathroom tiles with perkier colours and glossier textures. Once you start shopping, you may need to make decorative adaptations. For example, a friend went shopping for kitchen units, confident in his own taste. He returned, dejected by 'other people's standards' – the kitchen units in his price range were to his mind 'shoddy bits of mass-produced chipboard'. He had not found what he really wanted. It was important that he considered exactly what that was and he explained he wanted pale, textured, lime-rubbed oak – rustic and handmade, with weight and texture. He could not afford to commission a carpenter so he decided to buy the inexpensive units and crackle paint them himself. The kitchen was quite easy to achieve once he had defined his requirements.

Shopping takes time, patience, persistence and, at times, an unnatural optimism. Nevertheless the more clearly you have understood your own taste the better you will be able to use and adapt what you find when you shop. It will take time, too, to pace out the colours of several rooms. You will need to decide whether you want each room or area to be of equal colour weight – like mid-blue, mid-grey, mid-green and so on, or whether you want sharp contrasts on surfaces, or possibly decorative themes, or whether you want to decorate the whole house in various tones of one colour. You may find all rooms facing in an easterly direction refreshing in blueish tones, and all those facing west warmly comfortable in yellowish tones – but then you will need to bridge the spaces in between.

Now, start with the room you most want to decorate. Get to know what it feels like. Sit in it at various times of day. Imagine the room in use. Get those who will share it with you to discuss their ideas. Establish the purpose of the room and plan the practical use of your space – its storage facilities and flow of traffic. This is essential if you are not to be perpetually uncomfortable. Make a budget for decorating but keep in mind that *choosing*

takes time, effort and energy and that choosing a less expensive option in preference to your more expensive first choice could cause untold disappointment and expense later on when you find that you cannot live with the results.

With your representative or real furniture, existing objects, container of colour and textural ideas, check to see if your basic scheme is still apt for your room. Make a list of your major purchases – furnishing fabric: printed or woven; floors: carpeted or hard, patterned or stencilled; walls: painted, textured or papered. Only you can decide which of these surfaces is easiest for you to handle first. Generally, I like to *know* the texture and colour idea for the floor, then I like to start choosing from a patterned fabric. In one length of fabric you can usually find both pleasing colour harmony and the key decorative style.

Experiment with areas of colour so that you see the changes from day to artificial light and the changes of light and shade. The smallest tin of paint available or a tiny sampler tin is a good investment in the search for the version of the colour you want. Cover as large an area as possible – preferably the corner of a room. Living for a short time with a strange patch on a wall is a small sacrifice for the confidence it gives when you paint the rest of the room.

It is not easy to know the effect of a colour from one patch, but it is virtually impossible to know it from a small sample on a colour chart. Try as many patches as are necessary – the results could surprise you.

The expanse of colour is also crucial. If an entire room is to be painted in one colour, then remember that what will emerge is a range of that colour, differing in areas of light and shadow and against other colours, textures and objects.

When choosing wallpaper, take the same approach as for choosing a paint colour – get as large a sample as you can or buy a single roll and look at it in the room in various conditions of light. If possible, take objects with you when shopping – be it a cushion which contains the colours of the room or any other object which sums up its essence.

In most shops, fabric is hung insensitively; it is frequently creased and dirty and equally frequently hung too close to other unsympathetic designs. Take care to isolate the fabrics and to concentrate on each one. Choose a few that work with your object – buy a length of your two or three favourites and take cuttings of doubtful choices so that they can all be considered at home.

Keep *looking* while in the course of dec-

orating. When you get down to the detail of your room, you may be pleasantly surprised by the architraves, skirting (baseboards), the quality of natural light or the shape of the fireplace. You may be unpleasantly disappointed by elements you thought were superb and should be highlighted; if so, do something about it.

Finally, you will have a freshly finished, pristine room. Ironically, it may seem too crisp, too clean, too perfect. It will mellow through time: surfaces become scratched, rubbed, stained. Usually this happens long before you need or wish to start decorating again, so add yet another consideration when you choose things for your home – how they will age. If you approach decorating with a clear sense of how you will live in the room – which brings us back to the importance of listing what you *do* in your home – then remembering how the room will mellow should be part of any choices that follow.

1 *A restful room created with great confidence and style. The dominant theme is produced by the richly patterned woven fabrics in strong colours, used for upholstery and cushions, and the powerful design of the carpet.*

2, 3 *The project here was to furnish a room, which had been structurally altered, as a dining room. The new supporting steel beams had rigid lines, leaving the room hard and characterless.*

The basic ideas for the decorative scheme came from a shiny, black painted plate and a shiny, patterned, dark Malayan table. As the still-life shows, the shininess became a dominant element once tin foil, a shiny pâpier maché plate and shiny, decorative cutlery were added.

When these were looked at in conjunction with the room, the outstanding problem was to soften the hard lines of the new building work. At first, a soft carpet was chosen; although it was the right colour, it was too soft and worked badly with the austere architectural features. Obviously it was far better to go for crispness – which is a kinder version of the hardness – rather than defeat it with softness. The solution was found in a wallpaper which has firm, stamped motifs on it as if hand-painted. Using it in various, but complementary, colours and scales gave the room wit as well as continuity and the pattern relieved the overpowering hard structural lines. A Matisse print had added a contrast to the shininess of the inspirational still-life; in the room itself, the Matisse print brings gentle and colourful contrast to the black floor and table and unifies the shiny surfaces with the patterned walls.

FLOORS

Floors are literally the basis of your home, both practically and aesthetically. They are the surfaces where you, your family, pets and guests walk, sit and lie, where things are spilled or dropped and under which services such as water pipes and electrical cables run. A floor may be required to provide sound and heat insulation, or take heavy traffic; changing may involve a substantial investment.

Just as crucially, the floor is the setting for your furniture and possessions. Since it forms a very large part of the surface area of any room, its colour and texture will have a dominant effect on the overall decorative scheme. Large patterns, deep shades and borders will make a room look smaller; small patterns, light colours and plain surfaces will increase the impression of space. The type of floor also makes an important contribution to the character of your home – whether it is chosen to complement a style or period look or to make a bold, anachronistic statement.

All in all, there's a lot to be said for making the floor your first consideration. But even if this proves impractical, the choice of a floor certainly merits very careful thought. Pay close attention to the details – the junctions between different types of flooring or between walls and the floor – and don't neglect the overall view – the transition from level to level or from room to room.

The checklist has been designed to help you discover your preferences and your practical requirements. By the time you've considered both of these aspects fully, a floor can almost be self-selecting.

FLOORS
CHECKLIST

- Which activities take place in the area:
  - living?
  - cooking?
  - eating?
  - sleeping?
  - bathing?
  - washing?
  - play?
  - home workshop?
  - a combination of these?
- Which activities take place on the floor:
  - sitting?
  - lying?
  - playing?
  - dancing?
  - exercising?
  - other?
- Which areas are likely to get especially heavy wear?
- Is there direct access to the outdoors?
- Is there a possibility of overflow from:
  - baths?
  - sinks?
  - washing machines?
  - dishwashers?
  - house-plant watering?
- Are prams (baby carriages) or bicycles likely to be wheeled over the floor?
- Do you have pets which will shed hairs or make paw prints?
- Do you want the flooring to suit:
  - an existing decorative scheme?
  - your home's architectural character?
  - your furniture?
- Can you plan your decorative scheme around the floor?

- Is there a view into other areas with different floor coverings?
- How long do you want the flooring to last?
- Does the floor need special care?
- How much cleaning and maintenance will the flooring require?
- Do you want the floor to provide heat and/or sound insulation?
- Can the floor structure take the weight of the flooring you want?
- Are there signs of rot, infestation or damp in the timbers?
- Is there a damp-proof course and ventilation?
- Is there much disruption involved in installing the floor?
- Does any major work need to be done before the floor is laid:
  - rewiring?
  - plumbing?
  - installing central heating/cooling?
  - building work?
  - extensive decoration?
- Do you need access to under-floor services?
- If you have under-floor heating is your flooring compatible with it?
- Have you investigated cheaper alternatives?

A traditional slate and stone floor in an old Oxfordshire house has been rescued from dereliction, but with the intention of conserving it, rather than restoring it. The owners enjoy the aged surfaces of the floor and original marbled wall and their approach is to maintain the best aspects of the house as sensitively as possible.

Hard floors

Brick

Brick floors can look cosy and rustic (especially in reds, buffs or browns) or cool and chic (blues, purples, yellows). Green flint or lime bricks are a stylish, but rarer, possibility. Non-slip, waterproof, often stain- and grease-resistant, bricks are also much warmer than marble or ceramic tiles. They are suitable for ground floors only. Use types recommended for paving (brick paviors), otherwise the surface will quickly degrade. Thin brick tiles or slips can also be used.

Bricks can be laid in a variety of patterns or in conjunction with other surfaces – stone, for example. They look particularly good with rugs. Also useful for connecting a ground-level room to a garden, patio or outside area (but the bricks must be frost-resistant). Can be taken up walls for an easy-to-clean junction or used to clad sturdy kitchen units, for example, to unify visually.

Laying Must be laid on a damp-proof course and into a mortar bed with mortar joining. Some brick tiles can be laid on thin adhesive – check with supplier.

Treatment Sealing can be difficult – a lot depends on the type of brick. Since most have porous surfaces and it's hard to strip an absorbed seal, go carefully and ask the supplier for advice. Bricks can also be polished.

Ceramic tiles

These blocks of high-fired dust-pressed clay come in a huge range of styles. Sizes vary from tiny to foot-square; shapes include hexagonal, square, rectangular, Provençal (and choice is further extended by the different ways in which tiles can be laid); patterns range from flowery to geometric. Aside from the standard colours, unexpected shades include glossy greens, and the newer vitrified colour ranges include subtle tones, such as cloudy blues, greens and greys.

Handmade tiles are charmingly irregular in shape and pattern; mass-manufactured types have a precision aesthetic and accuracy of repeat. Some are machine-made, then hand-decorated. Textures vary too: many are relief-textured to make them less slippery. Most good ranges include matching wall-covering tiles, which give a sloped edge to the wall-floor junction for easier cleaning and organized appearance.

Although durability is high, surface patterns under thin glaze can get worn away. Obviously dishes will break when dropped on tiles; less obviously, if you drop hard, heavy objects the tiles may crack or chip. They are also cool to the feet (which is why they are so much used in hot climates) but can be used over under-floor heating. Can be a noisy surface and some people find them tiring.

Laying Must be laid on a level, solid floor such as a concrete sub-floor with cement or sand screed, or any other smooth sub-floor with a latex screed. These tiles are very heavy and place a great strain on suspended timber sub-floors, though a small bathroom, say, would have less of a loadbearing problem than a large one. If in doubt, call in a surveyor, or house inspector, to check loadbearing capacity, having calculated the number and weight of tiles. Timber floors must be covered with hardboard first.

Since these tiles are difficult to cut, space and set out, think carefully before you attempt to lay a floor yourself: badly laid tiles look awful, and may lift up and lead to water seepage, which could damage the sub-floor and cost a lot to put right.

Treatment Most tiles should not be sealed and high polish can make them dangerously slippery. A light polish looks good, but can, paradoxically, attract dirt. Generally soap or detergent and water are sufficient – harsh abrasives can damage glazed tiles. Beware also of glazed tiles which can become dangerously slippery when wet – don't use these where you are likely to spill water.

Pebbles/cobbles

An interesting way of treating a border or a lobby, especially for a seaside or country cottage. Pebbles and cobbles come in a wide range of colours and shapes. You could collect and grade your own, or obtain them from landscape suppliers. But they make a noisy, uneven and dirt-prone surface.

Laying Grade and embed in mortar on screed bed over damp course. Avoid jagged points.

Treatment Cobbles can be sealed, or treated with mixtures such as wax and linseed oil.

Marble

A luscious, hard-wearing, polished natural material, which comes in many beautiful, usually 'veined', shades, marble is also expensive, cold, difficult to cut, heavy and noisy when walked on. For ease of laying, it is now available in thin sheets or tiles, in very fine slices backed with epoxy resin and glass fibre, or over expanded polyurethane backed by steel.

Predominant colours are grey-veined white, white-veined black, and dozens of reds, ochres, greens.

Laying In cement bed on concrete sub-floor.

Treatment No surface treatment needed once marble has been polished industrially. Do not use strong acid or alkaline cleaners.

Well-worn brick.

Classic ceramic tiles.

Cobbled stone floor.

Marble tiles, slate diamonds.

Mosaic

This most ancient and elegant of floorings comes in glass silica, clay or marble, with glazed or unglazed finishes in the clay varieties. Mosaic makes very durable, hard, cool, potentially noisy floors – expensive, but with a tempting range of colours and designs.

Laying It comes on a peel-off backing to make laying easier. Edges can be tricky – it's best to carry on up the walls for a neat finish and to make cleaning easier. Otherwise, lay irregular ones as tightly to the edge as possible so the minimum of exposed grout shows – but it is far better to finish in flat-edged mosaics. It can also be used as narrow skirting (baseboards) in kitchen and bathroom. Because many types of mosaic have uneven surfaces it's absolutely essential to have a smooth, even, screeded sub-floor. Make sure grouting is even too, or dirt will collect in joints.

Treatment Wash, do not polish.

Quarry tiles

Traditionally associated with country homes, quarry tiles are usually square or rectangular and come in a range of colours similar to bricks. Made from unrefined, extruded, high-silica alumina clay, they are basic in appearance, and very hard and durable but a little softer than ceramic tiles. Simple treatments usually look best.

These tiles can be used with under-floor heating and can be surprisingly cheap – but there is a wide price range and a lot depends on thickness. Disadvantages: noisy, cold and will break almost everything you drop.

Laying Lay on screeded concrete sub-floor.

Treatment Quarries can be left as found; otherwise, consult the manufacturer if you want to seal. If this is suitable, seal immediately with a mixture of linseed oil and turpentine (one : four), cover with brown paper and leave for forty-eight hours. Subsequently sweep, wash, polish if you want – but take care not to make the floor slippery. Very worn quarries can be cleaned and then sealed with a water-based sealer – paint this on carefully as the surface will be worn unevenly. Don't seal waterproofed tiles with a polyurethane-type sealer – it will peel.

Slate

Slate floors, with their beautiful, slightly rippled surface, usually come in large slabs and in a range of greys, grey-blues and grey-greens evocative of the mountain regions from which they are hewn. Slate can be combined with other materials such as wood, but this is only successful if the slate is cut in regular geometric shapes. It makes a wonderful foil for rugs. Durability is very high if the slate is properly cut, and it is quite impervious to water. But it is also cold, hard, noisy and expensive, and can be slippery when wet unless it is the non-slip variety.

Laying Rather brittle and heavy to handle. Lay in cement bed on concrete.

Treatment Use a linseed oil and turpentine mix (one : four) as for quarry tiles. Sweep and wash. Emulsion polish is best. Can also be sealed with a water-based sealer.

Stone

With its medieval, rustic, even ecclesiastical overtones, a stone floor demands an appropriate setting. It's perfect for the corridors, lobbies, halls and kitchens of old houses – and some new ones. Varieties include sandstone, York stone, granite and limestone, all of which are available in slabs, but stone chippings cast with cement into slabs are a cheaper alternative. Stone is extremely hard-wearing but cold, hard, heavy and noisy and can look unattractive if stained. Costs vary according to type.

Laying Very hard for one person to manage. Must be laid in cement bed on concrete sub-floor with damp course. Can be ground flat like a marble floor.

Treatment Some stone is far more porous than others; therefore, some can be sealed, while others can't. Ask your supplier for advice. Sealers will change the colour and may chip off. Sweep, wash and polish.

Terrazzo

A very smooth, elegant, tough surface typically found in hotel lobbies, real terrazzo consists of plain or coloured marble chips set in concrete or cement and then ground smooth. Granite varieties and industrial versions are also obtainable; a new range combines dye-treated river-bed chips with strong resin to produce a hard nubbly carpet.

Because of terrazzo's strength, it can be very thin – 9mm ($\frac{3}{8}$in). It comes in tiles, slabs or can be laid by trowel *in situ*, and tends to be mottled, splodged or spattered rather than veined like natural marble. Usual colours include brown, black, red, grey and yellow mixed with white. Terrazzo is suitable for use with under-floor heating.

Laying The trowel-laid types must be installed professionally, and can extend up the wall. Tiles or slabs should be laid on screeded sub-floors; joints can be sealed with silicone.

Treatment Sweep and wash. Do not clean with strong acid or alkaline solutions.

Mosaic tiles.

Subtle-coloured quarry tiles.

Riven slate slabs.

Terrazzo hallway.

Flooring: function and flair

1 *Bricks are ideal for hallways leading to outside areas, or for patios. Pavior bricks (made for floors) are non-slip, waterproof, stain- and grease-resistant.*

2 *An unusual tough and durable surface is seen in the studio of a German artist. Sections of strong brown leather were stitched together to form a permanent flooring, which, in spite of fierce use, still looks good twenty years on.*

3 Cork is available only in a few natural colours but is tough and versatile. Use heavyweight tiles for floors, either pre-sealed, or painted after laying with polyurethane or acid catalyst sealer. An area of untreated cork has been left beside the bath in this spacious bathroom and makes a fitted bathmat.

4 New products add to possibilities for floors: heavy-density wood fibreboard is marbled and lacquered to give a tough finish; designs are based on the floors of seventeenth-century Venetian churches, and the floor is warmer and cheaper than real marble.

Semi-hard floors

Hardboard

A thin, fibrous sheet board made from softwood pulp, hardboard can be used as a very inexpensive floor in its own right, sealed or painted, or can provide a very good, even surface on which to lay another flooring. Comes in shades of brown. Not very durable in the long term, especially if water gets underneath or the seal wears away.

Laying If using as final floor, lay smooth side up and 'condition' before use by brushing water into reverse side, then stacking boards flat, back to back, in room they will be laid in for no longer than forty-eight hours. When fixed to a sub-floor with panel pins or grooved ring nails, they will dry and tighten to fit.

If fitting a final floor, begin in centre of room, slotting border in at edge. If laying on uneven floorboards as final covering, use a thick underlay. If laying for lining, lay from edge of room, rough side up, so pins sink in and a good 'key' surface is provided for adhesive. On uneven surfaces, pin at frequent (100-mm [4-in]) intervals.

Treatment Seal at once, or paint as for floorboards, if hardboard is used as a final covering. Subsequently sweep; wash if necessary, but with a damp cloth rather than using buckets of water and strong detergents.

Chipboard

Thicker than hardboard, chipboard is made from urea formaldehyde resins and wood-chips bonded under pressure. It is available either in tongue-and-grooved form for floors or in sheets and looks rather like cork when sealed. It's reasonably durable, an efficient insulator, warm and resilient and so is often used instead of wooden floorboards in new homes. Avoid using where water may be spilled.

Laying Fairly easy and quick since chipboard comes in large sections. Use woodworking adhesive to fix tongues into grooves, removing any excess adhesive *immediately* because of the dangers of permanent staining – in fact, it's best to paint on the first coat of sealer before you even start laying to minimize the risk of staining. Unlike floorboards, chipboard can't be removed for access to services under the floor, so provide suitable access traps (or make a hatch).

Treatment If chipboard is not sealed immediately, it will stain irreparably. Once allowed to get wet, it is permanently weakened. So seal thoroughly as for floorboards and care as for plywood (see *Wood floors*). Alternatively, for a soft, golden sheen, you could apply several coats of oil; tung oil is excellent for this.

Cork

Despite the relatively narrow colour range (light honey to dark brown), cork is a wonderfully versatile, lightweight but hard-wearing floor, warm, resilient, comfortable and quiet, with good insulating properties. Made from natural cork, compressed with binders and baked, it can be striped, gridded or patterned in appearance. Laying it with a border or in a chequered pattern will give variety.

Check that you have flooring grade cork – which can itself come in different thicknesses – not the cheaper wall tiles. Thicker grades give more resilience and insulation, but thinner grades laid on hardboard should be fine. A tougher version exists – tiles or planks, bonded with an impervious vinyl surface. Provided cork is laid and sealed properly, it should be reasonably durable. Do not use over under-floor heating: it will lift.

Laying Light and easy to cut, cork is reasonably quick to lay in regular-shaped rooms without too many obstacles. Lay on smooth floor. Use the recommended adhesive, with a proper serrated spreader so it is applied to the correct depth.

Treatment Untreated cork can be used successfully in bathrooms where its absorbent qualities are needed. Elsewhere, sealing is essential. Use several coats of polyurethane as soon as laid (matt probably looks better than gloss), or one or two coats of a tough acid catalyst sealer, for which you need to wear a mask. Pre-sealed tiles must be butted very closely together to prevent water seepage. Wash and occasionally emulsion polish. Avoid spirit-based chemicals.

Linoleum

A durable material, linoleum is made from a compound of natural ingredients including linseed oil, ground cork, wood, flour and resins, baked slowly at high temperatures and pressed on to a jute or hessian back. It is no longer the thin, brittle material of the post-war years but a really strong, flexible flooring which has benefited from new design ideas. It usually has a surface dressing and comes in sheet or tile, in good, plain colours, marbled or patterned. It is warm underfoot and resilient, but avoid getting water underneath since this will cause it to rise.

Laying Reasonably easy to cut, but, as with vinyl, large rolls may be daunting. Lay with the manufacturer's recommended adhesive on dry, even sub-floor, with a damp-proof course if on the ground-floor level. You'll need professional help for any complex patterning.

Cork tiles.

Cork veneer tiles.

Contrasting linos.

Vinyl floor tiles.

Treatment Just sweep, wash and polish the floor lightly with emulsion polish. Avoid strong alkali cleaning agents. Worn linoleum can be revamped with special lino paint after the surface has been thoroughly cleaned and then rubbed down.

Plastic

Available as woven matting or honeycomb duckboard – is surprisingly comfortable to bare feet. Some new varieties come in the form of small snap-together tiles: expensive, but stunning. Very durable and resilient, except for danger of melting when burned or if spirit solvents are splashed. It might fade in continual exposure to strong sunlight. Since water can obviously seep through gaps in open-holed varieties, it is probably best to lay this type on an impervious sub-floor. Plastic matting is cheap; more complex honeycomb types of plastic flooring are fairly expensive.

Laying Cut matting to fit; bind strip matting together for larger spaces with adhesive tape. Plastic tiles can be cut with a suitable sharp knife.

Treatment Wash with plain hot water. Dirt will fall through holed varieties, so you will need to invest in a powerful vacuum cleaner and be prepared to lift and clean underneath the flooring.

Vinyl

This versatile, workhorse flooring is produced in varying degrees of flexibility and in a huge number of patterns, thicknesses and textures, some simulating natural materials. Industrial grades – impregnated with quartz crystals or mineral shards – provide unusual stippled surfaces. Vinyl is also made with a relief surface.

Available in tiles or sheet form, vinyl is waterproof and resistant to oil, fat and most domestic chemicals, but not immune to burns or abrasion by grit. While the thicker or cushioned types are quiet, resilient and warm underfoot, thin vinyls may be cold and hard. Bigger widths mean a floor can be covered without seams. Vinyl can be used over under-floor heating.

Laying Easy to cut and lightweight, though dealing with giant rolls can be awkward. Usually wise to cut oversize and trim to fit, since it shrinks slightly *in situ*. Can be loose-laid or stuck down to the prepared sub-floor.

In winter, heat room in which vinyl will be laid – cold makes it brittle. Allow vinyl to acclimatize before cutting – don't buy and lay on the same day. If you need access beneath the floorboards, make a hatch – once fixed with glue, vinyl can't be lifted. Complex patterning may require professional laying.

Treatment Wash and rinse. Avoid build-up of emulsion polish.

Rubber/synthetic rubber

Much used in public places, rubber is now established as a tough, warm and very stylish floor for home use too. Available in single colours, marbled, or with relief patterns to aid its non-slip qualities. Generally durable and good at withstanding stiletto heels, but the natural type can react badly to some spirit-based chemicals.

Laying Lay on screeded concrete or smooth, even sub-floor. Synthetic rubber can be loose-laid on screed but will be colder underfoot. Must be cut carefully at edges.

Treatment Can apply thin metallized emulsion dressing to real rubber to enhance its appearance. Wash both types with warm water and mild detergents; watch out for dirt building up around relief patterns.

Coir

The thick, prickly fibre which comes from coconuts, coir is used to make many different varieties of matting. Tough, cheap, generally golden in colour, it is the perfect low-cost flooring solution for halls, stairs if it's tightly fitted (but beware: it can get shiny and slippery).

There are now some interesting versions with beautifully dyed sisal or other materials woven in. Often vinyl- or latex-backed to minimize dust penetration and make for greater durability, coir will last a long time, but may shed more dust as it ages and crumbles. Texture may be too abrasive and uncomfortable for bare feet.

Laying Easy to lay and cut to shape. For wall-to-wall coverage, stitch lengths together; bind edges with jute tape.

Treatment Vacuum clean. Loose matting can be taken up and beaten, scrubbed with soapless detergent. With unbacked versions, dirt falls through, so you need to clean underneath periodically.

Rush, seagrass and maize

These natural materials vary in texture – maize is the finest and the palest in colour. Woven squares can be sewn together into mats using fine twine, and there are many attractive weaves. Ideal for temporary accommodation. Plenty of cool charm. All types look good over other flooring, but do tend to create dust.

Laying Do not need underlay.

Treatment All deteriorate if too dry, so mist occasionally with a plant sprayer. Lift and sweep beneath, and snip off flaking ends.

Sheet vinyl flooring.

Rubber stud and wood.

Golden coir matting.

Rush matting.

Wood floors

New wood

Smooth, glowing, beautifully finished wood provides a durable and tranquil surface that looks equally good in the kitchen, bedroom or living room. The list of possible flooring woods, soft or hard, is long and poetic, ranging from the familiar spruce, fir or pine (soft) and oak, maple, afrormosia (hard) to the exotic or unusual – purple heart, willow, padouk, sapele. A timber merchant will help you to investigate all the possibilities. Similarly, woods are available in a variety of forms: softwood or hardwood boards in many different widths, pre-sealed wooden 'tiles' (often veneered softwood) and hardwood parquet (short pieces set in a formal, repeating pattern).

Durability is high, but stiletto heels and cigarette burns leave bad marks, especially if veneers are not sufficiently thick or hard. Wood is resilient, so there's 'give' and things won't necessarily break when dropped. And it continues to look good, even improve, as it ages. Too much dry heat may cause shrinking, and butt-jointed boards particularly may shrink and twist, so check the level of humidity. Frequent wetting may cause swelling and warping. Can be expensive.

Laying The major error amateurs make is to misjudge the position of joists and knock nails through electric cables and water pipes – make sure you know the layout of such services before you start. Tongue-and-grooved boards slot together and snap in place: not too hard once you've learned the knack. Wood block and wood mosaic should be laid on screeded concrete, ply or chipboard (over damp course on ground floors). Lay parquet and wood strip on level timber, ply or hardboard. There are also systems of solid wood fitted with metal clips and glue, which obviate the need for nails, and vinyl-bonded wood plank floors in a sandwich of cork core, veneer and PVC surface.

Treatment Vacuum clean or sweep; wash lightly. If not pre-sealed, seal carefully with polyurethane, acid catalyst sealer or oleo-resinous sealer. Otherwise, polish deeply, thoroughly and regularly.

Old wood

Bare floorboards, whether to be polished, stained or painted, must be in a decent condition to begin with and the work necessary to bring them up to a classy finish can be heavy. Floorboards are durable, but since they are exposed they also get dirty, damaged or splintery. Unless you have sealed gaps between boards, expect draughts to whistle up between ground-floor boards – but gap-filling material may turn a different colour when sealed or stained. However, don't be tempted to insulate below ground-level boards or block up sub-floor ventilation – this will lead to damp. (Check regularly that vent bricks haven't got blocked up.) Bare boards will be noisy and more expensive than you might think – hiring sanding equipment isn't cheap. And don't use cheap paints or stains – poor quality ones are a false economy.

Laying It is possible to fill gaps with old wood where you've taken out badly damaged boards. If the floor is butt-jointed, make sure the fit is as tight as possible. Punch nailheads below surface so they don't tear sandpaper.

Treatment First, give the floor a very thorough scrub with strong detergent and hot water (wear gloves). If the boards have always been covered, you may find you don't need to sand, apart from a quick manual rub with sandpaper (or scraper or paint remover) on stubborn stains. If the boards are very soiled or already have a surface coating, hire a sander and professional edging sander, after replacing damaged boards. If you want your finish to look really professional, cover up nail heads with stopping. Make sure the sander collects dust, empty the collecting bag regularly, and wear a mask. Sand along length of boards, not across, which will make scratches. Clean up all dust carefully with a slightly damp cloth when finished, then give a final clean with white spirit, leaving boards to dry thoroughly. You can seal straight away or bleach the boards and coat with polyurethane or white floor wax.

Boards can also be stained. This can look patchy unless applied very evenly – and you can only darken timber, not lighten it. Unusual dyes and coloured stains are available. Apply a final clear seal, unless you are using a wood seal with built-in colour, or polish boards repeatedly with a mixture of wax and linseed oil. Or several coats of oil will look good – give it time to soak in.

Painted boards are attractive too, though may not wear as well as sealed ones. You can use any good gloss or eggshell, but you'll get better results with proper floor paints, which usually contain polyurethane, acrylic or epoxy resin and dry to a hard finish. Yacht paint is particularly hard-wearing but takes a long time to dry. Make sure boards are meticulously clean, or the paint won't adhere properly. This can be applied in patterns if you're a careful worker, using floorboards as guidelines for stripes, or ready-made stencils.

Stripped and limed pine.

New oak parquet.

Stripped, varnished pine.

Old wooden parquet.

Plywood

Provided it is thick enough, timber-faced plywood can be cut into squares or bought ready tongued-and-grooved and laid like any other wood – on boarding in older houses but even directly on joists if you want to try it as a new floor. With a good finish it can look quite elegant or it can be painted or stained for a livelier effect. Not very impact- or wear-resistant for heavy traffic and must be thoroughly sealed or treated immediately. Comparatively inexpensive.

Laying Can be hard to cut precisely around odd shapes and hard to fix with nails: try using serrated-head hardboard nails. Ask supplier to cut to size. Lay on boards, joists if sufficiently thick, or bed in bitumastic on screeded concrete.

Treatment Seal, paint or stain and seal. Emulsion polish if you like. If staining, check that stain and seal are compatible – and make sure ply surface is laid in same direction. Sweep and wipe with damp cloth rather than scrubbing clean.

A maple floor works well in this modern apartment, created in what was once office space above a shop. The original pine floorboards were covered with this new wood floor.

Limed oak parquet.

Painted stripped wood.

Gloss paint on wood.

Stencilled wood.

Soft floors

Carpet

The range of carpet types may seem bewildering at first, but it's worth being familiar with at least the broad categories. On the other hand, don't be obsessed with a manufacturer's 'name'. Big retail groups offer excellent lines of carpet at good prices because they can guarantee their suppliers high sales.

A rough idea of the durability of a carpet can be gained by assessing the denseness, resilience and weight of its pile. Press your thumb into the pile to see how quickly it recovers – the quicker it does, the denser and more resilient the carpet, unless it is a shag (long-hair) type. The weight should be stated on the label. Short, dense-fibre carpets are probably the most durable: long strands and big loops may look bulky but actually weigh less.

Make sure the carpet you choose is the right quality for the situation in which you wish to use it – look at the label carefully and don't put a light-use carpet in your living room or on the stairs. Conversely, a room rarely used doesn't have to have a heavy-duty carpet. For an all-purpose carpet, an eighty-per cent wool, twenty-per cent nylon mixture is probably the best choice, but modern synthetic fibres have improved dramatically in quality.

Before buying carpet, work out roughly how many square metres (or yards) you need, so you can compare prices. If the retailer does not provide a measuring service, make a sketch plan so that you buy the correct amount. Check estimates to avoid the common fault of over-ordering. Patterned or bordered carpets will obviously need more yardage.

Plain carpets will show stains and shading, whereby some areas of pile become permanently reversed in the direction of the lie – though a hard-twist pile is much less susceptible to this rather inexplicable effect.

Underlay Unless the carpet is foam-backed, you'll need underlay, and it's important to choose a good one. Animal-fibre underlay has high resilience; it should have a weight of about 1kg per square metre (2½lb per square yard). Foam must be of a good quality – rub it with your thumb under medium pressure and reject it if it disintegrates. Foam should be laid over paper, paper felt or hardboard to prevent it from sticking to the floor. Do not use foam on stairs, but special pads or jute-backed crumb rubber.

Laying Don't attempt to lay fitted carpet yourself, unless it is fairly light-weight and foam-backed: this demands specialist skills.

Cleaning New carpets tend to produce fluff: for the first few weeks clean lightly with a hand-brush. Thereafter, vacuum regularly at least once a week to prevent dirt from being embedded at the base of the pile where it can rub and cut fibres loose.

To shampoo, follow manufacturer's instructions exactly. Spray extraction cleaning (often wrongly termed steam cleaning) is best left to the professionals. Remove stains right away.

Carpet terms

Axminster Name comes from loom on which the carpets are woven. This type of loom inserts pile tufts into the weave from above so that strands need not run along back – therefore, a great many colours can be used. The surface is cut pile, but may be long and shaggy, short and smooth, stubbly (where hard twist yarn is used) or carved.

Berber Originally meant a carpet with looped pile in natural, undyed wool, in the same shades used by Berbers of the North African desert. Now general term for nubbly, flecked carpets.

Body carpet Carpet less than 1.8m (6ft) wide. Used as runners in corridors, as stair carpet or seamed for awkward shapes.

Bonded Yarns or fibres are bonded into an adhesive base in one of several ways. Can be of superlative quality.

Bordered squares In fact usually rectangular, with the border around the perimeter. Can be turned to equalize wear.

Broadloom Carpet wider than 1.8m (6ft). The most common broadloom widths are 2.74m (9ft) and 3.66m (12ft), but can reach as much as 5.5m (18ft).

Brussels weave Tightly looped pile, uncut.

Carpet tiles Available in all carpet constructions, but usually plain. It is important that they possess guaranteed dimensional stability.

Cord Looks rather like corduroy; woven, with fibres carried along back, in wide range of colours. Often in artificial fibres or non-sheep animal hair. Hard-wearing.

Cut pile Strands of yarn are cut rather than looped into carpet.

Indian carpet Always off-white, the coarsely handwoven looped wool pile is knitted into the back. Good quality ones are durable.

Looped pile Uncut loops on the surface. The pile can be short or shaggy.

Shag pile Pile that is 25 to 50mm (1 to 2in) long. Do not use on stairs – heels can catch and it is dangerous. Gets dirtier more quickly than short pile and looks very unattractive if tangled. Cheaper types may disappoint.

Tufted Individual fibres are punched or otherwise fixed into the base material, which is usually 'sealed' with some sort of

Fitted colour.

Shag pile carpet.

Hard-wearing cord.

Striped colours.

waterproof backing. The pile may be looped, cut or both.

Wilton Like Axminster, derives its name from the loom on which it is made: this weaves the yarn in a continuous strand, so only a limited number of colours can be used. Smooth, velvety surface.

Types of non-wool fibre

Acrylic Most wool-like in appearance and the way it handles. Good wearing properties but not quite as resilient as wool. Dirt shows more readily than on wool and not so easy to clean by shampooing. New versions being treated to resist dirt.

Modacrylic More expensive than acrylic but has better anti-flammability properties. Unfortunately, the fibre is difficult to dye, so limited range of colours.

Nylon or polyamide High wear resistance. Some manufacturers abuse this by using only a low pile weight, which results in a cheaper carpet but one that looks good for a shorter time. Avoid nylon carpets of much less than 560g per square metre (20oz per square yard) to be on the safe side. And while yarns need to be crimped, watch out for those that have been over-crimped to give the impression of extra bulk. In the 'anti-soil' processes of recent years the material is coated to repel dirt, but once the coating breaks down, it can be far worse

than if there had been no coating in the first place. The process can be repeated on a laid carpet, however. Static can be helped by incorporating metal or carbon-coated fibres into the blend – or just by using a simple humidifier (a bowl of water, for example). Nylon is self-extinguishing, but a permanent hole or blemish will be left. About the same resilience as wool.

Polyester Because of its softness, used for shag or semi-shag. Durability and soil resistance about the same as acrylic, but lower resilience.

Polypropylene Hard-wearing, cheap, often blended with other fibres. Does not readily show dirt, but high flammability and not self-extinguishing. Often used for backings or, because it absorbs little moisture, plastic backed for kitchen or bathroom carpet.

Viscose rayon Cheap, not very hard-wearing, often mixed with other fibres to add bulk. Low resilience, low dirt resistance and easily flammable, but there are flame-resistant types.

Rugs

Every country has its traditional rugs, but modern machine-made rugs can be very handsome indeed. You can get contemporary rug makers to weave you a rug to order or sell you an unique creation from stock.

How the rug lies on the floor is important. A good quality rug should have underlay if it is going on bare boards. Secure light rugs on hard floor surfaces with mesh backing or nylon bonding strips – both to avoid dangerous slipping and to prevent rugs 'walking'.

Types of rugs

Belgian Copies of Persian and other types, plus some contemporary ones.

Braided rugs Made of strips of cotton or wool, plaited and coiled from the centre out, usually oval, sometimes round.

Caucasian Very distinctive; bright reds, blues, greens and beiges. Stylized figures and elaborately decorated, packed border.

Chinese Thick and rich, often in black, soft yellow, pink, peach, apricots and blues. Display familiar Chinese motifs.

Dhurry Usually handwoven cotton. Traditional Indian but 'discovered' in the past few decades: wide choice of colours, styles and sizes at reasonable prices. Beware of colours bleeding on to carpet beneath, so interline with fabric.

Flokati Made in Greece: heavy, shaggy pile wool rugs in white or off-white and a wide variety of sizes. Reasonably priced.

Kelim Tapestry woven from fairly harsh, thick wool. Made in Turkey, Iran and elsewhere:

Kurdish version is brighter, more mixed, usually with embroidery, and usually cheaper.

Numdah Mainly Indian origin. Very pretty, naive, soft and colourful. Cheap, but won't stand up to heavy wear.

Persian Very high-quality rugs, probably originating in Central Asia, still the centre of rug-producing area; wide variety available. Usually rectangular or long runners, knotted in wool. Often richly coloured (reds and blues are favourite grounds) with stylized motifs.

Rag A lineage back to at least the seventeenth century. They are not just folksy, can be sophisticated too.

Rya Shaggy pile Finnish carpets, in abstract designs.

Serape These come from Mexico, and are coarsely woven with fringed ends.

Turkish Usually from the Anatolian region. Often have pointed prayer arch at one end, sometimes flanked by two pillars of wisdom, but each region has its own distinctive look: Ushak, for example, has star designs with abstract flowers.

Turkoman or Bokhara Includes rugs woven in tribal areas of Turkmenistan, Uzbekistan, Kazakhstan, Afghanistan, Pakistan. Mainly red grounds are used, usually with the familiar octagonal 'gul' motif.

Pale dhurry on wood.

French tapestry rug.

Turkoman rugs.

Unusual kelims.

Decorative rugs

2 *The owners of this beautifully proportioned French room planned every aspect of decor to enhance its shape. The custom-made rug echoes the design of the chairs, while the use of muted colours throughout gives calm elegance to the salon. Strong geometric shapes are used even for the lattice lines of the blinds. The room provides an excellent background for a valued art collection, without becoming overly formal: soft Eileen Gray sofas ensure the right balance.*

3 *A fine oriental rug adds richness to an otherwise austere hallway.*

1 *Two wool rugs on a floor composed of inexpensive plywood squares that have been varnished many times to produce a reflective dimension to the room. The flat texture of the carpet and slight sheen of the leather chairs are highlighted in contrast and add to the 1930s theme.*

SURFACES AND FINISHES

Wall and ceiling surfaces offer as great an opportunity as furnishings to create the mood and character of a room. There is such a huge diversity of finishes available – from 'broken colour' paint effects to the ever-increasing range of manufactured surfaces, such as felt, foil and studded rubber. Even the once-exclusive hessian now comes in a paper-backed variety that is no more difficult to hang than wallpaper. Whatever atmosphere you want – light and airy, warm and cosy, dignified or exciting – colour, texture and pattern can provide it. You can show off a room's architectural features or play them down; or use *trompe l'oeil* to create features that do not exist or to alter proportions – for example, to 'raise' or 'lower' the ceiling. The finish can add life to a boring box of a room, serve as a neutral background for a collection of *objets d'art*, or co-ordinate the colours of existing furnishings.

It's a good idea to check whether you really like looking at the surface or finish you've chosen: before finally committing yourself, pin up wallpaper and fabric finishes, and test paints in an inconspicuous corner, allowing them to dry out, and don't forget to study them in both artificial and natural light.

Preparing surfaces

Surfaces should be in the best possible condition before decorating starts: deal with damp, for instance, and other serious problems first. Preparation *is* boring, time-consuming and may seem unproductive, but it makes all the difference to the end result.

All but the most decrepit plaster surfaces can be resurfaced: areas of bulging, crumbling or hollow-sounding plaster should be cut out and replaced, and hair-line cracks and small holes repaired with cellulose filler then sanded smooth when dry. Or the walls can be completely resurfaced by 'dry-lining' with plasterboard, or sheetrock.

Bare plaster is a satisfactory base for paper and paint. But if it is at all dirty, dusty, greasy or damp, the finish will simply not adhere to it properly. Previously painted and papered walls and ceilings should be stripped – using a chemical or steam stripper – washed down with water and detergent plus a drop of ammonia, or with sugar soap if the surface is glossy, and then rinsed and dried. If old paint is flaking, it should be stripped or burnt off.

The best finish requires a first-rate surface, which lining paper will provide. If the wall is to be papered, hang the lining paper horizontally for a better finish – this is called 'cross-lining'. If you are painting over old wallpaper, make sure it is firmly attached, otherwise the paint will loosen it further.

New plaster should be thoroughly dry before painting or papering. If it's to be painted, prime it with watered-down emulsion paint. If you are going to paper the wall, it should be sized with either a sizing solution or watered-down wallpaper paste; ideally, paper should not be hung for a year after.

Brickwork in good condition is often best left bare, but repointing may make a world of difference. Just seal or paint it to prevent it becoming a dust trap.

New and stripped wood should be rubbed down and primed before painting. Painted wood should be washed and 'keyed' by rubbing down; it need only be stripped off if it is cracked and flaking, or if extra paint will make a door or window stick. Use a blow-torch or hot-air stripper (which doesn't scorch) preferably; or a chemical paint stripper.

1 *Ancient cracks and flaws revealed when the room was stripped have been emphasized by a paint-washing technique.*
2 *A confident mix of surface finishes works to a dramatic and stylish effect in this bathroom. Glossy black brings out the strong white of the vitreous enamel and the fine marbling on the wall around the bath. A mirrored ceiling and glass accessories add more shine. Colour is introduced by the rug and painting.*

Visual tricks

Choosing colours, patterns and textures can be difficult; it can also be one of the most pleasurable aspects of decorating (see *A SURE SENSE OF STYLE*).

If the room hasn't got much character to start with, a strong pattern will instantly inject some. 'One bold pattern is enough' is a well-worn maxim; but if you've a good eye and loads of confidence, there is no reason to keep to it. The key is to concentrate on the room's good features, play down its less attractive points, and think in terms of the overall feeling you want to achieve.

When there is too much going on – walls at odd angles, sloping ceilings, staircases – a single treatment or pattern often helps to pull things together. Or you could underline the irregularities by distinguishing between one plane and another with different shades of the same colour, by using the same colour but in varying finishes and textures, or with complementary colours – look at paintings by the great colourists, such as Bonnard and Matisse, for inspiration.

Picture or dado rails can be useful to divide different finishes; if they have been removed, you could fake them with a stencilled border or simply with a painted stripe.

Continuing a colour or pattern from the ceiling down to picture-rail height, or colour-banding the walls, are ways of 'lowering' a ceiling that seems too high. Painting it a darker shade than the walls has a similar effect; if it is lighter, the room will appear to be higher. Shading, so that the walls darken as they rise to meet the darker ceiling, is a subtler approach but needs skill to do well.

Vertical stripes will make a room seem taller (horizontal stripes do the opposite), but if the wall is crooked, they will emphasize this. Stripes are best avoided altogether on ceilings, unless you want the illusion that you are living in a tent.

Picking out cornices in contrasting colours is a good way of adding interest at ceiling-height, especially if the walls are painted the same colour as the ceiling.

Distressed or broken-colour paint effects, such as sponging, stippling or dragging, will add depth to flat walls and help to disguise irregularities, such as uneven surfaces and poor plasterwork. Mirrors make space seem larger and more intriguing, and, if they are placed opposite or adjacent to windows, will increase the amount of light in a room.

If you prefer wallpaper to paint, remember that a large pattern usually needs a big wall, while a dainty pattern may look charming up close but could form an indistinguishable blur from the other side of the room.

1 *A detail on the previous page showed the walls and ceiling of this kitchen. The tarnished effect is the result of painstaking dripping, marbling, dragging and other paint effects using rich, golden colours and a verdigris mixture, carefully dripped below the dado line. Woodwork was finished in sage green and dragged.*

2 *Careful blotches of brown paint and finely drawn 'cracks' in black have given flat surfaces a sun-baked appearance, enhanced by the dark carpet, terracotta pots and the blue blinds, which filter the available light.*

3 *A visually exciting and economic effect created by hanging a canopy in the same black and white fabric that covers the bed. The neutral colours of the walls, platform and storage units provide an excellent background.*

4 *The dining room in a New York apartment. Ornament is linear, colour constrained, the overall result very human. The bare plaster has been colour-washed above the acid-etched brass channel inserted in the walls. False beams were added to the structural ones in the ceiling.*

Paint

If you can't find the exact colour you want, you can make up your own by adding artists' pigments to white or off-white paint.

Paint sense
When buying paint, get the correct amount at the outset and select tins with the same batch number; otherwise there might be slight variations in the colour. If the colour is ready-mixed, make a note of the batch number in case you have to reorder.

Paint the ceiling before you do the walls to avoid splashing new paint work. Paint on paper sometimes blisters – but this is usually temporary and the blister will disappear when the paper dries out. However, if the room is very warm, the paint blisters can dry before the paper does; in this case, turn off any heating and open a window to slow down the drying process.

Paint types

New types of paint are introduced all the time, and it is no longer a simple matter of choosing from water-based emulsions or oil-based gloss and eggshell. Briefly, the range can be broken down like this:

Oil-based gloss This is the traditional finish for woodwork and metal. It gives a hard, wipe-clean, high-sheen finish, but is slow-drying. Professional decorators

generally prefer it to non-drip paint (see below), because it can be brushed out to a finer finish; it is also glossier. The best results are achieved by first applying one to three coats of undercoat, with only a top coat of gloss. The darker the colour being covered, the more undercoat necessary.

Oil-based eggshell/satin finishes Satin-finish paints are suitable for interior walls, woodwork and metal. Trade eggshell is the most expensive and needs careful brushwork, but will give a very elegant surface. New surfaces should be primed, while previously painted surfaces need undercoat for a solid colour base.

Non-drip paint This popular paint, containing polyurethane, has a gel-like consistency. The gloss version can be applied more thickly than ordinary oil-based gloss, and is less liable to run. It has a tough finish, which is not as hard as liquid gloss but more elastic and so more resistant to chipping and abrasion. Although some versions incorporate an undercoat, one coat may not completely obliterate an earlier, darker colour.

Water-based emulsion This is the usual finish for walls and ceilings. Not as hard-wearing as oil-based paints, emulsions have the advantages of being easier to handle, much quicker to dry and requiring no special thinners

or brush cleaners. No undercoat is necessary; but several coats of emulsion may be needed to get a good finish. Absorbent surfaces benefit from being 'sized' with a thinned-down first coat. Two coats are usually enough, unless the starting colour was very dark; one will sometimes suffice. Some mixes are available to reduce condensation or prevent fungus or mould.

Finishes can be either matt or have a slight sheen (these are called 'satin' or 'silk'). The glossier surfaces are easier to clean; vinyls are easiest to apply and provide washable surfaces.

Acrylic emulsions An acrylic gloss has less of a sheen than an oil-based gloss, but has the advantage of a far shorter drying time and hardly any paint smell. There are also quick-drying acrylic primer undercoats, which mean that three coats can be applied on the same day.

Solid emulsion This comes in a tray that doubles as a roller tray. Reduces mess to the absolute minimum and reduces waste because the box is resealable. Good for ceilings, since it is non-drip. The range of colours is limited.

Textured emulsion The thickest emulsion of all, often used over poor surfaces and to cover hairline cracks. It is applied with a brush or roller; a random ragged effect is created by using a long-

pile roller, and it can also be made into more formalized decorative patterns. However, the effect can be cheap and nasty; the abrasive surface is difficult to clean, and to remove.

Primers Use the primer to suit the specific surface. Alternatively, universal oil-based primer can be used as a base for paint on wood, metal or new plaster; it seals a porous surface, binds a powdery one and gives the paint a surface it can adhere to. On new plaster, primer is essential to seal in the alkaline salts that will otherwise leach out. New or resinous wood also requires a knotting compound brushed on prior to priming to prevent resin bleeding from knots and spoiling the surface. There are specialist primers for such surfaces.

Wood stains These protect and colour wood, while retaining the surface texture and grain. An alternative to varnish where wood is not going to be subject to much hard wear; otherwise, use a waterproof polyurethane stain, which both stains and varnishes.

Varnish Synthetic varnishes (polyurethane or polyester) are easier to use than traditional ones. Available in matt, eggshell or gloss, they give woodwork a hard, clear finish, and protect wallpaper and paint work.

Blackboard paint Encourage children who like drawing on

Enamel gloss paint for doors.

Eggshell pastels, 1950s style.

Matt emulsions on rough plaster.

Blue stippling on white.

walls to limit their activities to one area. Blackboard paint can be applied to metal, hardboard or plaster surfaces, but the best base is a smooth, flat wood such as plywood. The surface should be primed before application.

Paint effects

Using special paint effects, you can texture and colour walls in ways that make them unique. Broken colour finishes used to be the province of skilled professional decorators, but the fashionable resurgence of these effects has led many people to try them for themselves.

There are two basic methods of applying paint effects. Paint is either added over a background colour – with a sponge or by spattering, for example. Or the top coat is partially removed – with rags, combs, stippling brushes and so on.

The different tools used to manipulate the paint produce quite different effects, and the colours you choose make each pattern individual. The overall effect can be expensive and luxurious, although the process is as cheap as the price of the paint.

Any of these effects can be used on woodwork as well as walls. But it's important not to overwhelm a room with special effects; tortoiseshell confined to a door or a fireplace might make an eye-catching feature from something quite plain, but used all over could easily look absolutely hideous.

Sponging A soft, cloudy effect is created by dabbing one or more wash colours over the base with a natural sponge. Or the glaze can be painted straight on to the base colour and the sponge dabbed over the top, creating a mottled effect as the sponge unevenly soaks up the wet paint.

Glaze, which has a transparent or semi-transparent finish, is available tinted or you can colour it yourself; or you can mix your own glazes from boiled linseed oil and turpentine.

Rag-rolling A rag used to 'distress' the paint gives the effect of crushed velvet. Rag-rolling involves forming a bunched rag into a loose sausage shape, and rolling it down the wet glaze or wash. Rags of different textures give different prints; cheesecloth, hessian, jute, linen and lace are all suitable.

Other effects can be produced with a rag. If it is bunched and pressed on the wall over the wet paint in different directions, the effect is soft and mottled. For the softest texture, the rag dipped into glaze is rubbed with a polishing motion into the wall until it forms a diffuse cloudiness.

Colour-washing A thin film of tinted wash – made from thinned-down water-based paint – applied with a big brush, in bold, sweeping strokes, over an emulsion background gives a luminous effect similar to distemper (the traditional colour-washing material made of powdered colours mixed with size or another emulsion); textures vary from translucent to almost opaque. The technique's artlessness is part of its charm.

Dragging A fairly firm brush dragged over a thin glaze produces a fine, stripy result with the irregularity of a natural fibre or grain. A second glaze coat dragged horizontally produces a texture like that of woven silk.

Stippling The effect is delicate – tiny freckles of colour over an even base – and is achieved in a number of ways. The slowest, traditional method uses a small, hard-bristled stippling brush pressed into the wet glaze, so that particles of the glaze lift off when the brush is removed. A dry rag can produce a similar effect; so can a paint roller pushed over the wet glaze, if care is taken to avoid skids.

Spattering An almost three-dimensional effect created by flicking specks of paint on to walls or woodwork. A coarse-bristled brush is used and the process can be fairly messy. The end result should be protected with a coat of varnish.

Advanced effects

The look of real materials can be faked using these techniques:

Marbling The effect is built up with thinned paint, but with the addition of techniques that recreate the patterns found in natural marble: these include drawing thin lines with a fine brush to mimic the veins found in some kinds of marble, and introducing a new, wet colour before the first has completely dried, for a natural, bleeding effect.

Graining Natural-looking wood grains are faked by drawing a comb or dry brush through wet glaze, and creating knots and heart wood lines with the edge of a cork and pieces of string pressed in the wet glaze.

Bambooing The distinctive markings of real bamboo can be emphasized by picking out the rings, knots and spines with paint, or simulated on woodwork that has a similar rounded quality; the effect can be intentionally realistic or obviously fake.

Tortoiseshelling The decorative practice of imitating the mottled and clouded shells of sea-turtles originated in Asia. It is difficult to do well, and can be a little overpowering on too large a scale.

Wet varnish applied to a base coat is manipulated into broken bands, lines of a darker colour are painted on top, then softened with a large, soft brush.

Three colours spray-gunned on grey.

Marbled door frame, stippled dado.

White walls, marbled furniture.

'Bamboo' painted on yellow emulsion.

Colours and textures

1 *An unusual muted shade of matt emulsion covers a rough plaster wall.*
2 *Clear, strong shades of paint have been used to define architectural details and enliven this hallway. A striking use of red gloss outlines the curved door recess.*

3 *A soft yellow wash on the walls is a good ground for an eclectic mix of styles in furniture and decorative objects.*
4 *In a bathroom, the walls have been given a grey wash of paint on bare plaster to provide a neutral background against which the various objects and fittings, such as the white towel rail and patterned floor, stand out.*

5 In this room careful attention has been paid to achieving a high-quality finish on every surface. The paintwork is gloss white and the walls are marbled to give a subtle texture.
6 Deep red does not dominate in a room flooded with daylight from full-length windows. On a dividing wall, strong blue outlines interior windows.

Walls: paper and painting

The variety of paper-backed surfaces available goes far beyond traditional wallpaper; it includes, for example, textured and thin fabrics, foils and woven cane. It ranges from tough and hard-wearing to those which should be treated with great care. It might be intended as a foundation for paint, or could even be more expensive than your central-heating system – if it is hand-blocked, for instance.

Before you decide on a paper, it is worth pinning up a sample to see if you really like looking at it. Another approach is to play around with samples of different colours and textures to get an idea of how flooring, curtains and so on are going to get along with each other.

Wallpaper sense

Always buy sufficient paper to complete the area you are decorating and take a note of its batch number so that if you have to reorder you avoid colour variation. Remember to allow for wastage and pattern repeats.

Generally, heavier wallpapers are easier to hang than lightweight ones, so think twice before opting for a cheap, lightweight paper.

Use the paste recommended by the manufacturer; as a general rule, heavy paper requires thicker paste. Usually, the paper shouldn't be hung immediately it has been pasted: most wallpaper expands after pasting, a process which takes at least five minutes; if it is still expanding while it is being hung, it will dry unevenly and shrinking will occur. It's a good idea to apply paste to the wall as well as the paper.

Wallpaper types

Printed papers The cheapest papers are usually machine-printed, thin, difficult to handle, prone to shrinking and stretching and not very hard-wearing. Better quality papers include the 'grounds', which are printed once with a pattern, and the 'duplexes', two layers of paper bonded together for better strength and texture. Hand-printed papers are very much more expensive, whether they are silk-screened, block-printed or stencilled, and it is worth getting a professional to hang them.

Printed papers come in three main categories: spongeable, washable and vinyl. Spongeable papers can be wiped down gently with soapy water; washable papers, which are covered with thin plastic film, allow cleaning down with water though not with detergent or abrasive; vinyls are much tougher, and because their thick plastic coating makes them 'scrubbable', are ideal in kitchens and bathrooms.

Heavyweight, embossed papers

These improve insulation and their texture disguises a poor surface. But they are difficult to remove, so are best regarded as long-term solutions. With the exception of lighter wood-chip papers, all these papers require well-prepared surfaces, ideally cross-lined.

Relief papers A wide variety of heavyweight papers embossed with wood-pulp relief is available. Finishes range from simple decorative patterns and random textures to fake finishes, such as basket weave or traditional plaster mouldings. These papers are usually painted after hanging; they are good at disguising poor surfaces – but are often irredeemably ugly.

There are several types of paper produced, including a high-relief one made with cotton fibre, vinyl-faced washable paper, and a deeply embossed, traditional version with its pattern – simulating wood panelling, tile or plasterwork – set in putty-like material on a paper backing. All of these papers should be painted, stained or glazed.

Wood-chip or ingrain paper has a random texture produced by chips of wood and other fibres sandwiched between two layers of paper. Economical and hard-wearing, it will cover small cracks and imperfections well, and is available patterned and with 'broken colour' paint finishes, as well as plain.

Decorative wallpaper borders are manufactured in stick-on strips. Most are bland, in neutral colours designed to go with almost anything, but some bolder examples can be found.

Natural fibres Many natural materials have been backed with paper to make them easy to hang: wood veneers, silk, canework, 'woven' mixtures, and even dried grasses. Two of the most successful examples are hessian- and cork-faced paper; the latter has a thin veneer of almost translucent cork on a coloured backing, which produces an interesting marbled effect. Many of these fibres – Japanese grasscloth, for instance – are delicate, so are suitable only for walls that are not going to get any rough wear, and they can be very difficult to clean. It is impossible to pattern-match with natural materials, so panels will be noticeable – make a feature of this with borders or beading.

Special-effect papers These range from printed fake effects – such as wood panelling, stonework, marble, fabrics, snake-skin and suede – to 'luxury-look' silver and gold foil papers, and include moiré silk paper with its delicate shading. Foils need a very flat, lined surface and should be attached with PVA adhesive.

A stencilled wall frieze.

Stencilled corner details.

Book endpaper for marbled effect.

A mural in pastel acrylics.

Wall painting

Stencils Hand-done stencilling has a naïve charm of its own. It is simple to do and can enliven uninteresting or awkward rooms. A stencilled border will highlight an architectural feature or break up a featureless wall. It can substitute for a picture rail, with the effect of lowering a very high ceiling; vertical stencilled patterns have the opposite effect.

Ready-cut stencil kits are available, or traditional patterns can be copied: simple patterns, rather than fussy or dainty ones, are easier to cut and look more effective.

The stencil is cut out of traditional oiled stencil board or clear acetate sheeting, and taped in place over registration points marked on the wall, so that the pattern fits accurately each time. Quick-drying paint should be used when more than one colour is being applied: a thinned acrylic over an ordinary emulsioned wall is a good choice, although emulsion, poster paint, thinned oil-based paint and signwriters' paint (Japan colour) are suitable too. It is important to use a good colour combination of stencil and base colour, otherwise the effect could jar.

Murals These can be based on pictures or photographs, scaled up using grids to fit the wall. A two-dimensional picture done well looks better than a failed attempt at depth and perspective, so, unless you are an artist of some talent, stick to something simple – or employ an artist of talent! Techniques can be mixed: for instance, stencilled patterns of plant designs can be incorporated into wall painting, perhaps; 'broken' colour finishes could be used to increase interest and add depth to flat colour – the only rule is not to overdo it.

Trompe l'oeil This means 'deceiving the eye': perspective and delicate shading contrive to create the illusion of solidity, or of another world beyond. At its simplest – the faked panelling of a flat door, for instance – a reasonable effect can be achieved with stippled shading by a careful novice. But complicated *trompe l'oeil* is best left to the experts.

Trompe l'oeil can be exploited to correct an unbalanced room or to create architectural interest that is lacking. Examples range from a vase of flowers in an imaginary niche, a cartouche above a door, an extra bookcase or an idyllic scene viewed through French windows.

A ferny pattern has been stencilled around this shaped wooden door, while the fake stone frame and dado were hand painted.

Trompe l'oeil *on a wall mural.*

Co-ordinated paper, frieze and fabrics.

Fabric ticking on walls.

Simulated hand-brush dragging.

Painted patterns

1 *A wall mural based on the plans of Le Corbusier's Villa Savoie.*
2 *A witty* trompe l'oeil.
3 *Beautiful painted wood panels in an eighteenth-century French château.*

4 *An enchanting Egyptian-style room, reconstructed from a theatre set for a Parisian home. The bedspread is a paisley cashmere shawl and the light is a French Gothic fitting. The carpet is modern, but the well-considered use of sympathetic colours gives coherence.*

Other surfaces

1 *Pressed metal sheeting with a basket-weave pattern is used on these walls.*
2 *Mirrored cupboard doors with frames to match the skylight.*
3 *Wooden battens filled with insulating 'beans' provide good texture and soundproofing.*

Wood This is attractive and a good insulator, combatting heat loss and noise. The most common wood lining is tongue-and-groove panelling, although veneer finishes are also used. Like all second surfaces, it is best batten-mounted to the wall and can be laid in a vertical, horizontal or diagonal pattern and stained, varnished or painted.

Other fabricated woods that can give an expensive look include faced woods – such as plywood and the thicker block-boards and laminboards – with a quality of veneer that varies according to how much you spend. Composite boards, some with an insulating core, are available faced with plywood or a plastic veneer. Inexpensive hardboard should not be dismissed; it can be stained, painted or varnished.

Fabrics Some fabrics, including hessian, felt, wool and silk, are available paper-backed and can be hung like wallpaper, although, in the case of delicate fabrics, special care may need to be taken not to stretch or mark them. The adhesion method varies according to the type of material you are using; it's essential to get instructions from the supplier before hanging the fabric.

Unbacked fabrics are more difficult to hang; often they are stapled to battens rather than stuck directly on to the wall surface. The advantage is that any material can be used, ranging from cheap calicoes and muslins to expensive and luxurious silks and velvets.

The acoustic qualities of a room can often be improved with a woven cloth finish on the walls.

Ceramic tiles These can be hand- or machine-made, plain or patterned, glazed or unglazed, smooth or textured; they are hard-wearing, easy to clean and an ideal surface behind work-tops, around the bath or lining a shower. The thin tiles that are made today are fixed with an adhesive rather than with the traditional mortar, making them easier to lay.

Ceramic tiles can be used on almost any surface that is clean, dry and stable – even over the top of firmly attached old tiles. Interesting effects can be created by co-ordinating tiles from pattern families – using special border tiles or coloured grouting, for instance – or alternating colours – traditional checkerboard patterns look good, or the tiles could be laid diagonally, in multi-coloured stripes, or even randomly for a patchwork effect.

Cork This not only insulates but looks and feels very warm. In rich

4 *Aluminium battens over plastic sheeting.*
5 *Tongue-and-groove panelling in a well-appointed loft room.*
6 *A metal screen defines the staircase area and draws the eye up to a Mackintosh 'Hill House' chair.*

natural patterns and colours, it comes in different textures and thicknesses; as tiles, panels, or paper-backed. Cork can be protected with a PVC or polyurethane coating, does not show the dirt and can be wiped down, but cannot stand up to a great deal of wear and tear, particularly in its more attractive unsealed form.

Vinyl Available as tiles and sheets and usually regarded as flooring material, vinyl is waterproof and washable, and therefore it is a useful wall surface for bathrooms and kitchens in particular – although do not use near any sources of direct heat because it may melt.

Synthetic rubber Sheeting made of synthetic rubber is a tough, washable surfacing material, and is available in many textures and colours.

Stainless steel and aluminium Expensive materials, both these metals are available as tiles and sheeting. They make an impressive splashback to a stainless steel sink, or can be used to link kitchen units. The tiles are fairly straightforward to fit, being flexible and soft enough to be cut with scissors.

Plastic laminate Although this is not a new material, improvements in printing and texturing technology have transformed plastic laminate into a decorative surface that should be looked at again.

It is made by bonding together layers of resin-impregnated paper, which is then plastic coated to produce a hard-wearing, easy-to-clean surface, which will stand up to heat.

Plastic laminates can be stuck directly to walls, but, because they require perfectly flat, smooth surfaces, it is usually more practical to mount the laminate on battening or on special plastic mounting strips, which are attached to the wall.

Mirrors Use mirrors to create the illusion of space, increase light and alter a room's perspective. Sheet mirror is expensive; and the larger the mirror the thicker it should be for safety's sake, and the better it must be secured – big areas of mirror sheeting are best mounted professionally.

Mirror tiling is far cheaper, but requires an absolutely flat surface if a disjointed, distorting image is to be avoided (but this can, in itself, be very attractive): batten-mounted plywood, for instance, makes a suitable base. Plastic mirrors and coloured acrylics are cheaper alternatives, although they look cheaper, not having the same quality of depth that glass-backed mirrors have.

FIREPLACES

For a while the traditional fireplace seemed to be a threatened species: with the advent of central heating, fireplaces were stripped out of many homes and only in a few was their overriding value as an architectural focus still appreciated. But the open fire is now undergoing a revival, and in many places the cosy glow of burning wood and coals can be found in at least one room. And when there are power cuts or winter is severe, it is a useful adjunct to your heating system.

There have been improvements in the efficiency of open fires: for instance, air ducts incorporated into the underside of the grate can supply air from the outside for combustion, thus avoiding warm air being drawn from the room for the purpose. And heating appliances set into the fireplace have become rather more attractive in the last decade or so. (See *HEATING*.)

Flame-effect fires Gas/coal and log flame-effect fires have now been developed which not only produce real flames but can comfortably heat an average-sized room.

At the same time, traditional gas fires have been fitted with realistic ceramic panels of coal and logs which glow and flicker with lively flames. Although bigger than the flame-effect fires, they can be set inside an opened-up fireplace recess.

Solid-fuel stoves Stoves burning solid fuel can provide continuous penetrating warmth throughout the house. A wide range of styles is now available, varying from enchanting period reproductions, both rural and classical in character, to elegantly simple modern ones. Some incorporate gas burners too, providing leaping flames behind the stove door, others back boilers for water and central heating.

The fireplace

All of this has served to bring back the fireplace as a major feature in the home. People are inevitably drawn to sit round a warm fire or stove during cold weather, and this is when the fireplace becomes the most important architectural feature of the room. So don't choose a fireplace or have one built before you have come to terms with the period and character of your house, and, more particularly, with that of the room itself. (See *ARCHITECTURAL CHARACTER*.)

Unless your house or apartment has had all its traditional features stripped out, be guided by the existing character. With new buildings as well as with old ones, scale is a most important factor: don't overwhelm tiny rooms with large fireplaces – inglenooks (recessed fireplaces with built-in seating) are an exception here, as they add apparent as well as actual volume to a room, and so are large kitchen fireplaces, which were built to house big cooking pots and still have space for drying wet shoes. Similarly, the character of a large room can be diminished by a small, undistinguished fireplace.

Mantelshelves

The mantelshelf needs to be positioned according to the proportions of the room. In houses with high ceilings the whole emphasis of the room is set at a high level. Ceilings – and furniture – in modern houses tend to be lower, allowing the mantelshelf to be set quite low. Make sure the fireplace is not made to look insignificant: this can be avoided by incorporating it into adjacent features, such as bookshelves and cupboards, and giving it a raised hearth.

Inglenooks

In cottages built from the early 1800s onwards, parlour and bedroom fireplaces are narrow, with vertical emphasis. In earlier cottages you may well find an inglenook behind a more recent fireplace. Even if it is not intact, a builder familiar with restoration work should be able to repair it for you. The underside of the lintel should be not less than 1.4m (54in) from the hearth. Opening up an inglenook adds to the sense of space in a room and enables you to set a free-standing fire or stove into the recess created.

The hearth

If you like your fire surround but the grate itself is unattractive or inefficient, an alternative to replacing it with another inset grate is to pull out the grate and its surrounding firebricks to give a recess about 900mm by 900mm (36in by 36in) by 380mm (15in) deep. This can then be lined with a material which can withstand the heat from a free-standing fire or stove – for example, slate, marble, bricks or tiles. The hearth can be matched to the lining or, if tiles are used as a lining, slate or marble could be used. Contrasting tiles for the hearth and lining can look fussy.

Opening up a fireplace

If you are opening up an old fireplace, check the flue carefully: linings must be fireproof and if they are cracked, or mortar has fallen out of brick and stone joints, the result could be a leakage of poisonous flue gases. The flue, which should have a special liner for certain types of stoves, should be thoroughly swept before use. Also, make sure the chimney is not sealed at the top.

1 *A modern oak fireplace with traditional overtones fits well into an Edwardian house.*
2 *An inexpensive fireplace made by using window architraves, then given a marbled paint finish.*
3 *Fireplace fakery: a concrete frame gives an abstract focus to a small bedroom.*
4 *Attractive asymmetry is the result of old building methods where fireplaces were often placed to one side of a chimney breast that carried the flue from the floor below. Here the feature is emphasized; a positive response to a potential problem.*

Fireplaces as focal points

6 *An imaginative modern design abandons traditional conventions by creating a window around a chimney. This fireplace is in a purpose-built summer house near Zürich.*

1 *Pre-cast concrete shapes, including even mantelshelf clutter, create a room sculpture.*
2 *European rococo grandeur is successfully incorporated into this room and contrasted with a quarry-tiled floor.*
3 *Simple ceramic tiles provide a backdrop to the studied display of ornaments.*
4 *Fifties fun in a New York loft: economic on space and decorative, the fire is also functional.*
5 *Hard-edged simplicity of building blocks and an iron stove.*

7 *A well-designed sculpted Travatine marble fireplace. Strong lines are complemented by 1930s wall lights.*
8 *A custom-made fire-screen in brassy metal contrasts successfully with the black marble surround.*
9 *An American architect adapted the traditional fireplace of a Mexican adobe for this cast concrete interior.*

10 *The original fireplace has been removed and a metallic finish applied to the chimney breast in a room which also has reflective surfaces on the ceiling and chairs.*
11 *The ultimate focal point, as striking as a work of art. A surround of strengthened glass and translucent onyx provides sophisticated natural light. The glow of the fire takes over by night. The flue is consigned to the outside of the building.*

WINDOWS AND DOORS

Windows are there to let in the light and the air and shut out the cold, a fact that often seems to be obscured by the way they are treated. They are important architectural features, too, and for centuries people have delighted in dressing them up in the most beautiful and finest ways possible.

There are so many options that it is often difficult to decide how to make the most of the windows. Take curtains, for instance. Materials can be left alone, lined, or given a patterned border or heading, left to hang rather flat, pleated, draped, be very full or flouncy, be perfectly plain and sculptural or heavily patterned and rather blousy: imagine, for instance, full-length lace curtains under an elaborate deep, V-shaped pelmet; chintzes of red and pink flowers lined with raspberry pink, which will blow in a breeze; or delicate unlined cotton combined with a strong-patterned softly draped valance.

Of course, curtains are not the only way of dressing a window. There are roller blinds, curtain blinds such as the Austrian or the Roman, and all the non-fabric blinds – made from split-cane, metal, wood, plastic or pleated paper. Then there are sheer and net fabrics, which can be used on their own or under other curtains.

You could hang stained-glass plaques and panels from the top of the window frame. A latticework screen will partially obscure the view and filter the light; green-fingered window dressers can grow a jungle of tall geraniums into the light, giving privacy and shade. If you have a particularly beautiful, secluded window, it might be best to leave it alone and concentrate interest on the frame or the view outside.

Doors and doorways are usually treated as the poor relations. Certainly, the best approaches are often the simplest; even so, there are many interesting possibilities – you could exploit the tension between the frame and the door, for example, by painting the outer frame a strong colour or by outlining it with several plain stripes. More elaborate treatments with clever paintwork can change the door's appearance quite dramatically – the use of slightly different shades of the same colour, for instance, or of simple stencilled patterns, or elaborately hand-painted panels, or you could use special paint effects such as spattering or tortoiseshelling.

It's worth remembering that how the insides of your windows are treated will affect the way they are seen from the outside. And that a door outlines the view from one room to another and, by its very nature, must always be a focal point.

A holiday retreat on a hilltop overlooking Melbourne, Australia. Original windows have been renovated and given a new finish of plain white paint, but all decoration stops there – the house does not contain a single curtain or blind. Throughout, the interior is stark and simple, as shown here in the dining room with its solid table and slate floor. The view stands out, framed like a work of art, and provides visual interest for the room.

Windows

Curtains may seem the obvious way to dress your windows. But they are not always the best way. The windows may look better with metal shutters, for example, or plain Venetian blinds; or a latticework screen may provide the privacy you need and, at the same time, improve the quality of light in the room.

It's usually best to treat groups of windows – even if they're an odd match – and bow or bay windows as one unit, with identical curtains or blinds. Full-length curtains or Venetian or pinoleum blinds look good on picture windows. If large windows are multi-paned, they don't need to be glazed with plain glass; the central panes could be clear, and the rest opaque – this will cut down the glare, softly filtering the light.

Beautifully shaped arched windows can be difficult to deal with. You could hang a blind or a café curtain to cover the straight sides of the window, leaving the arched top free. Or hang curtains high above the arch to fall right to the floor, extending them so they can be drawn right back beyond the window frame; do the same with a row of arched windows, but hang the curtains from ceiling height.

If you've windows high up on the wall, or skylights, don't cover them unless necess-ary; let them flood the room with light and at night allow you to see the star-studded sky.

Deep recessed windows only let in a limited amount of light: leave them bare and concentrate interest on the sills, which could hold collections of fascinating objects; or the recesses could be painted boldly – in a deep violet or bright yellow, perhaps – as a contrast to plain pale walls.

There are many imaginative ways of drawing attention to windows without using curtains or blinds. If the inner window frames are flat, they could be 'finished' with fine-lined or curved beading. A softer approach would be to grow vines from pots at either side of the window and train them around the frame; they will eventually meet to form an arch. Interest can be added to a row of tall windows by filling in the gaps between them with floor-to-ceiling columns, and unifying the whole by using the same surface and finish for the frames and columns.

For a three-dimensional effect, a wide second frame can be added in front of the existing one, suspended 150mm (6in) or so out into the room; it will appear to be floating, creating an interesting optical illusion, which can be further exploited by hanging Venetian blinds in the window behind. Or install wood and paper Japanese screens over a large picture window to turn a bright, glaring room into a restful retreat gently bathed in light.

Window grilles are often needed for security purposes. Try not to think of them as 'bars on the windows'; they could be painted white or a pale shade and livened up with pots of bright geraniums. If the grille's patterning is particularly delicate, then it should be emphasized, with dark, even black, paint.

You may need to shade a porch or verandah from the hot sun – hang crisp, dazzling white canvas curtains in the opening; or use bamboo or pinoleum blinds or cheerful broadly striped Roman blinds.

If you want to open up your house to increase the amount of light inside, you could install internal windows, a large glazed wall, or use glass bricks, which will give a certain visual depth to the wall, while still letting the light in, and they will provide more privacy and insulation than ordinary glass.

Whatever you do, don't ignore the view from the window. How you treat the windows will affect what you see when you look out to refresh yourself with a look at a world that is different from the one you're in.

1 *Lacy, white roses have been stencilled on to window panes to provide privacy as well as a delightful, old-fashioned finish for otherwise undistinguished windows.*
2 *Unconventional shutters create a modern, asymmetrical effect for an utterly plain window.*

3 *Chairs and windows in an elegant Parisian apartment have been draped with white cotton; combined with a wrought-iron screen, from a shop window display, they create an eerie atmosphere.*
4 *This kitchen has been built in what was a clock tower; the clock face forms this unusual window over the sink.*
5 *A deep recess to a lovely oval window in the corner of a Parisian garret – an atmospheric and romantic setting for an architect's office.*
6 *Dense, opaque glass forms small squares of light on a stairway.*

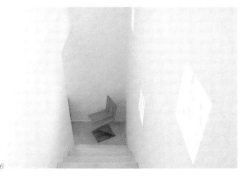

Curtains and curtain fabric

Curtains form a screen between you and the outside world, and they keep out the light, keep you warm and help reduce noise significantly. These practical matters are as important as the colour, design and texture of the curtain fabric.

Curtains should be either floor- or windowsill-length, otherwise they will ruin the proportions of the window. (Curtains that are overlength so that they fall in a sculptural mass on the floor look particularly good.) The exception is café curtains, which are hung on a pole or track placed half-way down the window.

If a window is unusually wide, you can compensate by extending the curtains to the floor or by stopping the rail at the edge of the frame so that the open curtains cover some of the glass. Sill-length curtains suit narrow windows, or the rail could be extended beyond the frame.

Pelmets and valances
Pelmets and valances fit over curtain headings and tracks. Pelmets are made of wood and either painted or covered with fabric, often in the same pattern as the curtains – but different, more adventurous patterns can look wonderful. Pelmets give curtains definition and can follow the architectural lines of a particularly beautiful window.

Valances give a softer effect than pelmets and usually consist of soft pleats or gathers falling across or down the side of the curtain in a shaped curve.

Headings
A heading is the gathering or pleating at the top of a curtain. The tape sewn on to the curtain back will determine both the shape and size of these gathers or pleats; or the heading can be hand stitched.

Pinch pleats and pencil pleats are the most popular headings. Pinch pleats are small clusters of pleats grouped at regular intervals; they suit fairly heavy, floor-to-ceiling curtains. Pencil pleats are tighter and run continuously across the curtain, and work well with lightweight net and sheer fabrics.

Gathered headings are a cross between pinch and pencil pleats, but should be reserved for short, light curtains; they look best with a pelmet or valance.

Looped headings, often used on café curtains, need to be made by hand – they are a cut-out scalloped shape. If there is a radiator behind the curtain, a looped heading will let the warm air circulate into the room.

Tie-backs
Tie-backs are both practical – they hold back the curtains to let the light in – and decorative. They can simply consist of a doubled straight piece of fabric, attached by rings to a hook on the window frame or wall; or can be very elaborate, with deep curves of cloth or floppy (or stiffened) bows and tassels. Thick Italian cord or pieces of silk or velvet can also be used.

Curtains with pleated or gathered headings could have tie-backs made in the same fabric – often with a piped or corded edge – or in a contrasting fabric. If a pelmet or valance has been used, then the tie-backs can be made in the same fabric. Or, instead of fabric tie-backs, you can use classic brass rosettes and hooks, which catch the curtain fabric behind them. These work well with double curtains.

Tracks
These range from plain, 'invisible' plastic tracks to sophisticated sectional metal ones with pull-cord mechanisms. Aluminium tracks can be bent to fit awkwardly shaped windows.

Generally, curtain tracks should be wider than the window frame so that the curtain can be drawn right back to let in the light; very thick curtains may need as much as 600mm (24in) on either side.

If the window extends right up to the ceiling or the curtains are made from a heavy fabric, it's a good idea to use ceiling-mounted track, which is stronger than a wall mount. Before you hang the curtains, make sure that the track is correctly and safely attached, so that it will take their weight.

Poles
An attractive alternative to tracking, curtain poles are available in brass and wood, and in a wide range of diameters.

Wooden poles are usually made of mahogany or pine, and you can buy unsealed ones that can be painted or stained. Or you may find an antique pole, complete with its original rings and often elaborate finials. Use a curtain that is a strong contrast to the pole – mahogany, for example, with yards of white muslin.

Curtain fabrics
There are so many curtain fabrics on the market that it's difficult to know where to start. You'll have to choose between plain ones – there are heavy linens and textured weaves, moirés, thick velvets and airy lawns – or a pattern – such as traditional floral prints, bright glazed chintzes, small clear-coloured geometrics or strong stripes.

Don't forget about scale when selecting fabric for curtains. Generally, a small room with small windows won't look its

Antique lace in harbourside house.

Strictly elegant drapes.

Pretty gingham tie-backs.

Exterior curtains to cut out the sun.

best with curtains made of a large-scale pattern, although a single-colour border or a plain blind beneath the curtain can sometimes soften the effect.

Equally, tall gracious windows will look less than impressive with a small, busy pattern, while horizontal stripes will distort their shape. Heavy fabrics, such as velvet, shouldn't be used for short curtains; they are best reserved for full-length curtains.

You could use old curtains; you can often find them in antique shops. The colours of old faded chintzes are quite lovely, and improve as they fade over the years. Old Victorian brocades and velvets, too, have a sheen and depth that are matched only by their very expensive modern equivalents. If the curtains are far too long for the window, then let them lie on the floor – this has the practical advantage of eliminating any draughts, and, in any case, it would be sacrilege to cut them up.

Look for textiles that don't immediately spring to mind as curtains, but would look good hanging up and framing a window – a paisley shawl, for example, hung diagonally across a window and caught at one side, with a plain full-length roller blind beneath; or a soft rug or kelim, too fragile to have on the floor, hung on a pole and caught with a brass loop.

How much fabric?

Never skimp on the quantity of material; generously full curtains look so much better. If you want to save money, choose a less expensive fabric. Calculate the amount of material you need by multiplying the length of the finished curtain plus allowances for hem and heading, by the number of curtain widths.

Work out the position and length of the track or pole before calculating the curtain length. Measure the distance from the curtain track to the sill or floor. For lightweight materials and sheer fabrics, allow an extra 150 to 250mm (6 to 10in) overall for hems and heading (250mm [10in] for heavy fabrics), and one extra pattern repeat for each curtain.

The number of fabric widths needed will depend on the type of heading you are going to use: you'll need twice the track length for the popular pencil and pinch pleats; while sheer fabrics need three times the track length. Also add another 37mm (1½in) for each side seam and each join.

Always check whether the fabric you've chosen is preshrunk; if it hasn't been, you should wash or dry clean it before the curtains are made.

Linings If you want curtains to keep out the light, they should be lined. There's no doubt, too, that lining makes a great difference to the way a curtain hangs. Linings are available in many colours; it is advisable to use white or cream under pale fabric – before buying, check to see whether it alters the colour. If you're using coloured linings, make sure they look good from outside, too.

Some linings have insulating qualities. One has a grey backing, so should only be used with dark fabrics; a white insulating lining is also available, but is too heavy to use with fabric blinds.

Interlining A soft, warm material that comes in various weights, interlining will considerably increase a curtain's insulating qualities, and make any curtain, however well headed or hung, fall much better.

Sheer fabrics

If you live cheek by jowl with your neighbours, or right on the street-front, sheer fabrics are almost a necessity. And they can be used as second curtains, hanging under chintzes or velvets, perhaps; they can be stretched over screens to permanently cover the lower part of the windows; or hang them on their own as café curtains.

There are sheer fabrics that shine, and ones that have the dull gauze texture of cheesecloth. There are self-stripes, semi-abstract patterns, burnt-out designs with a ghostly quality, and sheers with small coloured designs all over them. Many of these can be used for roller and Roman blinds, and they can look good gathered across a frame and used to diffuse the light.

The way that sheer fabrics affect the light is one of their most endearing qualities. Even in countries without too much sun, the light can be harsh, and sheer fabrics can soften and, in many cases, dilute it. A heavily patterned sheer curtain in a bedroom that faces the rising sun not only diffuses the morning light but has a soft dappling effect.

Lace Many of the laces available today are based on Victorian or Edwardian designs, including French window panels (narrower than usual to cover the width of the window only) and half-sized horizontal panels to go across the lower half of a kitchen or bathroom window. You can make roller blinds out of the harder wearing laces, such as Nottingham or Madras. Or lace could be hung over plain curtains, so that the pattern of the lace is accentuated.

If you like the look of old lace and would prefer the real thing, you should be able to find it in antique shops. Designs don't have to match: windows look very pretty with different patterns in each window – particularly if they are panels.

Classic modern designs, grey curtains.

Generous folds by bed and windows.

Crisp white fabric gathered up.

Bold patterns and colours.

Window dressing

1 *Pretty ties connect billowing clouds of cheesecloth to iron rails in a beautifully decorated hallway.*
2 *Fresh unlined cotton with a deep frill hung from a wooden rail by large brass rings; the simplicity is echoed in the modest, metal-ringed curtains for the four-poster bed.*
3 *A cool room of muted shades with flat patterned fabric at the windows, pinned back during daylight.*
4 *A Roman blind – subtle window dressing for an elegant room.*

5 *In a softly decorative bedroom with delicate stencils and linen-fold Tudor panelling behind the bed, the windows are defined by gentle folds of translucent fabric.*
6 *On an attractive arched window, plain blinds have been stencilled with a pattern repeated on the arch of an alcove.*

171

Blinds and shutters

Like curtains, blinds and shutters help to control heat, reduce noise and provide privacy. But where blinds and shutters come into their own is in their simple, modern lines, and the way they allow all types of windows to remain uncluttered.

They are relatively inexpensive and, because they are less over-powering than curtains, tend to work very well on small windows and in small rooms.

It is important to get their proportions right, though. Blinds usually look best when they are longer than they are wide; if you have a large window, hang several narrow blinds rather than one very wide one – this will give you more flexibility in controlling the light, as well as softening the effect of a big expanse of glass.

Roller blinds
Popular since the eighteenth century, roller blinds can be used plain and on their own, or they are sometimes matched with very formal curtains, or soft sheer ones for a more delicate effect.

You can make them yourself with a kit that is fairly simple to use, buy them ready-made from a stock range of sizes, or have them made to measure. Make sure you choose a suitable fabric – otherwise they may roll unevenly. A tightly woven flat cotton is a good choice, but use a waterproofed fabric in the kitchen or bathroom.

Plain blinds can look good with braid, fringing or coloured ribbon, but patterned ones are usually best left alone. A painted window frame picking out or echoing one of the blind's colours can look very effective, too.

Roman blinds
Although they look something like ordinary blinds when let down, Roman blinds draw up into series of broad flat pleats, giving a neat pelmet effect. They look good on their own, but they also work well with plain curtains. Roman blinds particularly suit dining or living rooms, and can be used to good effect to shade the sun from a balcony.

These blinds, which are usually made of curtain fabric, should be lined – this improves the way the pleats fall and, of course, keeps out more light.

You can make them yourself, although they are not as straightforward as roller blinds. Use broad stripes or patterns, plain calico, even sheer fabrics.

Austrian and festoon blinds
Austrian and festoon blinds, which are unlined, hang straight when let down, usually with a scalloped hem, but have a ballooned effect when drawn up (by cords, which run through looped tape at the back). Festoon blinds are not as full as Austrian. But they can both be rather ornate and lavish; some have frills at the sides and bottom, and ribbons as well – these can look good when left to rest about half-way up a window.

Wooden and paper blinds
Paper blinds are made out of tough, stiff, pleated paper; they are available in a range of colours, and are practical and decorative.

Wood and cane blinds come in several different forms. Pinoleum blinds are made from matchstick-like slats of wood, either stained in a dark colour or left in the original light wood colour, and woven together with cotton, but you can see through them. Wooden and bamboo-like blinds are very Somerset Maugham-ish and look wonderful with strong sunlight behind them.

Venetian blinds
Venetian blinds have lost their dowdy image, with their super-thin slats and clear perspex (acrylic) operating rods. Available in plastic, metal or wood, they come with colour co-ordinated cords and in many combinations of colours. Venetian blinds give a faceless window definition, and look good in a tall Victorian window with a deep reveal that frames the blind. They are difficult to clean. Wooden Venetian blinds, usually made of cedar, are expensive but give a wonderful mellow light to the room.

Vertical louvre blinds
These blinds – which are made of thin strips of canvas, wooden slats, silk or synthetic fabric – are attached at the top and bottom of a window. They pivot open or closed, and they can be drawn across to the sides of the window; they are often used on floor-to-ceiling windows.

Shutters
Shutters are an important asset in the right room. Not only do they look great when folded back on either side of a window, but they keep out the light when you want them to, they don't restrict the window at all, and they provide security and silence.

Louvres
Louvres can be extremely elegant when used full-height across one end of a room that has French windows, or they can be useful when you have odd-shaped adjacent windows that are difficult to deal with separately. Louvres can also be used to good effect on the outside of the windows and, when folded back, they can do much to enhance a dull external elevation.

1 *Venetian blinds used to unify.*　　2 *Austrian blinds of white brocade.*　　3 *Full-length, vertical blinds in white.*　　4 *Inexpensive, pleated paper blinds.*

5 *White Roman blinds filter daylight and offer a screen against an uninspiring view. Generous Victorian window frames with their original shutters have been carefully stripped and polished to give a fine texture and a strong decorative element that matches the floorboards in this austere room.*

6 *A new window, overlooking a terrace, was let into the deep walls of this bedroom, creating an excellent study area in what had been a dark corner.*

7 *Pulley blinds on a sloping wall of glass provide colour in this muted kitchen. A marble worktop is set against stained woodwork and stripped floorboards.*

8 *Over-sized studio windows are covered simply and effectively with folding fabric blinds.*

9 *Concertina wooden shutters in a panelled room. A plain roller blind filters daylight.*

Plain frames

1 *Bare windows appear to be mere holes cut in the plaster walls – virtually no frame is visible. The pattern of the wooden exercise ladder is repeated in the wooden stairway outside.*

2 *The original windows in an old stone farmhouse were replaced with rustic, hand-crafted frames in stained wood, which were specially made to blend well with the building.*

3 *Panelling around a window provides neat shelves and small storage compartments – an ingenious window frame in a bedroom designed to be used for more than mere sleeping.*

4 *With a view of the Manhattan skyline set in a metal frame, any adornment of this window would only take away from its impact.*
5 *A soaring lightwell in a north London terrace house. The architect owner has added dramatic folding floors for versatility.*

6 *The recess of this skylight in a small attic bathroom has been lined with mirrored glass, matching the bath wall to give an illusion of space as well as extra reflected light. The all-white colour scheme also works well in an area of limited space.*

7 *The gentle curves of linen pelmets over deep window recesses give a touch of decoration to a room of monastic understatement. The window surrounds appear to be stone but are, in fact, painted to give that effect.*

Doors

Doors have a special dual role to play – they create transitions and maintain privacy. And they can give interest to boring, plain walls. So, they deserve plenty of attention.

The door frame is an obvious starting point. You could paint the outer frame black or a very dark colour, contrasting it with white or pale walls, door and inner frame. You can give emphasis to the frame by stencilling a pattern around it, or paint a very broad, coloured stripe around the doorway, or use various special paint effects, such as marbling. For a classical appearance, you could add a wide decorative moulding over the head of the door, or fake one using *trompe l'oeil* techniques.

In many instances, it makes sense to treat the walls and doors similarly – if the door is undistinguished, for example; or when there is a dado, and all the woodwork, including the door, has the same colour or finish. If the door is surrounded by bookshelves, you could continue the shelves up to the ceiling and over the door, creating a whole wall of books, and then paint the wall, door and shelves the same colour.

You can play visual tricks by painting the doors with *trompe l'oeil*, concentrating on distorting perspectives. Or paint simple geometrical patterns on the doors – traditional Turkish patterns or more stylized Egyptian designs could be copied.

Glass doors add an extra dimension to a room. The patterning and size of the panes create their own decorative effects, and, of course, bring light into rooms which may otherwise be dark and unwelcoming. It is possible to replace the wooden panels on some doors with glass or mirror panes, or a window (transom light) can be inserted above the door to let in more light. If you want silence and privacy, a plain flush door can be lined with felt and covered with green baize.

Folding doors can solve space problems and look great too. Paint the two sides differently so that, when they fold back, a contrasting colour will be revealed – choose wonderful combinations such as sky blue and orange, or pink and apple green, or you could play safe with different shades of grey.

Curtains can be used instead of doors to divide off rooms – a pair of plain cream curtains made of unlined calico will brighten up a darkish opening, or use a strong pattern with an elaborate, contrasting heading. A sensible, old-fashioned remedy for draughts was to hang thick velvet curtains on the door itself, so that, when the door opens, they move too. In hot countries, bamboo or bead curtains are used in doorways to keep out flies – they make bell-like sounds in the breeze, while light shining through glass beads creates coloured floating patterns.

If you decide you want to dispense with doors altogether, but you still need to define the boundaries of the space, free-standing screens are an answer. There is a wide variety of types available: from beautifully decorative chinoiserie ones to streamlined versions, such as plain iron-framed screens with cream silk, or thick flat frames filled with black vertical wires.

1 *A chinoiserie interior in an eighteenth-century English mansion with an intricately patterned, hand-painted door and the original wallpaper.*
2 *The Clarté building in Geneva, designed by Le Corbusier, retains his original design details such as these reinforced glass-and-steel sliding doors, dividing a living room and study from the hall.*
3 *A roughly carved old wood door has been waxed and polished for textural effect.*

4 *Rooms that are divided by interior windows and glazed doors have a wonderful sense of light and space; particularly impressive in this Antwerp house with decorative, traditional stained glass in the upper 'windows'.*
5 *Smooth finishes – plaster walls, painted woodwork and plain flooring. In this stark simplicity, colour is important to define shapes and add interest.*

6 *A beautiful old door gains character as it ages and is now set in a superb glass surround.*
7 *In a London dockland conversion, the original warehouse double doors open on to a landing stage, allowing sensational views across the River Thames.*

CAMOUFLAGE

1 Hide ugly pipes and provide period character in a bathroom by fitting the basin into an old cupboard.

2 Lined in sheeting, with wooden poles supporting a tented ceiling, this small dining room has been inexpensively transformed.

3 Glazed wooden doors give character to a hallway. One has linen curtains that maintain a cottage feel while hiding ugly meter and fuse boxes.

4 A sumptuous silk parachute offers low-budget high style when matched with old boxes and chairs covered in sheeting and plastic.

5 *In a New York loft, the home office hides behind sliding glazed screen doors when not in use. When open (6), the office is perfectly situated in a semi-private alcove.*

7 *Kitchen plumbing and wiring are concealed effectively behind wall panels to match storage units.*

8 *A radiator given the same paint finish as the dado area behind.*

9 *A witty solution for a brick wall – the radiator has a fake brick finish.*

LIGHTING

Lighting can be the most important and economical element of home design. Almost any room can be made to look better and to function more effectively with the right lighting. Yet too often it is relegated to being an afterthought once a house has been completely decorated and all the furnishings have been selected.

Lighting is a complex subject. Consider natural light: the difference between the quality of bright, overhead sunlight and a misty dawn, or between a gloomy grey day and a clear night on full moon, is the difference in intensity of light and depth of shadow. With technological developments and innovative design, artificial lighting can imitate nature in its large range of effects. And the quality of artificial light, like natural light, is as much about shadow as about illumination. The two are equally important.

Since artificial light is usually dependent on electricity, it should be planned at a stage when electrical wiring is being installed, overhauled, or when it can be moved with the minimum of disruption. Deciding where to position lights, and the type of lights to purchase, is as difficult and as crucial a decision as you will face when designing a home (see *PLANNING*).

So, when planning lighting, you should always take into account: the quality of light required in a specific place, the type of fitting (fixture) that can offer that quality of light and the type of fitting that will suit the room stylistically. The decisions will affect every aspect of the room. Light and shadow can enhance or destroy decoration and furnishing choices. You can bring a room alive for activity and calm it for relaxation, or you can make it too uncomfortable for either.

Find out about lighting and about fittings within your budget. Plan lighting with as clear an idea as possible of the layout, furnishings and, above all, the functions of the room. Then give yourself scope for change – and for mistakes. Plan as many light sources as you can, plan to combine several types of fittings (and hence, qualities of light), and provide as many switches with dimmers for greatest possible control and flexibility.

Also take account of comfort and safety at all times: bad lighting can lead to serious accidents. The elderly and the very young are particularly vulnerable. Wires should not be placed where people might trip over them and fittings that are easily knocked over are equally dangerous. Accidents can also occur because areas are not adequately lit; this is especially important in kitchens and bathrooms, on stairs and for workshops.

A room designed to provide a theatrical setting – with entrances on and off from all sides, an overhanging balcony, and a bank of lights for changing the mood, spotlighting the action and highlighting the characters. An abundance of windows, glass doors and skylights give the same room maximum exposure to natural light by day.

Quality of light

Domestic interior lighting can be divided into three basic categories, related to the different visual requirements you may have.

General

Overall or background lighting, which provides illumination after dark. Since the function is to throw light on a wide area, general lighting can be achieved in two ways, either by using one central light source, from which light spreads out, or by using a variety of individual light sources.

Most homes are wired to have a central light hanging from the ceiling in the middle of each room to provide general lighting. This has great disadvantages because a central light usually gives an unattractive and dull quality to a room and is inflexible. More effective general lighting can be achieved by using several light sources – for example, downlights or spotlights fitted in the ceiling. In work areas, general light is often provided by fluorescent tubes, but they tend to produce glare and are often positioned so that you are working in your own shadow. Equally effective, and more attractive, is the use of several spotlights.

Task

Concentrated lighting used to illuminate one area brightly – for example, a work surface, desk or reading chair. Task lighting can also be used to highlight particular objects or features in a room such as paintings or plants.

Spotlights are particularly effective for this, whether they are fitted to the ceiling or walls, on floor stands or used as table lamps. Fluorescent tubes can also be used, and they are considerably better if they can be hidden – beneath wall units in kitchens to light work surfaces, for example, or behind shelves to light display objects. However, although less expensive, fluorescent tubes do not provide the quality of illumination that can be achieved with spotlights. This is particularly true since the advent of spotlights that throw out intense, narrow beams of light.

Atmospheric

Light used for effect, to provide shadow and subtle illumination. Lights placed low in the room and giving local illumination are used to this end – table lamps, floor lamps, wall lights. On the other hand, uplights also give subtle light that is reflected from the ceiling.

Spotlights, which are used for illuminating work or reading areas, paintings or architectural features, can become atmospheric when dimmed. The same applies to pendant lights used with a dimmer.

Dimmers

Flexibility is an essential ingredient for good lighting. Few rooms should be lit to the same intensity at all times. Dimmer controls for lighting are invaluable because they allow the intensity of light to be varied simply at the touch or turn of a switch. They are very easy to install and, in addition, it is possible to wire them to table and floor lights as well as to ceiling and wall fittings. Some fittings, such as low-voltage desk lamps, have dimmer switches attached.

Dimmers have the effect of cutting the voltage of electricity passing through the bulb; the result of this is not only to give varying intensities of light but also dramatically to lengthen the life of the light bulb and cut the amount of electricity used, especially if a bulb is switched on at the lowest possible level of brightness – that is, when the dimmer switch has been turned right down.

1 *General lighting from a variety of sources – each has been selected for its looks as well as the quality of light it provides. Concealed lighting plays on the ceiling, while 1930s-style wall lights and a modern uplight give further illumination. A giant 'electric plug' carries two fluorescent tubes and just outside the curved arch stands a modern floor lamp in chrome and glass.*

2

3

4

2 *The classic desk lamp on the bookcase offers two equally effective types of lighting with the minimum outlay on fittings and wiring. When turned to the chair it is the perfect reading light; when directed to the wall, as here, it provides low-level, general illumination that flatters the room and creates an intimate atmosphere.*

3 *Carefully planned, subtle and atmospheric lighting to entertain by or merely relax. The design of the room specifically lends itself to special effects, such as ground-level lighting below a raised platform and a built-in sofa.*

4 *Coloured lights have a spectacular effect in this minimal house, where flat surfaces and near-empty rooms are bathed in purple and green. This is lighting designed for impact not for practical illumination, and the fittings themselves are either hidden or utterly discreet.*

Lighting equipment

Bulbs

Technical advances in lighting centre on developing the light source – the bulb. It is also the bulb – although often in conjunction with the design of the fitting (fixture) – which determines the quality of light produced.

Tungsten (incandescent) Standard domestic filament bulbs are tungsten bulbs – the higher the wattage of the bulb, the hotter the filament burns and the brighter the light. They give a warm light which is well suited to domestic interiors and attractively illuminates colours. The best way to use them is to buy the highest wattage bulb suitable for the fitting and then control intensity with a dimmer switch. The standard tungsten bulbs disperse light – casting beams in all directions – which is controlled by the shade or fitting.

Reflector bulbs, which give directional light, are internally silvered for use in spotlights. Tungsten bulbs that are crown-silvered (top-silvered) reflect light back to the fitting and reduce glare. Crown-silvered bulbs used in a spotlight fitting with a parabolic reflector produce a narrow, adjustable beam.

Halogen (tungsten/halogen) All bulbs described as halogen are in fact tungsten/halogen, combining a tungsten filament and halogen gas. Linear halogen bulbs give a bright, white light which is up to twenty per cent more powerful than standard tungsten bulbs. They are particularly effective for uplighting where the light is directed to the ceiling and reflected back to the room.

Low-voltage Low-voltage halogen bulbs are far smaller than other bulbs but give a concentrated, crisp, bright white light. They operate on an electrical supply of twelve volts or less, so must be used in conjunction with a transformer (which reduces the mains voltage).

They produce a precise 'spot' of light – a controlled beam – which varies in width and intensity, depending on how the fitting reflects the light. Low-voltage fittings include surface spotlights, downlights and table lamps. They are excellent for accent and display lighting, for task lighting where close work – such as reading or embroidery – is involved, and for general lighting when used from several sources and controlled by a dimmer switch.

Existing light fittings designed for standard voltage bulbs can be converted for use with low-voltage bulbs. The low-voltage bulb is attached to a transformer that fits into a bayonet or Edison screw socket. But the result can be unsightly since the combination of low-voltage bulb and transformer is considerably larger than a standard tungsten bulb.

Fluorescent Straight fluorescent tubes come in a variety of lengths and can give either a cold, white light or warmer effects, depending on the colour tube you choose. It is important to check the quality of the light when buying these tubes, since names such as 'warm white' can be misleading; if the effect is cold and white, the result is harsh, glaring light that reduces shadow, flattens textures and can be hard on the eyes. These problems are reduced by fitting a filter – either a solid, translucent cover or a slatted panel – over the tube to disperse the light.

Circular or curved mini-fluorescent tubes are more flexible than straight tubes, since they can be adapted for various types of fitting. They have a very long life, use less electricity than tungsten bulbs (as do straight fluorescent tubes) and emit little heat, so can be used with a wide range of shades. This has enormously expanded the uses of fluorescent lighting for domestic purposes. Paper, ceramic, glass, steel and cloth have been designed to enclose, filter or deflect light from new types of fluorescent bulbs, improving both the appearance of fluorescent fittings and the quality of light they produce.

Fluorescent tubes cannot be used in conjunction with standard dimmer switches.

Neon Neon tubes can be shaped not only for sign writing in coloured light but also for providing unusual sculptural domestic lights – definitely decorative rather than functional, but adding a distinctive touch to an interior.

Fittings

Light fittings (fixtures) are designed around specific types of bulbs. Select for quality of light first, good looks second.

Downlights As their name suggests, downlights cast pools of light on the surface or floor immediately below the fitting (fixture); they are compact and are either surface-mounted or recessed into the ceiling. Depending on the type of bulb and fitting used, the effect of downlighting can range from a narrow beam of concentrated light (low-voltage halogen bulbs in recessed fittings) to a wider, less intense beam (a tungsten reflector bulb in a swivel, eyeball fitting), through to bathing an area with light (a standard tungsten bulb on a surface fitting).

Downlighting is extremely versatile. It can be used for general lighting, directional task lighting or for atmospheric background effect, and is especially effective when it is used with dimmer switches. The light is glare-free

1 *A tungsten uplight.*
2 *The whiter light of a tungsten halogen uplight.*
3 *A floor fitting for tungsten halogen.*
4 *A standard tungsten pendant.*
5 *A tungsten downlight.*
6 *A floor light with tungsten halogen bulb.*
7 *A tungsten parabolic spotlight.*
8 *A standard spotlight on a floor-stand fitting.*
9, 10 *Tungsten pendant globe and ceiling light.*
11 *A fluorescent tube.*
12 *A table lamp.*

and fittings are small and often unnoticeable in a room – an enormous advantage if you like clean lines and hate lampshades. They make good sense in areas with low ceilings or hallways where pendant lights might get knocked when furniture is moved. Recessed downlights are particularly discreet fittings, and, if there is an electrical outlet in the right place, they are easily fitted without causing disruption to ceiling plaster or the removal of floor covering above: a hole is cut in the ceiling, not much larger than that covered by a standard ceiling rose, and the wiring is connected as for other fittings. (Low-voltage fittings need a transformer, which involves using a professional electrician who will probably need access to wiring from the floor above.)

Pendants Light fittings that hang from the ceiling are called pendants. The effect – and quantity – of the light produced is dependent on the type of shade used, since the majority of these fittings use standard tungsten filament bulbs.

Light can be generally dispersed using a translucent shade – such as a glass globe or a paper lantern – that encloses the bulb. It can be directed downward using an opaque shade that is open at the bottom – a metal cone, for example. This is effec-

tive over a table and some pendants can be raised or lowered for greater flexibility. Lampshades that are open top and bottom give two-directional light.

If the electrical outlet in the ceiling is in the wrong place and cannot be moved, or if you like the effect of looped wiring, a looping block can be fitted to the ceiling to change the position of the pendant.

Once again, the range of effects is greatly increased by the use of dimmer switches.

Spotlights The range of spotlights available is wide; it is important to select the right type for effect and efficiency. On most fittings, the bulb is obscured from sight by a cowl but on some the bulb is exposed, so care must be taken in positioning the spot to avoid glare. Standard spotlights are best used for general illumination from the ceiling: because the beam is directed, spotlights bring out textures and colours more effectively than pendants or fluorescent tubes.

Mini-spotlights cast strong pools of light to a precise area and are effective for local lighting and highlighting. Spotlights with parabolic reflectors (using crown-silvered tungsten bulbs) give a more controlled and narrow beam. More expensive low-voltage spotlights take this one step further, producing an adjustable

beam of bright white light from the smallest possible fittings.

A single spotlight is useful only for task lighting. It is more versatile to use at least three spotlights aimed in different directions, from either a track carrying a row of spotlights or a twin or cluster fitting. Spotlights can also be mounted on the wall or used with a floor stand.

Uplights Uplighting provides soft, general illumination without glare by directing light at the ceiling or wall and then reflecting it back to the room. Uplights are often referred to as wall-washers. Obviously, uplighting cannot be used for task lighting, but it is excellent for general background illumination and for a subtle effect of light and shadow. However, it should be chosen with care, since the surface it floods with light will be highlighted. If your ceiling is the worst surface in the room, then choose light fittings that detract from it; but if you want to enhance plaster mouldings on ceiling cornices use uplighting.

A cool, bright light is achieved with halogen uplights and a warmer, less intense light with fittings taking standard tungsten bulbs. Used in conjunction with dimmers, uplights turned low can create a romantic, soft glow.

Table lamps Table lamps come in a wide range but with two

main functions: either as task lighting, such as desk lamps, or placed in a room to provide areas of low-height, local illumination.

The fitting is important: it is likely to be prominent and therefore should suit the style of the room. The type of light produced will depend on the type of fitting – a low-voltage halogen desk lamp is specially designed for paperwork and has the effect of a narrow beam spotlight; a table lamp consisting of no more than a clouded glass globe gives a completely different effect of diffused local light. There is a wide choice of styles and effects so choose carefully, considering the function of the lamp and the details of the fitting – its shape, colour and impact on a room.

Floor lights Lights raised on a stand are excellent task lights, especially for reading or other close work. The traditional standard lamp gives localized light below and general light above. The shade that is chosen for a standard lamp must complement the room.

Floor lights now include mounted spotlights and other directional lights, often using a table lamp fitting in conjunction with a floor stand.

Another possibility for subtle, localized lighting is to place a glass globe or other light on the floor behind an object.

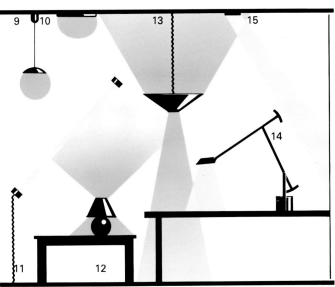

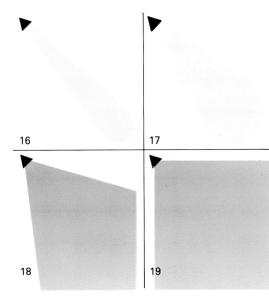

13 *A pendant casting light up and down.*
14 *Low-voltage tungsten halogen desk lamp.*
15 *Low-voltage ceiling spotlight.*
As a general guide to varying light sources:
16 *low-voltage tungsten halogen spotlights give a clean, narrow beam;*
17 *a tungsten halogen bulb gives clear white light;*
18 *a standard tungsten spotlight;*
19 *standard tungsten pendant or globe.*

Luminaires

1 *An outdoor lamp used effectively as the single artificial light source in the ultimate minimal bedroom.*

2 *Tungsten halogen provides a bright white light, particularly effective for uplights. This pair brings out every detail of decorative plaster moulding in the living room of an early nineteenth-century house.*

3 *Tungsten halogen tubes, unlike fluorescent ones, give a flattering light that is preferable for a bathroom.*

4 *Parabolic spotlights using silvered tungsten bulbs give a defined beam of light. These have been mounted in a conservatory to highlight plants and light the interior through a glass partition.*

186

5 *In this stylish dining room, only candlelight is used for gentle, sophisticated effect. The eighteenth-century Genoese chandelier is the room's centre-piece.*
6 *Low-voltage halogen bulbs are far smaller than other types; as a result, their fittings can be attractively discreet. Here, tiny lights have been mounted on to the frame of French doors, and they are supplemented by twin desk lamps for task lighting.*
7 *Pendant light fittings are especially useful over dining tables.*

Planning

The lighting for any room should be determined first and foremost by function – cooking, bathing, reading and eating, for example, require very different light levels. Architectural features, atmosphere and furnishings also need to be taken into account. Light can enhance the colour and texture of curtains and hangings and highlight pictures and objects; it can transform a bustling family room into a formal setting for entertaining. Remember that you have both illumination and shadow at your disposal.

Adjustable lighting from several sources is very important for rooms with more than one function. In any room, the most flexible and attractive lighting will result from mixing the various kinds of light and types of fitting.

Electrical wiring

Ideally, a lighting plan should be made before any decorating work is done so that, as far as possible, wiring can be hidden in the fabric of the building. However, even given the opportunity, most people find it daunting to finalize lighting plans at a very early stage of decoration, before colours and furnishings are chosen. The best solution is to ensure that the electrical wiring in your home is as flexible and adaptable as possible. Putting in extra socket outlets for lights may seem to cause more trouble and expense than it's worth. Yet disruption of wall surfaces and possibly flooring should be carefully weighed against the improvement that the right lighting will give (see *ELECTRICITY*).

The key is to consider lighting before any decorating is done. If, for example, you decide to fit several downlights in one room, the most sensible approach would be to make that decision before any work has been carried out on the ceiling.

If you are using table lamps and floor lights for local and accent lighting, consider wiring special lighting sockets to the main switch. This enables a central control at the door for switching lights on and off and for dimming them. These sockets can be placed where wall sockets go and can replace normal sockets.

Whatever your plans, consult an electrician and find out what rewiring is necessary. It may cause less disruption, and less expense, than you think.

Room specifications

Living rooms General diffused light, from downlights, uplights and pendants, should be combined with local, accent lighting from table and floor lights and spots. Dimmer switch control is invaluable to brighten and subdue the light for different activities and moods. If the room is used for office work, a desk lamp provides the best local light. For reading, ensure there is adequate light adjacent to comfortable chairs. Also consider objects, such as paintings or other treasures, which you would like highlighted by spots or picture lights.

Flexibility is vital in a living room, so, if possible, plan to have as many light sources as you can. Remember that you do not have to use them all. The choice of fittings is also important. They must suit the style and period of the room. Consider the fact that discreet, modern fittings can look far better in an elegant period setting than more obtrusive, decorative lamps.

Bedrooms Recessed ceiling downlights are unobtrusive and give the best overall light,  but you may prefer several low, shaded table lights to give a softer general illumination. Tracks with spotlights can be fixed to the ceiling, or near the desk and bed, if they are close to each other. For bedside reading, wall lights or mini-spots mounted on the wall are ideal since free-standing bedside lamps have to compete for space with clocks, radios, books and so on. Make sure you can see yourself adequately in mirrors. Built-in wardrobes or walk-in cupboards can be fitted with tubular filament lights operated either by pull-cord switches or automatically when the door opens (as on a refrigerator).

Bathrooms In most countries regulations covering electrical wiring in the bathroom are strict. If fittings are likely to get wet they should be enclosed to avoid possible shorting and electric shocks. A pull-cord switch is the only safe one inside the bathroom; if you want a dimmer switch, wire it outside the door. Ceiling-mounted downlights with internal reflectors give good light; wall-mounted fittings with glass shades are an alternative source of flattering light without glare. The basin (sink) or mirror area can be lit by a  combined light-and-shave socket (outlet). Fluorescent light is unflattering.

Kitchens General lighting for the kitchen should offer maximum adaptability of lighting level and direction for different activities. Eyeball downlights can be rotated to direct light exactly where needed. Alternatively, tracks (especially those with extendible systems) allow you to direct as many spotlights as you need on the oven, hob (cooking top), sink, table tops and work surfaces, and into cupboards.

Work surfaces must be highlighted for safe and efficient food preparation. Recessed fluorescent tubes built into wall-mounted

cabinets avoid the problem of the cook working in his or her own shadow. Systems of track holding a number of lights with independent switches are useful in kitchens, as are pivoting hinged fittings mounted under kitchen wall cabinets to provide downward illumination on work surfaces. If you also eat in the kitchen, put in a dimmer control to fade out kitchen clutter when you are eating, or consider a fitting that bounces light off the ceiling.

Stairs, passages and halls Wall lights for stairs should be placed to follow the treads. Stairs must be effectively lit for safety. On half-landings, a downward-directed beam should be used. A time switch can be fitted to ensure that the staircase is automatically lit at dusk, and a dimmer will provide low-level night-light. Small, long-life fluorescent fittings

are also highly effective and are economic in hallways.

Spotlights are not suitable for halls and stairs, because they can produce glare when seen from various angles.

Study areas Lighting must be designed to focus on the page or computer or typewriter keyboard. Low-voltage halogen light is easier on the eye than either fluorescent (although this is improved by reflector fittings that warm up the light) or standard tungsten light. Smaller, low-voltage bulbs have transformed desk lamps, which now are neater and take up less surface space. Computers require good general lighting that is at a similar intensity as the display screen. Glare on the screen must also be avoided. Remember that bookshelves and other areas of storage require lighting.

1 *In a room with attractive mouldings, a light has been fitted into a detail above the fireplace.*
2 *Downlights, fitted into the ceiling, provide excellent lighting for a bathroom where bulbs should be enclosed to avoid the possibility of them getting damp.*
3 *In this kitchen, light fittings have been hidden in storage units above the worktops. They provide good task lighting and attractive effects.*
4 *Intimacy can be created in a large room by low-level lighting, which illuminates only the seating area, while other lighting is controlled by dimmers.*
5 *In this room, a track carrying spotlights provides general illumination and highlights the picture, while interesting fittings carry local and low-level lighting.*
6 *A well-designed hospital lamp, created for use by a bed, works perfectly in this bedroom, shining down on a stunning Indian quilt.*

Lighting design

Lighting consultants can help you create schemes custom-made for your style of interior. They are as much a part of the home decorating business as interior designers.

John Cullen, who won the International Association of Lighting Designers' award for excellence in lighting design, has invented a system for the home that creates light beams – including hard-edged spots, wall-washes and split beams – using optical lenses attached to a single halogen light bulb. He has also designed a low-voltage general lighting system: light from clustered bulbs is bounced back off the ceiling to give a diffused overhead light.

When designing any lighting scheme, John Cullen considers exactly where the light should fall in relation to the architecture and furnishings, and then decides where the light sources should be in relation to the depth, height and size of the room. 'Light is the presentation of space. You need to consider effect, not form. Many people present space in terms of architectural form and then buy the objects that complete the decor, but they lose control of the lighting.' For evenly diffused general lighting, he uses free-standing floor lights or wall-mounted uplighters or wall-washers, but makes little use of tracks: 'Personally I think of them as an excuse for lack of planning – except where there is no alternative.' He believes that if you use down-

lights for general lighting, you will need task lights, too. Rather than use accent lights with shades, Cullen suggests decorative lamps for general lighting, and low-voltage fittings with reflectors that throw out precise beams to accent objects and areas of interest.

David Hersey brings an equally imaginative approach to domestic lighting from his background as one of Europe's leading theatrical lighting designers. 'Consider the balance of light and shade in every room. Evenly lit rooms can be boring. There are times when light cannot be seen, yet its presence creates atmosphere. In the theatre it is sometimes even the unifying element in the production.' One of his most ambitious theatrical schemes contained a mobile railway bridge carrying several banks of 'intelligent' lights controlled by computer. They could rack up and down, change colour, pivot and tilt to create a series of spectacular effects. 'With dimmers and spots on tracks, the amateur interior designer is starting to understand light and can be more experimental without additional complicated electrical work,' Hersey explains. He recommends fixing tracks straight across the middle of the ceiling or even down the walls, and replacing all light switches with dimmers to allow control of light intensity for mood. But he emphasizes that lights must be bright enough for work, indicating good directional task lighting.

Particularly aware of the problems of overhead lights, Hersey comments: 'If the beam comes down steeply, it creates ugly vertical shadows. In the theatre we find that if overhead lighting is used then actors can appear to have no eyes – just dark hollows.' Some smaller lamps are used domestically – for example, Hersey uses a baby floodlight with flaps, which can open to wash a whole wall with light or close to a narrow slit, giving a defined beam. For domestic lighting, he recommends using matt paint finishes on ceilings to soften the light. He also suggests crossing light beams at steep angles wherever the ceiling height allows it; this avoids direct glare from vertical beams of light. Downlighters should be carefully positioned and anti-glare devices, such as reflectors or rims, attached to fittings to give directional light; use warm gold reflectors for spots and some downlights.

David Hersey suggests balancing downlights with uplights. Use narrow beams of intense light to heighten textured surfaces, such as unplastered brick walls, and to define areas of a room. Other theatrical effects can be directly applied in domestic interiors. Consider dappled light in a dining area, for instance: 'It can give a marvellous leafy midsummer light.' A sheet with an irregular pattern of holes punched in it can be fitted inside a focusable spot to produce the effect.

1 Thick glass shelves allow hidden lighting from above to filter through to the worktop – an aesthetically pleasing and practical solution for a kitchen.
2 In the bathroom of the same apartment, an intense beam of light emanates from a low-voltage tungsten halogen fitting above the circular mirror.

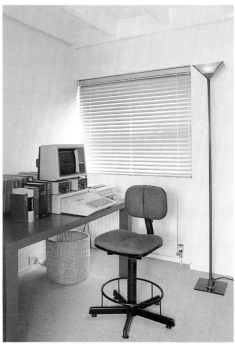

3 An over-large desk lamp floods the floor with light and, at the same time, provides excellent task lighting.
4 The screen of a home computer should receive no strong reflected or direct light, which makes it difficult to read. An uplight, providing good general illumination, is reflected back to the room from the ceiling, keeping the screen clearly defined.
5 This attractive kite fitting is well suited to a Japanese-style room of simplicity and character.

PART 3

CREATING ROOMS

*The colours in architect Charles Jencks's old
ranch house echo the sky, sea and sand of
California, while, at the same time, providing
cool relief from the heat.*

ENTRANCES, HALLS AND STAIRCASES

Entrances, halls and staircases are often seen as the leftover areas of the house, depositories for unwanted miscellany and clutter. Frequently, they are the last spaces to receive any consideration; most people tend to concentrate on rooms – bedrooms, living rooms, kitchens, bathrooms. Yet the transitional spaces of a house are heavily used and are vital in the impression the house makes on both visitors and occupants. Looking from an opened front door through into the house beyond, into areas of light and dark, and glimpsing different rooms and people, can be dramatic and fascinating. When designing and decorating entrances and passageways, you also need to be very practical, as they are always subject to considerable wear and tear.

Although each of these areas requires a different design approach, there are two common factors to consider when planning them. All are thoroughfares, and you must allow for the smooth flow from outside to inside, from public hall to private rooms, from upstairs to downstairs. Of course, movement – by adults, running children, pets, plumbers and carpenters – is a constant in all these spaces. So any clutter, slippery surfaces or constricted spaces will cause problems. Movement also creates wear, so finishes throughout these areas should be durable and easy to clean. And to avoid accidents, there should be ample lighting, especially on the staircases.

The other factor is more difficult to define, as it concerns more than just physical problems. How you move from one space to another affects the way you feel in the new space: the actual transition colours your impressions. So avoid abrupt changes and introduce each new space through careful gradation of light, surfaces and colour. Traditional house builders understood this instinctively: a porch or flight of steps to the front door creates a halfway area between the public street and the private interior of the house, while the movement from hallway to living room could, for example, involve a change from a stark wood floor to a quieter, carpeted one, which would be warmer to the foot and also to the eye.

The generous entrance of a nineteenth-century house. Oak panelling and an imposing stone fireplace were installed later. The present owners relieved the resulting gloom by bleaching and liming the oak and taking down the fireplace overmantel to reveal a section of Victorian hand-blocked wallpaper.

Entrances

First impressions are crucial. So the entrance is a key element in how the house as a whole appears to others. The front door marks the boundary from outside to inside, which can often mean from rain and cold to dryness and warmth. Ideally, there should be some shelter outside the front door. And a ledge is handy for putting down packages while you fumble for the keys.

The door itself is clearly important: a heavy wood door proclaims the solidity of the house, but perhaps you would rather convey openness and light with a partially glazed door, or modernity, with a glossy, flush-fitted one. In every case, consider both the security a front door offers as well as the impression it makes. And find door handles, bells and knockers that match the style of the door and the house.

Inside, there should be room to take off coats or to greet visitors. If the entrance is rather cramped, leave the area by the door fairly unencumbered: coat racks or umbrella stands can be placed farther into the entrance. The one essential just inside the door is a light switch. A small table near the entrance is a convenient place on which to leave mail, messages, newspapers and keys. If you have room, use the space for quickly discarded boots, bicycles, roller skates, umbrellas and the like.

Natural light flooding through a window by the door would be most welcome, and it enables you to see who is outside. Artificial light should come from several directions or be indirect so gloomy shadows are not cast. Although the entrance should be welcoming, remember that it is a semi-public space. Views from the open doorway should be partial or obstructed, otherwise those inside will feel disturbed whenever someone comes to the front door.

Surfaces should be extremely durable: rain, mud and snow will all find their way into the entrance. It's essential to have a large doormat so you can get mud and dampness off your shoes before you enter the house. A defined tiled or sealed wood area is an excellent floor covering; if you have a carpeted entrance, make sure that the colour will not show the dirt and the carpet is easy to clean. Remember, too, that the lower parts of the walls in the entrance are likely to get some rough treatment – from large furniture and boots scraping against the walls and bicycles leaning in the entrance. The Victorians solved this problem by using either tiles or panelling below the dado. A more modern solution might be to use heavy-duty washable wallpaper.

Oddly shaped areas, which entrances often are, benefit from strong definition. Take care to enhance architectural detail and to unify the area by means of decorative style. Each of these entrances achieves this in a different way.

1 The original door has been replaced in glass; the style, reminiscent of a fortified timber and iron door, is in keeping with the origins of this house, built in the sixteenth century as a monastery.

2 The entrance to this farmhouse in southern Spain has an old floor of brick tiles. Decorative details include the collection of gardening hats and a nineteenth-century painting of nearby Gibraltar. Traditional ceramics echo the colour scheme.

3 Inspiring simplicity on a grand scale in a 1930s house. The terrazzo flooring is dramatically enhanced by natural light and the plain wood door, and its sculptural quality is seen in the curved line of the staircase. The bareness of decoration emphasizes the fine architectural lines.

3

4

5

4 A simple entrance restored with care. The walls are painted to give a marbled effect. Woodwork has been bleached and limed, then French-polished in white. The wood floor is complemented by the muted green carpeting. The whole effect carefully blends real and simulated surfaces.

5 The outer entrance hall of a seventeenth-century Dutch house has a fine atmosphere created by the use of quality materials plus a drinking fountain to refresh weary visitors.

Halls

The hall threatens to become one of a house's dead spots unless you treat it more like a room. Clearly no one spends a lot of time in the hall; its main function is to provide a means of circulation from one room to another. But it can be transformed from a mere circulation space into an important part of the house.

The key element in enlivening a hall is light, which should, if possible, be natural. If there is no way of bringing natural light directly into your hall, consider opening up doors or interior 'windows' into other parts of the house where natural light is available. Artificial light in the hall should provide contrast: a long, uniformly bright hall is almost as bad as a dimly lit one. Light should be used to pick out features, such as seats, bookshelves, telephone and pictures.

These features provide an opportunity to do something other than just pass through: you might pick a book off a shelf, use the phone or look at a picture. But because the hall will still be used for circulation, do not cram it so full of diversions that it becomes a positive annoyance to use, as well as a potential safety hazard. Always leave room for easy access: if you have to sidle carefully past a table, it shouldn't be there.

If you are desperate for extra space in your house, you may have to seriously consider using the hall as an alternative room. The 'found' space in a hall – under the stairs, in an alcove or in a blind corner – can be used as a small study, a work-room or even a kitchenette. Another use for this space is for storing items such as books, bicycles and tools. Heavy outdoor clothes and footwear are also best kept in the hall.

As with the entrance, finishes will have to be durable because of the amount of movement through the hall. Your treatment of the floor in particular will make a major difference to how your hall is perceived. If the floor is the same as that in the adjoining rooms – wall-to-wall carpets, for example, or hardwood floors – then the hall will seem to be an extension of the rooms themselves rather than a separate part of the house. If you want to make a clear distinction between the hall and adjoining rooms, a change of floor surface should suffice. Or keep the doors closed.

In many houses, the hall has been created by a subdivision of the front room. Consider whether you need a hall at all; it might be possible to create a larger and more useful room by its removal. The entrance area could be closed off with glazed walls and door, for instance, yet remain light and still seem part of the room.

1 Homely antique furniture gives style to a small hallway and is a focus for decorative objects as well as functional storage.
2 A modern building using traditional materials and shapes for a clean-lined elegant hallway. Strong geometrical shapes are used in the quarry tiles and the decorative woodwork for the door and landing. A sharp beam from a recessed downlight suggests the airy light of a Mediterranean house, the inspiration for the architect's design.

3 *The hallway can be used for other purposes, such as a dining area. This plan makes good use of space and adds to the enjoyment of a fine view.*

4 *A hallway with grand architectural proportions carefully restored and simply decorated with strong modern paintings.*
5 *In the same hall, an old saddle horse stands in the space created by removing an understairs cupboard.*

Staircases

Stairs are one of the most dramatic elements of your house. They are used for entrances and exits, for chance conversations, for unusual views through to other rooms. In addition, the change of level created by stairs is inherently a scene of activity, of motion. But stairs also create difficult design problems, and safety, in particular, should be a key consideration.

Like halls, stairs should be treated as an active element of the house rather than as a mere functional space for moving from one floor to another. One of the best ways to encourage this is to make them as open as possible: allow views through to other rooms, to halls, to different levels. The staircase itself should have a feeling of openness rather than of enclosure. Stairs will always look and feel better if they are in a double-height space, particularly if there is some natural light flooding in from above. If your house has a confined staircase with a low ceiling, try to create the illusion of openness by opening up views to the sides or by using light colour schemes. Another option would be to partially glaze a surrounding wall.

Whichever treatment you choose, the type of artificial lighting is important. Low levels of light are acceptable and can be perfectly safe, providing that there is a clear distinction between riser and tread. The worst possible light for a staircase is flat and shadowless. Positioning of lights in and around a staircase can be difficult: try to avoid spotlights glaring into people's eyes as they climb up or down the stairs.

Stairs can be used for purposes other than just moving up and down. They can be gathering places. Several wide stairs at the bottom of the staircase give people a place where they can sit and talk, or perhaps just observe the activity taking place in other parts of the house.

When choosing materials, it's important to take account of the level of safety they offer. Polished wood stairs can look beautiful, but if you have children, are elderly, or just enjoy walking around in your stockinged feet, they may prove too slippery for safe use. The same applies to painted wooden staircases. Scrubbed wooden treads with painted and stenciled risers were a traditional Shaker treatment, and are less treacherous. Carpeted stairs are a common solution, but as with halls, make sure you choose a carpet that is easy to clean: both the colour and fibre are important considerations here. A carpet runner can be laid on the staircase, using either carpet rods, which the Victorians favoured, or various forms of under-carpet gripper.

Other materials can be used for stairs, depending on the general character of your house. Some modern houses have concrete stairs, although without some covering these can be cold and will invariably be extremely hard on your shoes. A traditional Mediterranean solution is to use ceramic tiles on a masonry (or, more recently, concrete) structure, and then edge the steps with wood. In hot climates, the tiles are gratifyingly cool, as well as being decorative, hard-wearing and very easy to clean. Mirrored risers, or no risers at all, will make the stairs look as if they are floating in space. Steel stairs are also used, and so are traditional cast-iron spiral stairs, which were common in nineteenth-century gardens, but are not recommended if you have small children.

For both quality of light and enjoyment of views, windows along the stairs are a very good idea. There are various other ways of enlivening the spaces surrounding the stairs. Landings can accommodate various features, such as a small desk, bookshelves or plants; if they are large enough, they could be used as living rooms, or they may be ideal for storage. Lining the walls of the stairs themselves with anything that juts out (such as bookshelves) may prove rather annoying, unless you have a very wide staircase. But the walls can be used for collections of small objects or, of course, for hanging paintings or photographs.

1 *Outer space inspired the design theme for this hallway where the lean straight lines have been broken up by a painted mural and simple accessories.*
2 *Simple decor and the spare lines of an open staircase are complemented by objects in glass and wood.*

3 *An unusual metal staircase, moulded and varnished under heat, dramatically reduces staircase bulk.*
4 *This wrought-iron garden gate was found in France and was used to define a landing near an iron staircase.*

5 *Prefabricated interiors can create interesting angles and economize on space. Splashes of colour offset the neutrality of the walls.*
6 *The wooden staircase is dark and glossy; in contrast, the lower stairs are natural concrete.*

LIVING ROOMS

Parlour, salon, drawing room, front room, best room, lounge, reception room … the variety of names given to living rooms reflects the variety of approaches. Each name conjures up a slightly different atmosphere, but they can all be divided into two distinct types of room: a formal setting for use only when entertaining, and the more relaxed centre for family life.

If you feel the need for an adult, formal room for special occasions only think twice before using the best room in your house, because a room like this is empty most of the time. On the other hand, creating a formal setting and then expecting life to continue as normal, without any damage to the room's pristine appearance, is asking far too much of any family. Should you succeed in imposing a regime strict enough to protect the carpets, furniture and ornaments, undoubtedly any feeling of ease or relaxation would quickly vanish – and, surely, relaxation is the key to a successful living room.

There are many ways to achieve a stylish living area that can be used comfortably on a day-to-day basis and also doubles as the setting for parties and gatherings. Careful planning is required, though, and so is ridding yourself of all preconceived notions of what is 'right' or 'wrong' for a living room. Before making major decisions or purchases, consider these essential points:

Activities Most living rooms are hives of (often conflicting) activities; if some of these can be transferred to other parts of the house, even temporarily, pressure on the living room will be relieved. Could the stereo system or the television set be moved to another room, for instance?

Whatever the activities, comfortable seating will be a priority. So, too, will lighting and storage. If you entertain frequently, you'll need several tables or surfaces for refreshments. Stacking tables or shelving near the seating serve the purpose admirably and have the added advantage of leaving the space clear for other activities once the guests leave.

Flow Easy access to the doors, light switches, windows, telephone, television and stereo are essential. Furniture – the sofas, chairs and tables – should form 'islands', out of the mainstream of these established patterns of circulation. Grouping the furniture – two or three small chairs and a table, for example – is better than scattering pieces about at random; getting rid of furniture you no longer want or need is better still.

A real living room, unlike photographs of interiors in glossy magazines, is never static, and changes as it responds to a family's changing needs. Flow patterns alter, too, as furniture, appliances and equipment are rearranged or replaced. Planning how people can move easily around and through a room is crucial; so, too, is a flexible attitude – you should be prepared to change if the plan does not work in practice.

Layout Living rooms that have a single, formal function are few and far between; most play host to a wide range of activities. It often helps to portion out the space, so several people can happily co-exist, doing different things at the same time. It's a good idea, also, to create comfortable nooks and crannies in a living room, however small; these will be natural gathering places, and, at the same time, comforting if you are alone. You could use the furniture as low walling to establish subdivisions within the larger space; or, in a really large area, screens or dividers may be needed to create small, interesting places. Make sure the seating is comfortable.

On the other hand, some homes, especially those with small, interconnecting rooms, feel like rabbit warrens, confused and overcrowded. In this case, a living room may attract more activity and life if it is enlarged and opened up – by removing a wall to join two rooms into one, enlarging an arched passage between two rooms or replacing an opaque door with a semi-transparent one.

Features Just as you can build a good fashion wardrobe around a few timeless, top-quality outfits, so a room will benefit most if you spend your money on the fundamentals. This is a far better approach than to keep adding small accessories, in the hope of compensating for basics in bad condition or for the fact that the room has no outstanding qualities.

Is a graceful bay window the best feature? Make it a focal point by the arrangement of seating and dramatic lighting. Emphasize interesting architectural details with colour and sympathetic choice of furniture, whether historically 'correct' or boldly contrasting.

If your living room is lacking any inherent features, then you have a blank canvas on which to work, and you can choose the style, or combination of styles, that you like best. Living rooms aren't meant to be museums, so if you have your heart set on a modern fireplace, but your home is in a characterless 1930s development, there is nothing to stop you. Or you could add a beautifully polished wood floor, a richly patterned carpet or a large-scale storage system, which visually commands a whole wall and creates a stage setting for the objects it contains.

1 *The living area of a Paris loft, an empty space suffused with light where each object, each piece of furniture, has a particular impact, and the unusual shape of the room is outlined by wooden beams. The effect is one of serene comfort.*

2 *The exposed timbers of a converted English barn give such striking definition – all decoration and furnishing have been kept to a sympathetic minimum. Originally, the magnificent structure of the beams gave a top-heavy feel to the room and there was a lack of natural light, because the barn was designed for storing not living. Both problems were solved by opening up the gable end and installing a full-length window.*

2

Formal rooms are for
calm relaxation as well
as entertaining. So
comfort is as important
as style and everything
in the room needs a
place where it can be
seen and appreciated.
1 English country-
house style in Paris.
This room is like a
garden all year round.
2 White on white
accentuates the
proportions and details
of this room where
every object is in
harmony with every
other.
3 A fine-proportioned
Georgian 'drawing
room' in London; it
provides a formal
setting which here has
been relaxed by an
eclectic mix of
comfortable furniture,
sparse decoration and
the surprise of a French
fireplace. The pale walls
and bleached pine floor
are enriched by the
deeply coloured oriental
paintings.
4 The formal
arrangement of this
room is not without
flexibility. Seating,
occasional tables and
ornamental objects can
all be rearranged easily
for large gatherings or
small groups of friends.

4

Location

Living rooms, once again, are becoming places for living: for relaxing, playing with the children, entertaining, eating, and, in some cases, cooking, not necessarily simultaneously but with harmony in one space. As the heart of the house, the living room deserves extra attention.

Although there are traditional locations for a living room within a house, and architects' plans will clearly and firmly label an area as a living room, don't be misled into thinking that there are not other options open to you. Planning changes to your home should definitely include considering changes to the room layout and room functions.

In every house, there is a place where people instinctively congregate, and sometimes this is not where you – or the architect – intended. It may be the geographical centre of the house, the room with the best natural light or the one with the most exciting view. It may even be the kitchen, especially if it is large, light and you have children. Try not to ignore or fight this natural selection process,

and, if necessary, relocate the living room in what is clearly the heart of family life – in the kitchen, for example, add an easy chair if there is room, hang pictures on the walls, and make sure the lighting is flexible enough to provide the clarity needed for preparing food and a softer, lower intensity for eating and generally relaxing. (Dimmer switches and a few table lamps or other forms of low-level lighting should cover all possibilities.)

It could be that the room that is presently designated as the living room would be better used as a study, bedroom or playroom. If the view from your ground-level living-room window leaves much to be desired, why not move the living room up one storey, to look out through leafy trees, perhaps, instead of at fast-moving, noisy traffic?

Traditional layouts call for the living room to be located at the front of the house, so it is quick and easy to get to. If, on the other hand, your house faces away from the sun and its front room is dark and dim, you may value a warm, sunlit room enough to break with

tradition and reverse the layout, in spite of the longer trek. This has the advantage of easy access to the back garden, which is usually more private than a front one – particularly in a large city, where the front of a house can be a very public and exposed place – and is where there is likely to be play-space for your children, a patio for outdoor entertaining, or a garden that needs tending.

Some very successful living rooms remain at the front of the house, but 'turn their backs' on the outside world completely. With shutters or curtains, these rooms can look inwards: huge, colourful posters or paintings of landscapes provide 'views' out, while keeping the room open and airy in feeling.

It may be that the best room for living in at one stage of a family's life is not the best room ten years later, when the children are grown and the number and nature of living-room activities have altered. The important thing is to be aware of the changing patterns and be flexible enough to develop – even move – your living room in response.

1 *Twin sofas solve seating problems simply; their bright horse-blanket covers echo the colours of the fireplace.*
2 *An open-plan design with a U-shaped sitting area for relaxation and entertaining.*
3 *Studio and sitting room are elegantly separated and dividers carry storage.*
4 *A relaxed sitting area just off the main traffic flow in the open entrance of a Greek house.*

Planning

Certain features in a living room will make the space comfortable and attractive to those who use it. Some combinations of features – like some individual ones – tend to work better than others, depending on the size and layout of the room, and on the people using it. There are, though, no hard and fast rules, and a successful formula for one family's living room might prove a dismal failure for another's, because their requirements or aspirations for the style and use of the room may be quite different. Still, most living rooms share a common purpose and the following guidelines set out the basics for planning a room that functions well.

The first essential is seating and, like the room itself, the seating has to meet many needs – working, relaxing, entertaining, even dining. The most comfortable living rooms allow people to follow their instincts and form a circle – however loosely – when they gather together. A group around a fireplace is an ideal example. The seating, or some of it, should be easy to rearrange for entertaining groups of various sizes, and so that some pairs, or even single seats, can be set up outside the main circle. For this reason, two-seater sofas are far more useful than larger, three-seater ones, which tend to be too heavy to move, take up a lot of space and provide unsociable, three-in-a-row, seating.

Tables should be on hand, possibly stacked away when not in use, and should be sturdy enough not to tip over. In the case of a combined kitchen and living room, a big table at the centre becomes the focus for life revolving around it. The larger the table the better – various members of the family can then use parts of it for different jobs at the same time.

Storage of some form or another will be necessary, whether for books, the paperwork of daily life, records, tapes or even drinks and glasses. Treat storage as a positive element in the design, not as an afterthought. Use large-scale shelving units at any level. At low level, they should skirt the walls and provide horizontal surfaces for storage, display or even working. Position a large, vertical storage unit with all the care you would take in hanging a painting. If the shelving is open, arrange the contents with equal care and consideration – rows of books provide flashes of colour, and punctuation can be added in the form of cut flowers in vases, clocks or collections of favourite objects.

If the room is used for watching television, try to make the set or the main seating easy to move, so that the television can be viewed by one person, a small group or a large gathering. Beware of letting it dominate the room, whether it's in use or not, or control the room's layout. Television can quickly take on the role of an uninvited guest – and particularly if various members of the household have conflicting views on what they want to watch. A living room should be a place where people can watch television as a group, but where they can equally well turn it aside for other events, such as games, visitors, quiet reads, work or for meals.

If the room is small, consider dual-purpose or adaptable furniture: a trestle table, sofa bed, extra folding chairs that can, if necessary, be stored away when not in use. Whatever the size of the room, a firm line should be taken with inherited pieces. If they are too large or overbearing, lend them to someone with the space – and inclination – to accommodate them. Store or sell unloved furniture in preference to enduring it.

If the room seems too crowded, but you *are* fond of all its contents, try rearranging the furniture before taking the drastic step of throwing a treasured piece away. Perhaps placing a sofa at a different angle across the room solves the problem, or cutting a table down from dining size to coffee-table proportions might help.

Having a small-scale plan of your living room drawn out on graph paper, with all the doors, windows, cupboards and permanent features marked on it, is a great help in organizing the room. Measure your existing furniture and cut movable shapes, to scale, from pieces of graph paper. You can then spend time happily trying out several solutions in miniature before actually deciding which layout is best for your room. This will save you the trouble of moving large, heavy pieces of furniture from one unsuitable spot to another even less suitable one. If you are thinking of buying new furniture, it's a good idea to get manufacturers' catalogues and work out dimensions, cut out paper models to scale, then try them out on the room plan before committing yourself to buying.

Lightly marking in the flow patterns – say, from one door to another, or from a door to major pieces of furniture or appliances – is a further refinement of graph-paper planning, and an invaluable one. Correcting mistakes in two dimensions is always easier than solving problems once the room is arranged.

There are also 'tricks of the trade', useful in sorting out some common living-room problems. Placing all the seating directly facing a view, for example, is more obvious – and often less attractive – than arranging it at a slight angle to the view. A fireplace is a good focal point but often means that you're sitting with your back to the windows; if there's no other option, then placing a large mirror above the fireplace can help to visually incorporate the window and the view. Likewise, a large mirror placed at right angles to a window doubles the image and increases the feeling of space and openness in a room.

Windows in two walls can improve the quality of space and light, especially if the only other window in the room is a large, floor-to-ceiling one, which tends to make everything appear in silhouette.

A door located exactly in the middle of a room is less exciting than one placed at one end – the room will open up when you enter it, rather than each side pulling for your attention.

In many living rooms, the single alteration that would make the most difference would be to lower the windowsills, so that when you are sitting down you can see the foreground view, as well as the sky.

Another improvement on the theme of 'lowering', but quick and virtually cost-free, is to hang the paintings, prints or posters lower – these are usually hung too high, resulting in a rather formal, unrelaxed feel, at odds with domestic character. If you have several small pictures, group them tightly rather than dispersing them evenly around the walls. A small picture to one side of a fireplace is a charming and informal alternative to a picture directly above the mantel.

Besides these fundamental points, some of which involve structural alterations, there are other factors, more easily adjusted, that have equal importance in planning a living room. These include lighting, surface finishes and colour, and are covered in detail elsewhere in this book.

Few people have the opportunity, or the funds, to 'do' a living room from scratch, and all at one time. More often, it is a case of working with what is already there and trying to improve upon it, incorporating new elements as they become necessary or affordable, or as your tastes change and develop. Whatever the time-scale of putting plan into action, and whatever the financial resources, remember that creating a functional and attractive living room is never an isolated exercise. Activities allowed or encouraged elsewhere in the house – whether working, playing, eating, watching television, listening to music, reading or talking – relieve the pressure on the living room; the more various rooms overlap in purpose and function, the more successful the living room, and the house as a whole.

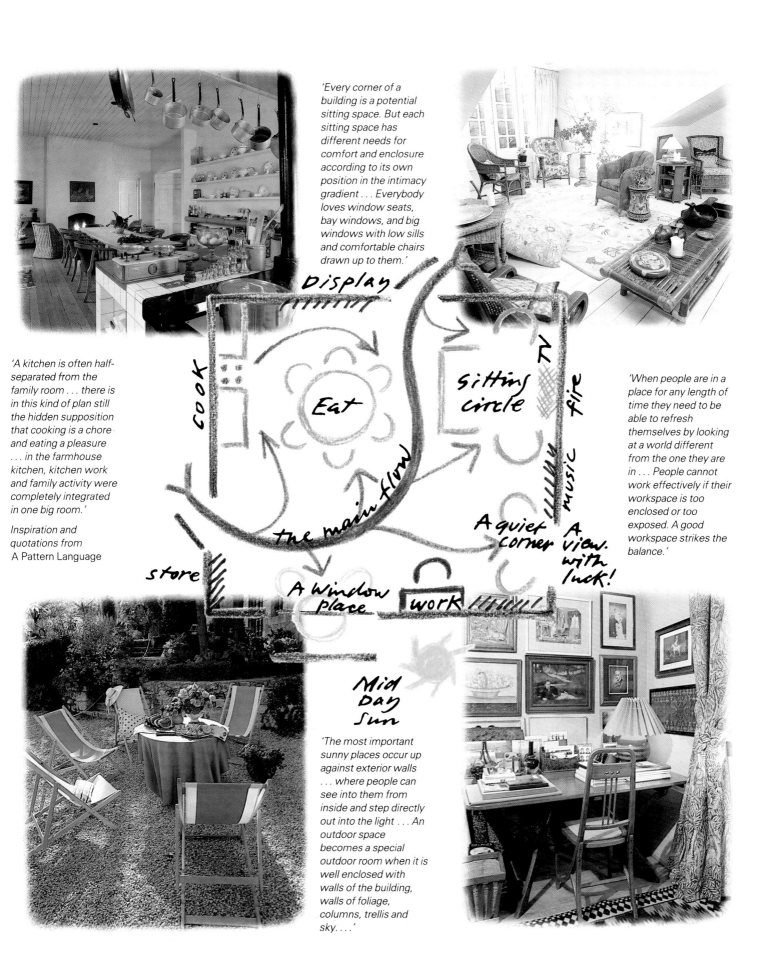

'Every corner of a building is a potential sitting space. But each sitting space has different needs for comfort and enclosure according to its own position in the intimacy gradient . . . Everybody loves window seats, bay windows, and big windows with low sills and comfortable chairs drawn up to them.'

'A kitchen is often half-separated from the family room . . . there is in this kind of plan still the hidden supposition that cooking is a chore and eating a pleasure . . . in the farmhouse kitchen, kitchen work and family activity were completely integrated in one big room.'

Inspiration and quotations from A Pattern Language

'When people are in a place for any length of time they need to be able to refresh themselves by looking at a world different from the one they are in . . . People cannot work effectively if their workspace is too enclosed or too exposed. A good workspace strikes the balance.'

Display

cook

Eat

Sitting circle

TV

fire

music

the main flow

store

A quiet corner

A view. with luck!

A Window place

work

Mid Day Sun

'The most important sunny places occur up against exterior walls . . . where people can see into them from inside and step directly out into the light . . . An outdoor space becomes a special outdoor room when it is well enclosed with walls of the building, walls of foliage, columns, trellis and sky. . . .'

Layout

1 *Busy contrasts from furniture and decorative objects can look great but excess clutter would ruin this room where the very opposite approach has been taken. It's cool, it's sunny, and a very liveable room.*

2 *A semi-basement transformed into a bright open living room.*

3 *A staircase adds scale, interest and heavy traffic flow – the furniture has been placed for ease of movement.*

4 *An adobe in New Mexico stays true to tradition, but a modern roof-light is disguised behind wooden beams.*
5 *Curved 1950s furniture falls into a natural seating circle.*

5

6

7

8

6 *A room arranged for style – with a Le Corbusier chair against an almost bare wall.*
7 *A room designed for reading and contemplation. An upright chair and a table not intended for mere coffee are as prominent as the sofa.*
8 *The living area of a loft – defined by the layout of furniture.*

Budget

Lack of finance brings with it a discipline that will be helpful to good design, as long as the priorities are right. Be strong-willed enough to invest the money you have on basics – structural repairs, re-wiring, new plastering, floor finishes or heating. The fabric of the room should take precedence over the furniture; a beautiful uncluttered room, structurally sound and its surfaces finished to a high standard, can be wonderfully easy to live in.

The furniture it contains – however much or little – is an important investment, and worth choosing with great care. (Statistics show that people buy furniture with roughly a ten-year expectancy.) Remember that good design isn't necessarily expensive, and that worn, old furniture can be preferable to cheap compromises or new tat. Hide a comfortable sofa covered in an ugly fabric with a nice rug, or take the trouble to learn how to re-cover it. Nondescript wood furniture might be improved if it is stripped, or painted to blend in with other colours in the room. If you don't mind, or even prefer, the slightly unconventional, then low-cost furniture can be had in

the form of wooden folding outdoor chairs, or mass-produced (but well-designed) furniture for schools, factories, offices.

Can't afford good paintings? As an alternative to the conventional and predictable travel posters or museum prints, why not hang up utility objects instead? Skis, oars or rackets for example, shiny, new or well-worn, or beautifully designed cooking utensils.

If you cannot immediately afford to have, say, the curtains of your choice, then make do with plain paper blinds or cheap calico until your chosen material is affordable.

Seasonal sales are a great boon if you know what you want – stake out the item and then wait patiently for it to appear in the sales. But avoid 'sale fever' – an impromptu, irrational purchase made simply because it was cheap; the chances are you'll regret it, and the money frittered away can't be spent on what you really want or need.

Certain natural materials, whether new or old, have an inherent appeal, and they are far more valuable visually than their actual cost would imply. Wood, rough woven cotton,

clear glass and stoneware objects can be bought quite cheaply, and, if they are well selected and arranged, can give a room tranquillity and coherence.

And some materials have a natural appeal, so certain colours and colour combinations can be the cheapest way to help overcome a limited budget. Ample use of white, with fresh and lively supporting colours, is one solution; choosing a series of closely related neutrals – greys, creams, pastels – is another. Flashes of colour are then provided by decorative accessories, seasonal flowers – and the people within the room.

If you see your stay as short-term, or know that the carpet you hope to buy is still some years away, make a 'carpet' of colour, using gloss paint. Add rugs for interest.

Small-scale objects – candles, flowers, lamps, cushions and curios of all sorts – add life and personality to a room, provided they don't become clutter. Plants in terracotta pots add life, in a very real sense – many will go on for years, giving you growing returns for your initial modest investment.

1

1 *Surprisingly comfortable, inexpensive furniture, basic shelving and a unifying colour scheme are the good sense behind this room. The flair comes from careful attention to detail – a strong pattern on the blinds, displayed objects that suit the furniture style, a well-finished floor and good lighting.*

2 *Investment in one large flourishing plant and bold, colourful fabric recovering an old sofa make a lively and inexpensive living area.*

3 *A restored Edwardian house: grey is the unifying and elegant ground for the room. Diffuse natural light though plain Holland blinds enhances the soft effect of the stippled walls.*

4 *Rectangles of sheet vinyl in bright colours provide a strongly stylish but utterly practical basis for a room, which needs nothing more than simple furniture and decorative highlights.*

Family rooms

It is a fact of life that young children tend to want to be where adults are, so, if you have them, your living room must combine practicality with style. To make the room pleasant to be in, yet keep it from degenerating into a nursery playroom, requires more common sense and forethought than money.

There is, for example, little point in using anything but washable loose covers and spongeable surfaces. (Proprietary wallpaper sealer is a good idea, and increases the range of wallpapers you can sensibly use.) Trying to prevent sticky finger-marks rather than being able to deal with them easily adds unnecessary tension to family life.

In a room that comfortably accommodates children as well as adults, good facilities for reducing clutter are essential. Big wicker laundry baskets are attractive and easy to scoop large toys into. An old-fashioned travelling trunk is another option, but be careful of tiny fingers getting caught when the lid is shut. Deep, stable bookcases, to hold chil-

dren's large-sized books, and low-level cupboards, with boxes inside to contain the jumble, make transforming a room from cluttered to cleared very easy. As children grow, storage facilities can be refined to include smaller containers for bits and pieces – puzzles, plastic building blocks, marbles, coloured crayons, pens, and so on. If tidying up can be presented as a pleasurable activity, almost a game, children participate more willingly in creating an ordered environment, and your workload becomes easier.

Non-slip flooring, lighting arrangements that cannot easily be knocked over and care in the choice and placement of electrical equipment generally prevent accidents for adults as well as children, and can make the difference between relaxing and being on perpetual 'guard duty'.

Family life need not mean a stripped-down barrack-type atmosphere. High shelves can feature colourful, delicate possessions in safety, and many children's toys, well de-

signed and not necessarily expensive, are attractive and decorative in their own right.

Comfortable, portable seating is sensible. Fold-away chairs and ottomans allow you to set up your own instant corner for a quiet read, while allowing children to build camps and caves to their hearts' content. You can provide small chairs or cushions for toddlers, but be prepared for them to prefer 'grown-up' furniture, and to use it whenever they can. (Banishing heavy, glass-topped coffee tables should be one of the first things you do if you have children – they are cumbersome, dangerous to infants, and show up smudges with almost theatrical clarity.)

No matter how successfully your family room is organized and furnished, make places elsewhere in the house for moments of private retreat. A desk or comfortable chair in the bedroom, or even on a hall landing, gives you the option to get away from it all from time to time, and return refreshed to the living room and family life.

1 *A room where a large family can gather for talking, eating, cooking, watching television and relaxing. An open-plan kitchen/dining room must be practical – easy to clean, for example – but comfortable chairs, a glowing open fire and a long table to gather around mean that this is also a living room and the hub of the house.*

2 *A farmhouse in southern Spain contains every element required for informal living. The warm colours of the beams are echoed in the rugs, and a collection of traditional plates, pictures and personal treasures has been carefully chosen. The overall effect is of a random, relaxed and affectionate family living room.*

2

Sources of inspiration

Creating a personal style is a gradual process; it develops from your own experience, surroundings, interests and – that most elusive of concepts – taste. Imitating a style slavishly rarely results in anything more than being historically correct.

Where to start? A house built in a particular architectural style can offer inspiration, and often does. A beautiful Tudor, Georgian or Modernist house, for example, can start off an absorbing quest for aesthetically sympathetic contents to fill it. The materials and furnishings might be contemporary with the building or a total and unexpected contrast. The spaciousness, scale and ornate detail of grand interiors, for example, often lend themselves to entirely modern furnishings.

Houses that are architecturally neutral offer you the opportunity to develop a strong feeling of your choice: a '1950s look', for instance, in a small, functional apartment, can be inexpensive and practical.

Historical styles seldom fall completely out of favour, but retreat from or return to prominence at different times. British interiors are good examples: many are nostalgic reminders of past glories, recreating the comfort and informality of a country cottage parlour, perhaps, or the classical elegance of a Georgian drawing room. But British style is ultimately an eclectic one, and unashamedly so. With their background of exploration, colonization, trade and navigation, the British have long been exposed to the domestic styles and cultures of other countries, and the result has been a comfortable adaptation and blending of many styles. This philosophy, of incorporating the best in form, colour, scale, material and texture, wherever it comes from, historically or geographically, is a healthy one: India, China, Japan, Scandinavia, Bauhaus Germany, the Mediterranean and Middle East, Africa and South America have all had periods of being in high fashion.

Today, incorporating 'things foreign' into the home scene is a smaller scale operation, but no less valid. Turkish, Indian and Chinese carpets enhance formal and informal settings alike. Bold North African shapes and patterns set the scene for modern interiors, and a sparse, Scandinavian purity can enhance a beautiful wood floor. An exquisite pair of Japanese vases can offer inspiration for the colour theme of a living room; a collection of blue-and-white china might complement a chintzy English sitting room perfectly.

The more surprising the mix, the more striking and individual, but it should all add up to a thematic whole, rather than remaining a collection of isolated and disparate objects. Often, the background of a room can visually weave together separate components: linked textural themes such as rush matting, straw baskets and bamboo blinds will create unity. Roughly textured wall surfaces together with natural flooring can give coherence to a room of plain cottons and varnished woods and provide an interesting contrast as well.

Besides the historical and ethnic sources of style, both of which can be rather anonymous if overdone, must be your own, highly personal viewpoint. The most important thing is to learn the difference between mimicking style and mastering it. The former is a sterile, academic exercise, often dependent on money and an almost maniacal determination to 'get it right'. The latter is a slower, more hesitant process, but ultimately a far more rewarding one, both in terms of creating personal, pleasant surroundings and the ongoing pleasure of using them.

1 *The cool clarity of strong lines, fine woods and natural colours is the Modernist blueprint for a beautiful and functional room. The furniture has been planned as an integral part of the structure so nothing intrudes on the geometric forms of the basic design.*

2 *Colonial splendour with palms, high arched windows and furniture that would look as happy on a shaded verandah.*

3 *Ultra-modern Memphis furniture mixed with fashionable 1950s retro' pieces. Cacti and geometric carpets, with mirrored walls and primitive sculpture, carry the style through the room.*

4 *A room in Provence where natural textures, dried herbs, a gravel floor and strong functional objects replay the landscape outside. Sunlight streams in through the windows, giving the essential Mediterranean quality to this perfect room.*

Living-room style

1 *Monochrome elegance: the carpet and chairs are by Eileen Gray and matched with a grey leather sofa. A print of a Hockney drawing is mounted on stainless steel. In the foreground stands a Fortuny umbrella lamp.*
2 *Eclectic taste: every item a beautiful object in itself and an integral part of the room's whole effect. The background decoration is essentially simple – plain walls, polished floor, glossy ceiling, a fireplace bared down to a metallic frame.*

3 *A strong combination of red and black. The 1930s scallop-shaped armchair, glossy piano, and modern chaise longue (by Rob Eckhardt) are set against an expensive abstract by Barbara Stoelite.*

4 *Soft textures and warm colours, a collection of art objects, an open fire – working together to create a gracious, relaxing but very stylish room.*

5 *Classicism on a grand scale. The walls are marbled not delicately but strongly, the chairs are not draped in white cloth but wrapped in it, the rugs add colour and the bust is set on a marble plinth.*

COLLECTIONS

Born collectors have little difficulty in decorating their homes; the dynamic jumble of their acquisitions fills every corner with interest. If genuine commitment, self control, and a bit of knowledge guide their purchases, the resulting collection should be a visually unified one, and an attractive addition to the living-room scene or to other rooms.

Collections need not be expensive, nor desperately erudite. It's generally not feasible to emulate the 'designer look' featured in glossy magazines, when the owners of the interiors featured are often dealers in the very commodities they display. As the genuine antique commands a more and more astronomical price, the not-so-antique becomes the quarry for most collectors. It is comforting to know that the mere passage of time leads to changing attitudes and makes the thing that was once scorned valuable.

Just as the Edwardians condemned the taste of their Victorian predecessors, and the china produced in the 1930s was once considered the height of kitsch but is now making its way into antique stores and top auction rooms, so some of today's 'junk' will inevitably be tomorrow's desirables. Early plastic, for instance, is starting to become fashionable, but is still very much affordable. An astute eye, patience and interest can often compensate for lack of funds and result in a collection that is both unique and stylish.

The flair with which you display the collection is as important as the items that comprise it. The china of the 1930s looks pretty on a pine dresser, for example, but takes on another character altogether on a thick glass shelf in a modern setting. Lighting helps to add focus, and with some collections – and with glass, especially – special lighting effects can greatly enhance the attraction. Quite mundane objects take on a new interest if given a stage setting: a collection of matchbook covers or cigarette cards displayed in an ornate frame, for example.

Collections need not be passive. Tools can be gathered to form a decoration, with pieces 'temporarily withdrawn' for active use. The brightly coloured wools of a knitting fanatic, or the drawing materials, brushes and paints of the Sunday painter, can be thoughtfully displayed on a shelf or table.

One of the most important parts of collecting – if a collection is conceived as a room decoration – is knowing exactly when to stop.

Collections should never encroach upon the primary purpose of a living room – which is to be lived in, comfortably, by all members of the family. If a collection begins to commandeer work surfaces as well as shelves, a reassessment is called for. Could some of the overflow be accommodated in another room of the house, or – as a visual extension of the living room – into the hall beyond? The problem may be that storage for ordinary clutter is sadly inadequate.

If you have genuinely run out of space but still get pleasure from the ongoing process of building a collection, replace quantity with quality, 'trading up' two or three more modest pieces for one outstanding one.

Though your primary obligation is to the people who use the living room, you have an obligation to the objects you collect, whatever their value. Watercolours and delicate fabrics need to be kept out of direct sunlight, or they will fade. Keep breakable objects out of reach of small children, and very fragile or small items may need a glass case for protection from dust as well as the rough and tumble of everyday life.

1 *A deep alcove with traditionally curved shelves is colour-washed in pink and yellow, providing a strong backdrop for a collection of nineteenth-century English china.*
2 *Each of these twelve compartments contains a separate composition of objects, adding up to a very individualized display.*

3 *Brilliant colour glazes with hand-painted upholstered chairs.*
4 *Automobilia – a collection of old toy cars.*
5 *Fitted glass shelving below stairs contains antique ceramics and old wooden boxes.*
6 *An elegant, subdued collection of fine antique wooden boxes.*
7 *An oriental folding screen provides a beautiful backdrop for artist's paraphernalia.*
8 *A grouping of twentieth-century china matched with a contemporary art work.*
9 *Sponge-patterned, nineteenth-century country earthenware.*

Designing displays

1 Bevelled mirrors – uninspiring individually but creating an intriguing collection with multiple reflections.
2 A set of pictures look good hung together and unhindered by other objects – these are Richard Smith prints.
3 A monochromatic collection of hand mirrors and old master engravings.

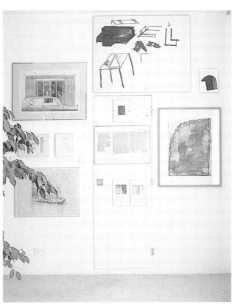

4 *An eclectic collection of objects, each of individual interest, and unified by their interesting patterns and textures.*
5 *Turn-of-the-century brass and copper frames, richly coloured against white boarded walls.*
6 *A graphic collection artfully positioned to camouflage an undistinguished door.*

KITCHENS

The kitchen is one of the most important centres of any household; it is not simply a work space in which many hours are spent, but it is also a room for the whole family to live in and entertain friends. In the past 200 years or so, the kitchen became relegated to the status of a cramped work-room, but the traditional kitchen, with the hearth as the natural heart of the home, has now made its comeback, thanks largely to open-plan design and the benefits of technological developments.

The first and most important step in planning is to decide on the sort of kitchen and the type of room you would like, and then to relate this to the rest of the house. It may be worthwhile spending time and money creating extra space and light, even if this involves relocating or extending the kitchen, perhaps by incorporating an adjacent utility room. It is also worth considering whether you really need a separate dining room: why remove the pleasure of watching others cook or of conversation while you work?

Careful planning should make cooking more efficient and enjoyable. Most contemporary design is based on guidelines following the principle of a 'work triangle' drawn between the three main activity areas of the kitchen: water supply, cooking zone and food storage. First, each activity area should be an integrated, self-contained unit with its own storage space; second, through traffic should be kept clear of the work triangle, especially the route between the cooker (stove) and the sink; third, activity areas should be logically related to one another for economy of movement. Good lighting and ventilation are essential both for an efficient work centre and for relaxation.

Since the appearance of electrical appliances in the 1930s, the kitchen has evolved into a machine- and gadget-oriented space. However, remember that it is a mistake to overload a kitchen with appliances ill-suited to your requirements, budget or style of cooking. Decide at the outset which appliances you need now, or are likely to require in the future: they can be expensive and will have a considerable bearing on your total budget; they also take up valuable space while requiring imaginative planning of electrical wiring and work surfaces.

A spacious old kitchen was restored by laying a ceramic floor in a classic pattern, installing simple cupboards, renovating the original solid-fuel stove and discovering a sturdy, old table and giant station clock.

KITCHENS
CHECKLIST

■ Which activities are you going to cater for in your kitchen:
- • domestic food preparation and cooking?
- • food storage?
- • everyday eating?
- • entertaining?
- • cooking professionally?
- • laundry?

■ How many people do you need to cater for?

■ Is your kitchen:
- • properly sited in relation to the house, or would it serve your needs better if it were moved?
- • spacious enough for the activities, appliances and storage required, or does it need extending?

■ What are your priorities:
- • food preparation with maximum speed, convenience and efficiency?
- • cooking on gas, electricity or a solid-fuel stove?
- • fitting a kitchen into a problematic shape or space?
- • the creation of a particular colour scheme or design style?
- • a clear division between the cooking and dining areas?
- • the use of the kitchen as a comfortable family centre?
- • safety for children?
- • usability by disabled or elderly people?
- • hygiene with animals?

■ What is the size of your budget?

■ Should you plan to complete the work at once, or in stages?

■ Do you need to consider the effect of any changes on the overall value of the property?

■ How long do you expect the kitchen to last?

■ Which of the following appliances do you want now, or in the future:
- • cooker (stove)?
- • wall oven?
- • free-standing hob (cooking top)?
- • solid-fuel stove?
- • microwave oven?
- • refrigerator?
- • freezer?
- • waste disposer?
- • dishwasher?
- • washing machine?
- • clothes drier?
- • waste (trash) compactor?
- • television?
- • radio?
- • stereo system?

■ How much storage space will you require for:
- • fresh food and groceries?
- • frozen food?
- • wine?
- • portable cooking appliances and utensils?
- • cutlery and china?
- • cleaning products and equipment?
- • laundry products and equipment?

■ Do you have clear preferences for:
- • open-shelf or cupboard storage?
- • built-in cabinets or free-standing cupboards?

Kitchen finishes

Contemporary kitchen style is created in part by practical considerations: all surfaces and materials must be resistant to water, steam, grease and smells, and should be easy to clean. But in recent years, with the return of the kitchen as a general living space, the clinically rational kitchen, synthesizing both design and function, has been softened by a greater emphasis on comfort, a warm atmosphere and traditional features.

Whatever your taste, there is always plenty of scope to give a room both individuality and character. Modify existing features: the chimney cavity of an old fireplace might be used to house a built-in oven, cupboard, charcoal-wood barbecue or extension speakers for a hi-fi system; a high ceiling can be boxed in to conceal pipes, cables and ventilator ducting. Always consider what looks good on display and what is best hidden behind closed doors. Kitchen utensils can be attractively displayed. Choose simple, easily moved furniture and leave plenty of space for circulation.

Walls

Many flooring materials, including cork, ceramic tiles, wood and vinyl, can be used imaginatively for kitchen walls since they are waterproof and insulated against heat loss. Impermeable vinyl or washable wallpapers should be stuck down with a fungicidal adhesive to prevent mould from forming. If you are using paint, prepare the surface well, choose a washable finish and add an extra coat for durability.

Floors

You might choose a kitchen floor for its softness underfoot; cork and vinyl are easy to clean and absorb sound, and rubber is quiet when walked on as well as being virtually indestructible. A harder floor, made of ceramic or quarry tiles, terrazzo, slate or marble, will be hard-wearing and look good, but can be cold and tiring underfoot and not always suitable for timber, as opposed to concrete, sub-floors. Polished wood is long-lasting and warm underfoot, but it needs frequent resealing in areas of heavy wear and can be slippery. Carpet is a problem for cleaning; use synthetics in kitchens.

Work surfaces

Laminates are the most widely used, all-purpose working surfaces in manufactured units; they can be contoured to eliminate awkward joints and sharp counter edges. More expensive options are artificial marble surfaces, ceramic and quarry tiles, or mosaic, bedded in mastic; well-sealed hardwood,

marble, slate, granite and terrazzo are beautiful but need more care. Stainless steel need not be restricted to sink surrounds; it is very hard-wearing and hygienic, and consequently often found in professional kitchens where it is used in conjunction with solid wooden chopping boards.

Lighting

Imaginative lighting is absolutely essential, particularly if the kitchen is used for eating and social life; recessed and adjustable fittings are useful because of their adaptability in such dual-purpose rooms. Natural

daylight is a bonus, and doors opening out to the garden can be partly glazed, but general and specific artificial lighting is always needed. Cabinets, drawers and work surfaces should be lit so you can work without being in your own, or others, shadow.

Windows

Louvred windows are a good choice for a kitchen: they improve general ventilation and adapt well to rapid changes in temperature. If you want curtains, they should be flameproof and kept clear of the cooking area. However, roller or Venetian blinds are far better because

they are less absorbent and allow you to control the amount of light entering the room. Dispense with curtains and blinds altogether if the view is good, although the room will lose warmth in winter and direct sunshine can be difficult to control. And bare windows do not look particularly attractive at night.

Heating

Conventional radiators and storage heaters often waste valuable kitchen wall space; instead, use a system with thermostatically controlled wall, ceiling or floor heating, or use small electric or gas heaters.

1 *Natural colours – off-whites and browns – and a stone floor create a homely style. The oil-fired stove was moved under the window and the existing chimney used for storage.*
2 *A strong colour theme: subtle, muted clay tiles on the walls, grey and gold ceramic floor tiles, toning shades for painted doors and drawers. The deep architrave creates a shelf for decorative objects and carries lighting and ventilation.*
3 *Stainless steel is associated with restaurant kitchens. In this apartment it provides a sleek, expensive-looking finish for the compact fitted kitchen and is hygienic and practical.*

Kitchen style

1 *An old oak table is the centre-piece for a traditional kitchen set around the walls; the chimney is used effectively for air extraction.*

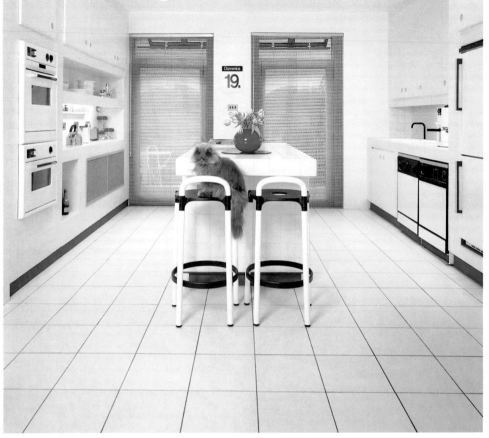

2 *A similar layout, in stark modern style using bright white tiles and fitted units. The centre-piece is an island unit carrying work surface, eating bar and storage.*
3 *A cordon-bleu cook recreated the elegance of a traditional French kitchen using modern components – melamine-topped table, fitted, purpose-built pressed-wood cupboards, pre-formed shelving, and a luxurious brass-trimmed cooker that runs off wood, coal, gas or electricity. The still-life is genuine eighteenth century.*

4 *Black melamine provides the darkest background on work surfaces and doors in contrast to old pine cupboards and metal utensils. The cutlery is second-hand, restaurant silver plate.*
5 *An ingenious island unit in a kitchen created by a Beverley Hills designer. The surface is terrazzo which can be moulded as required. The massive stove is a restaurant model.*

6 *The alternative to slick fitted units – stylish, inexpensive, free-standing furniture.*
7 *Less is more: great character derives from simplicity in this island-plan kitchen.*

Kitchen layout

The layout of a kitchen, both horizontal and vertical, should always be designed around the individual room and your own needs, preferences and ways of working. There are, however, five basic types of floor plan. Remember that you will almost certainly need to adapt these basic types.

The single-line kitchen With appliances and cupboards lined up along one wall, this fits into very limited space; the sink should be located in the middle, with the refrigerator and cooker (stove) at either end and built-under appliances used to maximize the amount of work surface.

The galley, or corridor, kitchen Arranged along two facing walls, this should have the sink and cooker (stove) on the same side of the kitchen. The width of the corridor must provide door clearance and adequate space for bending down.

The L-shaped kitchen This is good for open-plan and small, square rooms, and should have the sink in the middle of the work triangle for ease of movement.

The U-shaped kitchen One of the most workable arrangements with uninterrupted space for food preparation and serving. The sink is usually in the centre with the refrigerator and cooker (stove) on either side.

The island kitchen This layout needs plenty of space and careful design to ensure economy of movement. It is chosen by many professional cooks for its adaptability to different work sequences and large work flows. The island can double as a room divider.

The essentials

Whichever layout you decide on, the following components must be included:

Work surfaces Adequate work surfaces should be carefully planned (see *Work centres: cooking*). The main food preparation area, usually situated between the sink and hob (cooking top), should be large enough to serve up a meal.

Cooking equipment Cookers (stoves), or separate ovens with hobs (the cooking top, which incorporates gas burners, electric hot-plates, ceramic tops and other types of burners and grills), should be located so that pans can be carried back and forth easily to the sink; for working comfort, avoid placing this equipment in corners. A hob should not be under a wall cupboard or by a curtained window.

Sinks The sink should be close to the dishes, cups, cutlery and pans in daily use. Avoid plumbing a sink into a corner, and remember that dishwashers should be near the sink and waste disposer.

Storage space Tall units should not interrupt the countertop. Elevation must be considered: wall storage offers easier access and needs less door clearance than low shelves or cupboards, but allow good clearance of work surfaces. Line up the vertical divisions between corresponding wall and base units and avoid gaps between appliances and units. These waste space and are difficult to clean; instead, they should be put to good use. Careful planning is required also to ensure corner spaces are properly utilized.

1 *In a spacious kitchen, an island plan makes good use of abundant central areas with storage above and below.*
2 *A narrow corridor can be successful as a kitchen if the layout is kept linear (the table folds down at one end, making best use of a view).*
3 *The popular U-shaped kitchen layout provides a work surface near the sink and the dining area.*
4 *A kitchen in a Victorian house keeps to period; the quality of detailing needs special care in a small space.*

3

4

KITCHEN PLANS

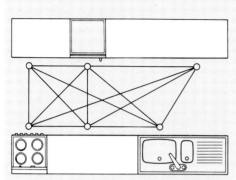

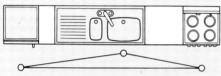

The traditional concept of kitchen planning is based on a triangle joining three work centres – hob (cooking top), sink and fridge – and this area should not be a thoroughfare. No two centres should be more than a double-arm span apart, to avoid tiring, nor should they be uncomfortably close.

Single-line kitchen
A linear plan is good if the back wall is long enough, and if the kitchen is used as a passage. Ideally situated below a window.

Galley kitchen
Not recommended unless built against a dead end or window; essentially for a one- or two-person apartment or house.

L-shaped kitchen
This is currently a popular plan as it combines well with a living area and overcomes any shortage of wall space.

U-shaped kitchen
A U-shape is ideal for a small area, an alcove where the cook works alone, or for an open-plan room with a kitchen area.

Island kitchen
This plan suits people who cook with style, and prefer to make the activity itself a room focus. It calls for careful planning.

Work centres: cooking

The cooking and main food preparation area is the heart of the kitchen. It needs very careful consideration since each of the wide range of alternatives has distinct benefits and disadvantages, depending on your cooking requirements.

In recent years many people have abandoned free-standing all-in-one cookers (stoves) for separate built-in oven and hob (burner) units. This arrangement is more expensive, but adapts better to individual needs and saves space. The choice between a built-under and eye-level oven must depend on the amount of space you have, whether you prefer one over the other, and so on. Some people still choose a traditional solid-fuel cooker, which doubles as a room, and even water, heater.

Gas and electric cookers, with either single or double ovens, can now incorporate hot-air or microwave systems, self-cleaning ovens, rotisseries and ducted fume extractors, and you will have to decide which of these justifies the additional expense. In a hot-air, or fan, oven the traditional radiant element is replaced by a heating element in the cavity between the oven and the outer wall. The uniform heat produced allows much larger quantities of food to be evenly baked or grilled (broiled) at once, without it having to be taken out of the oven and turned.

A microwave oven cooks or heats up food in a fraction of the time a normal oven takes and is particularly useful if you buy or cook in bulk for the freezer. However, even with a browning capacity, it cannot produce food with the same flavour or texture as more slowly cooked food and should be primarily regarded as a back-up system. In cooking by induction, which has been used in the food industry for many years, the steel or cast-iron container is heated by way of a magnetic field so that the element heats up only when a pan is placed on it. This makes it both safe and energy saving – only the part of the element in contact with the pan uses power.

Most hob units, or cooking tops, can be set into a worktop, leaving the space underneath for storage. If you are very short on space and cook simply, there are fold-down tops available. At the other end of the scale, there are combined gas and electric hobs, integral fume extractors, and modular systems, including charcoal grills and deep-frying pans, which can also be set into the countertop. If safety for children is a priority, a single-line hob can be run along the back of a work surface, and if you are fitting a cooking hood with an extractor fan or filter over the hob, remember that its height varies, depending on whether gas or electricity is used.

Ceramic hobs incorporate electric elements into an easily cleaned ceramic glass sheet; those with tungsten halogen light filaments allow heat levels to be changed instantly and, like gas burners, can be finely controlled and show the intensity of heat.

Work surfaces

Whatever work surface you choose for the kitchen (see *Kitchen finishes*), areas adjacent to the cooking hobs should ideally be heat resistant. If you can afford to further vary the surface for special purposes, consider the possibilities of building in a wooden butcher's block for chopping, or a cool marble or slate slab for pastry making.

Main worktops should be 500 to 600mm (20 to 24in) deep, while smaller work areas should be at least 300mm (12in) wide, but preferably larger.

The height of worktops, which usually varies from 850 to 900mm (34 to 36in), should be carefully adjusted to your own height for chopping, mixing and whisking at the right level. Some units have adjustable legs for this purpose; with others you can choose between plinths (bases) of several different heights to allow changes in counter level. Enough clearance should be left between counter and wall units – probably 400 to 500mm (16 to 20in) – to accommodate portable appliances, such as a blender.

HOB POSITION

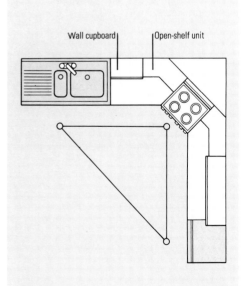

Wall cupboard | Open-shelf unit

A good alternative layout for a kitchen is to place the hob (cooking top) across a corner. The space wasted is not as great as would first appear. The great advantage is that the surfaces at each side of the oven are more accessible – and safer.

HEIGHT OF WORK SURFACES

It is a mistake to plan a kitchen with all the units at uniform heights. Delicate, complex tasks, such as cake-icing or making hot drinks, need a higher surface – more than the standard 900mm (36in) offered. Heavier tasks – kneading bread, hacking into cabbages, rolling out pastry – call on upper-arm and back muscles, so the work surface needs to be correspondingly lower.

Even with manufactured units, it is possible to vary height by using different widths of plinth at the base of the units, if the cupboards themselves are not available in various heights.

Alternatively, create a higher work surface by building up the existing units, for instance with a thick slab of wood for chopping.

With lower work areas, allow for extra clearance above so that your head does not bang against wall-mounted cupboards or shelves.

and n[...]
compa[...]
can be[...]
expens[...]

Fume[...]
The po[...]
return[...]
have m[...]
remova[...]
more i[...]
smells[...]
though[...]
machin[...]
sation:[...]
fumes[...]
general[...]
fitted to[...]
tively, t[...]
hoods [...]
the out[...]
air. The[...]
trusive.[...]

The [...]
part of[...]
hob ele[...]
which[...]
underne[...]
of the k[...]

1 *New hobs are available in a wide range of combinations, like this electric glass ceramic hob with two rings for braising, two metal rings for speed, and a barbecue grill. A hob ventilator is sandwiched between to suck away fumes. Other models incorporate gas and electric plates in one hob; deep fryers can be substituted for barbecue grills.*
2 *A nineteenth-century French marble shop counter provides an island work surface with deep-drawer storage space.*

3 *An expensive but beautiful island area with a marble work surface. A low-level inset has been created for the hob; it demonstrates that varying levels for different tasks can be attractive as well as practical.*
4 *In a small kitchen, the same tiling behind shelves, on walls and on the floor unifies the decorative effect. A fold-down table provides a space-saving work surface, and the narrow shelves offer easily accessible display storage.*

Storage space

Kitchen storage should be planned around appropriate activity areas, bearing in mind frequency of use and any special storage requirements. Space for everyday pans and utensils, including a safe knife-rack or drawer, should be found near the food preparation area; detergents and dishcloths should always be kept separately near the sink; china should preferably be close to both the sink, or dishwasher, and the serving area. Tools, storage jars and most other kitchen items are too attractive to hide and are usually more conveniently accessible when stacked on open shelves and racks or hung on wall hooks. (However, this will work only in kitchens with good air extraction and in areas not plagued by dirty city pollution.) If you have a particular space or shape problem, it may be worth considering the expense of a custom-built kitchen.

Food storage

The spacious, old-fashioned larder or pantry which pre-dated the refrigerator has certainly not outlived its usefulness for food storage. Incorporate an existing larder into any new kitchen scheme; if you decide to build one, position it on the cool side of the house with low-level, fly-proof gauze air vents. Different foods require different conditions: those spoiled by high humidity – such as dried herbs and spices, biscuits and sugar – need dry, warm storage. On the other hand, fruit and vegetables, other perishables and wine are best kept in a cool, well-ventilated and preferably dark space.

Refrigerators are available to fit under countertops or as large, free-standing appliances incorporating spacious freezer compartments, ice-making equipment and other features. The main consideration will be the capacity you need; whether you choose left-, or right-hand opening doors, make sure that they can be fully opened to remove shelves and vegetable bins. Matching freezers and refrigerators are usually made so that they can be stacked vertically or horizontally to give a compact arrangement. Top-opening freezers are bulkier but useful for long-term storage for large households. They need not be located in the kitchen itself.

Shelves and cupboards

Shelves above eye-level should generally graduate in depth so that you can always reach to the back. Swing-out racks occupying part of the cupboard space but leaving accessible single-line storage are a good idea; so, too, are narrow shelves built inside cupboard doors. A row at the back of the

work counter allows everyday cooking tools and appliances to be ready at hand.

Lower-level units can incorporate pull-out fittings: racks, trays, bins and drawers; revolving carousel fittings to utilize awkward corner space; even tables and ironing boards. Do make sure that all such fittings roll smoothly on runners.

Hinged doors give better access to cupboards than sliding doors, which are only effective for lengths over 800mm (32in), but they should be as narrow as possible on wall units to prevent injuries. Roller-shutter doors are only suitable for low cupboards since they require a degree of physical effort to operate.

Standard units

There are three basic types of standard kitchen unit: base, tall and wall, plus units made to house built-in appliances, which may have integrated doors or co-ordinating front panels. Dimensions are usually in accordance with accepted international standards so that it is possible to co-ordinate different brands of appliances and cabinets. If doors of varying dimensions have to be introduced, use no more than two sizes. Lengths of units range from 300 to 1200mm (12 to 48in), rising in increments of 100mm (4in), although some manufacturers also produce half-module units of 350 or 450mm (14 or 18in) which allow greater flexibility. Always check that the depth of the units is sufficient for your requirements – for instance, be certain that your largest dinner plate will fit inside the units. Base and tall units are generally 600mm (24in) deep externally, and wall units are 300 to 350mm (12 to 14in) deep.

1 *New hobs are available in a wide range of combinations, like this electric glass ceramic hob with two rings for braising, two metal rings for speed, and a barbecue grill. A hob ventilator is sandwiched between to suck away fumes. Other models incorporate gas and electric plates in one hob; deep fryers can be substituted for barbecue grills.*

2 *A nineteenth-century French marble shop counter provides an island work surface with deep-drawer storage space.*

3 *An expensive but beautiful island area with a marble work surface. A low-level inset has been created for the hob; it demonstrates that varying levels for different tasks can be attractive as well as practical.*

4 *In a small kitchen, the same tiling behind shelves, on walls and on the floor unifies the decorative effect. A fold-down table provides a space-saving work surface, and the narrow shelves offer easily accessible display storage.*

Work centres: washing-up and disposal

It is always expensive to alter plumbing, so the position of the sink will be largely determined by the location of the water supply and waste connections. Standard sinks are available in stainless steel or vitreous enamel, which is slightly less hard-wearing. If money is no object, a custom-made teak sink is a possible alternative. Recent innovations in plastics technology have produced finishes which are claimed to be non-staining, non-scratch, and to provide a truly durable and attractive alternative to enamel.

With various combinations of bowls and half-bowls available, it is important to select for your particular requirements. A double bowl, allowing simultaneous washing-up and rinsing, food preparation, soaking and so on, and a large drainer for leaving dishes to dry hygienically without wiping are well worth the extra investment, as are half bowls for strainer waste or waste disposal units.

There are three basic types of sink unit:

Lay-on sink/drainer Combined sink and drainer designed to fit on top of a standard kitchen unit. They come in various combinations of bowls, half-bowls and drainers and are usually in stainless steel.

Inset bowl and drainer Separate units designed to be set into a counter; the bowl may be set in flush or have a raised outer rim, which can be problematic because spilt water cannot drain back into the sink.

Inset sink/drainer, or sink centre This takes up less space and usually includes a second half- or full bowl, large waste outlet and matching taps within the sink apron. Wire baskets for rinsing and chopping boards which fit over the sink or drainer are also available as accessories.

If you cannot avoid having a washing machine or other laundry equipment in the kitchen, it should be kept well clear of the food preparation area and ideally have a quite separate sink.

Taps (faucets)

Mixer taps, which control both the water flow and temperature mix, are useful; those with Teflon-mounted ceramic discs or rotating stainless-steel balls don't drip and have no washers to be replaced when worn. Useful extras are a replaceable aerator to provide a smooth stream of water with no hard deposits, and a spray/brush attachment for rinsing dishes. Taps fitted to the wall are a good idea if you are short of work space. Make sure there is adequate clearance underneath the taps for tall pots and buckets.

Dishwashers

Washing-up is done more effectively by machine because the water temperature is higher, but dishwashers are only economical if you have the space and will make good use of them; remember also that they can discolour china and damage delicate cutlery. If you do a lot of cooking, buy a machine with a special programme for pots and pans.

Waste disposers

The problem of waste disposal can be reduced by separating out items that can be recycled and, if you have a garden, used for compost. Whether or not you have a waste disposer, you will need a large rubbish bin; it is best situated under or next to the sink. If possible, try to make use of a convenient corner or recess, or house a pull-out bin in a cupboard.

Waste disposers cannot devour many artificial materials but deal well with food; they require a second sink with a fast-running cold-water supply, and a waste-pipe with easy bends to prevent blockages. Reversible grinders are a useful feature to help unjam blocked material. To ensure that disposers do not smell, a good trap or water seal on the waste-pipe is important.

If there is a really large volume of rubbish

1 *Double sinks, with a half-bowl for preparing and draining vegetables. The window space has been cleverly utilized with a simple stainless-steel rail and butcher's hooks carrying pots and pans, while not obstructing the light.*
2 *A plate rack over a traditional ceramic sink is hygienic, time saving and attractive.*
3 *Modern sinks have numerous accessories – a single sink with basket, vegetable half-bowl and drainer may be a better use of space than a double sink.*

and no garden, you might consider a trash compactor, which compresses garbage and can be fitted in a cupboard, but this is an expensive alternative.

Fume and steam extractors

The popularity of open-plan design and the return of the kitchen as a household centre have made good ventilation and the efficient removal of cooking fumes and steam far more important than is often realized. Most smells originate from the cooking area, although sinks, dishwashers and washing machines can also be a problem for condensation: the best solution is to remove the fumes at source as far as possible. For general ventilation, extractor fans can be fitted to an exterior wall or window. Alternatively, these can be incorporated into cooker hoods placed over the hob, either ducted to the outside or with filters for re-circulation of air. The latest designs are sleek and unobtrusive.

The best fume extractors are an integral part of the hob. Vents located between the hob elements swallow the cooking fumes which are ducted downwards and then underneath the floor or else through the rear of the kitchen unit to the outside.

SINK HEIGHT

A factor often overlooked in choosing a sink unit is that it is best to be able to work without having to bend to reach the bottom of the bowl. Also take note that many new sinks are intended as supplements only to dishwashers, with small bowls, and little draining space.

4 *Some new extractors are slim enough to fit under wall-hung cupboards; the vapour screen is pulled out thereby switching on the appliance. The fan is housed in a boxed area.*

5 *Fume extractors can combine function with elegance; this glass-hooded model is ideal for an island work area, providing a hanging rail and lighting centre as well as clean air.*
6 *A bold solution to the air-filtering problem: a sculptured, purpose-built hood in stainless steel.*

Storage space

Kitchen storage should be planned around appropriate activity areas, bearing in mind frequency of use and any special storage requirements. Space for everyday pans and utensils, including a safe knife-rack or drawer, should be found near the food preparation area; detergents and dishcloths should always be kept separately near the sink; china should preferably be close to both the sink, or dishwasher, and the serving area. Tools, storage jars and most other kitchen items are too attractive to hide and are usually more conveniently accessible when stacked on open shelves and racks or hung on wall hooks. (However, this will work only in kitchens with good air extraction and in areas not plagued by dirty city pollution.) If you have a particular space or shape problem, it may be worth considering the expense of a custom-built kitchen.

Food storage

The spacious, old-fashioned larder or pantry which pre-dated the refrigerator has certainly not outlived its usefulness for food storage. Incorporate an existing larder into any new kitchen scheme; if you decide to build one, position it on the cool side of the house with low-level, fly-proof gauze air vents. Different foods require different conditions: those spoiled by high humidity – such as dried herbs and spices, biscuits and sugar – need dry, warm storage. On the other hand, fruit and vegetables, other perishables and wine are best kept in a cool, well-ventilated and preferably dark space.

Refrigerators are available to fit under countertops or as large, free-standing appliances incorporating spacious freezer compartments, ice-making equipment and other features. The main consideration will be the capacity you need; whether you choose left-, or right-hand opening doors, make sure that they can be fully opened to remove shelves and vegetable bins. Matching freezers and refrigerators are usually made so that they can be stacked vertically or horizontally to give a compact arrangement. Top-opening freezers are bulkier but useful for long-term storage for large households. They need not be located in the kitchen itself.

Shelves and cupboards

Shelves above eye-level should generally graduate in depth so that you can always reach to the back. Swing-out racks occupying part of the cupboard space but leaving accessible single-line storage are a good idea; so, too, are narrow shelves built inside cupboard doors. A row at the back of the

work counter allows everyday cooking tools and appliances to be ready at hand.

Lower-level units can incorporate pull-out fittings: racks, trays, bins and drawers; revolving carousel fittings to utilize awkward corner space; even tables and ironing boards. Do make sure that all such fittings roll smoothly on runners.

Hinged doors give better access to cupboards than sliding doors, which are only effective for lengths over 800mm (32in), but they should be as narrow as possible on wall units to prevent injuries. Roller-shutter doors are only suitable for low cupboards since they require a degree of physical effort to operate.

Standard units

There are three basic types of standard kitchen unit: base, tall and wall, plus units made to house built-in appliances, which may have integrated doors or co-ordinating front panels. Dimensions are usually in accordance with accepted international standards so that it is possible to co-ordinate different brands of appliances and cabinets. If doors of varying dimensions have to be introduced, use no more than two sizes. Lengths of units range from 300 to 1200mm (12 to 48in), rising in increments of 100mm (4in), although some manufacturers also produce half-module units of 350 or 450mm (14 or 18in) which allow greater flexibility. Always check that the depth of the units is sufficient for your requirements – for instance, be certain that your largest dinner plate will fit inside the units. Base and tall units are generally 600mm (24in) deep externally, and wall units are 300 to 350mm (12 to 14in) deep.

1 *Nothing can replace the traditional larder for practical storage. Cold and dark, fitted with shelves, racks and strong hooks, it provides space for keeping fresh food, maturing smoked meats, and stacking tins and jars.*
2 *New cupboards with baskets and racks inside doors and slide-out trays for lower shelves make good use of space.*
3 *Narrow shelving that allows all objects to be seen at a glance is practical and decorative.*

4 *A mixed storage system often works best: open shelves hold objects for display, closed cupboards conceal less attractive items. One door is louvred for ventilation, the other solid for storing bottles and tins. Drawers have been purpose-built to various depths.*
5 *Fine crystal glasses line up on narrow glass shelves, kept dust-free behind hinged glass panes for doors. The step ladder is used to reach high shelves.*

Creative kitchens

1 *An antique dealer in Sydney fills her pale kitchen cupboards with home-made preserves, produced for their decorative value as much as for their delicious taste. A lovely item of furniture such as this is one of the advantages of not using standard kitchen fixtures.*

2 *A French loft conversion with display at a level of simple elegance. White melamine shelves above the sink are back-lit and hold glassware. One L-shaped unit consists of a worktop and sink, with bulky equipment underneath and an open end for china display. The metal shelving unit takes decorative bowls and preserves and any mundane objects are hidden inside the few closed cupboards.*

3 *Very little was altered in this Florentine country house. Building work was minimal but important: installing double glazing and roof insulation. The kitchen is a beautiful room, and glass shelving units and a basic island work station do nothing to interrupt its dimensions.*

4 *A southern Spanish kitchen with an abundance of produce and decoration. A kitchen made up of individually chosen parts creates a unique style, more difficult to achieve with mass-produced units.*
5 *A wall-mounted step-ladder for pots and pans is practical, pleasing.*

6 *A suspended plate rack – a fine solution for drainage and display.*
7 *Kitchen collection: a mass of old utensils, which create an interesting display and are also in daily use.*

239

The Conrans' kitchens

The essential quality of a successful kitchen, more important than whether it is clean, and modern, or furnished as comfortably as a country sitting room, is whether it is a room that is enjoyable to spend time in. If the room is pleasant, the cook will often have company.

Traditionally, the kitchen was the heart of the house; early and primitive dwellings consisted of little else. It was here that people sheltered, spun, brewed, baked, ate, gossiped, brought up infants, rested and kept warm by the fire in old age.

In the more recent past, the cook has been shoved out of sight in some dingy or clinical, unimportant room, but now we have returned to the idea that the kitchen is in fact the most important room of all. Children and animals are drawn to it, friends feel most at their ease there. If it is properly set out, they come and go, talking or helping or following their own activities – homework or whatever – and still leave room for the cook to get on with things without feeling flustered.

As a family, we spend a good deal of time in our kitchens, in the country and in our small London terrace house. A new venture for us is a converted farmhouse in Provence where we have tried to design the ideal kitchen.

Kitchen life is a very rich and important side of existence, and should be made as enjoyable and as sensual as possible. The big bowls of tomatoes and aubergines, the bunches of herbs and flowers are as important to the eye as the tiles you choose for the walls or floor, and, even if you haven't got enormous funds, a rather ordinary kitchen can be brought to life by the happy placing of a comfortable chair and an eye for details.

Caroline Conran

1, 2 Our spacious country kitchen in an old billiard room. The far end of the room is dominated by a wonderful, free-standing, oil-fired stove – always ready to cook, to warm you after a cold walk or to dry tea-towels. I keep an old Turkey carpet by it for comfort. This is a living room with an open fire, armchairs and a television at the other end; it's at its best when there is plenty of evidence of a flourishing garden and meals being cooked.

3 *In Provence, our kitchen has two tables made specially for the room – one for dining and one an excellent chopping table. The ovens, hobs and grill are set into a long worktop and it is easy for two or three people to cook and move about at once. Across the room is a marble shelf with a mirror behind it (4) for fruit and vegetables, and specially designed racks carry china.*

5, 6 *In towns, the speed of life makes leisurely cooking seem out of place, so in London I cook fast using machines. The small kitchen functions like a galley in a ship, with plates and storage along one side, working space and equipment on the other. At first it lacked atmosphere, but once I had gathered a collection of favourite cookery books, found a place for a tray of drinks, installed a telephone, put up a picture or two and started growing plants, then I looked forward to cooking in my immaculate kitchen.*

241

EATING ROOMS

The room where you eat is often the centre of activity and the heart of the house. And the table is a focal point for solitary and communal activities – for conversation, playing board games, doing homework or jigsaw puzzles, and for the pleasure of eating.

Obviously, the furniture should be comfortable enough to encourage these diverse gatherings and activities; the surroundings are as important. Meals, the main *raison d'être* of eating rooms, should be relaxed occasions, conducive to lingering long after the food is finished – no-one will want to sit at the table longer than necessary if the lights are uncomfortably bright, the chairs hard, or the layout of the room awkward and unmanageable. Understanding what makes an eating room work, and how to adapt these principles to suit your particular needs, is important to the success of that room, and to the home as a whole.

The kitchen and eating space should be sensibly linked, with a minimum of hazards. If it is a trauma or physical challenge to transport a meal from the kitchen to the table, or to clear away the dishes, then the atmosphere in the eating room will suffer accordingly.

The formula for a successful eating room lies not in one particular style or layout, but varies according to the size of your family and its age span, whether you entertain a lot, and also according to the physical limitations of your home. The concept of a separate, formal dining room is redundant in many homes today, replaced by areas for eating in another room – or more than one, perhaps. The kitchen, living room, hall, possibly a bedroom, all offer potential eating spaces and, even in temperate climates, the garden or balcony is a seasonal option. Replacements for a self-contained eating room need not be second best, but ingenious solutions in their own right. The eating room always needs to be near the kitchen, but being hidebound by conventions may unnecessarily limit your choices. The checklist should help you realize the potential eating rooms in your house, help you improve the one you have or plan a new one, and clarify what is important about a space for eating in.

The ideal eating room could double as a playroom, study or private gallery, to display pictures or collections of small-scale objects, or it can be a haven for plants. The functional aspects need not preclude the exuberant or the frivolous: a successful eating room can be a showcase for your creativity and ingenuity, in both food and design.

EATING ROOMS
CHECKLIST

- Why do you eat where you do?
- Could you eat elsewhere?
- Is it possible to eat outside in comfort?
- What do you like/dislike about your eating area?
- How many people usually eat in this area?
- Can the area be extended to accommodate a larger number of people?
- How often is it used, and for how long?
- When is it most often in use:
  - breakfast?
  - lunch-time?
  - daylight?
  - evening?
- Is the space self-contained?
- Is it used for other purposes?

- Do you want continuity or separation between kitchen and dining areas?
- Do you need to integrate or isolate the eating area from the rest of the room it is in?
- Is there easy access to the kitchen?
- Is it easy to ferry food, cutlery and dishes between the table and the kitchen?
- Is the space easily maintained?
- Is it always on view, or in continual use?
- Is it subjected to a lot of wear and tear?
- What priority does the eating area have compared with other rooms?
- How much are you prepared to spend on it?
- How do you envisage your ideal eating area?

A formal setting for entertaining; bright daylight transforms it, reflecting off the pale elements of the room, while the Abutilon plant flourishes. A calm place for uninterrupted devotion to food.

Location

Eating rooms of today are quite likely to be incorporated into the living room or kitchen. In conventional modern houses, the short leg of an L-shaped living room is often devoted to an eating area; in kitchens, one stretch of a long wall, fitted with a narrow counter and bar stools, becomes the 'breakfast room'.

In older houses, originally designed with separate, self-contained dining rooms, it is common practice to 'open up' the interconnecting living and eating rooms to give one large living room, more generously proportioned.

Where separate eating rooms do exist, they are frequently given additional roles, usually as a secondary alternative to the living room. A dining room can become a quiet backwater where homework can be done at the table, or books read in a comfortable chair. A small desk in the dining room means one less person in the living room, and less chance of conflicting activities. This multiple usage of the eating room is doubly important if the living room is small, or the family is large with a wide range of age groups and interests. Unless formal dining is a major feature of your life, never try to maintain the isolated splendour of a separate dining room at the expense of the rest of the house.

Although the proximity of the kitchen is of prime importance, many houses often offer unexpected spots or corners for eating in. The hallway of an older house, for example, may be wide enough for a drop-leaf table and folding chairs, which can be hung up when not in use. Likewise, the landing may well be sunnier and more spacious than a conventional eating area; ornamental screens can be used to stop any draughts. A small table and comfortable chairs in a bedroom can be the ideal place for early-morning breakfast or a late supper.

Eating in a conservatory, or sunroom, is a special treat; in early spring and late autumn, when the sun is pleasant but the outside air cold, you can enjoy the feeling of being in a garden and still be comfortable. In fine weather, use the garden, verandah or balcony for outdoor eating.

The eating room is the most chameleon-like of all the rooms in the house: just as the ideal living room may alter its appearance, or even its position in the house, as your needs change, so will the eating room. If you have very young children, you may choose to use the eating room as a playroom, too, and then later, as the children grow, turn it into an eating room/study. If you're prepared to be adaptable, it could become one of the most useful rooms in the house.

1 *A dining area defined by only the table and chairs, close to the kitchen and with a practical floor.*
2 *Eating in the kitchen – literally.*
3 *A French country dining room.*
4 *Simply stylish – black-and-white tiles offset a white table beside the kitchen.*

5 *A tiny table, set against the window of a French country bedroom, where breakfast is laid for two. Eating in rooms other than those usually associated with food is sometimes essential, often practical and always pleasant, provided you can sit down at a table and enjoy a meal in comfort rather than trying to balance a tray on your knees. This arrangement will double as a study area.*

6 *A black wire screen partly divides the dining and living areas in a sparse apartment created in black and white. A glass-topped table designed by Le Corbusier stands on an Eileen Gray carpet. Above it, on a wall that partitions off the kitchen, is a Jim Dine print.*

Planning

The table is the centre of any eating area. There should be ample room to move around it when serving a meal. Often placing the table to one side of a room, or even against a wall, is the best choice; it can be pulled out when numbers necessitate, or when you want to extend it or raise the drop leaves.

A round table will accommodate more people comfortably than a rectangular one, and conveys a feeling of informality as there is no 'head' of table. Where space is at an absolute premium, corner tables or small tables that fit into bay windows or other recesses are worth considering; so are narrow bars or countertops running along at right angles to the walls.

Your choice of table should be influenced by utility as much as style. Remember, elegant table-cloths can disguise the most mundane surfacing underneath, if the occasion calls for it.

In former times, complete dining-room suites – a table, chairs and sideboard – were the norm. But you can successfully combine Victorian chairs with a contemporary white melamine table, perhaps, or modern Italian steel and leather chairs with a blond oak table. Chairs themselves could be mixed and matched, as long as they have a common visual theme.

Choose chairs that are comfortable, and allow plenty of room for knees between the seat and the table's under-rail. Chairs with arms may be more comfortable, but they take up more room and might not fit so easily under the table when the meal is over. In tiny spaces, chairs that stack and fold up are sensible, although only a few are really comfortable. Banquettes – permanently fixed, upholstered benches – are another possibility. Stools are space savers, too, and can be tucked under bars or countertops when not in use, but make sure footrests are provided for comfort.

If you eat in the living room and chairs have to do double duty, they should have reasonably firm back supports and be easy to carry from one part of the room to another.

If you have the room, a sideboard is useful for storing cutlery, china and glasses; the top, usually considerably higher than the table, is the ideal place to carve meat, and it's where you can keep the condiments, and leave the salads, fruits, cheeses and the wine for following courses. Where space is more limited, low, narrow built-in cupboards might be a better choice. If you're using the room for other purposes – sewing or homework, for example – there should be ample storage which is quick and easy to get at, so the table

can be cleared for meals in a matter of minutes.

Open shelves are display shelves, whether intentionally or by default. Dishes should be stacked or organized neatly. Favourite pieces of china can be displayed more prominently, vertically on shelving. Cabinets with glass doors look good and will protect the contents from dust and accidental knocks, although the glass itself will need regular cleaning.

The lighting should emphasize the importance of the table, while additional, secondary lighting can be used to illuminate displays or pictures on the walls. There should always be enough light so you can see what you're eating, but it shouldn't be harsh; dimmer switches are invaluable in creating the right mood. A central, over-the-table light with a high-watt bulb should have the bottom half of the bulb silvered, to avoid glare.

If there is a doorway between the eating

room and kitchen, a door that swings both ways is sensible, as long as there is enough 'swinging' space – but it needs a window, otherwise you might have a nasty collision with someone opening it the other way. Vertically folding louvred doors need less space, while horizontally divided stable doors combine access with a certain amount of privacy.

A trolley can be highly functional; it's invaluable for wheeling in dishes of food. If the eating room is above the kitchen, it may be worth considering the installation of a dumb waiter.

When the eating room is part of the kitchen or living room, then you may want to isolate the eating area. Waist-high storage units will define it and provide storage and worktop facilities at the same time. Or decorative screens could be used to enclose the eating area for special meals.

1 *A specially designed drinks trolley lives in the hall to be wheeled between living and dining rooms.*
2 *A contemporary version of the traditional sideboard gives essential space for serving and clearing in a formal dining room.*
3 *Converting a basement has provided an open expanse for a dining table. The area beneath the stairs (4) is fitted with shelves and wine racks, creating an attractive display, practical storage and a serving surface.*

5 *The beautiful curved shapes of a kitchen finished in terrazzo harmonize with the cool greys and silver of the dining area beyond.*
6 *American, nineteenth-century country style for the informal dining area of a weekend home on Long Island. A rustic atmosphere, created by the exposed wooden frames of the cabin and the kitchen units, is accentuated by old pottery and other objects displayed on open shelves.*

Eating-room style

The functional approach to eating-room style is the best starting point. Uncluttered space, however large or small, provides the setting for the main attractions: delicious food and friendly conversation. The way the space is used in different societies and in various types of eating places can be inspirational; you can take the elements you like and that would really work in your environment, mix them with flair, and produce a room that is strikingly different. But there should be a smooth transition in style, mood and tempo from the eating room to its neighbour.

The austerity of the Japanese tea ceremony room is a good source of inspiration: light wood; neutral matting or carpeting; pale colours or white; and paper or fabric screens and lampshades that produce diffused light. Furniture is kept to a minimum and the proportions of the room are paramount.

An interesting contrast is the 'high-tech' use of clean-lined materials, such as steel, rubber, glass and plastic, in accordance with the principle 'less is more'. But unremitting technological and industrial imagery can be cold and inhuman – alien and anonymous once the first thrill has worn off. Taking away the hardest edges by introducing soft, warm-coloured carpets, perhaps, or fabric blinds, is one way to 'domesticate' and personalize it.

Farmhouse eating rooms also rely on robust simplicity and honest use of materials, but convey warmth and coziness. Farmhouse-type furniture tends to be large and you can translate it carefully into scaled-down objects and images: wooden shelves reminiscent of a full-sized dresser; a small but perfect wood-and-tile wash-stand; high-backed chairs with rush seating instead of heavier farmhouse chairs. Lighting is soft and diffuse and the overall feel is one of gentle accumulation of objects rather than a contrived imposition of style.

If the room you eat in is bathed in light, make the most of it. White or warm terracotta-coloured walls, Mediterranean-style, with the woodwork painted surprisingly bright contrasting colours; mellow woods and simple furniture; blue-and-white ceramic tiles or clear glazed ones; stone or ceramic flooring with colourful rugs; baskets of fruit and vegetables; fine muslin curtains to filter the light, under bright Provençal cottons, all add up to a powerful, hot-climate image. It is a combination that invites the presence of plants – a jungle of specimen shrubs, trees and climbing plants in pots. Place the plants near a window, so the leaves filter the light.

There is a lot to be learned from small restaurants – French brasseries and bistros,

for instance. They are designed for comfort, efficiency, durability and a welcoming atmosphere. Minimal space is maximized by the brasserie-type bar, which is used for storage, for displaying and serving food, as well as for eating. Small cast-iron and wood-topped tables combine sturdiness, utility and charm – qualities equally desirable in a domestic setting. Mirrors increase the feeling of space, and a single fabric can be used for table-cloths, napkins and curtains. Tableware is simple and stackable, and looks as good on the home front as in a restaurant.

You may have the space you need for a separate dining room. The absence of any other purpose to the room, actual or implied, brings with it a certain formality. In particular, the preparation of food and kitchen activities are excluded from view; cooking implements, so much a part of informal eating rooms, have no place in this environment.

A formal dining room can be richly coloured, or sombre and artificially lit, or it can be bright, airy and full of sunshine. But it is first and foremost a room that is all about eating – the food and its presentation may be simple, but its distribution and consumption are well-ordered activities, done to a set and predictable pattern – and it is where the act of eating together becomes a stylish ceremony.

1 *A converted warehouse in London. The dining table is positioned so the adjoining kitchen is partly obscured – away from the sink and cooking area. Exposed pipes and wires have been rationalized to give the room a clean, minimal style. The full-length, arched windows flood the area with light and brightly illuminate the broad expanse of polished wood floor, which is perhaps the most important element in any minimal room.*

2 *Each object in this spacious room was chosen for its antique elegance.*
3 *Delicate charm created with pretty objects and decorative finishes. A plain trestle table is covered in old linen with scalloped edges and cut-work motifs. The floral frieze is based on an early twentieth-century design, and the 1920s bead lampshade suits the nostalgic style.*

4 *Earthy country living – antler hat-pegs, animal prints, sturdy Victorian furniture in a small English cottage.*
5 *An enthusiast for Japanese interiors built this almost authentic dining room; note the loudspeakers in the ceiling.*

Family eating rooms

Although the primary function of a meal is to consume food, family meals are also social events, perhaps the only time in the day when parents and children can sit and talk comfortably. Relaxed, congenial surroundings are vital, and the eating area must be sturdy and resilient enough to accommodate children and their spillings, while attractive enough to be used for adult entertaining. If you are fortunate to have more than one eating area in your house, then the problem is easy to solve: one eating area can be 'child-proofed' and the other assigned for 'adults only'. However, it is far more likely to be a question of compromise, with one eating area serving adults and children alike.

Washable surfaces are the key to relaxed dining with children. If the eating area is part of the kitchen – often an ideal arrangement where very young children are concerned – then wall tiles, such as rough hewn quarry tiles, in shades of russet, brick red and brown, or pristine white, glazed china tiles, are as attractive as they are suitable. Or vinyl wall-papers can be elegant yet totally child-proof.

Carpeting is never absolutely necessary, but is considered by many to be an essential part of comfortable living. Beautifully polished wood floors can be just as elegant, and cork and quarry tiles have their own informal charm, but if your heart is set on carpeting, then choose a durable one with a pattern or even a slight fleck to the weave; these show stains far less than pale, single-coloured carpets. Plastic sheeting under the chair (and throwing span!) of a small child may look less than picture perfect, but protects the carpet from the worst bombardments.

Not only food lands on the floor, but also cutlery, plates and glasses. It is simply not worth the continual tension involved to use expensive china and fine glass at this stage. You should be able to find good-looking, inexpensive tableware – china and glasses attractive enough to live with which won't break the bank when they break. Another option is to have one dinner service for the adults in the family and have another set that is reserved especially for the children: it could be plain, inexpensive plates in a mixture of bright colours, for example, and brightly coloured plastic tumblers.

The table itself must be fully protected if it's a 'good' one – it is certainly sensible to use protective pads. White laminated plastic tables stand up well to the wear and tear of family life and can still look good if dressed up with crystal and china for adult entertaining. Old wooden pine or oak tables are equally impervious, but transparent protective coating against the worst stains – red wine as well as baby food – is in order.

Checked plastic table-cloths or solid-coloured oilcloths may provide the civilized feeling that you long for, while not committing you to endless hours of washing and ironing. Unless you are a glutton for punishment, linen napkins are best left for special occasions, and easy-care poly-cotton ones provided for day-to-day meals.

If the cabinets or sideboard in your eating room contain precious things – best china and crystal, for example – it would be wise to make sure that tiny hands cannot open the doors and turn out the contents.

1 *The basement of a terrace house has been dug out – the increased space is used to good effect. The U-shaped units divide the room so that the central area is used for cooking, food preparation and washing-up, while either end of the room is free for eating. At one end is a relaxed round table for family get-togethers and formal meals. At the other, an ingenious breakfast bar that slides out from under the worktop is situated beside a window that catches the morning light.*

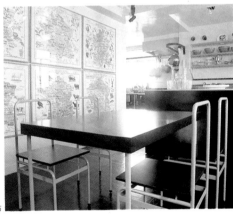

2 *Practical and atmospheric – a vast wooden table doubles as the work surface and centre of all life in a French country retreat.*

3 *A long low room, reminiscent of a cave but brightened by sunshine and white walls. A tribe can be seated at the lengthy table.*

4 *A small galley kitchen off a compact dining area with an unusual corner window.*

5 *Wipe-clean floors and surfaces – essential in a family room and never more so than one with a bold black finish, which provides great contrast to the bright white walls and colourful horticultural maps of France.*

Outdoor eating rooms

Wherever you live, whatever the climate, there will always be perfect summer days when you will want to eat outdoors. And the better the climate, the more sense it makes to plan your garden, terrace or balcony so that you have the option of eating outdoors. You'll need a degree of privacy, a reasonably level surface, adequate seating and some shelter from winds or the blazing sun. High walls, hedges, fences and shrubbery will act as a windbreak and screen, while forming 'walls' of an outdoor room and providing a sense of enclosure that can make eating outdoors more enjoyable.

It helps if the eating area is not too far from the kitchen; otherwise, the cook and helpers will be faced with seemingly endless treks back and forth. The path from kitchen to eating area should be smooth and even, with a minimum of level changes and tricky corners to negotiate. Of course, you can always cook outside on a barbecue – choose one for its looks as well as function. An open fireplace is simply made of fireproof bricks; you could even go as far as building a bread oven in the garden – it looks good and bakes wonderful pizzas. A nice view is another 'optional extra': if the view is less than

perfect, then an inward-looking, self-contained area – a vine-covered pergola, perhaps – could be a better solution, again walled in by hedges, shrubs, walls or fences.

You may be able to follow the sun and the seasons around the garden with a series of outdoor eating rooms: an east-facing sheltered 'breakfast' spot, to catch the early morning sun; a place that faces south (or north, in the Southern Hemisphere) for afternoon warmth, with dappled shade provided by trees or a pergola; and a west-facing 'room' to catch the last of the afternoon sun, where you can relax with tea, drinks or dinner. If this approach is not possible – and for most people it won't be – then choose the best spot in terms of sunlight and proximity to the kitchen.

Furniture should be durable and heavy enough to withstand the elements, or else light and portable. Solid oak or teak are good examples of the former (wooden furniture should be slatted to allow for drainage of rainwater); folding canvas chairs or directors' chairs fit the second category. White-painted wood will look charming against a background of greenery, but will need regular repainting. Add brightly coloured cushions

and pillows for extra comfort and visual interest. Above all, seating should be as attractive and as comfortable as possible.

Adults and children alike enjoy sitting on smooth lawns, preferably on a garden blanket to avoid grass stains. Low walls or benches provide additional informal seating, and so do wide, low steps.

There is nothing more magical than a summer evening meal, served outdoors. If you want permanent electric lighting, it's best to get professional advice. Candles, flares and fairy lights can look great and could be augmented discreetly by lighting from within the house.

There are several quite different approaches you can take with tableware. Earthenware pottery – in the terracottas, the green and yellow opaque glazes of the Mediterranean, or bright and hand-painted – is perfect. Or use light, unbreakable melamine plates and bowls in neutrals or bright colours. For dramatic evenings, set the table with your best silver, china, crystal and table linen.

However colourful and sweetly scented the garden is, vases of cut flowers or bowls of fresh and fragrant herbs are always a perfect finishing touch.

1 *An outdoor room shaded with slatted blinds that match duckboard flooring and wooden seats. The dappled sunlight completes a delightful setting for summer eating.*

2 *An inspiring location put to best use in this superb outdoor room.*
3 *Another wonderful view, if you can look beyond the enticing open-air buffet.*
4 *A small balcony complete with barbecue and hanging baskets to hold ingredients.*

5 *A laden table for an outdoor feast in beautiful surroundings.*
6 *Candlelight creates the mood for an intimate balcony meal.*

BEDROOMS

More than any other room in the house, your bedroom is the place where you can shut the door on the world, strip off all the trappings of the day and surround yourself with things that give you pleasure. It should be a haven – perhaps a love nest, a work-room or a second sitting room. What is most important is that it should be wonderfully comfortable and re-laxing.

Remember, your bedroom is the most personal place in the house; plan it so that it's a room that you look forward to sleeping, waking and living in.

The primary function of a bedroom is to provide you with somewhere to sleep. But, for many people, it is a multi-purpose room, with secondary functions that are almost as important. But if sleeping is the main activity you plan for the room, your task will be much simpler. You can allow the bed to be the dominant feature in whatever style suits you best – from four-poster luxury to bold futon simplicity. All other furniture can be kept to the minimum, and the decorations can be chosen, bearing in mind that it is essentially a night-time room that is seen mainly under artificial lighting.

If the bedroom is also to be your work-room, say, or double as a living room, the emphasis will shift from the bed to reflect the room's other function. You may even want to disguise the bed altogether. Turning it into a room that is inviting in daytime, as well as at night, means rethinking colours and furnish-ings. Lighting requirements multiply, more furniture is needed, and the bed moves off-stage a little – although it is still the most important piece of furniture in the house, often the difference between a good and a bad night's sleep, and should be chosen with the utmost care.

The smaller the space you have to work with, the more carefully you must plan your bedroom, especially if it has to work for you in a number of different ways. Good planning at the beginning, with an emphasis on comfort and storage, will save a lot of problems later on in the decorating process.

Whatever other role it may have, and whether it is large or small, a bedroom is concerned with moods. This is where you must be able to fall asleep easily; when you wake up, you should see the new day – and your bedroom – in the best possible light. And, of course, this could be a room for making love in, so invest in the best bed you can afford, fit soft carpet, choose colours and patterns that you love and you're sure you can live with, and make sure that the lighting is subtle and flattering, as well as practical.

1 *The guest bedroom of a converted chapel in southern France is a calm retreat. The rustic simplicity of the room has been maintained with an old iron bed, plaster walls, a wood floor, and tones of grey and cream, plus a few carefully selected objects.*
2 *Simplicity offers the best use of a small space – attractive basic colours, functional furniture and little else.*

BEDROOMS
CHECKLIST

- Is the room for one person, or to be shared?
- How near is it to the bathroom/toilet?
- Would it be possible to install an *en suite* bathroom/shower?
- Is the room to have a second purpose?
- How much storage space do you need?
- Do you want built-in or free-standing storage?
- Do you want a separate dressing room?
- Does the room get the sun in the morning or evening, or never?
- Do you prefer to wake in a dark or light room?
- Is the room soundproof, or will you need heavy curtains and carpet to cut down noise?
- Is there room for visitors, children's friends to stay overnight?
- What kind of flooring do you want?
- Are there enough socket outlets near the bed?
- Is there a switch to control all the lighting by the bed?
- What facilities do you want close to the bed:
  - telephone?
  - tea/coffee-maker?
  - stereo?
  - radio?
  - alarm?
  - television/video?

Beds and bedding

The bed

Your bed is undoubtedly the most important piece of furniture you own. You spend about a third of your life lying on it and if it's poor quality, your waking life can be affected. Beds that are old, lumpy, far too soft or unyieldingly rigid are bad for your spine and don't allow the restful sleep you need for good health.

The best kind of bed is the one that feels right to you. Whether firm or softer, it should give you adequate support. Those who suffer from backache tend to prefer a firm bed. When you test a bed, the heaviest parts of your body should make an impression; you should feel comfortable but the bed should not be so soft that it moulds itself to your shape. Double beds that have two connecting mattresses offer a chance for couples to each find their perfect level of comfort.

However good your bed, the expected life is only between ten and fifteen years. The exception is a bed with a wooden base: the base will last indefinitely, although the mattress will need to be changed.

When buying a bed, always shop around, and don't be embarrassed to lie on a bed to test it: take ten minutes or so to get its feel while lying in your usual sleeping position. Look for a bed that is at least 150mm (6in) longer than the taller person sleeping in it, and wide enough for you to be able to link hands behind your head without your elbows hanging over the edge.

Once you have chosen the right base and mattress, you can dress up the basic shape to create whatever effect you want.

The bed base

Bases come in three types:
Firm-edge The springs are attached to a wooden outer frame. This is a good choice if the bed is to double as a seating unit, because wear on the outer edge of the mattress is limited.
Sprung-edge The springs are mounted on a wooden base and are continued right to the edge of the base. This type of base is more expensive, but tends to prolong the life of the mattress.
Wooden A cheaper and perfectly adequate alternative, as a good mattress will provide all the support you need. Look for flexibly mounted slatted bases made from laminated wood with a sealing coat of lacquer. A central support for a double bed should be used to stop the slats sagging. Some solid bases are called 'orthopaedic', which is not a medical definition – it refers to the fact that these are harder than usual. Pallet bases are made for use with futon mattresses; they're low slung and slatted.

The mattress

As a rough guide, the more you pay for a mattress, the better quality you get. In a sprung mattress, price is determined by the quality and number of springs, as well as the stuffing and covering. Foam mattresses also come in different grades – the more superior, of course, being most expensive.

Whatever type of mattress you choose, the covering material should be made of natural fibres so that the mattress can breathe. Synthetic fibres tend to be slippery, so bedclothes have a tendency to slide off.

Mattresses, like bases, come in three main types:
Pocket-sprung Each spring is set individually into a calico pocket and moves independently, which means the springs only give where weight is applied. This makes them ideal for double beds: when one person moves, the other's part of the mattress remains relatively undisturbed. If the couple are of uneven weights, the heavier partner won't cause the mattress to slope. For these reasons, this is the most expensive of the mattress options.
Open-sprung The most common type of sprung mattress, this has a system of continuously interlinked springs that operate as one unit, allowing the press- ure to be spread evenly through- out the mattress. On a double bed, it will hammock towards the heavier person. Posture spring- ing is a more sophisticated and expensive version of open springing.
Foam Top choice for people who suffer from dust-induced aller- gies, although the synthetic foam can be hot to lie on in the summer. The best quality foam can be as expensive as a sprung mattress: cheap foam is usually thin and unyielding. Not suitable if you smoke in bed.

Bedding

There's a hard choice to be made between sheets and blankets, and easy, convenient duvets (quilts). You should think about comfort, preference, cost and look; also consider the implica- tions of time and maintenance. The traditional bed needs much more time to keep it looking good: you might love the idea of a bed with crisp linen sheets and layers of beautiful blankets, but, if you're always pressed for time, ironing the sheets will be a chore, and probably you'll leave the bed rumpled and unmade.

Duvets (quilts)

A duvet, or quilt, is simply a lightweight filling caught in a bag, which is then enclosed in a re- movable cover. The duvet insu-

American quilt with kelim rug

Fine lined black iron four-poster

A cheerful wool blanket

Traditional embroidery, brass bed

lates and warms you without weighing you down. Most duvets are constructed with vertically channelled seams, so that the filling is evenly distributed.

What most people like best about duvets is their warmth and lightness. And, of course, the other advantage is that, with a fitted bottom sheet, a bed can be made in a matter of seconds. Choose a duvet that is at the very least 450mm (18in) wider than the bed.

Unlike blankets, duvets are virtually dust-free; some have non-allergenic fillings.

Down Pure down fillings are the best of all. Eider duck down is the very best and most expensive, followed by white goose, and then ordinary duck down. Down is taken from the breast of the bird, is supremely light and warm (its natural function is to insulate the bird) and has no quill shaft to coarsen its softness.

Down and feather combinations Feather is inferior to down – it is heavier, and its insulating properties are not as good. So, the greater the proportion of down to feather, the warmer and lighter the duvet will be. If a filling is listed as 'down and feather' there will be more down than in a 'feather and down' combination.

Wool Combed wool fillings are very warm, but much heavier than feather or synthetic fillings.

They can't be washed, but must be dry-cleaned.

Synthetics These fillings are very much cheaper than any natural ones, so, if you're going for synthetics, it's worth buying from the more expensive types. Cheaper fillings don't mould themselves to the shape of the body well, so are not as warm. But synthetics are the most easily washable duvets and are good for people allergic to feathers.

Blankets

Convenient as duvets are, for many they will never replace the traditional blankets, which come in beautiful colours and patterns and in a mixture of fibres.

When you are buying blankets, make sure they are long enough to tuck in comfortably.

Wool At the luxury end of the range, there are merino wool, cashmere and long-pile mohair blankets. All are light, soft and warm. Cheaper, all-wool blankets tend to be heavier.

Cotton Cotton blankets are usually cellular – that is, woven into a honeycomb design. They are very light and warm, but should be used in conjunction with a normal-weave top blanket.

Synthetics These are easy to care for, and the more expensive, branded synthetics are hard-wearing. They trap heat, but

don't breathe in the same way as natural fibres, so they can make you over-heated.

Bed-linen

These days, sheets, pillowcases and duvet covers come in all sorts of design and colour combinations. It is usually recommended that duvets are not covered with a bedspread, so the design of the bed-linen makes an important contribution to the look of the room. If buying bed-linen before finally deciding how to decorate the room, play safe with white or a plain colour. You can choose from a number of different fabrics.

Linen Linen is expensive, but worth buying if you can afford it simply because it lasts practically forever, improves with age, and is actually stronger when wet, which means that repeated washings won't weaken it. On the minus side, it must be ironed after washing.

Cotton There are different qualities of cotton. The finest grade, percale, is like silk; but all cottons are also good and hard-wearing. Like linen, it should be ironed, unless treated with an easy-care finish. The exception is brushed cotton (which is very warm and comfortable in winter, but not so pleasant in summer).

Cotton/synthetic blends The feel and look of these sheets is

very similar to cotton, but the synthetic content makes them easy to care for.

Synthetic These are usually all-nylon. Easy-care, but they feel off-putting: slippery but slightly rough, can be very hot to sleep in and produce static electricity.

Pillows

The test of a good pillow is quite simple: balance it on one hand and it should hold its shape; if it droops, then it is too soft or old. (The exception is a foam pillow – it doesn't droop, but is uncomfortable to sleep on.) The type of filling affects the price – an expensive one will keep its shape longer.

Down Usually down from duck or goose is used. The most expensive pillows, they are exceptionally soft, light and resilient.

Down and feather mixtures The feather content makes the pillow firmer. As with duvets, combinations labelled 'down and feather' have more down than feather.

Polyesters Much cheaper than the natural fillings, these also have the advantage of being germ-repellent, non-allergenic and washable. Some have the softness and resilience of natural filling.

Latex Also germ-resistant, non-allergenic and washable. But pillows are very springy, which can be unpleasant.

Elegant, high-level bed alcove

A bright and inexpensive canopy

A sumptuous, draped four-poster

Simpicity and flexibility – a futon

Decoration and design

1 *A Milan workshed converted to a magnificent open-plan home. A simple partition placed below the exposed gables provides a clean, white backdrop to the white bed. Beyond it is the bathroom area (2), using a fine old double sink found discarded on a rubbish tip.*
3 *Restrained harmony, with a considered mixture of traditional decorative patterns, each with a harmonizing curved design.*

4 An 'explorer's' camp bed, complete with dyed mosquito net and matching sheeting, fits well into a corner eyrie of an Australian loft. A simple wooden chair is painted to match the ceiling.

5 Great style derives from this attractive arrangement of beautiful but inexpensive second-hand items, including an unusual glazed screen which lets in the light from the handsome bay window. They look their best in a room with the plainest decoration.

259

Bedroom style

For some people, the morning atmosphere of a bedroom is the most important. Sunlight – or the lack of it – can affect the way you start the day. The impression of light in a bedroom can be increased by using a colour that will enhance even the gentlest winter sun – warm pinks and yellows, for instance. Greens and blues have the reverse effect, giving the room a cool, fresh feel. Pure white reflects the light and provides a good backdrop for bright, patterned fabrics.

If you want a comforting, relaxing room, you'll find that the softest colours will work best – from warm light tones to the earthy, friendly colours such as terracotta, tobacco and honey.

The sorts of colours and patterns you choose for a bedroom can feel quite inappropriate if you're using the room for another purpose; on the other hand, too vivid and bright a colour scheme might be disturbing when you want to relax or have to use the room as a sick-room. So you'll probably need to compromise a little, if you're planning a dual-purpose room.

Ceilings

Since this is the one room in which the ceiling is likely to be looked at almost as much as the walls, you could make a feature of it. Choose a dominant colour from the room's scheme, or a contrasting one, or pick out the mouldings in a complementary colour. Another option is to stencil a pattern around the edges of the ceiling, or, if you have the ability, fresco it. Alternatively, you could cover it with mirror, although there is a danger that it will end up looking like a New Orleans brothel.

Pattern choices

The bed is a large piece of furniture; covered with patterned fabric it could easily dominate the room, so other patterns and textures should be chosen with this in mind. Patterns can be flowery, abstract or paisleys; Indonesian batiks could be combined with woven striped cottons and soft, fine muslins; plain calico bedspreads are versatile and can be livened up with a mixture of wonderfully patterned cushions. Mix soft earth colours and intricate patterns – reds, golds and browns look good with polished floors and Oriental rugs.

The most common choices for bedspreads in the past were lovely old quilts, often embroidered or made of patchwork, and these are still popular today. But you can be more imaginative – for example, an intricate antique shawl, a fragile rug, or a patchwork of old fabric can be folded in a triangle at the end of the bed over a plain-coloured bedspread.

Floors

Wall-to-wall carpeting is an obvious choice for a room where you spend much of the time barefoot, and it doesn't have to be expensive. A bedroom carpet is not subject to much wear, so needn't be of the highest quality; neither does it have to be a 'sensible' colour or pattern.

What is most important is that the floor is smooth and warm underfoot. Stripped and polished floorboards or cork tiles are possibilities, as is a cushioned vinyl floor. If you have decided against using carpet, rugs add areas of softness and colour to any flooring.

1 *On a platform overlooking the dining room of a Wiltshire cottage is this extravagantly colourful four-poster. The surrounding rust-red walls carry a subtle traditional pattern. The bed posts were once street lamps and they carry a canopy of appliquéd cotton roof-cloth from India, enriched with silk tassels. The bed is further draped with a collection of patterned rugs and blankets in toning red and black, and ornate velvet cushions.*

2 *A clever use of red quilting gives strong definition to the bed in a minimal room designed to give focus to the coloured objects in it. The table is laminated in blue and the floor painted with white gloss.*

3 *Yards of white netting hung on bamboo poles and catching the sunshine from the roof-light add romance to a simple attic bedroom. The pale blue of the carpet is emphasized by the darker blue Venetian blinds covering floor-level interior windows.*

4 *English country-house style: every object in this elegant, traditionally furnished bedroom is finely crafted. An arabesque theme runs through the decoration – in the antique Indian carpet, the crewel-embroidered bedcover, and the carved bench.*

Bedroom furniture

Bedrooms can get untidy very quickly. In smallish rooms where space is at a premium, it is especially important that every available bit of space can be used fully. Use the space under the bed, for example, for storing things that you don't need everyday.

Built-in cupboards and drawers look neat, and can be custom-made to suit your requirements exactly. You can buy cheaper fitted storage units, many of which come with a comprehensive range of pull-out drawers, adjustable clothes racks, hooks and shoe racks. Shallow drawers are more effective than deep drawers, and see-through perspex (acrylic) or wire drawers allow you to keep track of where your socks and shirts are.

Units can be 'customized' by changing the handles or painting the doors. Or replace the doors with mirrored ones to increase the feeling of light and space.

But fitted and built-in storage units don't suit every room, and, in any case, you may prefer the look of traditional free-standing chests of drawers, dressing tables and so on. It is often quite easy to increase their storage capacity; with a wardrobe, for instance, if the clothes you hang up are short, you can add another lower rail to double the amount of hanging space, or fit some shelves in the empty space underneath.

If you tend to throw your clothes on the floor on the way to bed, keep a chair nearby so they won't look quite so unruly.

By the bedside

Design for convenience: you'll need plenty of bedside-table space for reading lamp, telephone, books and water glasses. If you are fond of listening to music, make sure the controls of your radio and stereo systems are within reach of the bed, and choose a television set with a remote control.

Whether you write novels in bed, as Marcel Proust did, or are simply fond of breakfasting there, a sturdy bed table will be more stable than a tray. The ones used in hospitals are adjustable with wheels, so can be pushed out of the way when not in use; they are not particularly beautiful, however, but could be the model for a custom-made one.

Dressing rooms

If you have the space, consider equipping a dressing room. It doesn't have to be attached to the bedroom – any small and unused room will do. The storage can be more utilitarian than that you would choose for the bedroom – manufacturers' dress racks for your clothes, for instance, and shelves for the clothes that are to be folded away.

1 *A modern storage system of wire rack shelving which can be assembled to form practical and attractive open storage for clothes. Alternatively, it could be placed inside a cupboard.*

2 *A narrow corridor connects a bathroom and bedroom (3) and acts as a compact storage area for clothes and accessories. It has been fitted with custom-made drawers and shelves to create an ingenious walk-in wardrobe and dressing room.*
4 *A bookworm's ideal bed – complete with attached bookshelf.*

5 *Taking a Japanese theme in a bedroom has led to careful detailing in wood and a spacious clothes cupboard fronted with wood and paper 'screens'.*
6 *An alcove in the same room is fitted with neat multi-purpose shelves and drawers. The sliding screens on the windows match those on the wardrobe.*

Bedroom atmosphere

You can alter the whole feel of a room at the flick of a light switch. Getting the lights right can be complicated, particularly if your bedroom serves a different purpose come daytime. The key is to choose a lighting system that is versatile – one that can be adjusted easily, is controlled by readily accessible switches, preferably dimmers, and gives a soft, romantic light. At the same time, you'll need adequate lighting for dressing, making-up, reading and so on.

It's a great bore to have to get out of bed to switch out the light. Make sure you have on-off switches by the bed, as well as by the door, to control all the lighting in the room. A bedside lamp on each side of a double bed is better than a single light – one person can read, when the other wants to sleep.

Concealed strip lighting fitted round the edge of the room gives a gentle and indirect light that can be complemented by bedside lamps or spotlights. Adjustable wall spotlights can be used to throw light off the ceiling or can be pointed downwards for bed-time reading. Ceiling-mounted tracking is versatile; individual spots can be moved to highlight any feature in the room.

Your clothes cupboard (closet) could benefit from its own concealed lighting. The mirror above a dressing table or bedroom basin (sink) should be well lit for make-up and shaving purposes, ideally by a strip-light with a diffusing shade. The light should be in front of you so that it shines on your face, rather than behind you.

Natural light

Just as important as artificial lighting is how you treat natural light. If you like to wake up to a bright room, you could hang soft muslin curtains, light blinds or, perhaps, fine, unlined cotton over your windows. You may be able to dispense with curtains altogether, particularly if you have a bedroom that opens on to a balcony (but position your bed so that you don't wake up directly facing a bright window, which could give you a bad headache). The disadvantage of treating windows in these ways, however, is that you miss out on the insulation qualities of heavy, lined curtains.

For those who prefer to sleep in a darkened room, outside shutters provide a good alternative to curtains and blinds; they let in air yet block out the light.

An unjustly neglected source of bedroom light is an open fire; it produces a warm, subtle glow of the most romantic kind. If you're lucky enough to have a fireplace in your bedroom, make sure you use it!

1

2

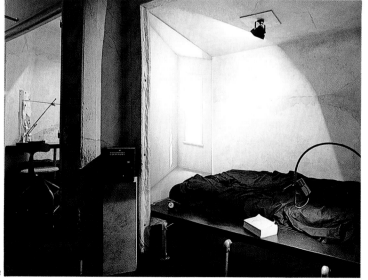

3

1 *Bedrooms require adequate light sources that are both practical, for reading in bed, and relaxing. This is achieved here with modern twin floor lamps, while a third lamp lights the table opposite.*
2 *Tungsten halogen tubes give gentle light perfectly suited to this strongly designed bedroom, where the disused fireplace serves as a bedhead.*

3 *'Distressed' walls enhance the cave-like atmosphere of this attic room. A single spotlight casts an interesting shadow that highlights the shape; the curved arm of a reading lamp provides adjustable light to read by.*

4

5

4 The carefully preserved rustic atmosphere in a mountain chalet calls for candlelight as a final, authentic touch. This is a romantic way to light bedrooms, but special attention must be given to safety.

5 Tizio lamps adorn a storage unit, which has been designed to make good use of a narrow room.

6 Few objects can beat the atmospheric impact of an old four-poster bed draped with flowing fabric. This magnificent nineteenth-century bed in an Indian house is covered with striped gauze, in harmony with the blue sprigs on the bedding material, and it is matched with a swivel mirror of similar vintage. The final touch for tropical atmosphere is the ceiling fan.

6

BATHROOMS

The bathroom is invariably one of the most awkward rooms in the house to design and decorate successfully; most are so small they demand rigorous planning and compromise to make them even workable, while larger rooms need equally careful treatment if they are not to look bare and clinical. You must get the functional aspects right in a room that must be for relaxation.

Moving the bathroom can be expensive. But its location is crucial, so it could be money well spent. Consider carefully whether your present bathroom is conveniently placed. It should be easily accessible from the bedrooms; ideally, with a separate toilet near the living area. If you have a large household, a second bathroom or shower room will be a good idea; it could be connected to a bedroom. Even the smallest, most awkward space can be fitted with a corner bath or sit-down tub, compact shower and pull-out bidet. If you're building the bathroom from scratch, leave out the toilet and give it a room of its own; or add an extra toilet and shower room.

When you plan a new bathroom – preferably in consultation with an architect or plumber familiar with local building and water regulations – you must consider the layout of existing water pipes, sewage outlets and air exhaust ducts. Extensive alterations to any of these can add considerably to the costs (see *PLUMBING*). Use materials that are moisture-proof – never uncoated wallpapers, matt emulsion paint, corrodible metal or jute-backed carpets – and any joints or cracks should be well sealed with silicone sealants and caulks.

The bathroom can be leisurely and luxurious, or simply streamlined; it may have to double as a laundry with fitted washing machine and drier; or, if it has plenty of floor space, may be the ideal area in which to do your exercises.

While the bathroom must be functional and efficient, it would be a pity to ignore the therapeutic and pleasurable aspects of bathing when you are planning this room. Remember that this is where you can really unwind after an exhausting day. It should be a place where you can pamper yourself – treat it as a haven of peace and solitude; add a comfortable chair for languishing in after a hot bath and heated rails to warm towels, which will help ease the transition from steaming hot water to normal room temperature; install good lighting so you can read as well as groom yourself, and make sure all your bottles and lotions and loofahs are within arm's reach of the bath and shower.

1 *Grey marble 'slips' and white ceramic tiles underline the spatial quality of this beautiful bathroom. The mirror and towel rail came originally from London's Savoy Hotel.*
2 *A turn-of-the-century Milan house has been restored to the monochrome style of the original design. There are few touches of colour in the building, and none at all in the impressive black-and-white tiled bathroom.*

BATHROOMS
CHECKLIST

- How many bathrooms, showers and toilets do you need?
- Is/are your present bathroom/s well located?
- Do you want the toilet in the bathroom, or in a separate room?
- Will extensive plumbing work be required?
- How much hot water do you need? Is your present system adequate?
- Are you installing new bathroom fixtures?
- What fixtures do you need?
- Do you prefer showers to baths, or do you want both?
- What type of taps (faucets) do you want?
- What type of storage do you require, and how much?
- Do you need to make special safety provisions for old people or small children?
- Are the wall and floor surfaces suitable for the hot steamy atmosphere?
- Is the bathroom centrally heated, or does it need a separate room heater?
- What type of lighting do you need?
- Do you want shaver socket outlets?
- What accessories do you need?

Bathroom layout

Bathrooms, like kitchens, are expensive compared to the other rooms in the house. The fixtures are permanent, so it's important to get the layout right. This room must be functional, easy to keep clean, and durable; at the same time, it should be comfortable and pleasurable.

When you're planning your bathroom, use scale plans of both the room and fixtures to work out the most effective scheme. Remember to allow space for doors and windows to open; work out the position of taps, lights and thermostats; and make sure that bidets, basins (sinks) and toilets have knee and elbow room. If you are fitting laundry equipment, always provide good ventilation and drains for overflows. You'll need plenty of space for towels and household linen, hair driers, shavers and lotions. Towel rails should be within easy reach of the bath or shower. Shelves for soap and shampoo are usually incorporated into modern baths; wider shelves can be built around the bath for plants and reading material.

The only option with a small bathroom is to use every bit of space as economically as possible. A vanity unit around the basin and boxed-in toilet cistern and pipework look neater and add extra shelf and cupboard storage. Basins, toilets and bidets can be wall-hung and storage units can be built into odd spaces or corners. If you don't have room for a conventional bath, install a corner bath or sit-down tub. Other space savers are sliding doors or blinds to conceal shelving, while, for the visual effect of extra space, mirrors work miracles – use sheets or mirror tiles over a compact wall to double the space. The back of the door can be hung with mirrors, clothes hooks or wire storage racks, and if the room has a high ceiling, store extra towels and linen up high on a slatted, pulley-operated rack.

You have rather more scope to create a relaxing, enjoyable atmosphere in a larger room – but isolating the bath, basin, bidet and toilet on separate walls may not be the most convenient or attractive arrangement. If there's a view – and privacy – position the bath near the window so that you can enjoy it. Free-standing cast-iron or pressed steel baths can be left to dominate a room. Or build a low platform around the bath to give it a sunken feeling. If you have space, add a comfortable piece of furniture – a sofa or *chaise longue* – or exercise equipment.

A shower cubicle or toilet can be fitted into a hall cupboard. It's not essential to allow full head-height over the full length of a bath – you could fit one under a sloping attic roof, for example, or underneath a staircase.

Safety

Water and electricity are a dangerous combination. Electrical socket outlets are either not permitted in bathrooms, or must be a specified distance from taps (faucets) and be fitted with waterproof covers – regulations vary from country to country (special shaver points are usually allowed). Electric light bulbs should be enclosed – they could short-circuit if damp. Lights, extractors and heaters should be operated by pull switches or from outside the room.

Check that floors, baths and bathmats have non-slip surfaces or backing and install hand-rails (towel rails are not sturdy enough) around bath, bidet and toilet. Glass doors or screens should be shatter-proof. Medicine cabinets should be fitted with child-proof catches, and keep strong disinfectants and cleaning materials locked away or out of reach. Rounded corners and smooth surfaces is the most sensible plan.

1 *Charm and precision have gone into the creation of this bathroom in a French family home. Practical white-tiled walls, with blue tiles forming a band of decorative checks and two generous hand basins. The lighting above twin mirrors is both subtle and effective. Antique furniture in natural materials – wood, rush, bone – provides contrast and character.*

2 *An outside feel achieved by location and by design.*
3 *A free-standing shower and toilet unit makes good use of limited space.*

4 *Another small space well organized to hold shower, bath and basins in great style.*
5 *An arched fanlight and sculptured ceiling make this narrow room private and pleasing, as do the fine bathroom fixtures.*

Bathroom fixtures

Many of today's bathroom fixtures come with special co-ordinated accessories and towels, and there is a wide variety of sizes to fit even the most awkward spaces. If you can't afford to replace your existing fixtures, it is often possible to repair cracks or chips, remove lime scales and reglaze – this is best tackled by a re-surfacing specialist.

Bathtubs

Traditional cast-iron and pressed steel baths with vitreous-enamelled finishes are stable and long-lasting, and moderately expensive; they are available in standard shapes and a reasonable number of colours. Not as good-looking but cheaper, are baths made from acrylic plastic; these are available in a wide variety of colours, are resistant to chipping and warm to the touch; they can become dull and are susceptible to scratching, however. Other plastic baths are made of glass-reinforced polyester, a stronger, more rigid material than acrylic – many of the designs are ugly, but one handsome exception is a reproduction of an old-fashioned free-standing bath with claw feet. Stainless steel is another option, although it may be difficult to find; hospital suppliers usually have it. Marble is an expensive, but attractive choice; it can be custom-made to fit your bathroom.

The average bath is between about 1.7 and 1.83m (66 and 72in) long. If space is limited and you really prefer a bath to a shower, there are small versions available, including a sit-down tub, which is smaller and deeper with a built-in seat. Conventional baths can be fitted with a seat or are available gently contoured at one end. If you are tempted by an extra large bath, remember it will be more expensive to fill.

Sunken baths are not always practical on upper floors; before installing one, get a structural engineer to check whether the floor structure will be able to support its weight. Low baths can be tiring to clean and make bathing children difficult, but suit rooms with limited headroom. An alternative is to set the bath in a low platform, which can be designed to include storage too.

Showers

Showers are more economical to use than baths. If possible, install a separate shower cubicle, and position the controls outside the shower, so they can be pre-set before entering. Ready-made cubicles are available in a wide range of styles from glass to acrylic; some have integral seats, heated towel rails and soap shelves. They can be difficult to integrate into an existing bathroom, however. A good-looking alternative is a custom-built, tiled alcove. If you are combining the bath and shower, choose a flat-bottomed bath with a non-slip surface, as wide as possible, and make sure that the surrounding walls, ceiling and floor are adequately waterproofed. Add a fitted glass or plastic screen or a plastic-lined shower curtain to protect the rest of the bathroom from splashes.

The shower controls should be fitted by a qualified electrician and plumber. The controls can be operated manually or automatically, and separate from or combined with the bath taps (faucets). Many include thermostatic controls which, once set, maintain the water temperature, whether or not a tap is turned on elsewhere in the house. More sophisticated dual controls set both the temperature and the rate of flow, and will stop the water flow automatically if the pressure drops below a certain level.

Shower heads can be hand-held units, adjustable to suit the height of each user; or they can be fixed – these look neater because all the workings are hidden behind the wall, but, although the direction of the heads can be changed, they are less flexible than hand-held types. Another option is a 'shower massage', a shower head that delivers water in bursts, rather than in a continuous stream; it can be either fixed or hand-held.

The electronic impulse shower is in the luxury class. It is made of pierced vertical tubes and adjustable sprays and looks uncommonly like the old-fashioned Victorian shower. It releases high-powered jets of water, alternating hot and cold, which spray the whole body and act rather like a massage. The temperature of the hot water is thermostatically controlled, while the length of each burst of water is adjustable. The unit can be used for an ordinary shower as well.

Basins (sinks)

Choose a basin that is as large as space permits – deep enough from front to back to enable you to bend over easily when washing your face and hair, and wide enough to accommodate wet, dripping elbows – and has a generous-sized rim to accommodate shampoos and the like, plus recesses for soap. If there are tap holes, check they are in the position you want them; otherwise buy a basin without holes and drill your own. It should be set at a comfortable height, either supported on a pedestal or vanity unit, or else wall-mounted. If wall-mounted, make sure that

A well-appointed capsule bathroom.

Custom-designed marble luxury.

Free-standing modern basin unit.

Moulded plastic shower unit.

the basin is securely fixed to a load-bearing wall or that it is supported by metal brackets.

Toilets

Most toilet bowls are made from glazed vitreous china, and are available in a wide range of colours and designs. With syphonic-flushed units, the contents are sucked quietly and quickly down the drain; a reverse-trap unit operates in a similar way and requires a smaller bowl. Wash-down toilets are cheaper, take up less space, but are noisier; water is flushed around the rim of the bowl to clear any waste. A low-level pan encourages a more natural squatting position; this is becoming increasingly popular.

Low-level cisterns are close coupled to the pan or concealed behind a partition wall. There are slim cisterns available to fit into a space only 150mm (6in) deep, or there are panel shapes with a top-press flush projecting only 114mm (4½in).

Bidets

Bidets are standard bathroom equipment in Europe, and are highly recommended if you have the space. Like toilets, they are usually made from vitreous china and are available to match other bathroom fixtures. Separate hot and cold supply pipes and a vented soil pipe are legal require-ments. Bidets can be either tap filled or supplied from under the brim. They need plenty of room at the sides for legs and at the back for knees; this may mean leaving a gap of about 100mm (4in) between the wall and the back of the bidet with some models. Pull-out designs are available if you are very short of space.

Taps (faucets)

Taps can be fixed to the wall or mounted on the bath or bowl. The more sophisticated mixer units come with or without shower attachments and thermostatic controls; they can be lever-operated, push-button or turned, and sometimes have adjustable swivel spouts. Make sure that the taps are easy to handle, especially with soapy hands, and that they direct water accurately into the bowl or bath. Many modern taps are very difficult to clean; certainly the old-fashioned cross-head taps and some wall-mounted controls are hard to beat on this score.

Gothic splendour in a nineteenth-century Camargue country house. The marble bath is suitably accompanied by elegant wrought-iron chairs and light fittings, brass 'swan-head' taps, and custom-made wood panelling and mirrored cupboard doors shaped like Gothic-arch windows.

Sunken bath and shower in one.

Antique cast-iron bath on marble plinth.

Sauna and cold plunge.

Wall-to-wall bath in a tiny room.

Bathroom basics

Bathrooms have to withstand considerable wear and tear from extremes of temperature, steam and moisture; any surface decoration needs to be tough, waterproof and easy to clean. Practical does not have to mean hard and clinical, however – you can achieve a soft, luxurious look without too much expense.

Walls

Paint is the cheapest and easiest way to decorate bathroom walls provided they are in reasonable condition. Eggshell or silk finish is preferable to gloss, which tends to aggravate condensation and should be restricted to woodwork. Washable or spongeable wallpapers are suitable, or a non-waterpoof paper can be protected with polyurethane varnish. Papers are not recommended for use in showers; use perspex, plastic laminate, shatter-proof glass or tiles here. Ceramic, glass or mosaic tiles provide an excellent waterproof and easy-to-clean surface. If you cannot afford to tile the whole room, use them to make a splashback over the bath and basin. Another, less clinical, choice is tongue-and-groove boarding, which can be waterproofed with polyurethane varnish.

Floors

Bathroom floors need to be water-resistant and also easy to clean. Cushioned vinyl is comfortable and practical, and is available in wide sheets to minimize joins where moisture could seep in; vinyl tiles are less practical on this count, but useful for awkward-shaped floors. Cork floors are hard-wearing and warm to the touch, and blend well with natural wood fixtures; cork is usually treated to avoid staining, but the bathroom is the one area where it can be left untreated. Duck-boarding is a less comfortable but highly practical choice.

Some synthetic carpets are specially recommended for bathroom use, and tufted, foam-backed carpets, carpet tiles and cotton rugs can also be used. But avoid permanently fixing a wall-to-wall carpet; leave it so that it can be lifted to dry if necessary.

Stone or ceramic tile floors are hard-wearing, but cold and uncomfortable underfoot and really need under-floor heating. Marble is too slippery unless combined with rugs, but quartzite and riven slate have a natural slip-resistant finish, while a non-slip aggregate can be added to terrazzo.

Lighting

Good direct lighting is essential for shaving, grooming or applying make-up, perhaps combined with a more subtle indirect light for leisurely bathing. Spotlights or downlights recessed in the ceiling are neater and safer than pendant lights, although downlights can cast quite a harsh, unflattering light. Lights at the mirror area should be aimed at the face – film-star style bulbs or fluorescent tubes behind louvred shades give an excellent if cruelly accurate light, while some ready-made mirrored cabinets have built-in lighting. A low-wattage night-light is a useful safety precaution. All lights must be operated by pull cords for safety.

Windows

You will almost certainly need some sort of screening at the window. Etched, opaque or stained glass is much prettier than reeded or frosted types, but is not really practical for large windows. A soft, filtered effect can be created by using louvres, pinoleum blinds, wooden shutters or glass shelves filled with plants, while a simple café curtain on the lower half of the window won't cut out all the natural light – remember, when using thin, semi-translucent screening, to position the lighting so there is no silhouette effect. Washable roller blinds are good in bathrooms; pleated Roman or festoon blinds or long curtains are suited to large rooms with few steam problems and plenty of space. In a small bathroom with limited wall space, replacing the window panes with mirror glass is an excellent alternative to curtains or blinds.

Heating

If you have a centrally operated heating system, use it to heat towel rails as well. Or electrically heated rails are available. Another bathroom heating option is to install wall-mounted fan heaters – well out of reach of anyone standing in the bath and operated only by pull cords. A small radiator between the bath and the bath panel is a good warming device provided you fit the panel with air vents. A hot-water cylinder in a bathroom cupboard will help heat the room and keep towels and linen warm.

Condensation

Good ventilation is vital in the bathroom to combat steam and condensation. Keeping the room warm helps; a ventilation outlet or extractor fan is a necessity in internal rooms – it should activate automatically when the door is opened or the light switched on.

Some surface materials, such as cork, tend to absorb moisture and so are less affected by surface condensation than ceramic tiles or gloss paint will be.

1 In a predominantly white tiled bathroom, a simple and classic pattern motif is created with black tiles and black grouting.
2 Well-designed tongue-and-groove panelling is painted to match the walls in a sunny pale cream bathroom with toning honey-coloured rush matting.
3 Furniture and fixtures take full advantage of a spacious attic bathroom. The shape and character are enhanced with glossy black woodwork and radiator and a polished wood floor.

4

5

4 Elegant but inexpensive varnished chipboard provides a panelled finish for the basin and bath – complete with shower attachment and fitted glass splash screen.
5 The luxury of a raised bathroom partly screened off from a bedroom comes both from the layout and the choice of deep-pile carpet, mosaic tiles edged in gold and a turquoise colour scheme which provides a calm, aquatic atmosphere reminiscent of Roman baths in exotic Mediterranean locations.
6 The largest room in a German artist's house was converted into this grand bathroom of unpolished pink and grey granite. Mirrors were banished.

6

Storage and accessories

All the accoutrements of washing and grooming need to be close at hand in the bathroom. And there is no reason why they should be hidden away – open shelving and wire racks can look every bit as smart as custom-built cupboards or cabinets.

Timber or melamine-coated chipboard shelves are more practical than the traditional toughened glass ones, which look great but need constant cleaning. A plastic-coated wire-rack system with shelves and baskets is ideal for small rooms where cupboards may look too heavy and dominant.

If you prefer to hide your clutter away, shelves can be screened with slatted or roller blinds to match the colour scheme. Steam-proof cupboards and cabinets for bathrooms are available, often with a wide range of special built-in features and gadgets and in every style, from treated mahogany to streamlined laminates.

There is nothing worse than underestimating your storage needs; in a bathroom, bottles and lotions must be within easy reach of the bath, shower and basin (sink), and they should be on a stable surface so they won't fall over and spill. You'll need shelves or cupboards by the basin for toothpaste, brushes and toiletries; disinfectants, bleach and other strong cleaners should be stored well out of reach of young children, preferably in cupboards with child-proof catches. The medical cabinet is traditionally kept in the bathroom; it needs a child-proof catch at the very least, but preferably a lock. Another option is all-in-one mirrored cabinets; they come with extras, such as built-in shaver points, fluorescent lighting or even with heated units, which will prevent the mirrors from steaming up.

Accessories, from chrome and porcelain via wood to plastic primaries, are very much a matter of personal taste. The essentials are obvious: towel rails; soap dishes; tooth-brush holders and mugs; toilet-roll holders; waste bins and laundry baskets. Choose towels and bathmats in colours that suit the rest of the room.

If you've the space, add a chair or seat – or perhaps a fold-down sauna-style seat if space is limited – so you can relax after an invigorating shower or bath. If you want your bathroom to be full of greenery, make sure you pick plants that enjoy the damp, warm atmosphere – philodendrons, spathiphyllums and anthuriums are good choices for a shady room; while begonias, coleus (flaming nettles) and other variegated or coloured-leaved plants thrive in bathrooms that are normally flooded with natural light.

1 *A beautifully finished bathroom, given grand scale by a large mirror beside the bath and a towel rail which runs the full width of the room – made from a shop clothes rail.*

2 *A careful mixture of old and new. Modern basin and taps with a marble splashback, antique iron towel rail and the original stripped floor and door.*
3 *A shiny black basin unit designed in Italy.*
4 *Practical and attractive laminate, with a granite-like quality, works well with the stainless-steel fixtures.*

5 *A stylish arrangement and fine fixtures: porcelain double-basin stand, chrome taps and fittings, an oval mirror. Quality bathroom equipment like this needs only simple white tiles in the background.*

6 *A small, nondescript bathroom given wit and style through the careful selection and position of accessories – some functional, some not.*

7 *The period charm of an antique basin and stone-tiled floor is maintained with plain white tiling and a glazed corner cupboard.*

8 *A delightful bathroom created with second-hand pieces offset by painted brick walls and a pretty rug. The sink is set into a Victorian washstand.*

9 *A collection of antique barbers' combs has been hung on towelling-covered walls. Pine shelyes hold interesting old bottles and the beamed ceiling is of fine wood.*

10 *A self-contained double-basin unit. Shaver sockets are set in and the lights are wired into the large circular mirrors.*

Bathroom luxury

When designing a bathroom you have to work within certain limitations – the fixtures, the most permanent elements of the room, must be functional, although you should choose them for their appearance as well; the materials you use must be durable and easy to care for. But you still have a lot of scope for developing your own style. You can mix textures and colours – soft flooring with chrome and reflective glass panels, for instance. Or concentrate on one material – wonderfully coloured mosaics on walls and floors, perhaps, or all-over tiles or terrazzo. Strong colour schemes – black and white, say, or bright red and shocking pink – can work well in a bathroom, whereas they could easily overpower a living room or bedroom.

A comfortable, functional environment, well done with a definite style, has a basic luxury of its own. But you needn't confine yourself to conventional bathroom fixtures. The greatest luxury of all is a really large bath that allows almost total submersion. There are baths with inset whirlpools – they bombard the body with high-pressure jets of water to produce a stimulating massage and look like over-sized conventional baths.

Steam plants are used for cleaning the pores and improving circulation. They are available in kit form for home use and can be used with any bath or shower, provided it is enclosed to keep the steam in. The kit consumes very little water or electricity and can be followed by a warm or cold shower for invigorating effect.

Outside the bathroom

Although not normally situated in bathrooms, saunas and hot tubs shouldn't be forgotten.

Saunas produce dry heat, which causes the body to perspire, cleansing the skin and soothing aching muscles. They are available in kit form, don't take up a large amount of room, and usually come complete with wall and ceiling panels of Finnish pinewood insulated with rock wool, double-glazed door and adjustable vents to provide fresh air as needed. The sauna is heated by a stove, with thermostatically controlled elements that heat volcanic rocks and gradually build up an intense dry heat.

Hot tubs are based on the same principle and are usually installed outside on a sheltered patio or by a swimming pool, or indoors in a conservatory (sunroom) or basement. Designed for groups of people to enjoy together, the wooden tubs are deep and circular, with seats all round. They look their best sunk into wooden decking or stone paving surrounded by large tubs of exotic plants.

1 *A roof-top whirlpool in California; varnished boat decking and sail-shaped walls, with brilliant white, yellow and blue paintwork, give it a nautical feel.*

2 *Given the space, what can be more luxurious than to convert a large room into a bathroom and add items which give it the feel of a spacious private study. A room for bathing, reading, writing, working, thinking and languishing.*

3 *Simple luxury: two industrial basins, built-in double baths, and white tiling – everywhere.*

4 *Two expensive materials for a streamlined effect: stainless steel and marble combine function and good looks.*

5 *A great view is a luxury in itself, as in this Bengali country house. The bathroom itself is peaceful, cool and utterly simple with subtle decorative touches, such as the old water jug and wash bowl, the flowers and brass buckets.*

CHILDREN'S ROOMS

When planning an environment for children, always put safety first. Children, particularly the very young, are imaginative but inexperienced, with an inquisitive nature that over-rules what little common sense they do possess. Use the safety checklist when planning a child's room.

There are national safety standards for children's furniture, so when buying always check whether these standards are met – there should be an approved label attached to the product. Your own common sense should always form the 'second opinion', because items which are technically safe in certain circumstances may be treacherous in others: for example, a Moses basket deemed suitable for a baby up to the age of three months will be unsafe for your two-month-old.

The location

A new baby doesn't really need a room of her or his own. One corner of the parent's room is an ideal location. But if you are planning a nursery, it should be close enough to the parent's bedroom so the baby can be heard.

By the time the baby starts to crawl, there should be less or no need for night feeds and the time is ripe for a separate bedroom,

giving the parents a chance for a return to normality, and the child a sense of independence, however tentative.

As children grow and others arrive on the scene, bedrooms change their occupants, their nature and even their position in the house. A nursery can revert to a guest or sewing room in the natural course of events, or a playroom can become a bedroom/study.

The siting of the room depends on the layout of the house, the child's age and the number of other children in the family. Ideally, the bedroom of a young child should be away from the hubbub of the living room.

Older children, especially teenagers, actually prefer physical distance from their parents and the intimations of freedom and independence the isolation brings. In large houses, one floor might be given over to teenagers or, if space and finances allow, a self-contained apartment within the home.

It is best to avoid the permanent fixtures and fittings of childhood that rapidly become outgrown or redundant – built-in small-scale furniture or painted fairy-tale murals, for example – there are nearly always temporary equivalents easily removed or dismantled when the need arises.

SAFETY
CHECKLIST

ELECTRICITY

- Fit socket outlets with safety covers.
- Permanent electrical fittings should have no exposed leads.

HEATING/LIGHTING

- Fit radiators and fires with guards that completely enclose them.
- Do not use a paraffin or oil-burning heater.
- Use wall-mounted or surface-mounted lights.

FURNITURE

- A cot should be sturdy, with no protruding parts. Spacing between the cot bars should be 37–50mm (1½–2in); if drop-sided, there should be an automatic locking device.
- Fit a secure safety rail to a small child's bed.
- Never put a child under four in a top bunk; the top bunk must have a safety rail; the ladder must be secure.

- Never position a chair or bed under a window.
- Chairs should be stable and sturdy.
- Free-standing bookcases and cabinets should be screwed to the wall.
- Never place a baby's bouncer or reclining chair on a table or bed, where it can tip off.

WINDOWS AND DOORWAYS

- Use safety glass for low-level panes.
- Fit windows with safety catches.
- If you use fixed double glazing, make sure it can be opened easily in an emergency.
- Use vertical bars for windows; the bars must be quickly detached in emergency.
- Fit a gate at the top of stairs.

SURFACES

- Paint should be lead-free; other surfaces non-toxic.
- Avoid sharp or splintery edges.

A child's bedroom in the home of a distinguished architect. Every item has been custom designed and built to a strong decorative theme.

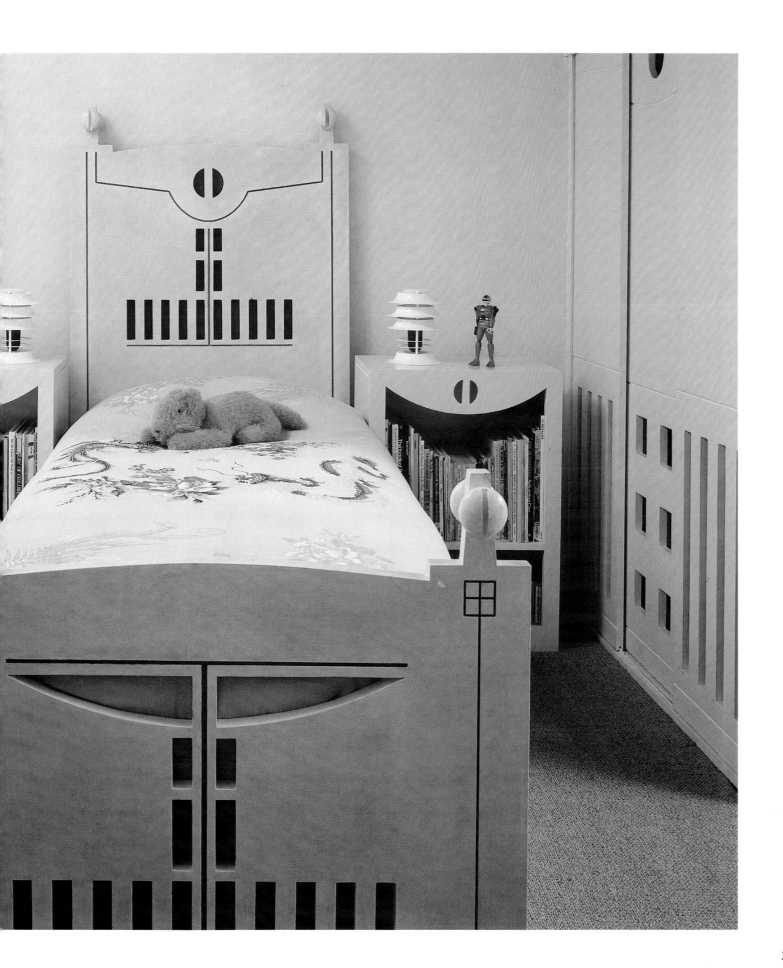

Nursery basics

With a baby's bedroom, it's a good idea to get the basics right at the start. Do any structural alterations, install heating, lighting and socket outlets with an eye on future needs. Then you can turn your attention to the more enjoyable decisions: choosing colours, textures, furniture and fixtures.

The baby's toys, clothes, toiletries and bits and bobs generally will add visual liveliness to the room; and you can change wall hangings, pictures and mobiles regularly.

If you want to wallpaper the walls rather than paint them, then choose a plain paper or a small-scale print that the child won't tire of easily. If you do have your heart set on a large-patterned child's wallpaper, make sure you have the resources – in terms of time, effort and money – to replace it when its initial magic has worn off. In any case, the wallpaper should be washable, probably vinyl.

It is usually easier to re-paint a room than to re-wallpaper it, a point very much worth keeping in mind. You can also clean a painted wall fairly effectively if you use a washable paint (see *SURFACES AND FINISHES*).

There is no doubt that hand-painted murals look stunning, but a professionally painted mural can be very expensive, and will most likely interest the child for a limited time only. But, if you have flair and inclination, you can paint a mural yourself, using books as a source of inspiration, or glue a book, page by page, to the wall and seal with varnish.

The floor should be comfortable, warm, easily cleaned and durable. For very young children, a washable floor is essential. Carpeting will very quickly become stained. Cushioned vinyl or cork are much more sensible; they are both easy to clean and they provide a good surface for first attempts at crawling. An inexpensive rag rug or dhurry – fitted with non-slip adhesive strips – can add a soft, warm touch.

The windows will need curtains or blinds that can block out all light when it is time for the baby to sleep. This doesn't necessarily mean dark or mournful materials – light-coloured curtains can be interlined or can be used in conjunction with a dark blind. Artificial lighting needs thoughtful planning. Ceilings and wall lights are safer than free-standing ones. Dimmers will give you the option of the clinical brightness necessary for cleaning and seeing to the baby's needs, or a soft, 'night light' effect.

Choose furniture for strength, safety, flexibility, durability and good looks. Baskets and swinging cribs are pretty and very young babies do like a sense of enclosure, but a cot or crib is a longer term proposition and can be used from the start. If it has several adjustable levels for the mattress, you save yourself backache by raising it to the highest level while the baby is young. Once the baby becomes active, though, you must lower the mattress to its lowest setting, to prevent escape attempts.

Sensible storage for very young children should be adult-orientated, for ease of changing, feeding, bathing and dressing. A chest of drawers is more useful than a wardrobe, as babies' clothes tend to be folded rather than hung up. Don't be tempted into buying a tiny, scaled-down chest of drawers, as it quickly outlives its usefulness and its diminutive point is probably lost on the baby anyway. If you feel a large chest of drawers is too heavy-looking, then paint it white or a pale colour. The top can be fitted with a padded waterproof mat for changing the baby. An open shelf nearby is very useful to store all the necessary creams and ointments within easy reach. There are special changing trolleys available, with swing-out sections for storage and pockets for lotions and cotton wool, but these are soon outgrown.

Shelves for displaying toys and stuffed animals should be placed where the baby can see and enjoy them from the cot.

This is a room that you will spend a lot of time in, often just sitting, nursing your baby. So add an easy, comfortable chair; perhaps a special, low-legged Victorian 'nursing chair'.

1 Colourful motifs and decorative images are particularly effective if incorporated into the design of a useful object – such as this lively ABC shelving unit. The basic decoration of the room has been left plain and simple.
2 A charming small-scale wardrobe, specially designed for a child's first room and beautifully blended with the muted colour scheme.

3

4

3 *Nursery furniture that can be adapted as the child grows is a good investment. This colourful unit, with toning toy boxes and a metal grid for hanging things from, has an adjustable top that will convert to a desk at school age.*

4 *A strong cot, high chair and changing unit are essential nursery basics. This sturdy wooden design with blue printed cotton is pretty without being dainty and has inspired the colour scheme for the room.*

Transition

Unlike babies, toddlers don't stay where you put them, but spend their time investigating the world around them, and extending the limits of their knowledge and skills. This is a natural process and a necessary one; but it can be tiring on parents. Though this stage is relatively short, a house that has been adapted to meet the needs of growing toddlers makes the job of parenting easier and more enjoyable. For the pre-school child, the bedroom is also a playroom. The child will still prefer to be wherever you are, but if the room is attractive and functional, many happy hours will be spent there. This has the advantage of relieving the living room of pressure and keeping it slightly more adult.

Once a child is out of a cot, an adult-sized bed, fitted with safety rails, is a better long-term buy than a child's bed. If your child has his or her heart set on a train- or boat-shaped bed, you could build bed-ends out of plywood. Bunk beds and pre-school children are a dangerous combination, but you could buy the bunks now, remove the ladder and use the upper bunk for storage only.

There is a good case to be made for scaled-down children's chairs and tables, to be used for scribbling, modelling, jigsaw puzzles and tea parties. Ideally, the table-top should be at the elbow height of the sitting child, whose feet should touch the floor. An alternative would be an inexpensive, low-level work surface that can be raised as the child grows.

For storage, the best idea is to choose a system that can be added to and adjusted in the future. Make sure it is tough and stable, as toddlers and young children will climb or swing on whatever is in reach. Storage should be low enough for young hands to reach, simple to open, easy to shut and large enough to fit everything. Toys and books can be stored on low-level shelves. A large toy box on wheels can be rolled from room to room and stored under a bed when not in use; if sturdy and fitted with a lid, it can become a play bus or boat.

Pre-school children need plenty of floor space in a bedroom: initially for practising crawling and walking, later for building with blocks, riding in pedal cars and being busy generally. Although the floor should be warm, comfortable and draught-free, the first choice is still cushioned vinyl, cork or soft linoleum; they can all be cleaned off easily and replaced with carpet when the child gets a little older. Provide a couple of giant bean-bag seats, for curling up in and looking at books.

In terms of decoration, a young child will have ideas of her or his own. This is the time when children are enchanted by animals, fairies and story-book characters, and large posters and wall friezes could be a source of great fascination. Place the pictures low on the walls, at children's eye level, on a strip of cork tiles running round the room or a felt-covered noticeboard. Include a scribble-on blackboard surface at this height, too.

Walls, too, need to be finished in a surface that is tough and easy to clean: washable paints, cork tiles or wallpapers. Wallpapers must be well pasted down; if the corners are lifting off, young fingers will certainly be tempted to have a go at peeling the rest.

Soft furnishings provide the ideal excuse for bright colours and patterns; the bed-linen, curtains or blinds can be nursery prints – they are easier to replace when the child tires of them than wallpaper or murals.

1, 2 *This nursery furniture is designed to be easily rearranged when the child outgrows the nursery. The cot and changing unit can be made into a desk and bed, and only the wardrobe remains in its original form. Bright colours are a lively alternative to traditional nursery pastels. The painted walls in the nursery are washable; the vinyl wallpaper is equally practical when the room is transformed for the school-age child. The strong cord carpet will withstand years of wear and tear.*

3 *Adjustable and expandable storage units are a sensible investment for children. The small chair is the only furniture which will be outgrown, but it is an inexpensive and much appreciated item.*
4 *A small child's room designed for fun and practicality. The sturdy wooden bed has useful storage drawers below and the canopy gives a feeling of security to a child getting used to a bed. Children enjoy painting, so a large roll of paper is handy. The flooring is washable, including the bright rug, and a toning, cloud-shaped radiator shield protects a small child from scorching.*

Children's furniture

1 *Practical children's furniture can also be fun. These chairs, complete with handy drawers under the cushioned seats, look exciting with their primary colours and interesting shape. They can be safely used to form a house, cave, train or other play objects.*

2 *It's a lucky child who sleeps in a bed as pretty as these traditional Finnish ones. The pine frames can be extended as the children grow. The floor is simply painted with gloss white to match the plain white walls, making a beautiful environment to grow up in.*

3 *Animal sleeping bags – easy to make and great to sleep in. They are especially useful for the ever-popular overnight stay with friends or for camping out at home.*

4 *Keeping the decoration simple and selecting furniture with easy-care surfaces is a practical approach for children's bedrooms. Colour and visual interest are usually added by the children themselves through their toys and other clutter or, as in this room, can be injected with a striped duvet cover and matching pillowcases.*

5 *For those who enjoy the effect of murals but lack the nerve or skill to paint them, hand-stencilled furniture offers another satisfaction. A large toy box is a good solution for storage since it offers instant tidying away; keep it at a low level so that children can do the job themselves.*

The school-age child

For a child, starting school is a great step in life, and her or his bedroom should reflect this transition, although the change will probably be gradual rather than sudden. A bedroom that has been well designed for a younger child will need adding to and re-arranging rather than drastic alterations. More storage will be necessary, some of it on a small scale. Children at this age are intrigued by minutiae: stamp collections, miniature glass animals, chemistry sets and so on. Compartmentalized storage – such as tins, small wicker baskets, glass jars, narrow shelves – all provide reasonable storage for small-scale items. Low-level shelving can be used for display now, as well as storage, and cork and felt-covered noticeboards can be raised as the child grows.

Hanging space for clothes becomes important: rods should be low enough for the child to reach. Beds and storage systems can be combined – divans with drawers, for example, or bunk beds incorporating desks, storage units or even cupboards. Beds could be built into the wall and come down at night, or stacked one beneath the other.

A desk and chair should be provided, although the child, at least in the early school years, may well want to do homework near you. As she or he gets older, the desk in the bedroom will gradually win out over the kitchen table. Make sure there is adequate lighting by the table and that it is safe.

Allow the child a say in choosing the paint colour or the wallpaper, though fiercely patterned wallpaper should be gently discouraged. If he or she is involved in these decisions, the chances are the room will be treated with greater care and consideration. Wall surfaces should be durable enough to take endless changes of posters.

Sharing

Children often have to share a room, whether they like it or not. It's best to give each a clearly defined area. The room needn't be divided exactly equally: the ages and interests of the children should be the determining factor. But make it clear at the start whose area is whose, going so far, if it's necessary, as having a demarcation line – folding screens, curtains or a low bookcase. Make sure each child has a desk and sufficient storage space within his or her area.

All children need some privacy: try to arrange the furniture so they are not always facing each other and, if possible, provide separate lighting, which will help to cut down arguments when one wants to read while the other is trying to sleep.

1 *A radical approach to a child's room. The bed is built on a platform and reached via a sturdy ladder. Below is a specially designed bathroom with low-level basins – by a playroom designed to look like a small gymnasium, complete with black court lines and a basketball net.*
2 *School-age children are avid collectors, so provide storage for the display of precious objects. A practical room encourages the habit of private study but it need not be drab; this room has been carefully created with strong colours and the old school desk is purely for decoration.*

3 *A wonderful environment for children has been created in an attic, using hammocks as well as a bed raised above cupboards, with plenty of space left for desks and shelving displays.*
4 *Clutter can be stored attractively: the colour of these baskets encourages a child to put everything in the right place – yet it is all close at hand, to be grabbed when needed.*
5 *Good design makes the best use of limited space with strong built-in furniture, decorated to give an air of sophistication. High-tech style, platform beds and built-in worktops are well suited to a child's room.*

Teenage bedrooms

A room of one's own will help make the growing-up process easier. Most teenagers feel they have left childhood behind, and want a more adult room – a living room-cum-study-cum-bedroom. They will need more independence – and room where they can work, entertain, sleep and make noise without interference from adults.

Your attitude to your teenager's room is as important as the room itself, particularly when it comes to tidiness: simply provide as much storage as you can and keep the door closed if the room upsets you. Likewise, respect her or his privacy and don't barge in unasked or go in and tidy up yourself.

It's worth, at this stage of your child's life, considering major alterations – building an extension (complete with *en suite* bathroom, if possible); converting an unused attic, basement or garage. Or you could change a study or workroom into a teenage bedroom.

One of the priorities will probably be to make the bed look less like a bed. Divans are obviously ideal; they can be used for seating as well as sleeping, and often provide storage space underneath. A sleeping platform is a good way of keeping the floor space clear, but the ceiling must be reasonably high and there should be some form of ventilation. Built-in seating and an extra divan could double as a spare room for overnight guests. Big cushions are useful; so, too, is a folding bed, which can be kept in a cupboard when not in use, or a sofa bed.

To minimize arguments about noise, thick carpets and heavy curtains will deaden the sounds. Shelving of various depths is a good idea: deeper shelves for records, large books and stereo equipment; narrow ones to take paperbacks and tapes.

Clothing becomes an obsession at this age. Provide a built-in or free-standing wardrobe; a long rail across an alcove, or rails on wheels, like those in clothing shops, also work well.

A large work surface is essential, for study and for hobbies. A desk is one solution, with a filing cabinet to keep papers, pens and pencils. A flat worktop with office pigeon holes and brightly coloured trays standing in for drawers would be a good substitute.

A full-length mirror will be appreciated. Lighting should be flexible; fit dimmers on the light switches to provide mood changes, and make sure there is good light for reading by the desk and at the bedside.

Most teenagers will have all manner of electrical appliances – from televisions and hair driers to computers and typewriters. There should be enough socket outlets; adaptors can be dangerous.

Finally, remember that the room belongs to your child, not to you. The choice of posters, records and even furniture should be left to her or him – within reason, of course.

1

2

1 This platform bed makes the most of a small space but is beautifully decorative. The area below is packed with storage, but the simple device of using cut-outs for handles offers pretty motifs. Every detail is designed in harmony – the light fittings, window and skylight, picture frames edging the bed and the step-ladder backed by a curtain.
2 When rooms must be shared, dividing the territory can help reduce friction. A curtain provides demarcation and neutral walls give both occupants a chance to enjoy their own decoration.
3 An ideal teenage room with a separate entrance, in the basement of a Milan house. The platform bed is raised on old drainpipes, painted yellow, with ample space for displaying the stereo below. A wide built-in worktop runs the length of the room and serves as a desk.

WORK AND ACTIVITY

Careful design of work areas in the home is essential: you need to create an environment which is practical and safe, comfortable, stimulating and a pleasure to be in. The following pages cover a range of activities:

Home office deals with areas for paperwork, and includes special sections on home computers and on working at home.

Studio space offers design ideas for areas devoted to creative pursuits such as making music, painting and pottery, or activities such as keeping fit or developing photographs.

Utility rooms describes areas containing laundry equipment, household cleaning items, ironing and sewing facilities.

Workshops is concerned with rooms for wood- and metalwork, repairs and other mechanical projects;

You might not believe that you have the space or the need for a work area – but think again. A place in the house properly designed for special activities is more a necessity than

a luxury. Work-rooms are for fun, study and hobbies, as well as for essential tasks. They can provide privacy and solitude, or a safe and soundproof area in which noise and mess can be created without disturbing other members of the household.

If you do not have a whole room to spare, convert a basement, attic, landing, hallway or a disused outbuilding. A simple extension could be considered, above a garage, perhaps, or using a space beside the house – a side path often collects junk alongside unused coal bunkers and could be the perfect site for a utility room or workshop. You may be able to use part of a room – a bedroom, for instance, one end of the garage or a section of the living room or kitchen. And remember that a work-room can double up as a games room, or a guest bedroom, possibly.

Whatever the task, it will be easier and more pleasurable if done in a stimulating, practically organized area.

A monotone colour scheme and subdued local lighting help to minimize the untidy effect of work clutter in this fashion designer's home work-room. Modern design elements are in contrast to the classical setting of the room.

WORK AND ACTIVITY
CHECKLIST

- Which activities are you going to cater for:
  - home accounts and administration?
  - study for school or college?
  - cleaning clothes?
  - p inting?
  - making music?
  - exercising?
  - woodwork?
  - metalwork?
  - developing, printing and/or taking photographs?
  - motor-vehicle maintenance?
  - pottery?
  - sewing?
  - writing?
  - others?
- Will more than one activity take place in the room?
- Will the activity create mess in the rest of the house?
- What work surface is required?
- Will you sit, stand or do both when working?
- What equipment do you need?
- Which items and equipment need storage space?
- Which services do you need:
  - electricity?
  - water?
  - gas?
  - heating?
  - air extraction?
  - telephone?
- Do you need special lighting?
- Should the area be private and quiet?
- Is soundproofing necessary?
- Should the area be isolated or be close to the:
  - kitchen?
  - living room?
  - nursery?
  - bedroom?
  - bathroom?
  - garden?
  - doorbell?
  - telephone?
- Do you have a spare room to convert for an activity room?
- Can you build on an extension or do without space you now use for other purposes?
- Where would you do this work or activity if you had no special room or area?
- What are the potential dangers involved:
  - electricity?
  - dangerous tools?
  - poisonous substances?
  - fire hazards?
- Will children use the room?
  Think of their size and their safety when designing the room.
- Can you afford to establish a work area?
- Will the work area involve hidden costs, such as extra heating bills?

The home office: work area

The home office is for concentration, paper work and private retreat, so locate it, if possible, in the quietest part of your home. If you are planning an office in a section of another room, consider two important points: will it be possible to work without interruption, and will you be able to organize the office space so that work can be cleared out of sight when not in use?

The desk Because the desk is the work centre of the office, plan this area first. Place the desk near a window if you can: a view beyond the room can help relieve boredom. Make sure you have easy access to the desk and adequate space around it to move your chair. You should not feel hemmed in or find you are constantly banging against an obstacle every time you stretch or reach.

Storage Make a list of the items regularly used when working at the desk. It will probably include: pen and pencils; paper; other stationery items; telephone; desk lamp; calculator; filing trays; hanging files; typewriter; computer keyboard and screen; waste-paper container; personal mementoes; reference books. When planning a system of storage, remember that each item should be easy to reach from your chair, as well as being kept in order.

Minimum mess Design a storage system to suit you. If you are obsessive about tidiness, then opt for a system that allows you to place everything out of sight when not in use. Consider the following points:

- Fitted, co-ordinated storage units are neater than unmatched filing cabinets and free-standing cupboards.
- Check that doors open and drawers slide with ease.
- Make sure that stored items are easily located, seen, and reached.

Maximum display You may prefer to keep things out in the open. But there will be endless small items: organized, tidy display can turn into a nightmare of clutter, so follow these guidelines:

- Everything must have its place.
- Display is commonly used in shops – look out for ideas.
- Pegboards or metal grids allow objects to be hung around the desk.
- Do not cover the desk top with objects – remember that you have to leave enough room to work on it too.

1

WORKING IN COMFORT
DESKS AND HOME COMPUTERS

Avoid the easy temptation of assembling any old table and chair to serve as your desk. The stress of bad posture, particularly when working at a home computer or on a typewriter, is subtle and damaging. Choose a chair designed for office use with a curved back to support the spine. It should have an adjustable height, so that your legs rest flat on the chair and your feet flat on the floor. Provide a footrest if necessary. Select a slimline typewriter or keyboard so that your forearms are not angled up when your hands rest on the keys. A visual display screen should be viewed so that your head is held straight, not tilted forward or back.

Use a paper-holder, so that you do not have to bend your head to read, and place it at the same height as a screen, if you are using one, so that your eyes can focus easily when looking from one to the other. Make sure the lighting is not directly hitting a screen or creating a shadow on the desk. Invest in a suitable desk lamp with an adjustable arm. The desk itself should allow your legs to fit comfortably beneath it. Situate storage units containing items regularly used within easy reach from your chair. Remember that you will not always want to sit upright in order to type but will also want to sit back and read, so make sure you will be comfortable for both.

4

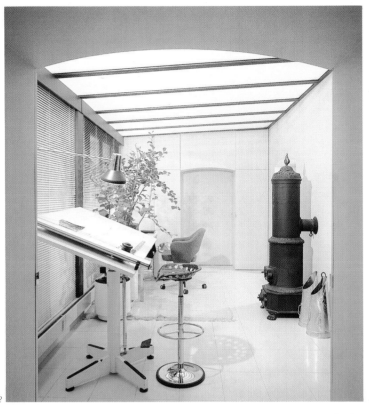

1 *Draped blinds allow for a good light source at the desk and provide shade and decoration in a small area.*
2 *Reinforced frosted glass gives a diffuse, soft light. The stove is beautiful and an inexpensive local heat source.*

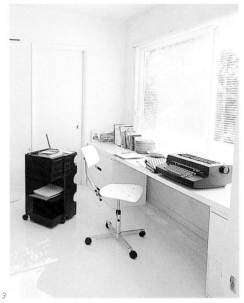

3 *A simple, functional arrangement where economy has not prevented good planning. A typewriter should not occupy the whole desk space; a chair on castors allows for maximum use of the work area. Likewise, all small objects needed from time to time are kept in a mobile unit, to save space on the work surface and prevent muddle. Adjustable blinds are excellent year-round window dressing.*

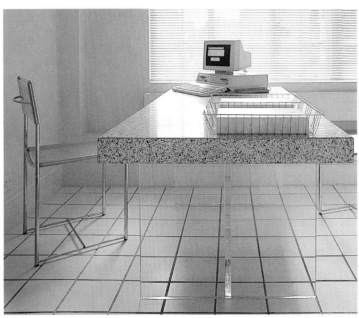

4 *A busy, open display of office objects is neatly organized on the desk, which is placed overlooking the central courtyard of a modern house.*
5 *In contrast, an American computer expert has a slab of granite for a desk, set on a perspex (acrylic) frame. In and out trays are filled with marhle blocks.*

The home office: style

Although rooms called private dens or studies conjure up very different images from ones referred to as home offices, they are used for precisely the same activities: personal paperwork, reading, study, solitude, household accounts, correspondence, and so on. The only difference is in the names and design styles they imply. A traditional study is lined with bookshelves, contains heavy, polished dark-wood furniture, and is filled with personal treasures. The home office suggests something streamlined, professional, modern and efficiently cool.

Details The objects in the room will have a large impact on the atmosphere of the room. The type of desk, lamp, shelving, storage, and even the style of the stationery items, office equipment, telephone, and anything else on show will contribute to the overall effect. But there is no need to be too rigid about style. You might find, for example, that a modern Italian desk lamp fits in well, even though your decor is Edwardian, your typewriter elegantly old and battered, and your desk traditional.

Co-ordination If your office area is only one part of a room, then you must consider the space as a whole and how you can coordinate its various functions with pleasing visual effect.

Personal style When the room is used by only one person, there is an opportunity to display collections and favourite objects. It is also a room that will evolve a personal style as you use it – start with the basics and keep the decoration simple. Pinboards, bookshelves, collections and all your office paraphernalia will live more happily in a simple room than in one where they all have to fight for attention with the patterned wallpaper, carpet and upholstery.

Lighting This is a place for study and paperwork, but that does not mean the lighting has to be glaring – create a gentle atmosphere by avoiding centre lights. If you do display a personal collection or have a fascinating – and useful – pinboard, then throw a little accent lighting on it to give the room a focus beyond the desk. The best task lighting for a desk is a desk lamp but there are alternatives: a downlight or ceiling spot.

Extras And do not forget that whatever you call the room, it can be a place for private retreat without detracting in the least from its serious work function. If you have the space, add an easy chair or sofa for moments when the paperwork is overwhelming, when you need a softer environment in which to concentrate, or when you simply want to be comfortably alone.

1 *A calm and inspiring room where creative thinking takes place rather than active work: a tidy study in Paris with minimal but quality furnishings.*
2 *A living room can incorporate a work zone too. The purpose-built alcove desk area is a decorative feature of the room. The window offers a view and the alcove creates a sense of privacy for concentration.*

3 *This work-room makes a strong statement of style and taste. 'Distressed' walls and automobile parts blend with a modern light and simple furniture.*
4 *A Tizio lamp figures in a simple, orderly office, where all the objects and fixtures are functional and share clean lines.*

Working at home

Traditionally, the professional home office was the writer's den or the busy executive's weekend work station. Today, more and more people are organizing a business or doing freelance office work full time in their homes. Undertaking a hard day's concentrated paperwork is very different from writing a letter with one eye on the television and the other on the kids. Distractions can be a serious problem. When you travel to and from work, shutting the office door means leaving the work behind. At home, the office can intrude on the rest of your life merely by its physical presence.

Your first consideration must be to separate work activity from domestic activity. Make a clear distinction by setting aside a permanent quiet area for work – not the kitchen table – and equip it properly. Make sure all signs of work in progress can be kept completely out of sight at the end of the working day, preferably behind a closed door.

The only way to prevent friends and family from assuming home work means you can be interrupted is to let them know your work hours – and stick to them. If possible, put in a separate phone, even a separate doorbell, for work use only.

If your work involves clients visiting your office, think carefully about where you locate it – you should present a professional front and avoid leading them past the kitchen or through a bedroom.

Those working at home can fall into the trap of trying to combine office work with housework, caring for children or even the odd hour of sunbathing. They are not compatible, so keep them completely separate.

Combatting these difficulties demands a mixture of organization and self-discipline. The rewards are independence and flexibility and the opportunity to work in an environment of your choice – a home office of your design.

Studio space

Nothing will encourage the pursuit of hobbies and activities more than having a properly equipped studio.

If your studio is for painting, sculpture, pottery, a photographic dark-room or other similar pursuit, its layout will depend on the scale of your work and the equipment and materials used. Walls, floors and all surfaces must be easily washed, stain-resistant or chosen to be ruined by accumulated residue from clay, paint, ink or chemicals.

Storage Allow lots of space for storage because the studio will contain a certain amount of clutter: display tubes of paint on a small trolley; paintings should be stacked vertically; a cupboard will be needed for tools and materials; chemicals and paint-dirtied rags are flammable and should not be stored in confined spaces.

Water supply A large sink is essential for potters and in dark-rooms. Fit a clay trap, or a sink filter, if necessary.

Work surface Organize the layout of the room in the correct working sequence. Your work surface should be large enough that you are able to stand back from it in order to judge work in progress.

Light Natural light from a north-facing window (or south-facing, in the Southern Hemisphere) is best for creative work. Supplement it with fluorescent lamps carrying 'daylight' tubes. Dark-rooms must be light-proof and require special 'safety' lights. Make sure lights are correctly positioned so you avoid eye-strain.

Safety Children will get enormous enjoyment from a studio where they can make a mess. But all toxic materials should be either locked away or stored out of reach and fit pull-cords, so that small wet hands are kept away from electric switches.

Noise If your studio is for making music, locate it away from party walls. Soundproof by filling wall cavities or lining the room with insulation. Double glaze windows, seal doors and floors, lay carpet, and adjust the acoustics by adding or removing sound-absorbing and sound-reflecting materials.

Exercise For safety and comfort, you need lots of space and no sharp edges. Floors must be non-slip – use well-sanded and sealed wood, cork or rubber. A mat is essential for floor exercises. Make sure that the room is well ventilated, preferably with a window (with curtains or blinds for privacy). The harder your equipment is to set up and put away, the less often you'll use it, so organize storage carefully and, if possible, keep equipment permanently set up. Visit health clubs and gyms for ideas about decor.

1 *Work areas in an unconverted family house, which, with its large high-ceilinged rooms, is an ideal location for a studio. The house is owned by an Italian furniture designer and here he works with students and apprentices. In what was once a bathroom, sample chair covers are dyed and stitched.*

2 *A true work/living environment has been created by an English sculptor, allowing space for work in progress and finished art to be displayed.*

3 *A work-room designed for a man who needs plenty of materials on hand for model making. The small extension is lined with hooks and fittings carrying objects and tools so that everything has its place and is easily reached.*

4 *A French journalist and broadcaster uses his work space as a leisure centre. With no time to pay visits to the gym, he trains at home and uses a flexible storage system to house his gear, his library and all his music and video equipment. This hobby room serves also as studio and music room. The whole room could be dismantled to move.*
5 *A printer has designed her studio to take maximum advantage of the light from a sea view; terrazzo flooring gives an elegant and durable surface, and ample shelf space has been allowed for favourite objects and sources of inspiration. A sturdy but mobile storage unit holds immediately accessible equipment.*

Utility rooms

The value of a good utility room has to be experienced to be appreciated: it is a separate area where all clothes can be washed, dried and ironed, all household cleaning equipment stored, sewing can be done in organized peace and endless essential but messy tasks are carried out away from easily damaged surfaces.

Space Washing machines and driers are bulky and you need clear front and rear access to them. Also allow room for drying racks, ironing boards (which can fold down from a wall), and for storing equipment such as vacuum cleaners, brooms and washing powder bought in bulk.

Services and safety You will need quick access to stopcocks (plugs) and pipes. Keep electric sockets (outlets) well away from water (and this includes the floor); and place them so that wires do not trail. The iron should have a socket of its own, so that you do not confuse plugs and can be certain it is disconnected after use – the socket should be at the same height as the ironing board. Always use a professional plumber and electrician to install machinery and to check the services regularly. Dangerous materials, such as bleach and cleaning fluids, must be kept out of reach of children, preferably in child-proof cupboards. Locking the utility room when not in use will keep children away from the fascinating collection of switches, machines and washing powders.

Cleaning clothes A double sink is useful for handwashing, soaking and bleaching, and should have good draining boards. Provide containers for dirty clothes, and for carrying washing from machine to drier or clothes line. A clear surface will aid sorting clothes. A drying rack is often essential even if you install a tumble drier and space is saved by using a rack which fits on the ceiling. A standing ironing board is useful.

Floors Laundry equipment tends to flood, so the floor should have a built-in drain, if possible. It must be durable and easily cleaned – in case you drop freshly ironed clothes on it.

Other uses

The utility room is a good location for boilers, freezers, water softeners and meters. It is the perfect place for storing shoe-cleaning equipment, stain removers and other household products.

Sewing and repairs If space allows, a corner can be used for a sewing machine and for storing paper patterns, pins, scissors, threads and other equipment. But a large table will be needed if you plan to do any pattern cutting in the utility room.

1 *Efficient modern equipment combined with traditional furniture and old laundry equipment make a spacious utility room functional and stylish.*
2 *Sleek, fitted storage units, part of a range to match a kitchen, house cleaning products and laundry equipment.*
3 *With careful planning, a small space can be used for more than one task or activity: here a laundry and ironing room doubles as a workshop area, with well-arranged lighting (built in over the work surface, adjustable for the laundry).*

Workshops

If you are interested in such activities as building furniture, taking on do-it-yourself tasks, and servicing or repairing your car, a workshop should be a priority.

Location Locate the workshop away from the main living areas of the house to avoid interrupting others with noise and vibration from machinery, and to control the spread of grease, wood shavings, and the like. If a separate area is not possible and the work you undertake doesn't require large pieces of machinery, then you could find a place to store tools and materials and to keep a portable workbench and a large dustsheet in part of another room – in the garage, perhaps, or the utility room. But do beware: it is rarely sensible to repair a motorcycle in the living room if you value your carpets, your up-holstery and your relationships.

Set up a work-room as soon as possible, if you are renovating a house. Where there is no space for a permanent workshop, use the room you will renovate last.

Noise To minimize noise, especially if the workshop adjoins the house, soundproof walls, double glaze windows and fit suppressors to electrical equipment. But do check that ventilation is adequate – you might need a fan or extractor. Also, connections to the house doorbell and a telephone might be necessary.

Floors The floor must be solid and preferably at ground level if you are going to install heavy machinery. In addition, it should be durable and easy to clean. Fill in any cracks to prevent losing any small parts and equipment you might drop. Concrete floors can be cold, so it's a good idea to use a small duckboard next to the workbench.

Tidiness You'll need large, strong rubbish containers for disposing of waste. Keep the workshop as clean as possible, and store brooms and cleaning equipment in a cupboard. Wood shavings and other rubbish are potential fire hazards.

Storage One of life's frustrating moments is to be halfway through a job and unable to find an essential tool: every tool should have its place. Display storage is best for things you use constantly; tools can be hung on grids or pegboards attached to wall fittings (magnetic knife holders are also useful for this). Make sure your storage areas are well lit for easy location of items.

Plastic baskets are useful for storing objects you need to carry around. Small items are best kept in removable sliding trays which fit storage cabinets. Dry storage should be available for any tools which are likely to rust – and remember to oil them regularly.

Workbench The workbench should be at a comfortable height – when you are standing beside it your elbows should be at bench height. It will need to take clamps and should be close to electric sockets for easy use of electric tools.

Lighting The workbench area should be well lit, but make sure there is no shadow over your hands when working. Portable lights are useful, especially for car maintenance, but make sure the bulb is well protected – lethal live wires will be exposed if it smashes.

Safety Safety should be a priority in the workshop. Use guards on dangerous equipment. Keep all electric sockets and leads away from water, and earth (ground) all equipment. Fit an earth-leakage detector to cut off the main electricity supply if faults develop. Take special care if you use electric, oil or paraffin heaters. Have a fire extinguisher in the workshop at all times, install a clearly marked electrical cut-off switch, and have an easily found first-aid box. Above all, keep children out by fixing high door handles and locking the room whenever it is empty. Install a telephone if you intend to spend long hours there alone – you may need emergency help.

1 *A woodwork studio where the chief rule for equipping has been followed: always spend as much as possible on sturdy workbenches, good lighting and floors. Quality equipment can be found second-hand: looks may be secondary to function. The tiled floor makes this workshop easy to keep clean. Fixed downlights and movable lamps provide flexible lighting and can be adjusted to avoid shadows falling on the immediate work surface. Electricity supplies to a workshop should be carefully installed for safety.*

2 *A fashion designer's workshop has walls of pinboards, paper-covered, renewable work surfaces and good task lighting. Materials, sketches and equipment are displayed for easy use.*
3 *A well-organized, temporary workshop established while a house is being fastidiously renovated.*

4 *A model maker's work-room with a purpose-built bench and tool rack.*
5 *These workbenches and storage units are bolted to solid walls, leaving space to slot tools neatly.*

ONE-ROOM LIVING

Having but one room to call home has become the almost quintessential condition of modern-day urban living. In Britain, the universal 'bed-sit' has a long association with grim poverty and being down and out, and, in the United States, studio and one-room dwellers are regarded as the poor relatives of those who are fortunate enough to have secured one-bedroom apartments. Large cities around the world have their share of undesirable but essential one-room living spaces for those who either want a nomadic existence or cannot afford more space. The result is that living in a single space presents a singularly unattractive image.

A single-room home has been a fact of life that one would not so much choose as agree to settle for, given no alternative. But there have been a number of recent developments that are contributing to a change in the status of one-room living: the single room need no longer be a place that you can simply make the best of, but a situation that you might conceivably delight in.

In most major cities, there are designers who are coping with the special demands of living in a tight space by using wit and imagination. Furniture manufacturers have also responded to what they perceive as a major trend in modern living arrangements.

The ubiquitous sofa bed is no longer a giveaway to the lack of a separate bedroom, for now there are many other ways that have been devised to camouflage a sleeping area. In addition, an array of folding furniture, low-voltage lighting and movable storage units are among the many designs and ideas that have been introduced in the market as the need has grown to make use of every inch.

Living in one room does not always mean getting by in a tiny area. Converted factories and warehouse spaces, even divided town houses, have produced a wide range of variations on the single-room theme. These expansive open-plan apartments in unusual buildings have given one-room living a new lease of life and a far more respectable, not to say highly desirable, image.

One-room living will never appeal to everyone. But for those who delight in the sense of being able to survey the whole house from a single vantage point, the lesson to be learned is that the size of the space does not necessarily determine the level of satisfaction. The person who, in search of more space to spread out, moves on from a single-room apartment to a cavernous loft may find that it was the comfortable cosiness of that small apartment that made living in one room so satisfying.

The attic home of a Japanese shoe designer. Every surface is white – walls, floor, shelves and so on – to help disguise the small dimensions of the room. Decoration consists only of a few displayed favourite objects. Being well-organized and scrupulously tidy are the prerequisites for living in one small room.

303

Design solutions

In past decades, when there was not such a severe shortage of urban housing, living in one room generally had only been a temporary state of affairs. The young professional expected to move up the career ladder and, as the salary rose, into a one- or two-bedroomed apartment; if there was a family, the additional space might be found a short commuting distance away from the central urban core.

But today's city dwellers are more apt to find that they are enjoying their centrally located homes and that it's not so easy or economical to move. Weighing the advantages and disadvantages, they decide that it makes more sense to stay where they are and fix up what they have – with or without the help of an architect or interior designer.

Concurrently, a new breed of designer has emerged, one who is ready and willing to help clients cope with adapting their small living spaces. These designers delight in the difficult project, perceiving it as an interesting challenge.

'It's important for people not to feel that they are being cheated by not having more space,' said Jean Weiner. 'It means making that space function well.' She should know. With Paul Shafer, her partner in a New York design company, she has devised intricate but workable solutions to seemingly impossibly small spaces.

The designers work at creating what they call 'sub-architecture', a design scheme that combines function with visual interest and includes ways to integrate lighting and storage and other functional needs. 'We often end up with people who need rooms that can change during the day,' Weiner explained. 'In the morning they need a place to get organized and to work. By the time evening rolls around, they want to entertain friends and relax.'

Sometimes the designers come up with moving parts – swing-out bookcases, sliding panels, storage cubes on castors, beds on pulleys. Often they use different levels as a design device – to provide extra seating and floor space as well as creating surfaces that can have multiple functions. 'Levels help in making the transition of a desk into a storage unit or closet. A lot of our work depends on which door you open, which door you pull out, which thing unfolds. We try and incorporate lighting. One can get a lot of variety at the flick of a switch.'

Weiner's attitude towards people who live in one room is particularly noteworthy. 'One-room living is an achievement,' she explained. 'It's not to be seen as an enforced condition or a sacrifice, but rather as a situation that can be dealt with with imagination and fun.'

In the last few years, Doug Frank, a young American interior designer, has completed so many one-room renovations that he was beginning to fear he would be typecast in that one speciality.

Taking clues from the successful minimalists, such as Joseph Paul D'Urso or Michael Schaible and Robert Bray, Frank took the attitude that it was not enough to move the furniture around but, rather, what was called for was a complete rethinking of space.

So, in a number of single-room apartments – many of them converted brownstones – Frank repositioned sleeping areas, had closets built behind dramatic curved walls, made the kitchens integral parts of the main space and designed seating that would be comfortable for both dining and just 'sitting around'.

The need to make an enormous number of demands on a small space can sometimes produce an innovative interior suited to very specific needs. A case in point was the situation faced by Henri Gueron, a New York architect who works at home, when his young son, Ivan, came to live with him.

Gueron had been able to cope with his son's gear when the boy was visiting him only weekends, but it seemed nearly impossible that the one-room studio could be made to serve not only as living space for an adult and a child, but also as Gueron's office. But Gueron found a way, and although his solution might not be suitable for everyone, he did make it work for himself and his son.

Privacy was an important factor; the main space was divided so that Ivan could have a tiny area to himself while his father worked and slept in the larger main living area. A series of carpeted levels organized the space and also provided storage. But Gueron emphasizes, as do many other one-room *habitués*, that 'neatness counts'. 'I'm always after Ivan to pick up his things,' the father noted. 'You just can't leave anything around.'

1 *Jean Weiner and Paul Shafer's design for this large space has involved building a platform with alcoves beneath for the kitchen and dining areas. Careful attention to detail ensured that the new partitions complement the original architectural style.*
2 *A typical Doug Frank design for one-room living, with a creative use of available space achieved using built-in storage units.*

3 *An ingenious split-level plan takes advantage of large windows for the raised sitting area. The dining table slides out of view when not in use and a home office is situated at a higher level.*

4 *A bedroom alcove can be screened off from the rest of the room by lowering blinds. Storage has been built beneath the bed platform and on one side of the alcove, behind curtains. The area beside the bed serves as a desk top by day.*

5 *Fantastic economy and planning makes full use of a small area: the steel gangway links two upper alcoves, providing a second bedroom and a compact conservatory (sun-room). A combination of natural and local lighting adds to the sense of space.*

6 *New York architect Henri Gueron adapted his one-room studio to include a small space for his son. The main area is office, living and bedroom for father.*

Dividing open spaces

While it might confound the imagination of someone struggling against the clutter in a home measuring 6m by 6m (20ft by 20ft), living in and organizing a too-large space sometimes can be as difficult and frustrating as dealing with too little room. The one thing that has helped many people deal with such a problem is the trend towards a more casual lifestyle, with increasingly relaxed communication between family members or residents and their guests.

For some, especially those who are lucky enough to have a grand open-flow layout, there is the freedom and sense of exhilaration that accompanies being unhampered by partitions and walls.

The glamour suggested by what appears to be an acre of wide-open loft space or by living below soaring cathedral ceilings has prompted some apartment dwellers to take steps that were pretty well unheard of a few years ago – namely removing walls to create single rooms out of houses and apartments that once comprised a more traditional sequence of spaces.

Gone are the entrance halls or foyers; banished are the living-room doors that separated that room from the dining room. The kitchen is visible; the bedroom sits nestled into a corner. Often, the bathroom is the only private and enclosed space that remains. Never mind. In one-room living – and especially in the case of lofts – making a dramatic statement is often the goal to which all concerned are working.

Often this type of life best suits those who prefer to live alone. The sense of never being able to 'get away from it all' is, of course, most prevalent when families share one space, despite generous dimensions and even the benefits to family harmony bestowed by the personal stereo. But the most devoted afficionados of open-loft living can be heard talking of late about 'privacy' and a 'space of my own'.

'Please knock before entering' on a teenager's room is warning enough for most parents. Although many siblings – even of opposite sexes – may share the same room for at least the first few years of their lives, having a private place where no-one else is allowed remains an almost universal, and understandable, goal. There is, in the end, something undeniably comforting in being able closely to define the parameters of a small area – whether it is a tiny office, a secluded area in which to read or a room where the baby is within earshot.

In some cases, the very adversity involved in pursuing that goal acts as an incentive by

challenging the designer. It helps to have a talent for thinking things through thoroughly, one of the specialities of a New York interior design firm headed by Barbara Ross and Barbara Schwartz. The company specializes in jigsaw-puzzle type plans, in which built-in storage and convertible sofas, along with double-duty surfaces, are all pulled together to create super-functional rooms.

'There's no excuse for a place not to work for any number of situations just because it's small,' said Ross, who convinced a client to redesign a Manhattan L-shaped studio so that it could be used both as a weekend *pied-á-terre* and as an *ad hoc* business office.

Setting a mirrored storage unit on an angle, the designers created a bedroom alcove that was separated from the main living area with a pull-down shade. A sofa doubles as a bed

for the client's young daughter and an irregularly shaped table is used both for dining and for business conferences.

The choice of materials – the finishes include marble and mirrors and the colour scheme involves a soothing shade of pale green – contributes to the impression of luxury that permeates the small but flexible interior.

The interiors of boats, anything from an ocean-going liner to a small yacht, are a constant source of inspiration to anybody planning to live in a small space. The ingenuity displayed by naval architects in making amenable living quarters in submarines and other warships, as well as the intelligent design of passenger aircraft and even space shuttles, can give many useful ideas to people who live in small spaces.

3

1 *Barbara Ross and Barbara Schwartz specialize in one-room designs. The pale green colour scheme and clever use of mirrors and angled fittings achieve an airy atmosphere.*
2 *Often, open spaces have large windows with an abundance of natural light, which facilitates multi-level design. Here, there is a bed platform and a room within a room for the small kitchen/dining area.*

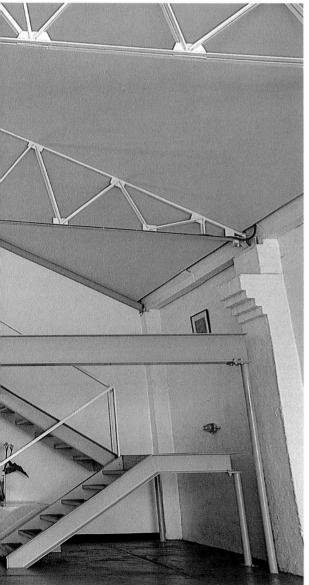

3 *A 1920s factory in Sydney was converted into a work and living area; the structure itself was used as a decorative theme.*
4 *The iron girder of the original mansard roof provides a sculptural centre for this Milan apartment.*
5 *Contrasts between the wooden beams and reflective surfaces provide dramatic impact in a London dockland warehouse.*

Open-plan layout

1 *A New York photographer utilizes the potential of her vast open loft for providing empty spaces. The bed is raised on a platform in an alcove (**2**) and much of her daily living requirements – including a home office complete with filing cabinets and a slide projector – are kept in the area beneath the bed. Most of the items in the loft are movable for greatest flexibility, allowing her to organize the main area as required.*

3 *This London apartment had been rather awkwardly converted in the 1950s when the second floors of two adjoining houses were connected to form one apartment. Designers Jan Kaplicki and David Nixon removed all non-loadbearing walls to create an open-plan environment. The bedroom area is defined by its raised platform carrying the bed, a striking uplight and a classic Rietveld 'Red and Blue' chair. The floor is made of aluminium sheeting glued to a chipboard sub-floor.*

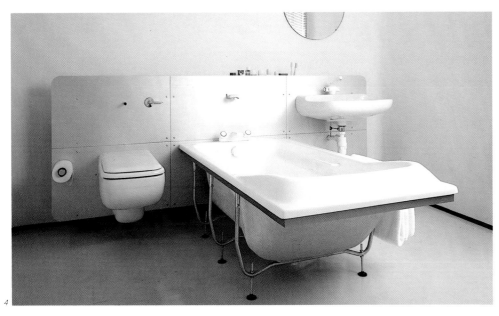

4 *The bathroom features an aluminium panel projecting from the wall, which hides pipes and stored items and carries a shelf for toiletries. The fittings hang from the panel and the floor is rubberized for easy cleaning.*

5 *The kitchen island carrying all basic equipment – sink and drainer, worktop, cooking top (burners), storage drawers, oven and dishwasher – was custom built for the apartment. Clean lines, open space and an absolute minimum of objects and displayed possessions make this the ultimate in minimal living.*

OUTDOOR ROOMS

The interior of the home, and especially the kitchen, is where most people spend as much money as they can afford. Improvements out of doors are often only considered as an afterthought, to be carried out cheaply when the carpets have been laid, the curtains hung and the money is running low. Yet the garden is what you will see every day from inside your home; it is where you will be at your most relaxed, soaking up the sun or enjoying the cool green shade. Even the tiniest scrap of space can be a place to work or to entertain, or just somewhere to sit and smell the flowers at the end of a hurried day. It can be somewhere for the children to play, or for grown-ups to exercise; it can be a living larder for keen cooks. With so many uses, the outdoor room ought to receive as much care and attention as the inside of the home, and you should include it in your planning, design and budget.

Start by deciding what the space should be for and what sort of atmosphere you want to create, just as you would with a room indoors. Should the garden reflect the style of the interior or be in complete contrast? Do you mind if it is at its best at only one point in the year, or would you rather it looked interesting all the time? If space is limited, it is often better to concentrate on one effect and do that well. So it would be more rewarding to choose a few months in the year when the flowers are to perform and show them off against a background of evergreens, so that the garden is not too dead looking in winter. Windows frame what can be the most dominating pictures in any room, so make sure that the view is what you want it to be and not just what happens to be there.

The conditions in your garden will also have an important bearing on your choice of plants. Soil deficiencies can be remedied to some extent, but the degree of sun or shade is more or less unalterable. However, remember that many gardens which are in total shade in the winter months often turn into semi-sunny ones when the sun climbs higher in the sky during the summer; shade can also be deliberately created. On the other hand, it is difficult to lessen the amount of shade when it is caused by neighbours' trees or the position of your own or others' houses; you will have to make the best of it by emphasizing the cool, dark atmosphere.

The final consideration is money. Gardening is not cheap and it is important to budget for paving, pots, garden furniture, compost and large plants. And if you are not able to look after your plants, somebody else will have to be paid to do it for you.

A small city for worship of the sun in the West Mesa of New Mexico, created by architect Antoine Predock in 1969. A series of apartments, windowless on their curving west-facing walls, were built with individual east-facing terraces. The extraordinary effects of altitude and sunlight were the source of interest for the owner of this room, where a sculptured wall and platform make a built-in sofa, a bed or study area. The place has a peaceful privacy, in harmony with the desert location.

311

Houseplants

Even if you have no garden at all, you need not do without plants. An increasingly wide range of plants is available for growing indoors, from easy-care varieties for lazy gardeners to unusual species that require a degree of pampering. Select plants accordingly to make sure they remain in good health – looking well is what matters most about houseplants. It is usually better to spend money on one really large flourishing plant than to compose one of those complicated displays of contrasting species. Such arrangements can look messy and disorganized unless you are very careful. It will be difficult to keep them all at their peak.

If you do have a garden, plants can spend part of the year outside and be brought indoors during the winter when the weather is harsh. A plain white slatted bench inside a window facing the sun can act as a reminder of the garden in the days when the real garden is not all that inviting. Large pots of lemon-scented leaf geraniums, for example, will make a green barrier between the room and the outside world and will smell like summer when the sun shines. Summer

flowers such as cornflowers and stocks can be grown outside until they are ready to flower. Large pots of lilac and philadelphus, or perhaps a winter jasmine tied into a tripod, which will pour down in a yellow winter fountain, can all live outside and then be brought inside for 'instant' blooms at the moment of flowering, but all these plants will need regular watering and feeding and some of their soil will have to be renewed once a year if they are to flower well. Myrtle and rosemary can be trained into little standards with clipped round heads and brought indoors for a special occasion. The important thing is to choose plants that suggest the garden, not the airport lounge.

Bulbs are easy – and cheap – to grow yourself and there are plenty of unusual ones you could choose that are rarely seen indoors. If space and time are short, it is worth buying the almost matured bulbs from a garden centre and planting them carefully in large china bowls with a bit of extra bulb fibre. Three hyacinths in a plastic pot are a cliché; on the other hand, a dozen in an old basin is a treat and a surprise. Single flowers are also

fun. One tobacco plant, an ornamental cabbage or lily can look very striking in a pot.

Since there is more time to study and appreciate plants indoors than in the garden, it is worth investing in some unusual varieties. If you want to show off, a well-grown bonsai or a large orchid will look stunning, but remember that a bonsai should spend most of its life out of doors. Cymbidiums, which flower in the winter months, are probably the most spectacular orchids; these and the cattleya hybrids can be grown with care in a south- or west-facing window (or, in the Southern Hemisphere, in a north- or east-facing one). Some trickier orchids might need the protection of a Wardian case or terrarium. Orchids generally dislike the fumes from gas heaters and do not thrive in draughts, but there are several types which can cope with shade.

If rare plants look out of place in family rooms, there is probably still nothing that can beat a row of geraniums in clay pots on a sunny windowsill. Indoor herb gardens also flourish in a bright kitchen and can be cropped year round.

1 *In a French fashion designer's room, purely decorated in white and gold, a large standard camellia gives a rich, dark contrast. One abundant plant will always have more style than a collection of struggling ones, and this one stands out even against other distinctive objects, such as the totem from Zaire.*

2 *A room decorated with flowers. The table centre-piece is fragile blue spring-flowering bulbs – grape hyacinths and miniature irises. A large palm fills one corner, a fiddle-leaved fig the other, and a cyperus stands in the window.*

3 *A pretty spring window decoration: white amaryllis, narcissi, hyacinths and crocus.*

4 *An orchid and a palm are well-selected for a room filled with exotic treasures: Egyptian sculpture, classic urns and a marble inlay table.*

5 *Primulas in abundance – intense colours on an equally rich textile.*

Window boxes and balconies

Around the world, the popularity of container gardening testifies to the effectiveness of this approach for brightening up odd corners and ledges. Think of Mediterranean towns for inspiration, where carnations grown in old olive oil tins and flourishing basil plants and vivid geraniums crowd balconies, windowsills and courtyards.

To be effective, window boxes, pots and tubs must be full and flowery, and this means giving them at least some attention once a day and sometimes more often. Watering must be reliable, and removing dead flower heads is vital; feeding at least once a week in the growing season will usually be necessary. Anyone who cannot spend the time in routine care would be better to plant a thin green line of box or ivy, which will only need a minimum of attention, under the windows.

It is equally important to consider whether the plants and their containers suit the character of the building. Classical designs – urns, tubs and some modern pots – look best against classical façades in fairly regular arrangements. Growing anything around a building of architectural distinction can upset the symmetry; romantic creepers may blur the outline. Roses are particularly unwieldy unless they are perfectly pruned and matched. Eccentric shapes and bushy climbers suit less formal buildings and may help to disguise an unattractive feature. Decide which note you want to strike by standing at the front of the house and looking at the whole façade before you put in a single plant. This is the impression that visitors and passers-by will have of the house and it is also the one to which you will come home day after day, so make sure it is the one you intended to give.

Select window boxes that are stable and secure and allow room for air to circulate so that the adjacent window frames and sills are in no danger from rot. The best boxes are made in light materials such as fibreglass or wood, and in plain rectangular designs. Loops and scallops can look fussy and may be hidden by greenery in any case. If, however, you opt to plant the window box with an upright evergreen, you should pay more attention to whether the box is pleasantly designed and in scale and sympathy with the building.

On balconies, the choice of plants can be governed more by personal taste rather than by the architecture of the building, because the display is more likely to be seen from inside than from the street. You should check how much extra weight a balcony can stand before loading it with plants – as a rough guide, containers should not be much larger than 400mm (16in) deep, but some balconies will not even bear this much weight.

Climbers round the windows and doors of a balcony can create the impression of overall greenery without taking up too much room. In recessed balconies, choose shade-lovers, such as honeysuckles and ivies. Formal wrought-iron balconies are probably best treated simply, with not too many trailing plants to hide the architectural details. Runner beans work well and have the added advantage of being edible! Larger balconies can be complete gardens in their own right; include plants at different levels.

Painting containers all one colour will give a feeling of unity if an assortment seems worrying. Pots in a strong colour – French blue, for example – filled with a range of grey and white plants will look sophisticated, bright flowers in pots painted tapestry green will give a more rustic air, or you could choose a colour which fits in with the colour scheme you have used indoors.

1 *City roof gardens, like this London terrace, need care to produce a good show. Deadheading of annuals and frequent watering are essential. Fuchsias, wax begonias, petunias and hydrangeas provide a bright display. Extra colour has been added with instant pots of French marigolds.*
2 *The owner of this small apartment, with a balcony overlooking the City of London, planted runner beans mixed with sweet peas to cover the exterior walls. Silver-leaved cinerarias provide a lacy, pale contrast. Herbs and other hardy annuals fill the beds.*

3 *Mediterranean sun encourages abundance in an enviable way, but even in duller climates the enjoyment of colour can be emulated. The beauty of this simple window box derives from the profusion of scarlet and pink geraniums.*
4 *Busy Lizzie (patient Lucy) fortunately grows well in cooler climates; the trick is to pinch out the tops frequently to achieve a bushy growth. Window boxes do need regular attention; water at least once a day, even more in the growing season.*

5 *Usually plant containers look best in natural colours, but a beautiful single pot, treated boldly with a glowing hue, sets off a plant that matches or contrasts with it.*

Conservatories

Conservatories, or sunrooms, provide a lovely transition from house to garden and, as well as being extremely appealing places, also make good practical sense. The warmth of the house wall heats the atmosphere so that minimal energy is needed; the conservatory in return acts as a buffer between the house and the elements. In early spring, when it may still be too cold to venture outside, it is possible to sit in a conservatory, surrounded by flowers, and feel that winter is beaten. Even a glass roof without sides, a glorified porch, will often provide enough protection for tender perennials and shrubs which might not survive the cold months in the open. A conservatory will also enable you to extend the gardening season or grow exotic species.

These days conservatories are available 'off-the-peg' in many shapes and styles, or you could have one designed and built to your own specifications. In either case, make sure that the conservatory will be big enough to accommodate a table and a few chairs.

Choice of flooring will help determine whether the conservatory echoes the house in style or belongs to the garden. For surfaces with an indoor look but which can withstand frequent wetting, quarry tiles, slate, marble, wooden decking, or yacht-painted and stencilled wooden floors are all suitable. Bricks, flagstones, paviors, or granite setts will be more reminiscent of the garden. Cobbles can be uncomfortable to walk on, so use these in moderation. Whatever floor is laid, make sure that it drains away from the house walls and out through the door, or through a drainage hole in the perimeter wall.

Although a conservatory is expensive to build, you must also budget for the extras which will do justice to the structure when it is finished. This means setting money aside for large pots and good plants. This is rather extravagant, and your gardening skills need to be very good; mature plants will be much harder to establish than small ones. Pots and tubs large enough to take a few permanent climbers and big feature plants are essential, as is the use of good quality compost. A few beds can be made at the edge of the conservatory, but build away from the house or perimeter wall, leaving a gap so that you do not bridge the damp course.

In the relatively small space of a conservatory it is important to establish a single mood. Don't mix jungle plants with delicate flowers, or grow spiky architectural plants if you want a romantic bower. But whatever style you choose, a few evergreens are always useful to provide a good foundation.

A changing display of pots gives more freedom than beds; non-performers can be pushed to the back or put outside while others take their turn. 'Staging' may be useful to show the smaller pots off to best advantage; this is no longer commonly available in wood but decorative types in wire or aluminium will make attractive *jardinières* for such small potted plants as cinerarias and auriculas, for those who like something demanding, or the easier-to-grow alpine strawberries and nasturtiums.

Watering, lighting and heating must also be taken into account. Water can be supplied simply via a tap or by sophisticated systems. In a shady conservatory or lean-to, it might be useful to invest in some 'grow' lights which can be screwed into a light fitting to provide artificial sunlight, but make sure they are waterproof.

Warming and lighting plants through the winter is often less of a problem than shading them in summer. If the conservatory is south-facing (or north-facing in the Southern Hemisphere), extra ventilators could be useful and blinds may also be needed, although if money is tight, proprietary paints to cloud the glass through the summer will do the job nearly as well; green is more effective than white. Alternatively, it is often easier to tack fine green plastic netting either inside or outside the glass. Strategically planted trees and shrubs outside (or a climber) will provide attractive 'living' shade.

Heating could be minimal unless you want a tropical effect or plan to use it in winter as a living area, but if a heating system is installed it will need a separate thermostat as well as a motorized valve separate from the domestic system so that it can operate twenty-four hours a day during the winter months.

Finally, no matter how sophisticated or expensive your equipment, you must be prepared to devote enough time to your plants. Be careful of overwatering, but, equally, of insufficient watering; in summer you should check this every day. There are devices on the market which will indicate when watering is necessary; automatic systems also remove some of the risk and responsibility, but they are expensive. Plants can be placed in saucers or on gravel, but if the weather turns cold and pots are left standing in water, there will be many casualties. Other time-consuming chores include feeding once a week in the growing season and dead-heading, without which plants will look neglected and will cease to flower. A couple of days each spring and autumn should also be set aside for special needs, including pruning, renewing compost and repotting.

1 *Marble slabs create a 'pool' trompe l'oeil beneath a dense canopy of mature plants.*

2 *With a room as beautiful as this one, containing a tessellated floor and graceful glazed roof, the plants need only act as a foil.*
3 *In contrast, a very simple, modern, prefabricated structure added to an attractive stone-walled house owned by a painter offers an alternative source of pleasure; the flower display is the focus. Variety of height is achieved by mixing wall-climbing plants with potted plants on different levels.*

Patios and terraces

A patio or terrace should be as luxurious as possible and as much a reflection of your personal taste as your living room. Here is where you should concentrate on seclusion. Provide a sense of enclosure with a low brick wall, a trellis, a hedge of an aromatic herb like rosemary or lavender, or simply with a row of pots – but do distinguish it from the rest of the garden in some way.

It is better to err on the generous side when planning a terrace or patio. Large defined spaces round a house help to integrate it with the rest of the landscape – nothing looks as ridiculous as a house perching on a small plateau of stone or concrete.

The best place for a sitting area is in the sun, near the house, so that it can be part of domestic life. Some shade will be important for summer meals but, since it is wise to keep trees at a distance from the house – they can undermine the foundations, and there could be a danger from falling branches – it is better to rely on awnings, pergolas or parasols to keep off the sun.

Scented plants and dramatic flowers (lilies are an obvious choice) should be included in any terrace planting, either in pots or in permanent positions, and evergreen shrubs can be used to keep the area looking furnished in winter – choisya, ceanothus and cistus (with resin-smelling leaves) will all look suitably exotic. For shady patios, plants with interesting leaves, such as fatsias, hostas, ferns and lilies of the valley, come into their own, interplanted with sweet-scented tobacco plants and ivy. A simple fountain on the wall, no more than a trickle of water running into a stone scoop or a large shell, will emphasize the cool, dark atmosphere and provide humidity for the plants.

The patio is the place where pots and tubs are most effective, particularly if you group them by an entrance or in a corner. Choose containers to fit in with the planting scheme. Clay pots look right anywhere, but plastic varieties do drain less quickly. White-washed clay pots can look very pretty if you want to avoid the earthy look of terracotta. Honey-coloured pottery, lead or fibreglass reproductions, wooden Versailles tubs (best for permanent tall plantings), stone urns and rustic wooden barrels are all possibilities. So are good glazed modern pots, but make sure they are frost-proof.

Tables can be of a hardwood such as teak, which weathers to grey, or in slate or marble if you want a classic, time-honoured look; painted softwood and plastics will add colour and cheer. A built-in barbecue is a good idea only if you eat and cook outside a great deal and if you positively like the utilitarian and domesticated note it strikes. Portable barbecues are just as practical and mean more space for plants and people.

Don't forget the personal touch. Outdoor sculpture or collections of *objets trouvés*, such as pebbles, fossils or interesting rocks, are ideal for display. Old chimney pots provide vertical interest, but look better unplanted. Almost anything which you find attractive and will stand the weather can add to the charm of your patio.

1 *This entrance in Barcelona creates a colourful welcome for visitors and a shady patio for the owners.*
2 *The harmonious effect of a wisteria canopy underplanted with irises gives a colourful contrast to plain paving on a French terrace.*

3 *An unusual mixture of silver-leaved cineraria and miniature variegated geraniums – a decorative summer planting against a leafy backdrop.*
4 *Climbing nasturtiums provide quick but temporary colour, while rambling roses soften the hard lines of a wooden verandah.*

5 *Seasonal plantings and interesting containers will give life to dreary patio corners. Here, fuchsias and spider plants make a striking scheme. Out of season, the beautiful old lead cistern has the stage to itself.*

6 *Patios require patience: establishing even fast-growing plants, such as rambler roses, take time. In this beautiful patio corner, a flower-covered rambling rose complements its less vigorous but more colourful neighbour – a climbing rose.*

7 *Vivid flowers, such as French marigolds, are often difficult to use in a garden as they easily overpower other plants. This single-flowered variety, however, works well here, with bright lilies and an unusual chair.*

Roof gardens

Although extreme skyline alterations may require permission from planning authorities in some parts of the world, roof gardens can be treated as quite distinct areas, in terms of design, from the house or the rest of the garden. But this freedom must be weighed against cultivation problems.

Wind will be a nuisance, and protection in the form of screens to filter the worst of the gusts is vital. Solid screens can cause more problems than they solve by creating areas of turbulence, and will need firm anchoring, but they may be necessary for comfort. If money is no object and the view is sensational, plate glass is a possibility. Wooden barriers such as trellises or palings are best fixed by a professional; remember that drilling into roof coverings is never sensible. A screen which needs almost no expertise to erect is a line of strong bamboos trapped into small holes which have been drilled into a piece of heavy timber. The weight of the wood acts as an anchor and the bamboos provide height for attaching climbers. A row of bay trees in large containers can make a dignified evergreen frame. In places with harsher climates, Portugal laurels (*Prunus lusitanica*) would look almost as good.

Flooring is a crucial consideration. You will need to check with an architect or structural engineer whether the roof has the load-bearing capacity for heavy pots and beds full of soil. An extra layer of protection will help spread the weight and keep the roof water-proof. It will also look more attractive than most roofing materials. Duckboarding can be made water-resistant and is available in various colours. Most paving is too heavy for a roof-top, but thinner slices of natural stone may be suitable. Ceramic tiles are a good choice, while astroturf is jollier.

Shade may be in short supply on an exposed roof; a pergola covered with wisteria or a vine is probably the best way to create it. It is possible to grow the odd tree in a large pot (birch is a good example), but tall plants can be stunted or deformed by wind and may well be out of scale with the rest of the planting. In sheltered, sunny roof gardens a parasol or a canvas awning will provide cover and introduce a holiday atmosphere, which could be played up with deckchairs, colourful geraniums and fuchsias. A framework made of 25-mm (1-in) tubing built off the roof on to which canvas sheets are laced during the summer is another alternative.

1 A person who started off knowing nothing about gardening cultivated this magnificent roof-top by following simple principles, learning from mistakes – and often breaking the rules. Everything is grown in tubs and the plants were selected for their versatility and impact – particular favourites are shrubs that offer pretty spring leaves, summer flowers, autumn colour and winter berries, and those with red blooms that glow under carefully designed lighting on summer nights. A roof-top of varying levels and distinct areas provides enormous potential for visual impact; the final touch is the handsome architectural lanterns, replicas of those that crown the domes of Brighton Pavilion.
2 A brilliant bower of bougainvillea, large pots of geraniums and a shady grape-vine on a sun-baked roof-top in Greece.
3 Another London roof garden, rich in foliage all year round. Spiky cordylines and a fan palm create focal points, while the narcissi and hyacinths provide welcome spring colour.

Small gardens

Resist the temptation to treat a small garden as a chance to display all your horticultural expertise, together with the entire stock of the local nursery. Keep it simple. Restricting your scheme to one theme or colour may seem unimaginative, but a garden will appear larger and more restful if the same type of plants and the same tones are repeated.

The smaller the space, the more important design becomes. Knowing what to leave out is the most difficult part, but some type of formal arrangement will help you to exert control. A formal design setting out a pattern of beds – a parterre or a knot garden, for example – works particularly well when the garden is often viewed from an upper window. These beds can be filled with herbs, vegetables or flowers, and edged with small hedges or ornamental tiles. A more modern look could be achieved by using blocks of flowers in different colours, without any edging. Even a cottage garden where the planting appears to be a muddle of favourite flowers needs some formal shape, such as topiary or a path between two flower-beds.

Gardens which contain no straight lines at all and rely on the curve are less successful on a small scale. Such gardens are designed to produce the sensation of wandering through a changing natural landscape, an effect that is rarely convincing in undersized gardens. But it is possible to introduce a romantic 'grotto' or a small, wooded corner in a shady place, a summer-cool and winter-green spot – very beguiling in a city garden.

Make sure your garden has enough privacy – a sense of enclosure is always important. Although trees shut out the neighbours, they rob the soil of nutrients and may cause excessive shade. Depending on the species, pollarding might be a good solution. Pleaching trees is also a good way of controlling growth: this results in a type of elevated hedge, which can be used to give height to a fence or a wall. Yew, if properly cared for, will grow up to 400mm (16in) per year; beech is not slow either and can be planted out when fairly well grown. Avoid the more obvious species, such as *Cupressus leylandii*.

In town gardens, space may be too limited to accommodate barriers which spread laterally as well as vertically, and here the height of walls and fences can be extended with trellises and the whole area covered in evergreens or close-growing climbers. The French create the most wonderful *trompe l'œil* effects with trellis used over a dull wall. Trellis traditionally comes in squares or diamonds, which may be too transparent for total screening if it is not completely hidden in

greenery, but it is not difficult to make a closer-woven, slightly unusual screen. One diamond-patterned panel can be superimposed on another to make smaller openings and a stronger screen; alternatively, an expanding trellis can be used half-opened, which gives a pinched lattice effect and is also stronger than the standard screen. Trellis must be fixed to strong battens nailed to the wall or fence and which reach to the same height as the trellis extension.

Screens or half-height barriers can also be made from wattle hurdles, palings, bamboos, large-meshed chicken wire covered with a dense evergreen, such as ivy, or espaliered fruit trees. Annual climbers – sweet peas, nasturtiums or runner beans, for example – can be trained up sticks to make a temporary summer screen to hide a children's corner, vegetable patch or anything else which upsets the unity of the garden design.

When space is very limited, lawns are probably a mistake, but if green is irresistible and the garden is sunny, camomile or thyme might be worth trying instead of grass. Bricks look warmer than paving in winter and can be

laid in different patterns, or combined with paving or cobbles, but make sure that the bricks you use are weather-proof. Different grades of coloured pebbles can be very effective, especially since plants will seed into this type of surface in a rather random and pleasing way. Paving stones are a conventional solution in a small garden; the best are made from natural materials but these rarely come cheap. Patterns of coloured tiles can look striking, especially if they match tiles used inside, but they must be frost-resistant.

Tiles are ideal in a minute front garden, creating an integrated effect that takes the hall out to the street. Careful choice of plants is important to counteract their dominating effect.

Edging is essential to separate earth from gravel and will make flower-beds look neater. Alternatives include low plants, tiles set on edge, flints, large cobbles, slates, treated oak slats or even shells. Old Victorian edgings for flower-beds in rope or scallop shapes look best of all, but are extremely hard to find. Painting concrete edgings with manure water or other fertilizer will encourage lichens.

1 *Make good use of a sunny spot by finding the right bench or chair to fit it. An old chimney pot is used as a plinth.*
2 *A path, bridging a water garden, disappears into rich foliage.*
3 *Circles of brick paviors break the long, narrow dimensions of a terrace-house garden. A profusion of greenery was achieved in two years with a careful choice of plants.*

4 *The unusual mixture of a pebble path and roof-tile edging against an abundant cottage garden.*
5 *Reminiscent of an Elizabethan knot garden, this plan is meant to be viewed from a height. Box-edged beds are filled with an informal mixed planting of shrubs and herbaceous plants.*
6 *A modern sculpture, perfect for a small garden: a water trellis by William Pye.*

Planting

There is not the same freedom over the choice of plants out of doors as there is in the controlled environment of a greenhouse or conservatory. For example, you will have to abandon plans for a garden full of summer flowers if dense canopies of shade cover the ground, but spring bulbs that appear before the leaves are on the trees may satisfy the craving for colour. Other factors apart from shade which might limit you include soil which dries out quickly, heavy and badly drained soil, excessive wind and extremely acid or alkaline soil. Check that any plant which you want to grow will flourish in the conditions you can offer.

It is probably better to limit the flowering season, unless the garden is to be made entirely from plants which have architectural qualities when they are not flowering. Include some evergreens and a few plants which depend on leaves rather than flowers for their effect but guard against having too many of these, or the overall effect may end up being rather municipal. Herbaceous plants and bulbs soften any planting scheme, but they are more work than shrubs and need massing if spottiness is to be avoided; it makes sense to concentrate their display against a background of more sober material.

Those who have no wish to grow plants at all should treat their garden as a room and furnish it with seats and a table, and provide a statue, tree or a handsome pot as a focal point. Such an arrangement can give as much pleasure as the most elaborate planting. For children, a play house with a picket fence and neat rows of vegetables and flowers is a good introduction to the pleasures of gardening, but supervision will be required. An ivy-covered climbing frame and a swing or a hammock, hanging from an arch or a pergola if there are no trees with suitable branches, are also good fun, but make sure they are safe and well anchored.

1 *Clusters of flowers against a dense background of shrubs and trees.*
2 *At Sissinghurst in Kent, a clematis has matured to provide a delicate backdrop to a beautiful garden seat.*
3 *Irises border a wonderfully decorative path.*

PLANTS
CHECKLIST

HOUSEPLANTS

Easy for warm rooms

- Begonia rex
- Howeia fosteriana
- Pelargonium
- Asparagus

Easy for cool rooms

- Jasminum polyanthum
- Ficus benjamina
- Gevillea robusta
- Abutilon

Harder to grow but easy in the right conditions

- Hoya carnosa
- Acacia dealbata
- Citrus
- Cymbidium
- Stephanotis
- Plumbago capensis
- Adiantum capillis veneris

Temporary effects

- Lilium longiflorum
- Narcissus 'Paper White'
- Vallota speciosa
- Primula
- Schizanthus
- Campanula isophylla
- Acidanthera
- Freesia
- Clivia

WINDOW BOXES

Permanent for sun

- Hebe 'Carl Teschner'
- Genista lydia
- Santolina incana
- Hedera (variegated forms)

Permanent for shade

- Buxus
- Viburnum davidii
- Vinca minor
- Aucuba japonica

CONSERVATORY

Cool green look

- Kentia fosteriana
- Fatsia japonica
- Sparmannia africana
- Fuchsia 'White Spider'
- Adiantum
- Campanula isophylla
- Nicotiana sylvestris

Sunny pretty look

- Plumbago capensis
- Acacia dealbata
- Jasminum polyanthum
- Pelargonium
- Helichrysum petiolatum
- Lapageria rosea
- Nerium oleander

ROOF GARDEN OR BALCONY

In sun

- Cytisus praecox
- Lavendula latifolia
- Ceanothus veitchianus
- Cistus laurifolius
- Jasminum officinale
- Vitis 'Brandt'
- Ceratostigma willmottianum

In shade

- Camellia
- Mahonia japonica
- Elaeagnus ebbingei
- Fuchsia magellanica
- Lonicera halliana
- Hedera colchica
- Helleborus corsicus

In wind

- Viburnum tinus
- Jasminum nudiflorum
- Genista hispanica
- Buxus sempervirens
- Hippophae rhamnoides
- Lonicera pileata

GARDEN

Top herbaceous plants

- Acanthus mollis
- Alchemilla mollis
- Artemisia 'Lambrook Silver'
- Geranium endressii 'Wargrave Pink'
- Viola cornuta 'Alba'
- Helleborus corsicus
- Campanula persicifolia
- Euphorbia robbiae
- Cyclamen neapolitanum
- Lychnis coronaria

Top shrubs

- Choisya ternata
- Daphne cneorum 'Somerset'
- Buxus sempervirens
- Philadelphus 'Belle Etoile'
- Viburnum bodnantense 'Dawn'
- Weigela florida 'Variegata'
- Hammamelis mollis 'Pallida'
- Cistus corbariensis
- Ceanothus 'Delight'
- Magnolia grandiflora
- Potentilla arbuscula

Sunny wallcoverings

- Jasminum officinale
- Humulus lupulus 'Aureus'
- Wisteria sinensis
- Rosa in variety
- Solanum crispum 'Album'
- Vitis vinifera 'Purpurea'
- Trachelospermum jasminoides

Shady wallcoverings

- Camellia
- Parthenocissus henryana
- Jasminum nudiflorum
- Rosa 'Mermaid'
- Hedera 'Gloire de Marengo'
- Hydrangea petiolaris
- Clematis montana 'Elizabeth'

Carpet plants

- Ajuga reptans
- Vinca major 'Variegata'
- Lamium maculatum
- Viola cornuta
- Cyclamen neapolitanum
- Convallaria majalis

Furniture plants

- Magnolia grandiflora
- Euphorbia wulfenii
- Rosmarinus officinalis
- Osmanthus delavayi
- Senecio greyi
- Juniperus hibernica

5

6

4 *An easily maintained garden takes its impact from the adjacent textures of bricks and leaves – herbs, ivy and carefully chosen climbers.*
5 *Euphorbias with two tubs of clipped box enhance a charming rural entrance.*
6 *Planting a small area creates an attractive view from inside.*

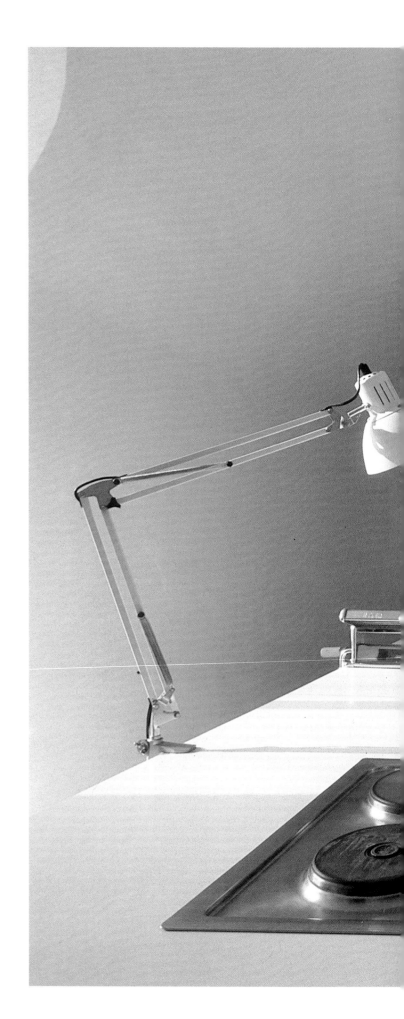

PART 4

ESSENTIALS

Our homes need certain essential domestic
services – the supply of electricity, gas and
water – without which they cannot function. It
is important to keep the wires and pipes, which
carry these essentials, out of sight, to emerge
from the fabric of the house exactly where you
want them. The sleek precision of a minimal
island kitchen bears witness to the fact that
good home design owes as much to basic
common sense as it does to aesthetic creativity.

SAFETY

Home is the place where most people take their safety for granted. Yet it is often the scene of serious accidents, some of which prove fatal. Statistics tell us that more than half of these fatalities are the result of falls, of which the majority affect those over sixty-five. But other causes include fire, poisoning (from gases and vapours, as well as from drugs and household chemicals), suffocation, choking, drowning and electrocution: a horrifying catalogue of disaster. At a less serious level, millions of people each year require medical assistance – even hospitalization – for injuries suffered in the home. But fatal or not, many of these accidents could certainly have been prevented.

Making your home a safe place to be is your responsibility. Prevention means careful planning in the first place: choosing home furnishings and equipment for their 'safety qualities' – the flame-retardant paint or upholstery fabric, for instance, the gas valve that can't be knocked on without lighting, the properly tested and wired electrical appliance, the non-slip floor finish and so on. The consumer movements in many countries have fought for – and achieved – legislation to set minimum safety standards. It is worth finding out about the standards that apply locally and looking for the appropriate labels. You shouldn't have to sacrifice good design for safety; truly good design recognizes the safety dimension. But only if we all continue to insist on it will shops, suppliers, builders and designers automatically build it into their products.

The external structure

When your home's structure is kept in good condition, accidents caused by falling masonry, crumbling brickwork and so on are unlikely to happen. Pay particular attention to access points. Good lighting and level, non-slip steps and paths are vital.

You, as a homeowner, can be held responsible for injuries suffered by other people on your property, regardless of whether they are your family, invited guests or uninvited deliverers of unwanted free offers.

Safety indoors

Sensible planning and careful maintenance pay dividends inside the house, too. Heating systems and the electrical supply need particular consideration.

Ventilation

Ventilation is important, because all fuels need a supply of air to burn and because by-products of the combustion process need to be removed. Open chimneys are not efficient enough for modern oil, solid-fuel or gas-burning appliances. Oil-fired and solid-fuel boilers and water heaters, which can produce carbon monoxide and sulphur dioxide, always need

their own closed systems. Gas-burning appliances can now have balanced flues which both draw in air and discharge the fumes.

It is also important to keep any chimneys, airbricks or ventilators in good order.

Signs of poor ventilation may not be obvious. Discoloration or staining around the top of gas fires or water heaters is an indication of defective flues. You may even experience unpleasant side effects, such as headaches.

Storage of flammable fuels is subject to regulations, which specify the type of storage necessary and where it ought to be situated; these regulations must be carefully observed.

Gas

Apart from the hazards of poor ventilation, the danger of gas today is from explosion. Gas can accumulate if there is a leak or an appliance gets turned on without being properly lit. Then any small spark, even from a burning cigarette or switching a light on and off, could ignite the gas/air mixture and make it explode.

You must have gas appliances and heating installed and serviced by an expert; don't cheat on maintenance.

Safety outside
1 *Well-maintained exterior fabric; well-secured cladding, roof tiles or slates, chimney stack, television aerial; guttering and drainpipes.*
2 *Well-planned access; steps in good condition; non-slip, level pathways. Adequate, well-sited outdoor lighting.*
3 *Glazed doors with toughened or laminated glass, avoiding injury if broken.*

4 *Adequate storage for flammable fuels, accounting for local regulations in position related to house.*
5 *Lockable outdoor store for tools, paints, varnishes, weedkiller, etc.*
6 *Upper-storey windows, up to 900mm (36in) from floor, should have safety catches or fixed vertical bars, which can be removed in an emergency.*
7 *Heavy-duty plugs and extension leads in good condition, for electrical tools used outdoors.*

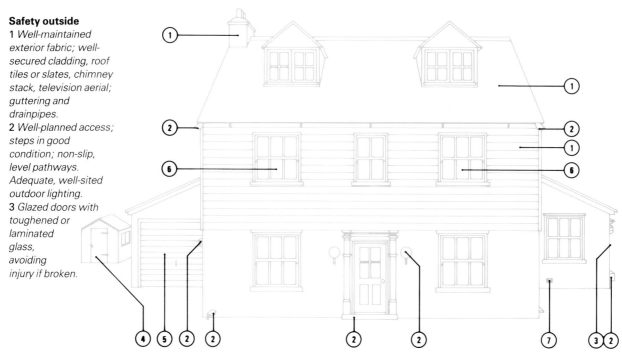

Most gas appliances come with built-in safety devices that make sure they cannot be turned on without being lit. These include lighting mechanisms that depend on an electrical spark rather than a pilot light.

You must know how to turn off the gas at the main supply valve – this must be sited so it can be easily turned off in a crisis.

Electricity

Although fatal accidents in the home caused by electrocution are fortunately rare, fires from faulty wiring, overloading, overheating or imperfect insulation present a very real hazard.

Using electricity safely means making sure that the whole system and individual appliances are in good working order.

Electrical systems All electrical systems must be installed to the proper standard – which means using a qualified electrician. The standards are set by professional bodies and also by law, and they vary from area to area. Have your system checked every five years and renewed after about twenty. If you have a jumble of wires, switches and fuses (electrical panels) for each unit – for the

cooker (stove), for the lighting, for example – the system is probably old and in need of attention.

When planning your system, make sure you have enough socket outlets for your needs in each room. Adaptors and trailing cords can cause accidents. A paucity of outlets is an indication of a badly designed installation that may need attention.

It is also a good practice to have more than one lighting circuit so that if there is a fault in a light fixture and the fuse blows you do not suffer a complete blackout.

Rodents can damage your wiring. If wires are stripped of their insulating plastic sheaths, they can result in electric shocks, blow fuses and even, in extreme cases, a fire. In an old house, periodic check-ups are advisable, particularly if you know mice or rats are about.

Electrical appliances Use electrical appliances correctly, following manufacturers' instructions. Plugs must be correctly wired. Make sure that each wire is firmly attached to the right terminal, and that the cord is in good condition and held in place by a grip. Check that plugs are fitted with the right fuses, ac-

cording to the manufacturers' specifications.

Since each country has developed its own standards, its own types of plugs and socket outlets and, most importantly, supplies electricity to consumers at different voltages and frequencies, electrical appliances made for one country cannot always be used in another without risk of overheating.

Overloading can occur if too many appliances are plugged into one outlet. Television sets, in particular, can overheat if you leave them plugged in all the time, whether or not the set is on. Power tools should have heavy-duty waterproof cables and plugs and socket outlets for outdoor work.

The bathroom is the one area of the house where you are most vulnerable to electrocution. There are often special regulations concerning types of light fixtures, power supply for washing machines or shower units and socket outlets for shavers; these regulations must be scrupulously observed.

Floors

Falls are a major danger at home and are very often due to an

uneven floor surface, loose tiles or frayed carpet, or rugs not securely anchored to polished floors. Prevention means making sure all floors throughout the house are level, non-slip and kept in good condition – especially on the stairs. If you like polished floors, use a non-slip polish – and anchor any rugs with a special rubber-backed underfelt. Make all changes of level obvious and well lit.

Storage

Cluttered, badly planned or nonexistent storage creates accidents and can be a fire hazard. It is often unhygienic, particularly in a kitchen. If your storage has to be high up, make sure you provide yourself with firm, stable steps, preferably with a handhold, for access.

Minimizing fire risks

Fire is probably the most feared of all home accidents and potentially the most devastating, threatening lives, possessions and the entire structure of your home. There is more risk from smoke and poisonous fumes than from heat and flames.

Most fires in private homes start in the kitchen, with oil left

Safety indoors
1 *Modernized electricity supply, properly earthed (grounded).*
2 *Electrical wiring installed to professional standards, checked every five years.*
3 *Sufficient socket outlets in all rooms.*
4 *Bathroom wired with special shaver socket outlet only.*
5 *All socket outlets, cords and appliances in good condition and conforming to safety standards.*
6 *Balanced flues where necessary for gas boilers, heaters or water heaters, or other ventilation.*

7 *All gas supplies fitted and maintained by competent installer.*
8 *Safety taps that cannot be knocked on inadvertently.*
9 *Level, non-slip floor covering in good condition.*
10 *Floor surfacing that is easy to keep clean.*
11 *Fire-resistant finishes for walls, furnishings and fabrics.*
12 *Lockable cabinet for medicines and drugs.*
13 *Storage for household cleaners, detergents, matches, etc. well out of reach of small children.*
14 *Adequate food storage, to protect from infestation.*

heating up in an unattended pan the chief culprit. (Oil spontaneously ignites when it reaches a certain temperature, so you need to take special care whenever you deep fry.) Other major causes are smoking, children playing with matches and electrical faults. Essential precautions include not smoking in bed; storing matches, lighters, candles and so on well out of children's reach; and keeping electrical appliances and wiring in good order. Make sure major appliances are unplugged when you go away, and unplug the television and stereo every night when you go to bed – except if manufacturers' instructions state otherwise.

Some structures will, of course, burn more readily than others: you need to take greater care in a wood-frame, wood-clad summer house than a house built of bricks and mortar! In many countries and cities, there are specific regulations about the use of different materials and it is essential to check up on these before you embark on major structural alterations.

Since the layout of a house or apartment can affect the way a fire spreads, regulations also apply to alterations that involve internal reorganization. The practice now is to try to contain a fire in the place where it starts – which is difficult in open-plan areas. There are fire-retardant specifications for internal walls, doors, paints and finishes which require that, for example, a door would take half an hour to burn through. If a door has no fire-retardant rating, just closing it will hold back a fire a short time and stop the passage of smoke. If a house has more than two floors and the stairs are the main escape route, it is a good idea to enclose the stairwell with walls and doors that meet fire-retardant specifications.

Unless you are a long way from the nearest fire station, it is not advisable to invest in elaborate fire-extinguishing equipment, for two reasons. Firstly, most home fire extinguishers can only put out a small fire, and, secondly, different fires do need different treatments; in addition, most of us, even if we have the right kind of extinguisher, have either forgotten how to use it or never really bothered to learn in the first place.

There is one exception: a fire blanket for the kitchen. This can successfully smother most fires which start at the stove – oil fires or cooking disasters, for instance – quickly and efficiently. Fire blankets made from glass fibre, non-melt polyamide and treated wool are all suitable.

If you do buy a fire extinguisher, there are several types from which to choose, and each is designed to tackle a specific job. These are the most common types produced for domestic use:

Water extinguishers These extinguishers deliver water under pressure and they are effective on ordinary combustible materials, such as wood, paper or cloth. These are not suitable for fires involving flammable liquids or live electrical apparatus.

Foam extinguishers and dry powder extinguishers These deal effectively with flammable liquids (fats, oils, spirits) but are very messy.

Carbon dioxide extinguishers, BCF or Halon extinguishers Spread gases to smother a small fire. They are useful for electrical fires because their gases do not damage electrical equipment, but they have to be used carefully because they are either toxic or asphyxiants.

Warning systems

The smoke detection and sprinkler systems now in many offices and public buildings are really too elaborate and expensive for you to consider installing in your home, although, in some areas, some sort of warning system is a legal requirement. There are battery-operated smoke alarms, now available at very moderate prices, which bleep a loud warning when smoke enters the mechanism; these should also warn you automatically when batteries are running low. They can be easily fixed to walls or ceilings at strategic points – but don't install them in the kitchen, because they will be set off every time you burn the onions.

Escape routes

It is essential to work out escape routes, especially from upper floors and bearing in mind the very young or not terribly agile. In some areas, an approved escape route is a legal requirement.

Most types of escape apparatus are too slow and too elaborate for home use. Outside fire escapes, although relatively straightforward for the very old, the very young and the panic-stricken to manage, are ex-

Fire safety
1 *Chimney swept.*
2 *Fire-resistant ceiling tiles for insulation.*
3 *Fixed fire-guards on all fires or heaters if children in house.*
4 *Flame-resistant nightwear.*
5 *Escape-route plan.*
6 *Matches kept out of children's reach.*
7 *Thermostatically controlled pans for deep frying.*
8 *Fire blanket near cooker (stove).*
9 *Airing for clothes away from heat source.*
10 *Blind not curtain near cooker (stove).*
11 *Boilers and water heaters serviced.*
12 *Gas appliances serviced.*

13 *Fire-retarding door between kitchen and stairs.*
14 *Fixed heating for hallway.*
15 *Flammable goods safely stored.*
16 *All appliances unplugged when house empty.*
17 *Flame-retardant covers for all upholstered furniture.*
18 *Sufficient sockets to avoid trailing cords.*
19 *No smoking in bed.*
20 *Electric blankets used as manufacturer specifies.*
21 *Adequate clothes storage.*
22 *Battery-operated smoke alarm.*
23 *Well-maintained electric wiring.*

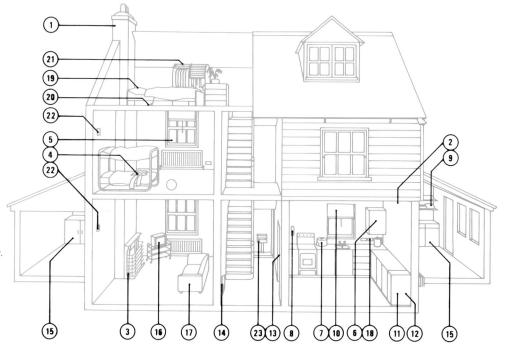

pensive and are an encouragement to burglars. The staircase could be the most practical route – hence the importance of the fire-retardant regulations and specifications for walls, doors and paints.

Tragedies have occurred because, as the last resort, people couldn't get out of the windows – either because there was not a big enough opening or double glazing had made the window impenetrable. It's important that every room, and particularly each bedroom, has a window which can open enough for escape.

Safety room by room
Hallways, stairs and landings
Planning for safety here is largely a matter of eliminating all unnecessary clutter and preventing falls by making the stairs safer – this means with firmly anchored coverings, no fraying carpets or loose stair-rods.

Insist that children do not leave their toys on the stairs and bicycles in the halls. You should make sure that the banisters are in good condition and there are good firm hand-holds. Since stairs are important as fire escape routes, good maintenance here is absolutely vital.

Living and dining rooms
The open fire is the most obvious danger point here: it is essential to fix a fire-guard in place when you are not in the room. Carelessness when smoking and poor electrical arrangements (not enough socket outlets, trailing or worn cords) can also be fire hazards. Modern upholstery, much of which is made from polyurethane foam, catches fire easily and gives off dangerous toxic fumes unless it is specially treated or covered with treated upholstery material. Look for fire-retardant labels when purchasing furniture or at least use a spray-on retardant according to the manufacturers' instructions.

Kitchens
The kitchen is where most home accidents occur, but a good work-plan, plenty of storage and easily cleaned work surfaces and finishes will automatically make it a safer place.

Deep frying is the activity most likely to cause an accident. If you particularly like deep frying, a safety measure would be to invest in an electric, thermostatically controlled deep fryer, or a special unit designed to deep fry safely.

Burns and scalds are other frequent accidents. The risks for children can be lessened by having a guard rail around the hob (elements) and buying stable wide-based cooking utensils, which you use on the back elements when children are around.

Electrical appliances proliferate in the modern kitchen, so the safe kitchen has plenty of socket outlets and appliances in good repair. Cords can get charred and dangerous if left too near a heat source. Cookers (stoves) and heaters need special outlets. If there is a boiler or water heater in the kitchen, special efforts must be made to ensure efficient ventilation.

Bedrooms
Bedrooms are safe havens – unless you smoke in bed!

It is important to have safe electrical appliances and plenty of socket outlets to eliminate the need for trailing cords. If you have an electric blanket, you should use it as the manufacturer instructs and have it regularly serviced.

Good storage is an advantage, especially if you have a radiant heater in the bedroom; clothes flung near a heat source or even

a scarf draped over a bedside light can catch fire all too easily – with tragic results.

A floor covering that is in good condition and is non-slip helps prevent falls.

Bathrooms
Safety in the bathroom is chiefly concerned with the correct use of electricity. Since electricity, water and people make a fatal combination, in most countries there are strict regulations laid down regarding light switches, socket outlets and the positioning of heaters.

You are advised not to put laundry equipment (washing machine and/or clothes drier) in the bathroom unless there is at least a space of 1.8m (6ft) between the appliances and the bath or shower, and the installation work should always be carried out by a qualified electrician and a qualified plumber.

Non-slip floors and hand-holds (grab bars) will minimize the risk of falling, particularly for the elderly. Non-slip surfaces for bathtubs and showers are also important. Drugs, medicines and household chemicals kept in the bathroom should be locked safely in a cabinet.

HOME MAINTENANCE SAFETY

- Major work involving the gas and electricity supply must be done by qualified professionals.
- Always turn off electricity supply at source when replacing an electrical fitting.
- Plan ahead when undertaking any task – accidents tend to occur if you are unprepared.
- Use the right tools for the job; keep clean and in good repair; follow makers' instructions.
- Tidy up as you go; lock away dangerous items; avoid piles of rubbish which can be tripped over or can cause a fire hazard.
- Never smoke when working.
- Keep children safely away when work is in progress.

- Teach older children the right way to use sharp blades, power tools and toxic materials and ensure that they undertake tasks only under adult guidance.
- Think before you act. Home repairs and decorating can be frustrating if you make mistakes or things go wrong. Keep calm.
- Do not take unnecessary risks; always seek professional help if you are unsure about safety.
- If you undertake a lot of do-it-yourself tasks, create a workroom designed for your needs with plenty of socket outlets, good storage, adequate lighting, a solid workbench, safety goggles and gloves and other protective clothing.

- Plan storage so that all equipment and materials are kept out of reach of children.
- Keep ladders in perfect repair; never place them at a dangerous angle or on uneven ground; do not overreach from a ladder.
- All adhesives must be used with great care.
- Keep clear of cutting blades and use sharp tools only on a sturdy bench or table.
- Power tools must be correctly wired and fused; use only properly installed socket outlets; unplug tools before changing parts and accessories and when not in use; never lift tools by their cable; use properly insulated extension cables.

- Check the position of hidden pipes and wiring before drilling into walls or floors.
- Do not attempt to reach high sections, for instance when decorating a stairwell or the upper exterior of a house, without suitable scaffolding or platforms. Never climb out on to a high windowsill.
- Do not undertake work alone if it may be dangerous. If a serious accident should occur, a second person can get help immediately.
- Take the trouble to learn basic first aid from a recognized authority and keep essential equipment and medicines, such as bandages and disinfectant, in a convenient place.

Special precautions

For babies, toddlers and young children

Safety for a tiny baby who has not yet learned to roll over or started to sit up and take notice means a warm, clean home with a parent (or other doting adult) in constant attendance.

The situation changes as soon as the baby can move about independently. The desire to explore will develop rapidly and, from then on, safety means minimizing the opportunities for the child to injure her- or himself – and, remember, they can also cause considerable damage to valued possessions. Most children learn quickly what they can and cannot do safely in their own home, but problems may arise with friends or younger siblings. While nothing can replace supervision – certainly up to the age of five ·or six and often longer – without doubt, careful planning will always make the supervisor's task that much easier.

One important guideline is the 1-m (39-in) rule: that is, move everything you don't want children to touch above this level – which will be out of their reach – and lock away everything that might do them harm. Fit protective covers over power and light socket outlets. Life is also simplified if rooms where children spend time are organized with an eye to their safety; where this is impractical, there is no option but to keep the children out.

For the elderly

About half the fatal accidents in the home happen to people over the age of sixty-five, so for this age-group, the safety dimension is obviously very important. Since falls are the most frequent accidents and are more serious in their effects on old people than they are on younger ones, it is important to pay special attention to lighting and floor coverings.

There are often accidents in the kitchen too, so a kitchen planned with safety in mind is vital. As reactions slow down and memory becomes less reliable, it helps to invest in automatic or thermostatically controlled electrical appliances so, for example, the kettle cannot boil dry.

The older one gets, the more important it is to have a comfortable ambient temperature – plan to have economical heating and very good insulation, so that the system is most efficient.

PESTS WHICH ARE PARASITES

FLEAS

Human fleas, cat fleas, bird fleas are most often found in houses. Cat fleas also bite humans – so do rat fleas.

Damage Larvae and pupae live away from host; adult emerges only when vibrations indicate presence of possible host. Adults bite to feed on blood of host, often causing intense irritation. Cat fleas thrive in central-heated, carpeted buildings.

Control/treatment Destroy larvae with long-lasting insecticide sprayed on carpets and upholstery, in corners and crevices. Vacuum thoroughly. For cat fleas, burn cat's bedding and spray all its sleeping places; treat infested pets with veterinary powder or shampoo; flea collars may limit further infestation. Clear birds' nests, if any, from roof and eaves.

BED BUGS

Damage Nymphs and adults feed on blood. Many people are sensitive to bites. Found in overcrowded, dirty rooms. Create an unpleasant smell.

Control/treatment Fumigation by specialist or thorough spraying with insecticide such as lindane, fenitrothion or iodofenphos. Bats and birds are host to related species – clear away birds' nests.

MOSQUITOES

Damage Bites cause irritation in temperate climates; in tropics, mosquitoes carry malaria, yellow fever, dengue fever, encephalitis, among other diseases.

Control/treatment Keep out of house with screens on windows, or use mosquito netting. Use insecticidal (pyrethrin) spray or aerosol on adults. Prevent breeding by pouring a little paraffin on surface of any stagnant water – which deprives pupae and larvae of air.

Safety for babies and toddlers

1 *Room scheme devised using a notional 1-m (39-in) high line: only objects children can play with, touch, eat or chew on are stored below this level.*
2 *Safety catches fitted to all windows, or vertical bars upstairs.*
3 *Cooker (stove) controls with safety switches; also positioned out of children's reach.*
4 *Hob (burner) guard to prevent pans spilling.*
5 *High, lockable storage for dangerous objects, household cleaners, detergents and medicines.*
6 *Safety catches for*

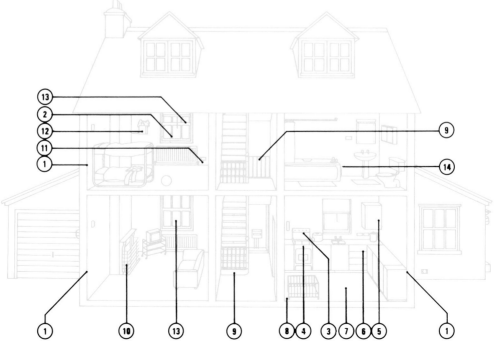

low-level cupboards containing fragile or potentially hazardous objects.
7 *Floor and work surfaces that are tough.*
8 *A play area in the kitchen outside the work triangle.*
9 *Gates on stairs to prevent falls.*
10 *Fire-guards that extend over any open fire or heater fixed firmly to wall behind.*
11 *Safety plugs in all socket outlets when not in use.*
12 *Night light.*
13 *Safety film over glass to hold broken glass in place.*
14 *Non-slip mats or base area for bath and shower.*

PESTS WHICH CONTAMINATE FOOD AND/OR SPREAD DISEASE

RODENTS

Damage Mice, in their search for food, leave droppings and urinate indiscriminately. They can spread salmonella, among other diseases. Rats, with homes in sewers, rubbish dumps, etc., spread more serious diseases – Weil's disease, rat-bite fever, trichonosis; probably foot-and-mouth disease on farms. Rat fleas brought bubonic plague to Europe in 14th century, still do in SE Asia and South America.

Control/treatment Keep food in cupboards or containers which are mouse-proof. If rodents persist, call your local environmental health department or a pest control company.

FLIES

Damage Feed on human food, but as they only have a sucking mouthpiece, they vomit and stamp on food (to make it 'edible') with their feet, with which they also forage on rubbish, sewage, etc. Houseflies breed on rotting organic matter, blowflies on meat or carrion. All flies may cause gastro-enteritis and typhoid. In warm climates they spread dysentery, ophthalmia, cholera, diphtheria.

Control/treatment Control with careful hygiene – put rubbish in closed bags or bins; never leave food out in summer. Keep flies out of house with screens at windows, or use aerosols (permethrin) or impregnated strips (dichlorvos). For cluster flies (which appear in autumn) – put insecticide into vacuum cleaner bag and vacuum.

COCKROACHES

Damage Emerge from cracks and crannies in buildings at night to feed and spread vomit and excreta as they go, leaving a foul smell and carrying a wide range of disease-causing organisms – food poisoning, cross-infections in hospitals and catering areas or kitchens.

Control/treatment Like warm humid places and infest blocks of apartments and offices, etc. For effective control, the insecticide needs to be placed where cockroaches hide – usually inaccessible except with specialist equipment. Follow-up treatments are necessary to kill nymphs hatching from hidden egg capsules.

LARDER PESTS

Biscuit beetle, drug store beetle, booklouse, flour beetle, grain weevil, flour moth

Damage These all feed on dry foods, such as cereals, pasta, powdered soups, and they contaminate food stored in larders, cupboards, etc.

Control/treatment Throw out contaminated food, clean larder or store cupboard and spray with insecticide for crawling insects.

HIDE BEETLES

Damage Scavengers of dead birds/animals. In homes they also eat bacon, ham, cheese.

Control/treatment Treat infestation with diazinon or other insecticide designed for crawling insects. Clear away birds' nests.

ANTS

Black garden ants

Damage Not known to spread any disease; will cluster over anything sweet.

Control/treatment Proprietary boric acid bait along path of entry gets taken back to nest and fed to queens and young, and destroys whole colony. Or use insecticidal lacquer or diazinon spray.

Pharaoh's ant

Damage Tropical species which can only live in central-heated buildings with high humidity. Feed on protein. Carry cross-infections and pathogenic organisms. Becoming commoner in Europe.

Control/treatment Difficult to eradicate as they are small – 2mm (1/12in) long – and hide in tiny cracks. Specialist firms use iodofenphos and spray boric acid or methoprene baits.

Safety for the elderly

1 *Level floors, in good condition, with non-slip surfaces.*
2 *Central heating with automatic controls for good ambient temperature; costs offset by good insulation.*
3 *Entryphone and telephone conveniently placed to avoid rushing to answer them.*
4 *Carefully planned bathroom, with non-slip floor, non-slip base to bath and shower and hand-holds.*
5 *Lever taps for those with weak hands.*
6 *Adequate lockable storage for medicines that is still easy to open with unsteady hands.*

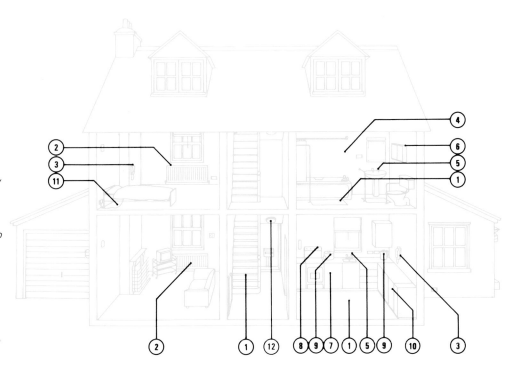

7 *Kitchen storage planned to minimize bending or climbing.*
8 *Safety gas or electric cooker controls, with knobs that are easy to manage, and with clear warning lights when turned on.*
9 *Small appliances, such as kettle or deep-frying pan, with automatic controls.*
10 *Extra storage, at convenient heights, to avoid clutter.*
11 *Electric blankets used as specified.*
12 *Extra lighting, especially on landings and stairs, to help prevent falls, and in living areas to make evening activities or reading easier.*

DESIGN FOR DISABLED PEOPLE

Planning a house or apartment to accommodate someone who has some type of disability is very similar to designing around the foibles of an able-bodied family. In fact, the very term 'disabled' is misleading since it embraces such a wide variety of conditions; and, of course, many disabilities tend to become the norm as one gets older.

It is perhaps more helpful to think of all aids and adaptations along the lines established by Professor Heinz Woolf at the Institute for Bio-Engineering, Brunel University, in England. He looks on an elderly man's need for a hoist to get in and out of a bath as very similar to his granddaughter's need for a hammer and nails to put up shelves: they both require tools to cope with the problems. One need is as normal as the other.

Certainly, very few disabilities now need to be a barrier to living an independent life among family and friends, in surroundings designed to offer the individual the chance to realize his or her potential as fully as possible. In the last two decades, designers and architects have begun to look at the problems caused by specific disabilities; new technologies are now being harnessed and manufacturers are beginning to produce special designs for the home that are suitable both for the use of disabled people and are easily incorporated into a house. Indeed, some architects and designers believe that features which specifically cater for disabled people – for example, the replacement of steps with ramps, generous corridor dimensions to allow for wheelchair users, and the placing of all electrical switches and controls at one convenient level – are more relaxing for everyone to use.

The need to consider the design of the home in relation to the household, the activities of all its members and the final effects that are required applies as much to a house or to an apartment where a disabled person lives as to any other home, and the general design points made elsewhere in this book must be considered.

The crucial difference is the need for a greater level of precision. While most housing is designed with a theoretical stereotype in mind, whose measurements we adapt to with lesser or greater degrees of success, the margin of error must be far smaller in design that is compensating for specific disabilities. John Penton, an architect with a special interest in the needs of disabled and elderly people, has emphasized the importance of rigorous analysis to find the solution that is right for each individual, and this will be the starting point for your planning.

Individual design

Every disability is different; no two people respond to a disability in the same way, so final design decisions and successful solutions must necessarily be completely individual. For those who have become disabled in later life and whose character, tastes and daily habits are more or less set, coping is principally a matter of adjustment, but for those born with a disability or who become seriously disabled as a result of illness or accident, solutions are likely to be more radical.

In either case, it is important to consider very thoroughly, and in as much detail as possible, exactly how the disabled person wants to live before any plans are made. One of the most practical ways to work out how, or whether, a house or apartment could successfully be adapted to his or her special needs is to work through a typical day with an eye to points of inconvenience or difficulty which require change. From this analysis of how the disabled member of the household – and everybody else – will manage, the design priorities will emerge and plans can be made around them.

It is also useful to learn from others; talking to people with similar problems always provides a useful second perspective. Advice from an occupational therapist is invaluable to help the disabled person realistically assess the limits of his or her physical capabilities. Organizations that concentrate on the specific disability can give advice on finding and choosing aids and adaptations. At this stage, when the criteria have been worked out, it is a good idea to discuss design ideas with an architect and, in the case of those who are severely disabled, to obtain some professional assessment from doctors, disabled people's organizations and so on.

Unfortunately, the more sophisticated the aids and the more radical the alterations needed, the more they will cost.

Few families, for example, have the means to create the ideal environment for a disabled child without financial help. It is therefore well worth investigating legal entitlements and approaching charitable organizations before proceeding too far with any plans; they should be able to give you advice on how to apply for financial help. Some local authorities have a statutory duty to provide grants, and sometimes housing, and government health services usually provide necessary aids, but the political climate will dictate how much funding is available at any given time.

Independence

One of the most important morale boosters for a disabled person is the ability to manage personal chores independently. It is perhaps the most important single factor of design which can materially improve the quality of daily life. Selwyn Goldsmith, an architect concerned with design for the disabled, has identified the different approaches to buildings where 'we put people apart with disabilities' and those which are 'an instrument of involvement and participation, of communication and understanding, mutual support and mutual regard'. Certainly, design can transform living space to give disabled people maximum independence. This, in turn, allows the elderly to remain in their own environment, disabled children to be brought up in a family atmosphere, and a greater proportion of disabled adults to live outside hospitals or other institutions.

Almost everybody with a disability, except those who need help getting in and out of a wheelchair, should be able to manage daily tasks independently with the aids to communication, mobility and which compensate for specific disabilities that are now available.

Surprisingly few major alterations should be needed: structural changes are usually only necessary where doors or rooms have to be altered to make wheelchair access and manoeuvrability possible. But certain design features developed with the disabled in mind will improve a house for everybody: level floors with non-slip surfaces; plenty of storage space systematically organized to minimize clutter; adequate lighting, heating and ventilation. Many appliances and furnishings adapted for specific disabilities are unobtrusive and can be very easily incorporated into any design scheme: seating to give a bad back proper support; telephone and doorbells that give visual signals; door handles and taps which can be easily turned by those with little strength in their hands; and electric clock vibrator alarms for the deaf. Do not forget, either, that many everyday labour-saving appliances and storage units – without specially adapted features – will increase the number of tasks a disabled person can carry out independently. It is useful to have all socket outlets, switches and handles at a level where they can be reached from a wheelchair or without bending.

Some of the hardest personal chores to manage alone are those linked to getting out of bed and dressing. An electrically operated bed means the position of the mattress can be varied to support the back or legs (or both) when climbing out of bed. Clothes are easily reached if they are kept on hanging racks or in transparent drawers on runners, which, in both cases, should pull out of the cupboard at the most convenient level. Dressing is made much easier by having somewhere comfortable to sit at the right height, and there are ingenious aids for putting on shoes and stockings when there is nobody to lend a hand. A chair in front of a well-lit mirror is important for applying make-up, and brushing hair in comfort.

The bathroom is another room that needs special attention. First, its location should be con-

sidered in relation to the bedroom. Proximity is absolutely essential when there has to be a hoist on an overhead track. Within the bathroom, there should always be plenty of space for easy movement and a floor with a non-slip surface. Often, the only other special fittings that are required are well-placed, large hand-holds and grab-bars along the edge of the bath, and a raised seat and hand-supports for the toilet. The basin may need to be set lower than normal. A platform at the end of the bath and either quarter-turn tap handles or electronic taps are often helpful for the elderly.

Wheelchair standards

The most radical and expensive alterations are those necessary to bring a house or apartment up to the design and dimension requirements for 'wheelchair standards'. These derive from the fact that someone in a wheelchair simply needs more space to move about in than someone who walks about.

Guidelines for public-financed housing often draw a distinction between wheelchair housing, for people confined to a wheelchair all the time, and mobility housing, for those who have some mobility around the house but who need a wheelchair to get about outside. Mobility housing requires space for a wheelchair to get in and out of a house, but in wheelchair housing space must be allowed for circulation and the problems of transfer inside as well. Individual cases will always present different problems and need different solutions, but there are general points to check when considering whether a house would be suitable or could be converted for wheelchair use.

Firstly, there are certain key dimensions: open doors should have a clearance of at least 775mm (33in). A standard wheelchair needs a turning circle of approximately 1.5m (60in) diameter; more, if it is larger. These

measurements obviously affect circulation from room to room, the design of hallways, kitchens and bathrooms, and any other spaces – the bedroom, for example – that involve transfer in and out of a wheelchair.

Secondly, stairs inside the house should be eliminated as much as possible. Ideally, the entrance, living room, kitchen, disabled person's bedroom and bathroom should be on the same level. It may be possible to build on an extra bedroom and bathroom at ground-floor level, but if there is no space to do this, an elevator or stair climber can be put in to move the wheelchair between levels. Then, there should be a bathroom, or at least a toilet, on each level.

Access is also vital. If a new entrance is being built, it should be designed with a flush threshold. Front steps can be replaced by a ramp, providing the gradient of the immediate approach is not too steep (maximum gradient is one in twelve); the back entrance may be easier to convert than the front one. An outdoor elevator or stair climber is another alternative, if there is space for one to be installed.

Special attention must also be paid to the garage. There are two main considerations: that there should be level, covered access to the garage directly from the house and, secondly, the garage should be large enough to allow for transferring from wheelchair to car, or for the wheelchair itself to be raised into the car.

Arrangements for getting in and out of a wheelchair depend on the individual. If a hoist is necessary, the positions of the bedroom and bathroom should take this into account. Bathrooms need to be generously sized to allow for transferring to the toilet, bath or shower.

The level of work surfaces, the positioning of appliances and the accessibility of storage space in the wheelchair cook's kitchen need special consideration. In addition, the floor space must be

planned very precisely, allowing room for the wheelchair to manoeuvre unless only one or two people are to be catered for, in which case a very compact kitchen – one that a wheelchair can enter frontwards and reverse out of – might be all that's required. The layout and work sequence which works best is L-shaped, and is spacious enough to allow the wheelchair to be turned through 180°.

Aids and activities

New technological developments, particularly in the field of electronics, are revolutionizing aids for those with special needs and are making it easier for disabled people to communicate with those around them, control their environment and interact with the outside world. Everybody with a personal computer will in future be able – at least in theory – to transmit and receive information, plug into information banks, call for help, learn new skills and subjects, control the immediate environment and organize his or her own shopping and banking.

Equally important, the philosophy which aims at providing disabled people with independence and the freedom to live ordinary lives as much as possible has opened up new attitudes and approaches, encouraging the enjoyment of everyday activities, such as cooking and gardening.

Mobility

Independent living depends on a person being able to get about when and, within reason, where he or she wants, without having to wait for help. The breakthrough for the many disabled people who have had to rely on someone else to push them, guide them, help them into a car or drive them even for the shortest journeys comes when they can do all this on their own.

Most buggies, run-abouts and powered wheelchairs use an electric motor with a rechargeable battery. Although these batteries have a limited range, they are silent, and both chairs and run-abouts are easily manoeuvrable with controls that can be managed with one hand, if necessary. The new, lightweight wheelchairs, originally developed for sports, are highly mobile. Some electric wheelchairs have kerb-climbers which can manage a step up to 125mm (5in); alternatively, there are portable folding ramps, and a variety of elevators and stair climbers that can be used inside and outside.

Cars off the production line may be specially adapted for disabled people by the manufacturers, or specialist companies will adapt suitable production models with a higher roof and a hydraulic ramp, so that a wheelchair can be wheeled in and anchored without any transfer problems. A few manufacturers are now making production-line models with a standard engine but additional design features for drivers with disabilities, so that it is unnecessary for them to leave a wheelchair.

For the partially sighted or completely blind, independent and unguided mobility has been greatly helped by sonic aids, but the long cane and the guide dog are not yet in danger of becoming redundant.

Communication

Communication aids for disabled people have developed very rapidly in the last decade or so, and imaginative learning programmes are helping disabled children develop to their fullest potential. Braille can be translated into print or speech (and linked to normal computer programme usage), speech can be presented visually and telephone communication can be transmitted to a visual display unit. There are now many ways to activate a keyboard – even by blinking – for those who find movement difficult, and it will soon be possible for those who cannot speak to activate speech synthesizers.

The use of microprocessors

has already made an enormous practical contribution to many people's lives: electronic alarms, infra-red blink switch systems, sound beacons, speaking thermometers for the blind and a range of telephone aids (inductive couplers, handsets with flashing lights and amplifiers, and cordless phones) are all examples of appliances that are now widely available and reasonably priced.

Seating

Completely individualized chairs which allow severely disabled children to sit unaided have demonstrated how good design helps physical development. Designers of chairs for more general production have also tried to incorporate these ergonomic principles and benefits into their work. One designer took plaster casts of a large sample of people with back conditions and drew up specifications for two chairs adapted to the back shapes of small and tall people.

Another chair intended to meet the needs of the individual, designed in Denmark, is made up from a set of interchangeable parts, which can be built into a frame to suit the person's shape. An electric motor will tilt the seat to help the seated person get up (in three different ways) or recline the whole chair at a comfortable angle, and there is a choice of backs and arm rests.

Cooking

Whatever special adaptations are needed, the basic kitchen layout should still be designed around the three main activity zones – the sink, the cooking equipment and the storage area (see *KITCHENS*). Any alterations will depend on exactly which members of the household will be doing the cooking and their type of disability.

Certain changes that are essential to enable a disabled person to use the kitchen will also benefit any household: the floor must be level, with a non-slip surface; the windows must

be easy to open; and the lighting should be carefully planned with all switches and controls easy to reach and preferably on the same level. Accessible storage will be at a premium: anything that does not need to be in the kitchen should be kept elsewhere, and storage drawers on wheels and carousel units could be fitted to maximize the amount of accessible storage.

For wheelchair cooks, or those who need to do at least part of the preparation sitting down, surface height is critical. It may be a good idea to fit surfaces at two different heights, for working either standing up or sitting down; while the ideal standing height is somewhere between 875mm (35in) and 1m (39in), a good height for seated working is likely to be lower, with adjustment for the individual's comfort. Allow space for knees to go under a surface designed for seated working and leave extra toe-space for a wheelchair user. Pull-out worktops – some are designed with holes to hold bowls and containers steady – are invaluable in a small kitchen. Sinks, wall ovens, hobs (cooking tops) and microwave ovens can all be fixed at the most convenient height (a split-level cooker gives maximum flexibility).

There are a number of useful aids, such as a bread-slicing gauge and Braille-marked cooker (stove) controls for people who are blind or partially sighted. However, ingenious ideas and techniques based on a highly methodical approach are often as useful in solving specific problems simply and with little or no expense; placing eggs or vegetables in a wire basket before putting them in a pan of boiling water, for example, eliminates the difficulty of retrieving and straining them later.

For those who do not have full use of their hands, or who have only one good hand, standard electric appliances, such as food processors and mixers, can compensate for lost strength or weak

grip. Touch controls or level-operated taps and appliances are easy to use. There are also many gadgets specially designed to help peel vegetables or open jars with only one hand or hold pans and bowls steady with shaky hands. Lifting heavy pans full of water out of a sink can be avoided by fitting a mixer tap with a high neck that can swing out over the draining board, thus enabling the pan to be filled on the same level as the hob. Choose lightweight pans and dishes that are easily carried in one hand.

Gardening

Gardening can be a therapeutic activity as well as a great pleasure – and can often be done by disabled people. There are a number of specialized organizations to help those with specific handicaps who want to go on with, or learn about, gardening. Blind people, for example, can use special techniques for planting, hosing and watering so that they can enjoy the sense of achievement gained from touching and smelling something they have grown themselves.

The first step should be to work out which aspects of gardening give the most pleasure and to consider realistically the kind of garden which can be managed successfully. If the work is to be shared with an able-bodied person, obviously the range of choices will be greater. When real enjoyment comes from being outside in the fresh air with plants and trees around, a garden that needs the minimum of attention should be planned; it could include a pleasant area for sitting out (with some sun and some shade), and shrubs, ground cover, small trees and perennials to give year-round variety.

On the other hand, for those who love grubbing about in the earth, there are many ways of gardening which abolish the need for heavy digging and back-breaking bending. Work can be made easier by concentrating on particular areas or keeping only a few beds intensively cultivated, and by using long-handled tools and special kneelers. Most labour-saving garden machinery (rotovators, electric hedge-cutters, petrol- or gas- driven trimmers and lawn mowers, for example) require considerable strength for safe and effective operation, so they may not be suitable.

An alternative is to raise the garden to worktop height and work standing or sitting in a wheelchair. Raised beds are an expensive solution (each bed has to be built on foundations to withstand the pressure of the soil it will contain), but may be worthwhile for avid gardeners. Remember, for a wheelchair gardener, the bed must be accessible from both sides: 1.2m (48in) is the most easily managed width. With four raised beds, a useful amount of vegetables and herbs can be grown and the crops rotated correctly in three, while the fourth bed is used for soft fruit. If the beds are filled originally with good soil and a layer of farmyard manure or mushroom compost is placed on top each year, no digging should be necessary.

However, there are a number of cheaper ways to achieve raised beds. Concrete drainage pipes, stacked tyres and low walls can all be built up to a convenient level and planted in the same way as raised beds: lime-hating plants grow well in beds built up from peat blocks (these must be kept well watered in dry weather).

Conservatory (sunroom) and greenhouse gardening is another possibility for the passionate but sedentary gardener, and it means it is pleasant to work in any weather. Staging can be arranged to suit the gardener; a comfortable worktop can be built for potting up plants. Propagation can be carried out with a mist propagator and it may be worth investing in automatic watering and temperature controls.

DEALING WITH DISABILITIES

COMPENSATING FOR SPECIFIC DIFFICULTIES

Partial sight or blindness

Structural adaptations
- Check that floors are level and in good condition, with non-slip surfaces.
- For partial sight: decorate with contrasting shades, textures and colours to show up doorways and furniture.

General aids
- Good, well-organized storage with sliding doors on cupboards.
- Bathroom equipment which is easy to keep clean.
- Special aids to help with cooking.
- For partial sight: good lighting and magnifiers.

Impaired hearing

General aids
- Kitchen/eating/work area allowing people to face one another when seated.
- Good light to help lip reading.
- Visual cues for doorbell, phone, etc.
- Induction loop for television and phone if necessary; cable television and teletext.
- Vibrator alarm clock.

Use of one hand only

General aids
- Kitchen aids for single-handed cooking.
- Food processors, electric can openers, dishwashers.
- Combination one-hand cutlery and plates with rims.
- Specially adapted car.

Limited grip and reach of both hands

General aids
- Kitchen with everything within easy reach.
- Ample work surface and socket outlets.
- Appliances for single-handed cooking to make work easier.

- Lightweight saucepans, dishes and possibly microwave oven.
- Lever handles on taps.
- Lever handles or touch latches on doors and cupboards.
- Big rocker switches or heat-sensitive switches.

Back problems or difficulty with bending

General aids
- Storage and work surfaces minimizing need for bending.
- Suitable chair.
- Special bed.
- Bath with hand-holds.

Limited activity; serious heart conditions or chest complaints, but mobile

Structural adaptations
- Abolish stairs or install elevator or stair climbers.
- Check that bedroom and bathroom are on the same floor.
- Check that entrance level with principal rooms has additional toilet.

General aids
- Seating in kitchen and other working areas.
- Compact layout for rooms in daily use and for work areas.
- Electrical appliances wherever possible for strenuous jobs.
- Entryphone, cordless phone extensions to avoid rush to answer phone or front door.

Reduced mobility; stick or frame needed, but not wheelchair

Structural adaptations
As above, plus:
- Check that floors are level, with non-slip floor surfaces.
- Check that doorways are wide enough for wheelchair access (900mm [36in]).
- Consider creating extra space for circulation.

General aids
- Any necessary adaptations in bathroom – hand-holds, etc.
- Chair that is easy to get up from.

Severely reduced mobility, but wheelchair not needed all the time

Structural adaptations
- Check that doorways are wide enough for wheelchair access (900mm [36in]).
- Check that adequate space exists for wheelchair in hallway.
- Check that entrance level with principal rooms has toilet/bathroom.
- Check that floors are level, with non-slip floor surfaces.
- Check that windows are low enough for seated person to see out.

General aids
- Door and window handles easy to use, within reach and aligned with switches and socket outlets.
- Kitchen worktops at convenient height – provisions made to work while seated.
- Lever taps.
- Bathroom adapted for individual with platform at head end of bath.

Wheelchair dependence

Structural adaptations
As above, plus:
- Check that entrance level with principal rooms has bedroom, bathroom, toilet.
- Check that hoists are installed wherever necessary.
- Check that adequate space exists for turning/circulation on entrance level.
- Check that bathroom and kitchen are adapted and designed for individual's needs.
- Check that garage is large enough and has direct access to house.

General aids
- Aids depend on individual's abilities and needs — to be worked out accordingly.

SPECIAL MEDICAL PROBLEMS

Home dialysis

Structural adaptations
- One room should be set aside and organized for dialysis.

Epilepsy

General aids
- All open fires guarded.
- Sharp-edged furniture avoided.

Incontinence

General aids
- Easily washable floors, chair and bed coverings.

ELECTRICITY

Essentials

Electricity is the most useful and convenient form of power in the home. At the flick of a switch it provides lighting, heating and hot water and will operate a full range of domestic appliances.

Where it comes from and how it is fed round the home is a mystery to most of us. The fact is that it is always there when it is wanted. The mysteries of electrical wiring lie buried in walls, under floors and in ceilings. The only obvious evidence of the extent of the supply comes from the siting of socket outlets, switches, light fittings and fixed appliances.

The design of electrical circuits and the siting of outlets is, naturally enough, related to the normal use to which they are likely to be put. Unfortunately, electricity demands vary from household to household, which means that a system designed for one user is unlikely to be totally suitable for another.

There is, however, no reason why you should have to suffer a situation that is inconvenient. It is quite possible to alter – or extend – the existing wiring arrangements, adding new fittings, increasing the number of outlets, moving existing ones or even taking the power supply into new areas.

Careful planning is most important. There is no point in making changes in the domestic wiring only to find in a few years that further facilities are required. So make sure all future requirements are taken into account. Of course, it is not always easy to anticipate what may be needed several years ahead, so it is wise to overestimate: it is far better to have extra socket outlets than not have enough later on.

Make a note of all the fittings, socket outlets and switches already installed. Where facilities seem inadequate, make a plan of that area and mark the location of existing electrical fittings and what changes need to be made. In the case of an extension, discuss what is required with the architect or builder and then consult a qualified electrician. Unless the alteration is a simple one, such as fitting a dimmer in place of an existing switch, advice from an electrician is a sensible and often necessary step to take.

Sound professional guidance is important from the point of view of safety, and to minimize the disruption that inevitably results from changes to the existing system. The way electricity is fed round the house means that surfaces are bound to be damaged; neat work by a qualified person will help, but the selection and method of routing new wiring will also play an important part in minimizing the problem.

Where it comes from

Electricity normally enters the home through underground cables; in some rural areas, electricity is supplied via overhead lines on pylons. In both cases, it is fed through a main fuse box and meter into the sealed distribution box (also called a consumer unit). From this unit, a number of circuits, each with their own specially rated fuse, carry the supply of electricity to the various parts of the home.

It is important to remember that the main sealed fuse and meter are the property of the local electricity board or utility. On no account should anyone else interfere with these fittings.

The size of the distribution box will depend on the number of circuits required. In an average-size, three-bedroom, two-storey home, there would normally be a minimum of five or six:

- two power circuits – one for each floor;
- two lighting circuits – one for each floor;
- one special circuit for an electrical cooker (stove);
- one special circuit for an immersion water heater, where fitted;

Extra circuits may well be needed where it is anticipated that the demand for electricity is going to be high. One obvious area is in the kitchen, where several high-powered appliances may be in use at any one time. If storage heaters are fitted, these will have to be supplied by a separate circuit, usually via a special economy-rate meter, recording on- and off-peak rate use.

Each circuit is protected by its own fuse, which may be of the rewirable or cartridge type, or the modern miniature circuit breaker – which is a more convenient device, since when that particular circuit is for any reason overloaded it will switch off and can be reset when the fault has been rectified. In the case of a cartridge, the fuse will blow and must then be replaced. (With rewirable ones, you should keep spare fuse wire handy and learn how to insert a length of wire; keep a torch by the fuse box.)

From the distribution box, the various circuits are wired through the home, connecting the relevant fittings, socket outlets and switches.

Planning

The very first decisions that have to be made are exactly what is needed in the way of new fittings and socket outlets, what will have to be moved or redirected and, possibly, what is obsolete. Depending on the amount of work involved and the age of the present system, the existing wiring may be able to be adapted and extensions taken from it; this is obviously preferable, since it will mean less disturbance to the decorations and normally involves much lower costs.

Where extensive new facilities are required, extra wiring circuits may have to be installed to cater for the increase in power demand. In extreme cases – where the wiring is very old or has been poorly installed, for example – it will be necessary to rewire the whole system. This, of course, is a major job that can involve a lot of disturbance. In such a situation, it is well worth considering what other jobs are needed around the home and co-ordinating these to create one major upheaval, rather than suffer one disruption after another.

Here are some points to consider in estimating the extent of the work required and how much planning to do:

- How old is the existing wiring and when was it last checked? As a guide, any system more than twenty-five years old should be replaced (and all wiring should be checked at least every five years).
- Do the new fittings or appliances need their own circuits? Remember, there are no short cuts. Where such installations need a separate circuit, do not connect them to existing ones.

• Where will new fittings or appliances be sited in relation to the distribution box? There may be alternative sites that make the routing of new cable much easier and less disruptive.

• Are the changes envisaged only to the lighting? In this case, unless you are planning a large number of fittings which would require a separate circuit, it may be possible to connect the new light fittings to the existing wiring or utilize the power circuit.

• Are there enough power socket outlets in each room? Ideally every appliance or fitting should be plugged into a separate socket outlet, rather than an adaptor. Equally, there should be an adequate number of socket outlets throughout the house (except in the bathroom) to avoid trailing cords and the use of extension cords. It is very often possible to add several socket outlets to existing power circuits; where a number of socket outlets are required or where the use of high-powered appliances is anticipated, a new circuit may well be necessary.

• Is there likely to be a risk of overloading existing circuits through the use of new appliances and fittings? Again, it may be necessary to wire in a new circuit or project extensions to an existing one. It is important to check loadings on a circuit with a qualified electrician.

These basic guidelines should help when it comes to making a decision on what work will be required to satisfy individual requirements.

Advice

Having decided what is needed and estimated the amount of work involved – for example, whether a simple extension is suitable, or whether new circuits are required, or the whole wiring needs replacing – professional help should be sought from a qualified electrician. The best way to ensure the right advice is through the local electricity board or utility.

ELECTRICAL WIRING
CHECKLIST

■ Could ducting be created to control wiring routes within the structure of the house, making future changes simpler?

■ How many socket outlets are needed in each room?

■ Have your power circuits got the capacity for all electric appliances and fittings, lights and equipment you might use at one time?

■ Have you designed your lighting in advance of finalizing electrical wiring to make certain light fittings are correctly placed and wired?

■ Low-voltage light fittings require a transformer – has this been taken into account?

■ Have you fully exploited the potential of track fittings for lights and power tracks for electrical equipment.

■ Have you positioned switches and controls – such as light dimmers – with careful consideration of safety and comfort, especially for children, disabled people and the elderly?

■ Have you considered using safety socket outlets which close off when not in use?

■ Trailing wires can be a serious hazard, as well as spoiling the look of a room. Ensure they are either buried in the structure of the building or firmly secured.

■ Computer wiring must be carefully planned so your system is not interrupted or affected by other services and wiring. Seek professional advice.

■ Are you considering computer control for your domestic systems – including heating, lights, security, water heating – and that this will involve complex wiring arrangements?

■ If you are considering a self-contained apartment within the house, have you taken into account that a separate electric wiring circuit will be needed?

■ Should your existing wiring be extended or renewed? If so, plan now for the changes which can be made as a result, such as improved lighting design, safe electrical fittings, getting rid of all trailing wires, placing extra socket outlets where required.

■ Have you also recognized that major redecoration could result from the upheaval of extending or renewing electrical wiring?

POWER CONSUMPTION
APPLIANCES

Equipment	Rating (KW)[1]
Deep-fry pan	1–2
Dishwasher (cold-fill)	2–3
Electric blanket	Less than ½
Electric drill	Less than ½
Fan	Less than ½
Freezer	Less than ½
Hair drier	½–¾
Heaters	1–3
Hi-fi system	Less than ½
Instant water heater	2–3
Iron	1
Kettle	3
Kitchen gadgets (can opener, coffee mill, mixer, waste disposer, etc.)	Less than ½
Lawn mower	Less than ½
Lift (elevator)	1–2
Microcomputer	Less than ½
Refrigerator	Less than ½
Shaver	Less than ½
Shower heater	2–3
Spin drier	Less than ½
Table light	Less than ½
Television	Less than ½
Tumble drier	2–3
Vacuum cleaner	½
Washing machine (cold fill)	2–3

[1]This is the power requirement. Consumption and thus running costs depend on how long the equipment runs at these ratings. In Britain, this is metered in 'units', measured in kilowatt hours (KWh).

Electrical wiring
British system:
1 *Electrical supply.*
2 *Distribution box.*
3 *Ground-floor ring circuit.*
4 *Socket outlet.*
5 *Spur.*
6 *Upper-floor ring circuit.*
7 *Ground-floor lighting circuit.*
8 *Upper-floor lighting circuit.*
9 *Spurs for attic socket outlets.*
10 *Earth cable for bonding.*

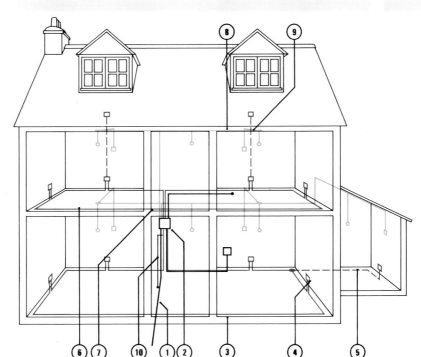

Lights

Lighting should always be considered not only from the practical point of providing essential light to see and work by, but also to highlight the features of a room and contribute to its atmosphere (see *LIGHTING*).

Ideally, each storey in the home will have its own lighting circuit, accommodating twelve 100-watt lamps; for any more you may have to install extra circuits.

Lighting circuits normally run above the ceiling and then down through the wall to the switches or wall fittings. When new lighting points and extra switches are required, connections are normally made to the lighting circuits at junction boxes or ceiling roses. The disruption this involves can be restricted to lifting floorboards from the room above and making holes in the ceiling to take overhead fittings. For wall fittings and switches, wiring would have to be taken down from the ceiling and this means feeding it through the cavity of a partition wall or channelling it down the plaster of a solid wall.

The great advantage with standard and table lamps and freestanding spotlights is that they require no special wiring and therefore cause no disturbance to the existing decorations.

In rooms with high ceilings, it may be necessary to fit a false or suspended one – particularly in solid upstairs floors, and in some apartment blocks – and all the necessary wiring can be carried in the gap above the new ceiling.

Extra switches are extremely useful in certain areas – hallways, staircases and landings, for example – where it is important for lights to be operated from different points. In a room with more than one door, switches should be placed by all access areas. Because such switches are mounted on the walls, however, fitting new ones will involve disturbing wall decorations.

If you're using low-energy bulbs, check whether special adaptors are needed; with standard or table lamps, connection is made by means of a plug-in socket adaptor; ceiling-hung lights have special fittings, which replace the ceiling rose but are wired up in a similar way and will not affect the existing circuit.

Certain areas make specific demands on lighting – both the kitchen and bathroom need special consideration (see below).

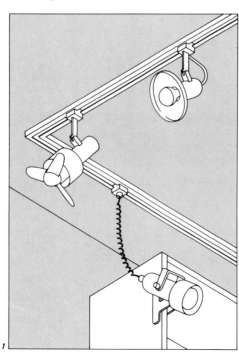

1 Lighting track enables light fittings to be connected to a direct supply of electricity anywhere along the track. It is most commonly used for spotlights but it can also connect to other low-wattage equipment, such as the fan shown here. In addition, a looped cable can be run from the track to a light fitting or other equipment at a high level in the room, for example, the spotlight attached to a wooden frame shown here.

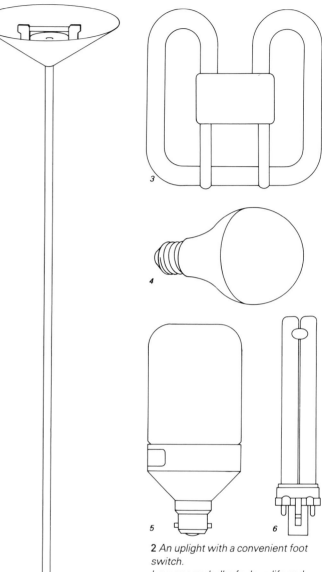

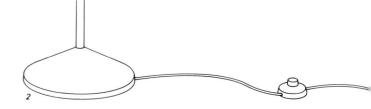

2 An uplight with a convenient foot switch.
Low-energy bulbs for long life and economy:
3, 5, 6 Mini-fluorescent lamps.
4 Low-voltage tungsten halogen bulb – it has special end caps and must be used with a transformer and in specially designed fittings.

Socket outlets

There are some useful guidelines about the siting of socket outlets to use when planning the electrical wiring:

● The simplest way of increasing the number of outlets is to replace a single socket with a double one; there is no major rewiring to do and only minor alterations need to be made around the existing outlet.

● When fitting socket outlets, install double rather than single ones.

● The ideal is to have at least one double socket on each wall of every room. This is particularly important in living rooms and one-room apartments, where the demand for power is likely to be high. Kitchens, however, need special consideration, while bathrooms should not have any standard outlets, for safety reasons.

● In larger areas of the home, such as living rooms and long hallways, there should be socket outlets at approximately 3-m (10-ft) intervals; the average length of cord on most vacuum cleaners is 1.5 to 4.5 m (5 to 15 ft).

● If partial or complete rewiring is required, socket outlets should be resited, if necessary. Where only a few extra outlets are needed, these can normally be connected to the existing power circuit.

Kitchens

Safety is a crucial factor in the kitchen, since not only are most of the high-powered appliances – cooker (stove), dishwasher, refrigerator and freezer, possibly a washing machine and drier – likely to be located there, but water and other liquids are always present.

It is particularly important to make sure that the kitchen is well lit, especially above the work surfaces. If you are using striplights to light work areas under built-in cabinets, connections will have to be made with the lighting circuit in the ceiling space, although it is often easier to make the connection through a fuse spur to a convenient socket outlet. Alternatively, the cable can run inside a cabinet, which will not disturb the decorations too much.

The power supply needs the most careful thought; it is important to work out the range of appliances and equipment likely to be used in the kitchen.

While it is not necessary to plan separate power socket outlets for all the items in the kitchen, you should have exclusive outlets for those in permanent use and enough outlets near the work surfaces for the portable appliances, some of which need their own circuits or individually fused outlets. Many of the socket outlets will be sited on the walls above work surfaces, rather than just above floor level, and some may be inside cabinets.

All cookers (stoves), hobs (cooking tops) and ovens must be connected directly with the distribution box, and their control switches must be within 2m (6½ft). Installation or repositioning of any of these appliances is therefore a major job and it requires careful planning of cable runs, particularly if they are being incorporated into island units.

Domestic microwave ovens are connected to normal socket outlets. Commercial models, however, have a much higher rating and must therefore have their own circuit.

Waste disposal units should always be wired to the power circuit through a fused switched connection unit, which is placed nearby. Cooker hoods and ventilation fans should be permanently wired to their own outlets.

Bathrooms

Safety regulations restricting the use of electrical outlets and fittings in bathrooms vary from country to country.

Lights, heaters and towel rails must be permanently wired to a fused connector unit out of reach of the bath and shower. Generally, socket outlets are not allowed, and the only permissible outlet is a special electric shaver socket, incorporating an isolating transformer. All switches should be of the pull-cord type, or placed outside the room.

There should be no surface wiring; cable runs must be through the ceiling space or recessed in the walls.

All metal parts and fittings should be earthed (grounded), including such items as water pipes, waste outlets, metal taps and other fittings. Care should be taken that new plastic fittings do not interrupt the metal-to-metal earth link.

Washing machines and driers should not be installed in a bathroom unless they are at least 1.8m (6ft) from the bath or shower; the installation should only be carried out by a qualified electrician working with a qualified plumber.

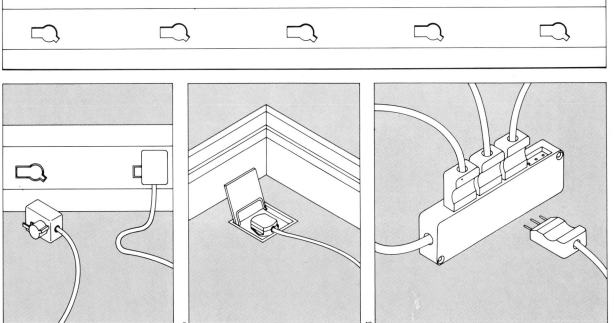

7 Power track can be used along the back of a work surface for electrical equipment.
8 Connection can be made with special safety plugs and sockets – the plug is turned through ninety degrees when inserted.
9 A floor socket outlet.
10 A compact switch block which takes special small plugs and can be used for tidy cable management of stereo equipment, computers and so on. Fixed near the equipment, it saves the necessity of having wires trailing to a wall socket outlet.

Heating

There is a wide range of electrical heating systems (see *HEATING*) and the amount of disruption caused in installation and rewiring varies enormously. Some systems providing general background heat will involve a major disturbance to decorations and some are only really practical to install when a house is being built; these include ceiling and under-floor heating.

Storage heaters require their own separate circuit. Although free-standing, they are wired direct to a connection point on the wall.

Wall-mounted panel heaters and skirting (baseboard) heaters involve wall connections to the power circuit and, because they are fixed in position, are usually permanently wired. Other free-standing heaters – oil-filled radiators and warm-air fan heaters, for example – pose few problems, since they can be plugged into a normal socket outlet.

Other types of electric fire providing direct heat are simply plugged into the normal power socket outlet.

Of course, the problem of wiring is not restricted just to electrical forms of heating. This kind of power is also required to control central heating fired by other fuels, such as oil, gas and solid fuel – time clocks, room thermostats, pumps and control valves, for example, will need electricity and must be wired in accordingly. Normally such controls, with the exception of room and radiator thermostats, will be sited near hot-water cylinders and boilers. In the case of a hot-water cylinder fitted in a separate cupboard, the wiring can be left exposed; the same applies with back boilers. All these controls can be wired into an existing power circuit.

An immersion water heater fitted to the hot-water cylinder will need its own circuit from the distribution box.

Instant water heaters are useful for remote plumbing fittings, such as out-of-the-way sinks where only small amounts of hot water are required, and for shower installations. Since power consumption can be high, a self-contained unit with its own circuit can be fitted; alternatively, other models can be wired straight into the power circuit. Normally, though, these appliances would be permanently wired into their own outlets.

Wiring outdoors

Running electricity outside the home is not as daunting a prospect as it may seem at first. Where a power supply is required in a garage, workshop or greenhouse, for example, one circuit is sufficient to feed the outbuilding. From there the supply can be split for power and lighting use.

The safest route for this supply cable – and for cables feeding garden lighting and swimming pools – is underground; special armoured cable should be used. If cables have to be run overhead, there will be restrictions to the minimum height for clearance, support and attachments.

The wiring inside outbuildings is best carried in galvanized steel or plastic conduits. Where a lighting circuit is taken off the power circuit, it should be protected with a separate fuse. In most cases, little or no attention need be paid to the appearance of the wiring, which means simple surface installation.

If individual appliances – electric lawnmowers, hedgecutters and chainsaws, for example – are being used outside, the power supply can be taken from a power circuit inside the home or from an outbuilding, but it is a good idea to have a socket outlet installed especially for this purpose and protected by a residual current circuit breaker, which will cut off the power if there is a leakage to earth (these devices are available either built into plugs or incorporated in power socket outlets; they can also be installed to protect the complete power circuit).

If the switches and socket outlets are outside, they must be waterproof or have screw-on caps to protect them from the elements. It is also sensible to site them in sheltered areas.

Wiring up apartments

Where there are several apartments within one building, these should be separately metered with their own wiring circuits. Although the general principles of wiring will apply, there are likely to be some additional items.

With a shared front door or main access, bells and possibly entryphones will need to be wired to the individual apartments. Where intercom services are needed, these can be plugged into the building's power socket outlets.

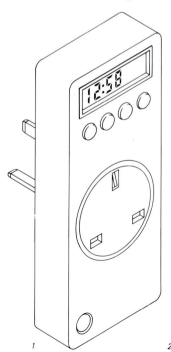

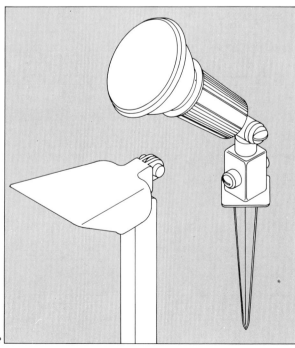

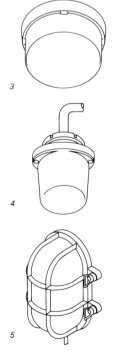

1 *Electronic time switch designed to be plugged into a power socket; it operates electrical equipment only at pre-selected times.*
Outdoor lighting:
2 *Light fittings on a spike for illuminating plants or paths.*
3 *Bulkhead fitting in a weatherproof casing.*
4 *Conduit entry outdoor light fitting.*
5 *Energy-saving oval bulkhead fitting which uses a mini-fluorescent bulb.*

Telephones/television

Electrical wiring is not, of course, the only wiring to be installed in the home. Other services, including telephones and televisions, need to be linked to the outside. These are often not planned with the overall design of the rest of the wiring in the home, so their installation can be inconvenient and unsightly.

With telephones, single wires connect individual receivers or link plug-in sockets. The wiring is often run along the top of skirting (baseboards), around the door frames and in the corners of rooms. Or it could be run through ducting (see below), although this must be screened to protect it from interference from electrical wiring, if the two are run together.

The television set needs to be connected to an aerial (antenna), unless the programmes are 'piped' in via a communal line. Television aerials are sited on or inside the roof of the building; it is therefore necessary to run a cable link to the set from there. Normally, this is done down the outside of the building. The cable is then fed through a convenient part of the wall or window and around the inside of the wall to the television set. Here again, ducting can be used to carry this cable.

Video recorders run off the normal power circuit supply, so there should be an adequate number of socket outlets near the television set.

With cable television, the size and route of the wiring is similar to that of the telephone, and runs to a socket outlet near the television set. Some systems incorporate a meter with the television, while in other cases the immediate area is served by a local 'kiosk' in the street. Rerouting similar to that used for telephone wires may be possible.

Ducting

Traditionally, wiring has been surface-mounted, run through floor and ceiling spaces or recessed into walls. The disadvantages of these methods are all too obvious. There is, however, another method which uses ducting. This is a special enclosure, which can be fitted either horizontally or vertically, through which cables can be fed. One design, shaped to look like skirting (baseboards), is fitted along the wall bottom.

This means that all surface wiring can be eliminated, and that future extensions or alterations to the wiring can be carried out more easily and with less disruption. Ducting can overcome routing problems caused by structural features such as exposed beams, solid floors or wall panelling. Certain systems incorporate sockets at regular intervals, and include secondary ducting to take additional wiring.

It is important, however, when considering the use of ducting, to bear in mind the compatibility of different types of wiring. This is necessary since the electrical current can, if run adjacent to certain other . types of wiring, upset the function of those systems. Protection is through 'screening', either using special wiring or enclosing in metal, wiring that would be affected.

Telephone cables, for example, usually need to be screened from electrical wiring, while the television aerial or cable television wiring doesn't. It's best to check this when installing any new equipment.

Information technology

The age of the microchip has revolutionized the field of communications and storage of information. How does this affect the existing domestic systems and are there problems installing such equipment as computers and display units?

Computing and communication need to be treated separately. To operate its function of storage and retrieval of information, a computer has to be connected to a clean power supply, one that has constant power at a constant rate. Normally, this means plugging in the relevant equipment to a socket outlet. If interference or faults occur, power changes might be affecting the equipment and it may be necessary to install a clean line.

Communication, the linking-up with an external source or supply, involves connection to a network and this is done mainly via the telephone system. Cable television is likely to play an ever-increasing role in this link-up.

For a computer system, several socket outlets are required to run the ancillary equipment, such as the monitor or screen, the disc or tape drive and the printer. Here a socket block or power track will eliminate trailing wires. Any other electrical equipment not directly involved with the computer should be screened to prevent faults occurring.

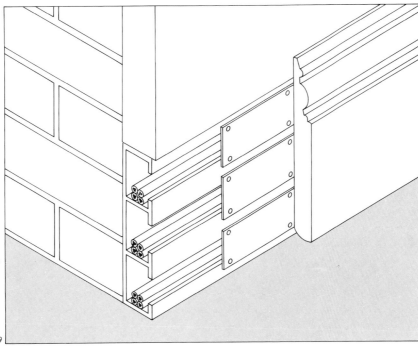

Outdoor safety
6 *When using electrical equipment outside, it can be connected to an outside socket such as this one, which is fitted with a residual current device.*
7 *A plug for outside use, with a residual current device.*
8 *A cable extension for outside use.*
9 *If power and computer data wiring are run in close proximity they require screened separation. This metal-enclosed ducting provides this and can be fitted behind skirting (baseboards).*

PLUMBING

Indirect system

The main diagram shows the usual household plumbing and central-heating system used in Britain. From the water authority stopcock, the rising main takes cold water to the cold-water storage cistern – the only normal connection from this is the necessary drinking supply to the kitchen cold-water tap. The cistern provides the supply to other cold-water taps, the toilet and the hot-water cylinder. A second cistern – the feed-and-expansion cistern – provides the cold-water for the central-heating system.

In the house illustrated, the hot water is heated 'indirectly' from the central-heating boiler, a motorized valve directing the flow either to the hot-water cylinder or to the radiators or, sometimes, to both. The hot water is taken from the top of the cylinder and vent pipes for both the hot-water cylinder and central-heating boiler allow air bubbles and steam to escape.

Direct system

An older system is shown in the smaller diagram. *All* the cold-water feeds are taken directly from the ring main, the hot water in this example being provided by a gas 'multi-point' heater; a feed-and-expansion cistern has been added for the central heating.

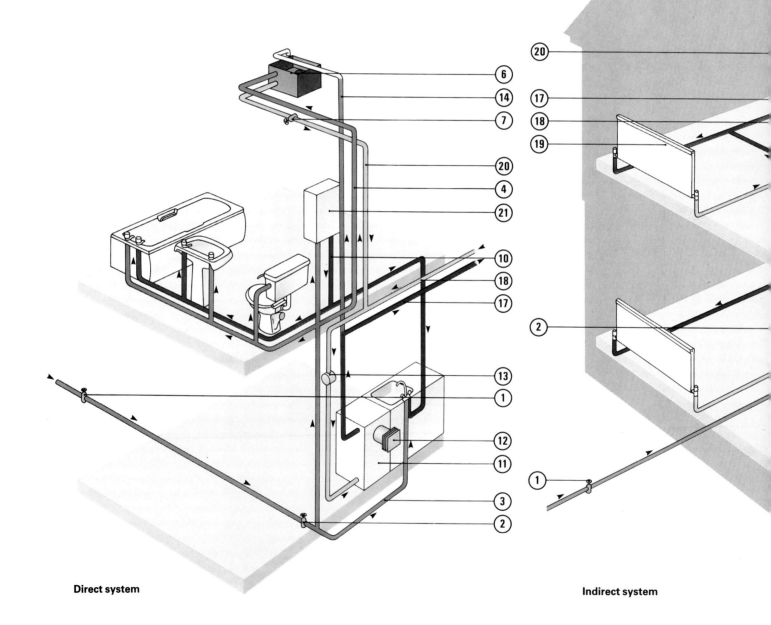

Direct system

Indirect system

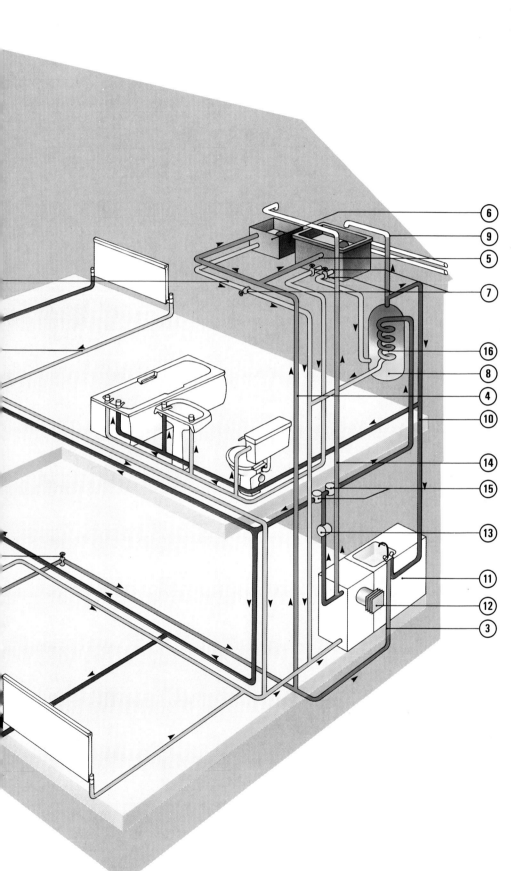

KEY

1 Water authority stopcock
2 Mains stopcock
3 Drinking water
4 Rising main
5 Cold-water cistern
6 Central-heating expansion cistern
7 Gatevalve
8 Hot-water cylinder
9 Hot-water vent pipe
10 Hot-water supply pipe
11 Central-heating boiler
12 Balanced flue
13 Pump
14 Central-heating vent pipe
15 Motorized valve(s)
16 Heat exchanger
17 Central-heating 'flow' pipe
18 Central-heating 'return' pipe
19 Radiator
20 Cold feed to central heating
21 Gas 'multipoint' water heater

SECURITY

No amount of expensive locks and alarms can stop a determined burglar, but loud warning noises, delays and clearly visible deterrents do discourage thieves, especially casual opportunists who are exploiting other people's carelessness and negligence. Good security and correctly fitted, quality locks are well worth the investment: insurance payments simply cannot compensate for the loss of irreplaceable items of sentimental value.

Security relies, to a large extent, on common-sense precautions: do not leave money or tempting valuables lying around, do not mark your address on sets of keys or carry them in your handbag or with any form of identity, and never leave a door-key under the mat, hanging on a string inside the letterbox or in any other hiding place – thieves may know exactly where to look. Finally, do not delude yourself that you own little of sufficient value to interest a thief: everyday household items, such as cameras, radios, televisions and electrical appliances, are prime targets because they can be disposed of so easily. Keep an inventory of valuables, with serial numbers of appliances and photographs of other items. Engrave bicycles, tennis rackets and other such items with your name and post (zip) code.

Ultra-violet marking is a less preferable alternative because the markings fade unless they are re-done every few months. Insurance policies should be index-linked and regularly updated to take into account any new purchases, and also to ensure that you are adequately covered. A 'new-for-old' policy is a good idea because it allows you to replace most items at their real cost; remember to check that value does not exceed the single-item limit and that the policy covers damage due to forced entrance.

Each home has its own special problems, so take advice from crime prevention officers and representatives of security firms, who will be able to advise you on the possibilities and the most effective measures for your needs. They will also be able to give you some idea of cost, which is obviously a prime consideration: there is no point, for example, in spending money on a quality padlock for a shed which houses a few plant pots, or in putting three locks on a front door if the frame is weak. You should also check any requirements specified by your insurance policy, otherwise any claims you make may not be paid.

Finally, remember that security relies on using the hardware you have installed: always lock up carefully; never be tempted to leave even the smallest window unlocked.

Vulnerable points

Target hardening – making vulnerable points more difficult to enter – and reducing the risks in potentially dangerous situations are essential for good security. To identify vulnerable points, try to work out how you would get in if you had locked yourself out. Can you, for example, climb in through a coal-hole, force entry in a basement area where there are no outside lights, or reach an unlocked skylight? Thieves often look for the quietest means of entry and try to get in by a vulnerable window – via the back of the house, a flat roof or a fire escape – first.

External doors and windows are obvious vulnerable points; pay particular attention to those out of sight of neighbours and passers-by, and windows located near flat roofs, drainpipes, adjoining walls and trees. But other danger points can easily be overlooked and left unprotected: bushes and hedges providing cover near the house, garden gates and garages or sheds with doors leading directly into the house, and tools or implements left around which can be of use to a burglar. Remember that prams and pushchairs (baby carriages and strollers) can be used to transport televisions and so on.

Identification of vulnerable points should include consideration of your household routines and situations in which there is an increased risk of forced entry. Try to disguise or, even better, avoid clearly visible routine and long absences, which can attract burglars, bearing in mind that the peak time for burglaries is daytime. A house should never look empty: messages on telephone answering machines should not suggest that you are absent, simply that you are unavailable for a short time.

Always try to ensure that a member of the household is at home when people are working there, and check the credentials or identity cards of window cleaners, workers and uniformed callers who arrive at the door; if in doubt, telephone the employers or appropriate authorities. If you are moving house or shifting household possessions, use a reputable company, check that they are insured for damage and loss and make a comprehensive inventory of goods. Similarly, contractors for renovation, redecoration or similar work must be chosen carefully since they have access to the house over a period of time. It may be worth changing the locks after they have gone.

Should your house-keys ever be stolen, inform the police immediately and consider changing the locks or fitting additional ones. Remember that even if the keys are returned, another set could easily have been cut. The keys to some locks are registered with the manufacturer so that copies can be made only against an authorized signature; however, registration is no guarantee against the keys being copied elsewhere.

Long absences

If you are going out for a full day or for an evening, make sure that all windows and doors are securely locked and set time switches for the lights if you expect to be home after dark. The general rule is that dogs should be locked into the house and cats locked out.

If you are going to be away for a long period, leave your valuables in a bank vault or safe deposit, cancel newspaper and milk deliveries, leave curtains and shutters half-open, set time switches for inside lights to come on at different times and leave on outside lights. A spare set of keys should be given, unmarked, to friends or neighbours; inform the police that you are going away and tell them who has the keys. Try not to let it be generally known in the neighbourhood that you will be away. It is worth asking a neighbour to report anything suspicious to the police and, if she or he is willing, to take in deliveries, remove any post that gets stuck in the letterbox and draw the curtains at night. If your set of keys is stolen while you are away, telephone neighbours and warn them.

Special precautions

Security for households with young children, elderly or disabled persons and anybody who lives either alone or in an isolated place needs special consideration. If you have young children, the lock of the front door should be out of their reach but the door chain or spy-hole door viewer within reach; however, it is safest to teach children never to open the door. When you go out without the children, make sure the baby-sitter (or the eldest child, if the children have reached the age to look after themselves) knows exactly where you are going and when you plan to return: leave the address and phone number, and the number of the nearest neighbours, printed next to all the telephones in case anything suspicious happens. (Also show the baby-sitter how to get out of the building if there is a fire.)

If you are elderly or disabled, or live alone or in an isolated spot, you should ideally have a door

viewer and an outside light switch next to the door, but if this is not possible have a door chain; always check the identity of callers. Keep the telephone number of a neighbour near the phone and do not be afraid to call the police if you see or hear anything suspicious. For the elderly and disabled, it is worth considering an intercom system to a friendly neighbour and/or membership of any neighbourhood watch schemes.

If you live alone, either do not put your name on the door bell or any entryphone or show two names. If you choose to be listed in the telephone directory give your initials only. Personal alarm systems, such as whistles and electronic alarms, are a cheap and extra precaution and can be easily carried in a pocket or on a belt.

Locks and bolts

Locks should be fitted to all windows and external doors. A loose or poorly fitted lock will not work efficiently, so it is worth consulting a professional locksmith who will know whether the door or window frame needs strengthening and will ensure the lock is securely in place. If a lock sticks,

always use a dry lubricant, not oil, available from hardware stores.

Window locks should be key-operated to prevent the possibility of the lock being released by hand through a small hole cut in the glass. Remember also to use non-returnable screws so that the lock cannot be removed if the glass is broken. Metal and wooden frames require different locks, catches and security bolts: those for metal frames lock either the frame or the window handle and can also be fitted to double-glazed windows (but, for safety reasons, it should be possible to open both sets of windows from the inside). Wooden-framed, casement and sash windows need different types of locks; catches are useful for narrow casement windows.

There are two main types of locks for doors: mortise and rim. Mortise locks are set into a rectangular cavity so that only the keyhole is visible on the surface; they are therefore more inaccessible to the burglar but they are only really strong enough on doors of at least 45mm (1¾in) thickness. Rim locks are surface mounted and therefore suitable for thinner doors as well. Both types should preferably have a

deadlocking action which, firstly, allows them to be locked from both sides, and, secondly, prevents them from either being opened and closed without a key, or being forced by a piece of plastic inserted between the door and the frame. These are especially important if a door has glass panels, if the lock can be reached from the letterbox or if there is a window above the door. A thief who manages to enter by another route, but hopes to carry things out through a door, should not be able to leave – unless a key has carelessly been left lying about. 'Hotel locks', incorporated into the door handle, are another option for inside doors but are usually ugly.

Bolts can be used for extra protection on both doors and windows. Surface-mounted bolts provide adequate security at night and are preferable because they can be opened more easily in case you need to leave the house quickly – in case of fire, for instance. It is wise not to deadlock these for the same reasons.

Keyholes can be covered by keyplates with a brass, or satin chrome finish, or they may be painted to match the colour of the door.

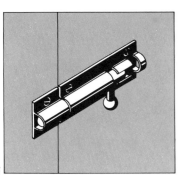
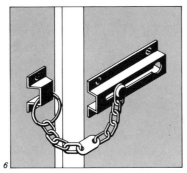
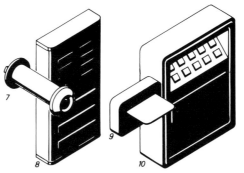
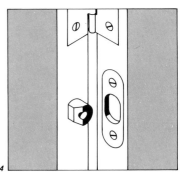
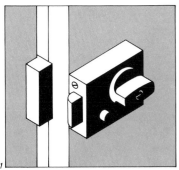
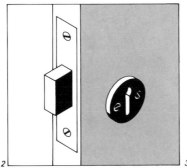

1 *High-security lock.*
2 *Mortise dead lock.*
3 *Two-bolt mortise lock.*
4 *Hinge bolt.*
5 *Door bolt.*
6 *Security door chain.*
7 *Door viewer with optional lens.*
8 *Entryphone.*
9 *Entry-card system.*
10 *Digital entry system.*

Doors

External doors should be made of metal (although you would probably only find these in converted commercial buildings) or solid-core wood, at least 45mm (1¾in) thick, close fitting (without gaps which would allow forced entry by leverage) and fitted with three strong, well-spaced, inward-opening hinges. The door and the frame should be of a similar strength.

Front and back doors should be particularly secure and well lit: two mortise locks and a rim dead lock, well spaced out, are a strong combination, with surface-mounted bolts at the top and bottom for extra security at night. Door chains should leave enough space to peer round the door; a simple temporary measure is a wooden wedge kept by the door. The locking surface of the door can be reinforced with a steel plate, which should be at least 25mm (1in) wide, 4mm (⅙in) thick and should overlap the locking area by at least 250mm (10in). Doors may also be fitted with diagonal bars, which are unattractive but very secure. External doors of apartment blocks or shared accommodation should be kept locked and key-holders strictly limited to residents; timers for light switches in shared halls and stairs should be positioned close to the door.

Internal doors should be kept closed at night and when the house is empty, but they should not be locked unless they are solid core. A locked internal door may deter a thief who has successfully broken into the house, but consider that it also suggests hidden treasure. Remember that emergency exit routes should be left unhindered. If one area of your home is particularly vulnerable and locks would not impede an emergency exit, you can fit key-operated mortise or rim locks.

Windows/glazed doors

Window frames should be close fitting and made of good-quality wood, steel or aluminium, with the glass set deep into the frame for strength. Windows that are rarely, or never, opened can be screwed together. Others may be fixed so that they open only a little way. Remember that wooden-framed sash windows need a lock on either side; some have a locking window stop to secure the window while allowing controlled ventilation, which is far safer for households with children.

If the house has shutters on the inside, these should be secured with a close-fitting metal cross-bar, and any gaps, where the bar could be levered up, should be protected by surface-mounted key-operated bolts at both the top and bottom of the shutter. Iron bars and grilles, although sometimes unsightly, can be useful for vulnerable ground-and lower ground-floor windows; at an extreme, metal gates which secure on the inside are available. Exterior grilles should be checked frequently for rust and the firmness of the brick or concrete surround. Where the windows open outwards, less obtrusive interior grilles, which may be painted, can be used: a folding, or concertina, grille can be hidden behind curtains. Some old grilles are attractive and can be highlighted as a decorative feature.

Sliding glazed doors need specially designed key-operated locks for aluminium frames on both the top and bottom door runners; and French windows should have three key-operated mortise bolts – at the top, centre and bottom – to avoid ruining the lines of the door.

Georgian glass wire and acrylic or polycarbonate sheet (also known as safety laminate) offer extra protection for very vulnerable windows or glazed doors. Georgian glass offers least protection since the wire can be cut if the glass is broken. Acrylic sheet, which is up to ten times as strong as glass, is very light and can therefore be fitted into a strong frame, but it is very expensive and can be easily burnt and scratched. Polycarbonate sheet is virtually unbreakable, but since it needs to be fitted over the entire window area with a surround of at least 8mm (⅓in) and must be screwed on to the main window or door frame because of its light weight, it is suitable only for a high-risk window where its unsightliness and permanent closure will not matter.

Further precautions
Entry systems

A door viewer of 180°, fitted at a height accessible to all members of the family, is a good protection device for any doors used frequently by callers.

Entryphones and intercoms are also useful to check the identity of visitors, particularly in

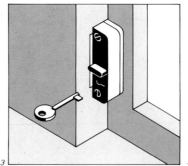

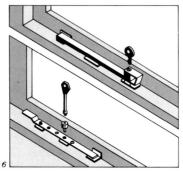

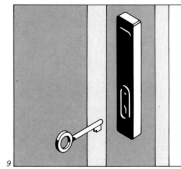

apartment blocks, but unknown callers should always be checked at the main front door, using a door chain and door viewer. Video systems, while expensive, do allow you to see exactly who is at the door without going down there. If there is a residential housekeeper or security guard in an apartment block, you should be able to contact him or her easily by a telephone or intercom system.

Light timers

Automatic light timers are an effective and reasonably cheap deterrent. It is worth spending a little extra on a switch that offers several settings, so that lights can be set for different times over a long period; more expensive timers that react to light and come on automatically at dusk are also available. Switches are most effective in the kitchen, living room and bedroom; they should not be installed in a hall, which is a thoroughfare rather than a place you would be sitting or working in.

If you have a home computer, you can link the lighting to the keyboard and programme the computer to switch the lights on and off; the computer can also control the heating and other services, burglar and fire alarms, and entry systems.

Burglar alarms

Alarms are essentially intended to draw attention to a burglar by a loud warning signal, but the box on an outside wall can also have a deterrent value. The most cost-effective system best adapted to your needs depends entirely on the premises; ask a security company and a crime prevention officer for their recommendations and then obtain at least three quotes on the system that seems most suitable. Have the system professionally installed, and make sure a neighbour has a key and is able to switch off the alarm if it is triggered accidentally.

The most common systems for domestic use are closed-circuit types, which use various detectors, including infra-red lights, pressure mats, ultrasonic sound and microwaves.

Open- or closed-circuit alarms These are triggered off when the opening of a window or door breaks or completes a circuit; the alarm bell rings for a set period and then switches itself off. Some models have a light out-side the front door which flashes after the alarm has switches itself off; others can be connected directly to a control room via the telephone.

Infra-red alarms These systems project a narrow beam of invisible light to a photo-electric cell in the receiving unit; the alarm is set off if the beam is broken. The alarm units, which should be fixed at entry points on the perimeter of the area to be protected and above the reach of domestic animals, should be concealed from intruders, who might otherwise crawl under, or step over, the beam.

Ultrasonic alarms These register the movement of a person within a protected area; since one alarm can protect only a limited area, it is often necessary to install more than one unit where there are several vulnerable points where forced entry may be possible.

Differential air-pressure alarms Changes in air pressure caused by an open door or window trigger these alarms; they cover limited areas and should be installed only where air leakage under doors and through windows is at a constant minimum.

Pressure-mat alarms These are activated by pressure on a mat hidden under a carpet but it is most important to site them carefully.

Safes

Safes are expensive and are difficult to install properly. It is probably more sensible to keep valuables in a bank safety box, but it is worth fitting one cupboard or room with very good locks and a strong door. Under-floor safes are probably the most appropriate type for domestic purposes.

Outside the house

Outdoor lighting is a good deterrent and helps to give personal protection: front and back doors should have a light controlled from the inside, positioned so that callers' faces are clearly illuminated. Drainpipes near windows can be painted with anti-scale paint which never dries but remains awkwardly tacky.

Garages and sheds should be well secured if they contain any implements that could aid a burglar: use a strong closed shackle lock or a hasp and staple lock and fit any internal garage doors leading to the house with strong dead locks. Ladders should always be chained to a wall ring.

Locks and bolts
1 *Locking window stop for securing sash window, allowing space for ventilation.*
2 *Dual-screw lock for sash window.*
3 *Casement-window frame lock for wood or metal.*
4 *Push-to-lock window catch for hinged or pivoted windows.*
5 *Security bolt for large wooden-frame casement windows.*
6 *Locking window catches and stops for hinged windows.*
7 *Locking window handle.*
8 *Lock for metal windows.*
9 *Patio-door lock.*

Home security devices
1 *Outdoor floodlights.*
2 *Passive infra-red, or ultrasonic motion, detectors.*
3 *Panic button.*
4 *Door contacts.*
5 *Inertia sensors on safes and furniture.*
6 *External alarm bell.*
7 *Internal alarm bell.*
8 *Control unit.*

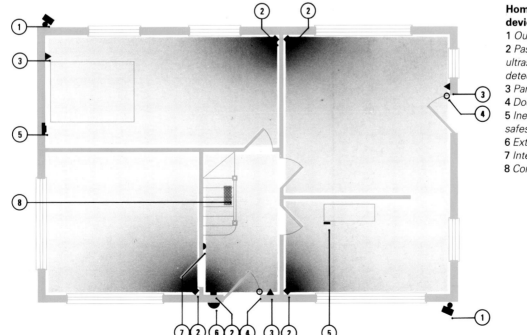

MAINTENANCE

There may not be a gaping hole in the roof of your house or mould growing on the walls, but it is always better to be on the look-out for problems in a house rather than to wait for them to make their presence felt. Serious structural problems need the experienced eye of an expert surveyor or structural engineer, but there is a lot the layperson can find out by a general survey.

Superficial symptoms may be due to something more serious. Remember, it is the *cause* of the problem that should be tackled. With this in mind, it is always worth tracing faults to their source and taking a second look at repair work, which should only be grounds for reassurance when you know that the job has been done properly. If you have not lived in the house for very long, it is as well to suspect that a repair might be simply covering something up.

Is the wood behind that reasonable-looking coat of paint sound? Try sticking a penknife in to make sure. Is that recent rendering (stucco) covering up cracks that result from structural movement? Look for fresh cracks.

Once you have cast your eye over your own repairs, have a look at the neighbours' properties. Houses of similar design and age are likely to have the same weaknesses. A fault evident next door, likewise repair work, should suggest an area worth checking on your own house.

Always seek specialist advice if you suspect a serious problem, though it is a good idea to understand what is involved. You will have to foot the bill.

The walls

A sound wall, performing properly, should be straight and plumb. While a small discrepancy in older houses might be expected, alarm bells should start ringing if the property is newly built. Examine door and window frames; they should be square and fixed firmly to the wall with no gaps.

Bowed walls are most often caused by moisture expansion of the brickwork and by the spreading of the roof structure, which is most visible at the top of the wall. If a wall is seriously out of true, consult an expert for the best remedy. Slightly bowed walls are an inconvenience rather than a problem.

Cracking

Cracks mean that movement has taken place. Small or hairline cracks need not cause too much concern in older houses (and many new houses will settle slightly). Larger cracks must be investigated.

Cracks in walls can be vertical, horizontal or diagonal ('stepped' down successive courses of brick or stone). They can be caused by movement of the ground, because it has been very wet or dry, or because a tree is growing near the building (or has recently been felled). Other causes include foundation failure, expansion of brickwork, failure of wall ties and spreading of the roof structure.

Cracks that are stable can be scraped out and filled, though this does nothing to cure the problem if movement is still taking place. Always examine pointing for new cracks. One way to test for continuing movement is to firmly cement a few thin strips of glass across the crack, leaving the glass clean and free above the line of the crack. A fracture line in the glass will show up if your fears are confirmed. This type of unstable crack may mean serious repairs such as underpinning.

Damp

It is only to be expected that older, solid walls will be more prone to penetrating damp than modern cavity walls. However, if damp patches are apparent on the inside after it has rained you should try to locate any sources which are making things worse. During heavy rainfall check for overflowing gutters, leaking or blocked downpipes. And look under windowsills: there should

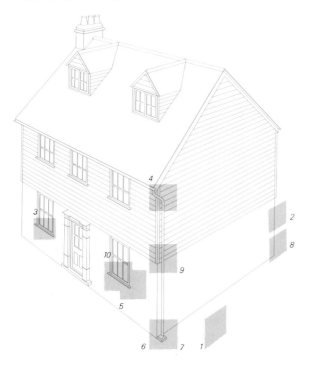

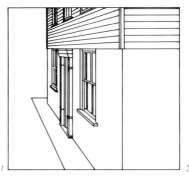

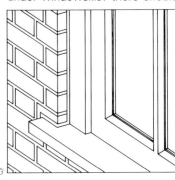

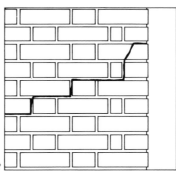

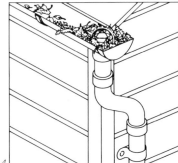

be a groove running along the underside of the sill which, if kept clear, will prevent water transmission to the walls. Also check overflow pipes from cold-water and toilet cisterns. If these are permanently dripping, the ball valves need attention.

Cavity walls should not give rise to any internal damp. If it does occur, the most likely cause is mortar bridging the cavity across wall ties – this may have been dropped during construction of the house.

The cures for penetrating damp – apart from repairing gutters, drainpipes and so on – are to plaster or clad the wall, or, in less serious cases, to apply a colourless silicone water repellent.

Rising damp

Rising damp should not be a problem in modern houses, in which damp-proof courses have invariably been installed. If there is a problem, the course has either failed or been bridged, perhaps by external rendering or by a flower-bed or pile of rubbish. You should be able to locate the damp-proof course about 150mm (6in) above ground level.

Many older properties have had a damp-proof treatment,
often in the form of water-resistant chemicals pumped into the base of the walls. Specialist firms offering this treatment give free surveys and estimates of the work necessary. Get several quotes; they may vary widely. And satisfy yourself that you are not dealing with a fly-by-night operation – a twenty-year guarantee is no good if the firm goes out of business.

Wall types
Brickwork

The bricks in sound brickwork should have a good surface. They should also be well pointed, which will help to prevent water penetration. Any loose or crumbly mortar should be raked out and replaced. The best way to clean brickwork is with a stiff brush and plain tap water (no soap or detergent). If you can find a piece of matching brick, this can be used to rub away at particularly grubby areas.

When brickwork has become porous, painting will help seal the wall, but it will need repainting periodically. White deposits on newer brickwork, known as efflorescence, are salts leaching out of the brick and will disappear with time. Spalling (splintering of
the brick faces) is more serious and is due to water freezing and expanding within the bricks. The only cure is to replace damaged bricks or, if damage is extreme, to render (stucco) the wall.

Render (stucco)

The condition of the wall behind rendering remains the important thing, although rendering will improve the weatherproofing of a wall and provide a good deal of protection where porosity is a problem. Bulging areas of render suggest that moisture has got in and weakened the bond between the render and the wall, or between the two layers of render. Tap the render to hear whether it sounds firm or hollow.

Large cracks (which may indicate movement of the wall beneath) should be filled with more render. A masonry paint will fill small cracks, though if the wall is flaky it should be prepared first with a special stabilizing primer.

Wooden cladding

Timber-framed houses, which often look just like traditional brick-built ones, are becoming increasingly popular these days. If you live in a timber-framed house, you mustn't forget that
the cavity walls incorporate a waterproof membrane that should not be punctured: do-it-yourself hobbyists should beware of any jobs that involve making a hole in an external wall, such as installing electric socket outlets. And, of course, the cavity must not be filled with insulation – unnecessary because the walls are already well insulated.

If painted, wooden cladding (clapboarding, weatherboarding) or wooden shingles can be treated as any other woodwork (see below). If it is left in its natural state, it will need periodic treatment with a wood preservative. Western red cedar contains its own preservative oils and weathers to an attractive silvery grey.

Always fix loose cladding with alloy or galvanized nails, as steel ones will stain.

Wood can be replaced by aluminium or plastic siding (for boarding) or asphalt shingles, but it is usually preferable to repair or replace the wood.

Roofs

The roof can be looked at in two ways: as a structure in itself, which must be stable, and as an envelope to keep out bad weather. Any interruptions to the

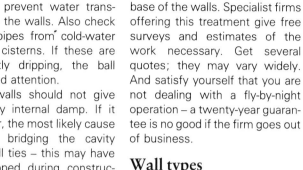

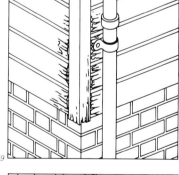

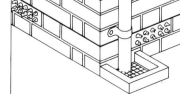

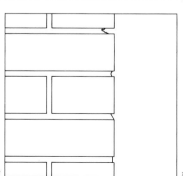

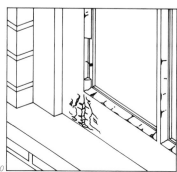

1 *Check the alignment of the house from a good vantage point.*
2 *Crack on wall could indicate subsidence.*
3 *Fill gaps between window frames and walls with non-settling mastic.*
4 **Do not** *allow gutters to be blocked; place mesh cowl over downpipe.*
5 *There should be a drip groove under windowsills.*
6 **Do not** *block holes in air bricks and keep drain holes free from blockage.*
7 **Do not** *allow build up of debris over damp-proof course or air bricks.*
8 *The top brick-and-mortar joint needs repointing. There are three common methods producing different profiles: (from top to bottom) ironed, weatherstruck, recessed.*
9 *Decaying clapboarding caused by a leaking downpipe.*
10 *Putty has decayed around the windows and the paint has decayed at the frame joint.*

simple surface presented by the tiles or slates of a roof, such as valley gutters, rooflights and particularly chimneys, can be regarded as potential sites for water penetration. Failing a detailed inspection using roof ladders, the next best thing is close scrutiny through binoculars.

If your roof is in a particularly sorry state, get the worst over with first – check to see whether it has affected the stability of supporting walls. In a badly sagging roof, where there is an evident sag across the whole roof (see below), check also for signs of movement in supporting walls. If the wall has been pushed outwards, bowing can be seen by looking along the roof. Bowing may send a wall out of plumb – a plumb-line is the obvious check, although it should be obvious to the naked eye.

When a wall has moved too far it will not be able to guarantee future stability so that even a new roof may not save the day. Clearly any decision on whether the problem is curable or not must be taken on the basis of professional advice.

A potentially disastrous 'improvement' to an old house, though not at all uncommon, is

the replacement of an old slate roof by a cheaper, but heavier, one of concrete tiles, which the old structure may not be able to support.

In older terraced (town or row houses) or in semi-detached houses, a hogged roof is usually easy to spot: the even surface of the roof is broken along the line of the party wall where the tiles or slates are tilting. This is a result of the roof sagging on either side of the party wall, or of wall settlement on both sides. Party walls are not exposed and support less of a load, so they are less likely to settle. In a terrace, you should look along the row to see if the same line of cock-eyed tiles is repeated. The only way to treat the problem is to immediately block up any gaps between tiles or slates with mastic to stop leaks.

Check the roof structure

Even when the roof is sagging badly, which may be most apparent along the ridge, you can still diagnose the situation yourself by examining roof timbers for failed joints and fastenings, or for rot. At the eaves, you will find a timber running along the inside edge of the external wall: this is

the wall-plate, and as it lies just behind the exposed eaves it is particularly prone to rot. Rafters and ceiling joists are both fixed here, so check if the rafters have moved over the wall-plate or if the wall-plate itself has moved relative to the wall. Alternatively, the cause might be located at the other end of the rafters. You should look for rot and subsequent failure where the rafters meet the ridge board (beam) that runs along the ridge of the roof. Remedial work is likely to be less trouble here than at the eaves.

A smaller depression or sag in the roof is probably due to local failure of the frame below. The rafters, running from the eaves to the ridge of the roof, are supported periodically by purlins (horizontal beams): these are the main structural members running along the length of the roof. In turn, the purlins will be supported by purlin struts, which rest on the wall below. Look for any defection in purlins and rafters; check also for twisting along the length of the purlins and bending or movement in the struts. An insufficient number of purlins, timber that was not strong enough for the job, or badly fixed struts can all contribute to this problem. Old

timber will dry out and weaken.

If things have not gone too far, treatment will involve jacking up the offending purlins to restore the line of the roof. Poorly designed gables may also put an excessive strain on purlins and so tend to force the roof to sag.

Not to be confused with sagging is rippling. A rippled roof will exhibit undulations on its surface, running from eaves to ridge. In an old roof, examine the tile battens: they may be failing with age between the rafters. Alternatively, a failed rafter will have increased the load on battens, which now cover a double span. If rafters were spaced too far apart in the first place, this will have had similar consequences.

In a modern house, you may find a trussed rafter roof. The roof space will be a network of timbers, prefabricated in a more finely balanced structure than the traditional roof. Apart from looking for signs of rot, look for bending in the supportive timbers running between ceiling and roof (struts), for well-fixed metal plates at joints and good jointing, particularly where the horizontal beams (ties) meet the rafters at the eaves. These latter joints prevent the roof spreading.

Roof structures
1 *Collar roof.*
2 *Purlin roof.*
3 *Roof altered for an attic conversion.*
4 *Trussed rafters.*

5 *Check if walls are straight from ground level.*
6 *Dipping in roof could be caused by subsidence.*
7 *Flashing around skylight needs repair.*
8 *Rippled roof could be caused by rafters placed too far apart. There are also slipped tiles and a missing tile.*
9 *Roof ridge sagging.*
10 *Chimney flanching is cracked and needs repair, as does unstable flashing.*

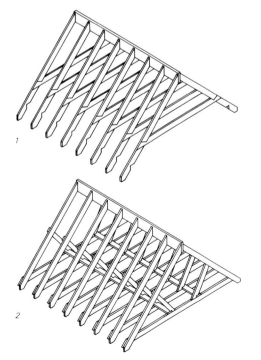

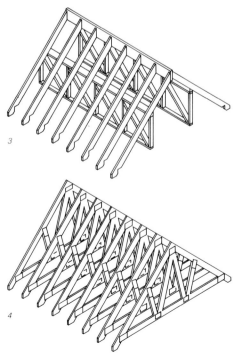

Chimneys

Chimneys have a hard life; they are not only exposed features, but must cope with alternating heat and cold and the corrosive mixture of soot and water.

Look at the lines of the chimney stack for signs of bowing or leaning. Mortar should also be in good condition and re-pointed if necessary. But, again, pointing repairs will not make the structure safe. If it is unsafe, get professional help as remedial work requires scaffolding.

Chimney pots should not be cracked and must be firmly bedded in the mortar 'flanching'. You do not want anything crashing down in a storm and damaging the roof. The flanching should be sound and slope outwards, as it serves to prevent water penetration of the stack.

There must be a good seal where the chimney stack meets the roof. The best way of achieving this is with stepped lead flashing pointed into the brickwork. A fillet (thin line) of cement is often found instead. This should be examined for cracking and for any gaps between the fillet and the stack. The same is true wherever a pitched roof meets a vertical wall – for instance, if party walls stand clear of the roof.

An obsolete chimney stack becomes more of a liability. If you wish to keep the chimney pot, it should be capped with a half-round ridge tile to maintain it in place and keep out rain but allow ventilation. The long-term answer to a disused stack is also capping: this generally means dismantling the stack to just above ridge level and fitting a concrete slab. Such a slab must be mounted on airbricks to permit ventilation, otherwise condensation inside the chimney may discolour interior walls.

Roof types

If you do decide to venture on to the roof, you will need adequate ladders: one that is secured on the ground and extends well beyond the gutter, and a roof ladder that will hook over the ridge of the roof. Gutters are not strong enough to support ladders, so extra care must be taken to find a point of support.

The ridge tiles along the roof ridges can sometimes be loosened by frost action and so allow rain penetration. Any loose tiles should be lifted and rebedded in mortar. Wetting the tiles first will prevent them from drying out the cement. Any coping stones on parapets or gable walls should be secure.

Shingle

A shingle roof, often of red cedar, can be regarded as a roof of wooden slates and should be similarly checked for a regular surface pattern, and in particular for any signs of rot.

Felt

Water should not collect on a flat roof covered in roofing felt (built-up roofing), but must be able to drain off. Check any joints in the roofing and look out for splits or blisters. Repairs can be made with a bituminous mastic, strengthened with a roofing felt for larger tears. Also check any flashing for security – self-adhesive bitumen flashing is now available; this can be used to repair small splits in the roof as well. A layer of gravel will prolong the life of a felted roof.

Asphalt

Ponding is not such a problem on asphalt. However, asphalt should be smooth and solid and on a solid base which is not subject to movement. Movement will crack the asphalt – a very fine crack can allow water penetration.

Slate

A good slate roof should present a smooth, even pattern. Missing slates are difficult to replace, because the nails that fix a slate are covered by the next slate up.

The do-it-yourself solution is to hire a tool called a slate ripper, which can be slipped between the slates and hooked over the inaccessible nails to cut them. With the damaged slate removed, a thin strip of lead, copper or zinc, called a tingle, can then be nailed between the adjacent slates to be covered. This must be long enough to bend up and over the bottom edge of the new slate to hold it in place.

When slates are flaking and crumbly and generally in poor condition, there is a budget alternative to reroofing: a thick coat of a special sealant can be applied that will cover the underside of the roof with a plastic skin. However, the sealant may reduce ventilation and may crack; it should not be applied to the roof top, it will ruin its appearance.

Simulated slates are generally thinner and darker than natural slate. Like natural slates, they

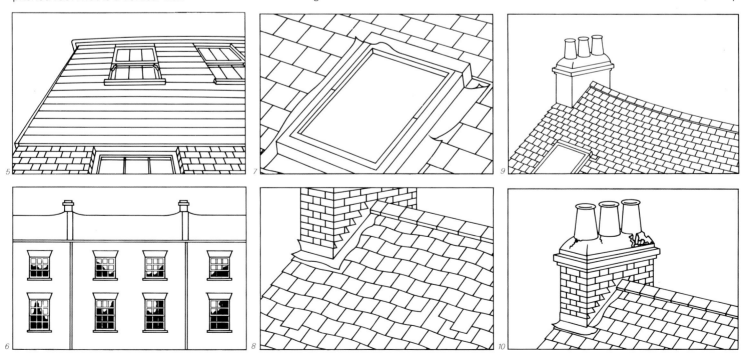

may be head-nailed or centre-nailed at each side and fixed at the joint of the two slates below. Some modern simulated slates are asbestos-free.

Tiles

Concrete tiles have become increasingly popular, being cheaper than slates. As with slates, you should look for an even pattern and any cracked or missing tiles. They are usually much easier to replace, however, being held in place by nibs hooked over a batten with nails every four or five rows only. A replacement can be slid in place while surrounding tiles are lifted slightly.

You should ensure that a replacement tile or patched area of roof does not break up the pattern of the roof, leaving gaps where it meets the old tiles. Clay tiles have been in decline as concrete ones take over, but they are still produced – if a replacement is not available you may be able to find a concrete tile with the right profile.

Metal

Copper can be found on old, particularly public, buildings. Tin has been used in the past, usually replaced by corrugated iron or by metal panels (standing seam roofs). Many garages and outbuildings have translucent plastic roofs. Check for possible leaks.

Eaves

The eaves of a house are always vulnerable. They are exposed and also act as the collection area for rain running off the roof; however, not being very accessible they are often neglected. The eaves' fascia board, on to which the gutters are fixed, is susceptible to rot if not maintained.

Guttering

Modern PVC gutters are often ribbed so that debris will not prevent the flow of water but, with any guttering, silt and leaves will need to be cleared out from time to time. Old cast-iron gutters and their supports may also look sound from the ground while being considerably corroded at the back. Where leaves are a problem, a plastic mesh guard can be fitted over the gutters. A wire or plastic cage fitted to the top of downpipes (downspouts) will keep off birds and nesting material – a common cause of blockages.

Watch how gutters and downpipes cope with heavy rain. Ideally you should take up a bucket of water or the garden hose (when it's not raining) and run it into the gutter at the point farthest from the downpipe. This may reveal any sag in the gutter, due to a failed bracket, or debris hindering the run-off. A small amount of debris can dramatically reduce a gutter's efficiency.

If you can get up there for a close examination, check the brackets fixing the gutter to the fascia board. Screws may have rusted away, in which case any holes in the board should be fitted with mastic and brackets repositioned. The gutter must retain a slight fall to its outlet, and have no sags.

A fascia board that has softened with rot must be taken down and a new board fitted. Do not be tempted to remove heavy cast-iron gutters on your own.

Areas of corrosion in the gutters should be removed back to the metal and the area treated with a rust inhibitor before it is made good with an epoxy filler – any rough patches or snags will collect debris. Leaking joints can be sealed with bitumen mastic. New PVC guttering should require no maintenance, but, on all gutters, beware of snow collecting against walls.

Drainage

Downpipes (downspouts) should be checked for leaking joints and for cracks, especially if they are old cast-iron pipes. Look for any damp patches on the wall behind. On older houses there may be a hopper (leader) head – a box on the wall into which pipes empty – that may get blocked by leaves or nesting material. Cast-iron downpipes usually have a slight gap where each section fits into the next. If there is a blockage, the leak will occur at the gap above the blockage, at least indicating where the trouble lies. At the bottom, water should be directed into an open gully or drain by an angled spout.

A soil pipe from the toilet, usually combined with the waste-pipe from basins (sinks) and baths, should have airtight joints. The top of the pipe should be fitted with a cage and should extend well above the level of any opening windows, which usually means it finishes above the eaves.

Drains must be fitted with a grate to stop rubbish falling in. If a level of water is visible in the drain, this indicates that the trap is intact and that water is not leaking away around the house.

The removal of the cover (manhole) over the inspection chamber (clean-out), followed by turning on taps and flushing the toilet, should quickly register as a steady flow of water, not a trickle. The interior of the chamber should be in good repair, otherwise material falling from crumbling walls may cause a blockage. If you do have reason to suspect that your drains are leaking, contact an environmental health inspector.

Woodwork

When the material is painted wood, the same advice holds for doors and windows, frames and any other exposed woodwork on the house. Once paint starts to crack, water will penetrate the wood, push off the paint further and expose the wood to rot. The treatment is to strip off the paint back to the bare wood, fill any cracks with a suitable filler, prime and repaint. Do not allow bare wood any time to get damp. Conversely, make sure that damp wood has dried out before painting it; painting damp wood will just lead to blistering of the new paint. If paintwork is simply fading or drab, then it can be rubbed down and repainted.

Wood with a natural finish should be re-treated before the surface starts to roughen and become grey looking. Whole ranges of sophisticated combined stainers and preservatives are available, with a variety of finishes. If the wood is cracked, wood fillers can give a reasonable colour match.

Rotten wood should always be cut out and replaced by new treated timber. If you discover a damp door or window frame, get it dried out. If the wood hardens up, fill any cracks and repaint; if it is soft so that a knife can be pushed in, the wood is rotten.

Check along the bottom of door frames – the most likely place to find rot. On casement windows, the weak spots are the bottom corners of the frame and of opening lights, the sill and the sill board running along on the inside. There should also be a good seal between wood and glazing. Any water penetration here can also lead to rot so dried out or missing putty should be replaced – and don't forget glazed doors.

Most of the above points apply equally well to metal windows (other than aluminium), except that for rot, you should read rust.

Look for any gaps between door and window frames and the wall; these can be a source or rot or damp walls. Fill with mastic, which remains flexible and can be painted, rather than putty or mortar.

Running along the underside of each windowsill, there should be a groove to discourage water transmission to the wall – this sometimes becomes clogged with paint. If there isn't one, it is worth fitting a strip of hardwood beading there which will do much the same job.

Sash windows are always worth careful inspection, as the hollow sash boxes built into the wall are susceptible to rot. If the window has a non-projecting sill, look for signs of rot at the junction of the sill and the stone sill beneath.

Bay windows can cause problems by not having the strength and depth of foundation of the surrounding wall. They can sometimes sink and pull away from the house, leaving gaps where rain may penetrate.

Rotten timber, if not visibly rotten, will not always be noticeable by deterioration of its painted surface. There may, however, be a dank smell and the appearance, upon investigation, of fungi or fungal strands running through the wood. It will offer little resistance to a knife blade.

There is often a certain amount of confusion between wet rot and dry rot. In both cases, wood must be damp for rot to get a hold initially, and rotten wood will eventually turn dry and brittle. But the great difference is that wet rot will stop once the wood has dried out; dry rot, however, once established, will continue to spread throughout a building even though the fabric may not be damp – travelling across brickwork and plaster if necessary.

Wood that has been treated with a good preservative will be able to withstand both fungal and beetle attack.

When treating rot, it is impor-tant to remember to deal with the *causes* of the dampness, as well as treating the symptoms.

Dry rot

Signs to look for in the wood are: a dull brown colour, cracking and warping, and a musty smell. Grey strands may be visible, or a growth resembling dirty cotton wool if the fungus is more developed. If it has got a hold, oval-shaped 'fruiting bodies' form and rusty red spots develop. Cracking will be across the grain of wood.

If discovered or suspected, dry rot must be dealt with as soon as possible and specialist advice should be sought. Treatment is a serious business and will involve the cutting out of all affected wood beyond the rot, which must then be burned. All affected plaster should be stripped off the wall at least 300mm (12in) beyond the attack. Other materials that show any sign of the fungus such as soil or rubble, should also be removed, and remaining surfaces should be treated with a fungicide. All new timber should be treated with a preservative.

Wet rot

All fungal infestations, if not dry rot, are commonly referred to as wet rot. Timber must have become damp for the rot to set in, so treatment consists of locating and removing the source of the damp, cutting out and replacing all affected wood, and treating remaining timbers with a fungicide. Improving the ventilation may help matters.

It is always better to insert a new piece of wood than to fill the whole area with filler, although there are treatments for hardening and filling small areas of rot. The replacement wood should be cut to size, glued in place using a waterproof resin adhesive and treated with a pesticide. Any small gaps can then be finished off with a filler and smoothed off.

Beetles

The only evidence most people ever have of a beetle attack is a lot of holes that they have left behind. Few people actually see a beetle. It is the young grub that eats away at the woodwork, and any holes are made by mature insects when they fly away. The grubs may have spent up to four years in there, depending on the species, having a feed at your expense. But the emergent beetles lay eggs again almost immediately, so infestation can easily spread to other areas.

The most widespread of all 'woodworm' is the common furniture beetle, which leaves behind it a characteristic circular borehole about 1.5mm ($\frac{1}{16}$ in) in diameter. It is difficult to tell if a beetle is still active, but tell-tale signs are new holes or recently deposited, tiny cigar-shaped pellets around the holes.

Other beetles are the much larger house longhorn beetle, whose calling card is an oval hole 6 to 10 mm ($\frac{1}{4}$ to $\frac{2}{5}$ in) wide; the powder post beetle, which attacks the sapwood of young hardwoods; and the death watch beetle. Termites can be a problem, particularly in areas of the United States.

The extent of damage to any structural timber can be tested by its resistance to a knife blade. If floor-boards have been badly affected, it is a good idea to check the floor joists below.

Several do-it-yourself treatments are available, as aerosol sprays or brush-on fluids. If the problem is widespread, you should seek professional advice. All woodwork/rot treatment firms give free surveys and estimates of work needed.

PESTS WHICH CAN DESTROY THE FABRIC OF YOUR HOUSE

RODENTS

Mice – house mice and field mice in winter. Rats and squirrels do similar damage – but more so.
Damage Cause structural damage by gnawing continually to keep their incisor teeth in shape – electrical wiring, cables, plastic pipes and so on.
Control/treatment Block entry holes to house with wire embedded in quick-setting cement.
Control: Proprietary mice bait which causes painless death; warfarin for squirrels.

BIRDS

Pigeons, starlings, gulls, sparrows.

Damage Their nests can block chimneys, gutters, downpipes, and break roof tiles so roof is attacked by rot. Flocks of pigeons and starlings damage masonry on city blocks. (Droppings and nests are breeding ground for flies, mites, carpet beetles, etc.)
Control/treatment Remove nests; fix loose tiles; clear gutters; protect eaves with wire mesh. Can be discouraged with repellent gel.

WOODWORM

Term covers the larvae of several species of wood-boring beetle. Usually the common furniture beetle; also the death watch, house longhorn and powder post beetles.
Damage Larvae spend years boring through structural timbers, floor-boards, furniture. Eventually woodworm destroys the wood. Only teak and Cuban mahogany are immune. Softwoods are very vulnerable. Death watch only attacks old hardwood beams. Signs are 2mm ($\frac{1}{12}$ in) exit holes.
Control/treatment Only use pre-treated timber for new work. Get all existing timbers surveyed and treated if woodworm is suspected. Treat infected furniture with woodworm killer and then use insecticidal polish at intervals on all polished wood. Control chemicals: dieldrin, lindane in proprietary woodworm killers.

CARPET BEETLES

The varied carpet beetle and fur beetle have 'woolly bear' larvae.
Damage 'Woolly bear' larvae feed on wool, hair, fur and feathers. Signs are round holes in carpets, blankets, clothes – often along seams. They also live among fluff and debris between floor-boards and shelving.
Control/treatment Proprietary moth-proofer on affected textiles and insecticidal powder puffed into crevices. Vacuum susceptible areas.

CLOTHES MOTHS

Common clothes moth and case-bearing clothes moth both have larvae that feed on wool. Brown house moth's larvae scavenges and eats textiles.
Damage Larvae digest wool, hair, fur, feathers, blankets, wool carpets, wool garments, upholstery – especially if soiled.
Control/treatment Moth proof carpets, upholstery, wool hangings, etc. Spray affected areas with moth-proofer. Store all woollens, well cleaned, in bags.

EXTERIOR MAINTENANCE CHECKLIST

WHEN TO MAKE CHECKS

In spring
■ See what damage the winter has wrought.

In autumn
■ Check to see what should be done to protect your house against the ravages of the following season.

EQUIPMENT

■ Always make sure equipment is in good condition. Some checks involve climbing a ladder; make certain that the ladder is properly secure and take no risks.

CHECKS AND REPAIRS

■ Simple checks and repairs, such as unblocking drain covers and checking roof beams in the loft, should not require professional assistance, but do not attempt checks or repairs which you cannot carry out effectively and safely. When in doubt, call in a professional expert.

CHIMNEYS

Chimney pots	If faulty
■ Are the pots fixed securely?	Re-mortar
■ Is the mortar flanching smooth and undamaged?	Re-mortar

Chimney stack	If faulty
■ Are the mortar joints in good condition?	Re-point
■ Are there any cracks in the chimney stack and is it leaning to one side?	Professional advice
■ Is the flashing, where the chimney meets the roof, in good condition?	Fit new flashing

DRAINS

	If faulty
■ Are all gulleys clear of debris?	Clear gulleys
■ Does water flow away properly?	Clear blockage/ professional advice
■ Is the concrete and brickwork of the manhole chambers in good condition?	Repair/ professional advice
■ Are manhole covers in good condition?	Replace

GUTTERS AND DRAINPIPES

	If faulty
■ Is there any debris (leaves, tennis balls etc) in the gutters?	Clear
■ Do the gutters run smoothly without sagging towards the downpipe (downspout)?	Refix gutters/ replace brackets
■ Does water flow away properly? *Check during rainfall or with a hose.*	Clear gutters/refix brackets
■ Are any gutters or downpipes split, rusting or coming away from the eaves?	Repair or replace gutters
■ Are the connections in the downpipe letting out water?	Fill with mastic

WALLS

Outside	If faulty
■ Are the walls straight and true?	Professional advice
■ Are there any cracks in the brickwork?	Professional advice
■ Is the rendering cracked or flaking off?	Replace/ professional advice
■ Are the bricks crumbling?	Render/clad or replace
■ Is there persistent efflorescence (white powder deposit) on old walls?	Professional advice
■ Is the mortar firm and in good condition?	Re-point
■ Are air bricks clear of debris?	Clear
■ Are there any large trees growing near the house?	Professional advice
■ Is there earth or concrete bridging the damp-proof course?	Remove

Inside	If faulty
■ Are there any damp patches on walls? *Check under windowsills or next to chimney breasts for signs of penetrating damp; check for a 'low-tide mark' which is a sign of rising damp.*	Professional advice
■ Are there signs of condensation within flue? *Check for damp patches on unused chimneys*	Ventilate chimney

ROOF

Outside	If faulty
■ Are there missing, slipped or cracked tiles or slates?	Replace tiles or slates
■ Are the ridge tiles bedded securely in their mortar?	Re-mortar
■ Is the roof sagging at any point?	Professional advice
■ Are the valleys between roof sections clear and in good condition?	Repair/fit new valleys
■ Are the flashings at roof junctions in good condition?	Fit new flashing

Inside	If faulty
■ Are there damp patches inside the loft or attic? *Check after heavy rainfall.*	Check roof/ repair
■ Are there signs of rot or other damage in any of the roof timbers?	Professional advice
■ Is the loft adequately ventilated?	Fit ventilation
■ Are there spaces at the eaves to allow air to flow?	Fit ventilation

FLAT ROOFS

Outside	If faulty
■ Are there splits or tears in the roofing felt?	Repair felt
■ Is the flashing between roof and house wall in good condition?	Replace flashing

Inside	If faulty
■ Are there any damp patches inside?	Check roof/ repair
■ Are there any signs of rot or other damage in any of the timbers?	Professional advice

WOOD AND METALWORK

Outside	If faulty
■ Is paintwork in good condition?	Repaint
■ Are there signs of rot or rust?	Replace rotted section
■ Are the joints in windows, doors secure?	Glue/ replace
■ Are there gaps between frames and walls?	Fill with mastic

INDEX